Standard Grade
COMPUTING STUDIES

WITH ANSWERS

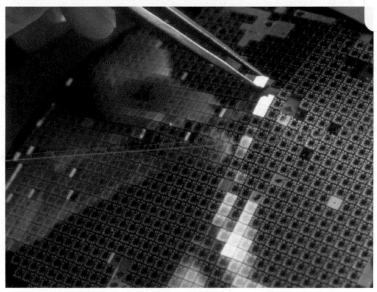

John Walsh

Cover Photograph: the cover photograph shows a processed silicon wafer containing hundreds of micromechanic pressure sensors. Tweezers are being used to remove faulty sensors, labelled by an automatic test device with a black dot of ink. These pressure sensors are destined for use in an on-board monitoring system in a car engine.

Hodder Gibson
2A Christie Street, Paisley, PA1 1NB

Dedication: To Helen, Peter John, Mary, Sarah, Siobhan and Cecilia

The Publishers would like to thank the following for permission to reproduce copyright material:
Photo credits: © David Sailors/Corbis; Alfred Pasieka/Science Photo Library; © Kevin Wilto/Eye Ubiquitous/Corbis; © Royalty-Free/Corbis; Chris Priest/Science Photo Library; Paul Shambroom/Science Photo Library; D. Roberts / Science Photo Library; © Hulton-Deutsch Collection/Corbis; © Tom Wagner/Corbis Saba; © Corbis Sygma; © James Leynse/Corbis; Ton Kinsbergen/Science Photo Library; "Mission Impossible" supplied by Capital Pictures; Matrix (C) Corbis Sygma; "Terminator 2" photo by Everett Collection/Rex Features; © Bioscrypt Inc; © Promethean ACTIVote; © Enstrom's Almond Toffee; © Index Limited; © LloydsTSB Online Banking.

Acknowledgements: The author would like to thank Alice Shanks for her help in the production of this book. The publishers would like to thank the following for permission to reproduce material in this book: Bradley Shanks; Independent on Sunday; Lloyds TSB. Box shots reprinted with permission from Microsoft Corporation; Box shot reprinted with permission of Quark, Inc. and its affiliates; Creative Inspire TD7700; Epson Global; Nokia 1100 by permission from Nokia.com; Smart Card Group, "Google Inc." Amazon.co.uk.

Although every effort has been made to ensure that website addresses are correct at time of going to press, Hodder Gibson cannot be held responsible for the content of any website mentioned in this book. It is sometimes possible to find a relocated web page by typing in the address of the home page for a website in the URL window of your browser.

While every effort has been made to check the instructions of practical work in this book, it is still the duty and legal obligation of schools to carry out their own risk assessments.

Orders: please contact Bookpoint Ltd, 130 Milton Park, Abingdon, Oxon OX14 4SB. Telephone: (44) 01235 827720. Fax: (44) 01235 400454. Lines are open from 9.00 – 6.00, Monday to Saturday, with a 24-hour message answering service. Visit our website at www.hodderheadline.co.uk. Hodder Gibson can be contacted direct on: Tel: 0141 848 1609; Fax: 0141 889 6315; email: hoddergibson@hodder.co.uk

© John Walsh 2004
First Edition Published 1994
Second Edition Published 2004
This Edition Published 2004 by
Hodder Gibson, a member of the Hodder Headline Group
2a Christie Street
Paisley PA1 1NB

Impression number	10 9 8 7 6 5 4 3 2 1
Year	2010 2009 2008 2007 2006 2005 2004

Cover photo by: Peter Menzel/Science Photo Library (T395/009)
Designed and typeset by Hardlines, Charlbury, Oxford
Printed in Italy for Hodder Gibson, a division of Hodder Headline, 2A Christie Street, Paisley PA1 1NB

A catalogue record for this title is available from the British Library

ISBN 0 340 885017

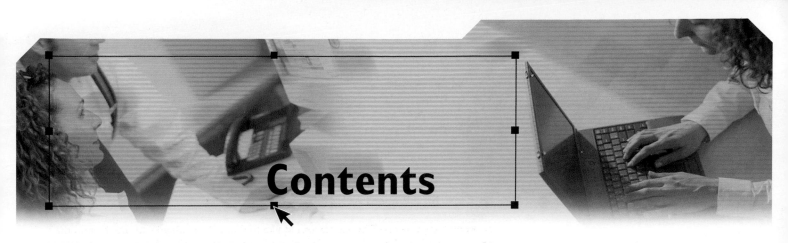

Contents

Chapter

Preface

This book is based upon the *Scottish Certificate of Education Standard Grade Computing Studies* arrangements document issued by the Scottish Qualifications Authority *to be examined in and after 2006*. It should be noted that this book is the author's own interpretation of the arrangements document.

Each chapter in the book matches a syllabus topic.

Programming is included, without adherence to any specific programming environment. This book is not intended to be a programming manual. Your teacher will provide support material tailored to the particular programming language which you will use.

The text is presented in a two-tier format, with the first part covering the requirements of Foundation and General levels and the highlighted sections aimed at Credit level. Each chapter contains questions designed to reinforce Knowledge and Understanding and Problem Solving. Although the questions are divided into these two categories, please note that some questions may not 'fit' precisely into a particular category. Pupils should note that the answers to the Knowledge and Understanding questions may be found in the text.

In addition, some suggested practical activities are included in certain chapters.

Key Points at the end of each chapter are included to aid revision.

An appendix provides a short glossary of Computing terms

Some historical aspects of the development of computer hardware and software and other "Did you know" snippets of information are spread throughout the book

Note that the sequence of chapters is not intended to constitute a recommended teaching order.

Words and phrases which are **emboldened** as far as possible relate directly to the detailed content pages of the Arrangements in Computing .....

Terms in italics are those that the author regards as being important, but are not in the detailed content pages.

John Walsh
March 2004

Hints and tips for examinations and tests

1   Take your time and read the question carefully. Make sure that you understand what it is you are being asked about.

2   Don't panic if you don't know the answer straight away, go on to the next question

3   Look at the number of marks available. For instance, if three marks are available, then you should make three different points in your answer, one for each mark.

4   Answers such as "*easier*" or "*faster*" will not be awarded any marks unless you give a reason to justify them, for instance "*It is faster to load a program from disk than from tape because...*"

5   As a rough guide, you should write at least one sentence for each mark.

6   Give as full an explanation as you can within the time available.

7   It doesn't harm your marks to include extra information in your answer if you have time.

8   Never leave any questions unanswered unless you run out of time. Blank spaces always get no marks.

9   Draw a diagram if it will help to clarify your answer.

Resist the temptation to leave the examination early just because you see others going out. Try to relax and look over your answers again, to make sure that you have attempted all of the questions.

1 General purpose packages

What is an application package?

The most common method of processing data with a computer system is by using the series of instructions stored in a **computer program** called an **application package**. There are a huge number of application packages, from games like *Tomb Raider* to spreadsheets like *Excel*.

What is a general purpose package?

Figure 1.1 *A selection of general purpose packages.*

There is an important difference between *Tomb Raider* and *Excel*. The game application has only one purpose — for the user to play a game. It is a single purpose package. You cannot add any information to the game. When you start playing all you can do is to follow the instructions and play it. On the other hand, you can use a spreadsheet application like Excel for many different purposes, but you must supply your own information to the spreadsheet before it is of any use to you. Application packages that require you to provide your own information like this are called **general purpose packages**.

Examples of general purpose packages are:

- word processing
- spreadsheet
- database
- graphics
- desk top publishing
- presentation and multimedia
- web page creation
- expert systems.

A selection of general purpose packages is shown in figure 1.1.

What does a general purpose package consist of?

If you said that a general purpose package was a computer program then you would be very close to the correct answer, but a general purpose package is more than just a computer program. When you buy a general purpose package it includes a CD-ROM

Figure 1.2 *The separate general purpose packages within Microsoft Office Professional.*

containing the program, but there is more than just the program on the CD-ROM. Other files which you would expect to find include:

- a manual (a book of instructions on how to use the package),
- a tutorial guide (a book containing a series of lessons which teach you how to use the package),
- a demonstration program to teach you how to use the package; this is usually easier to follow and much quicker than reading the manual!
- an installer program to install the software on your computer system,
- an uninstaller program to delete the software from your computer system.

The reason why these files are supplied in electronic form is to save the cost of printing and posting (books are heavy). If the user wants to read these on paper, then it is up to them to print the files out. Some software companies sell their programs as downloads from the Internet and this means that they do not even have to produce a CD-ROM.

You will use many different general purpose packages during your Computing course. Which packages you use will depend on what is available in your school or college.

Common features of most general purpose packages

Many general purpose packages use the same **commands**, such as:

- **RUN (OPEN APPLICATION PACKAGE)** This is the command that you give to the computer to start the program running.
- **NEW** This command creates a new, empty file, ready for you to put in your own information.
- **LOAD (OPEN FILE)** This command reads a particular file from backing storage, for example a hard disk.
- **SAVE FILE** With this command the computer writes a file to backing storage so that you can use it again later.
- **PRINT FILE** Using this command you can produce a hard copy (or printout) of your file. In some cases you may wish to print only part of the file, perhaps only page two out of a three-page document.

Many operations are also the same for different packages, for example:

- **INSERT** Put additional information in — perhaps insert an extra row or column of numbers into a spreadsheet.

- **AMEND** Change or correct spelling — for example, change their to there.
- **DELETE** You may remove material — for example, by deleting a paragraph from a document.
- **CHANGE TEXT APPEARANCE** Most packages allow you to change the way your text looks by using italics, bold, underlining or other styles. You can also usually change the typeface, or font.
- **COPY** Using COPY you can take a copy of part of your entire document and duplicate it somewhere else in the same document — or even in another document.
- **MOVE** You can take out part of the document and put it somewhere else in the same (or another) document.

Headers and footers

In addition to the features already mentioned, general purpose packages often allow you to place some information at the top and the bottom of each page of your document — these are known as the header (top) and the footer (bottom). Most of the pages in this book have a header, containing the chapter name and number, and a footer, containing the page number. The header and footer are typed only once at the start, when you are setting up the document, and will be printed on all of the pages. The general purpose package will automatically put the correct number on each page.

The human computer interface

Figure 1.3 *The human computer interface?*

The human computer interface (usually shortened to HCI) is the way the user and the program communicate with each other. Many different things could be regarded as part of the HCI, like the way the screen looks, or whether the program makes it clear to the users what they have to do next. An example of the HCI is shown in figure 1.3.

Programs that are easy to learn to use and help you understand as you are using them are called user-friendly programs.

EXAMPLE OF USER FRIENDLINESS

You are working on a computer and want to save your file. The instruction your package needs to do this is SAVE from the FILE menu.

But perhaps you are not really familiar with this package, or make the wrong choice and instead choose QUIT from the FILE menu.

A non-user-friendly system would not save your file if you made this mistake. The application package would quit and you would have lost all your data. But a user-friendly system would not quit straight away, it would ask you if you were sure that you wanted to quit, and whether or not you wanted to save your file before you quit the application.

Customising HCI

Changing the HCI of a general purpose package to suit the user is called customising the HCI. The HCI parameters control the many different ways in which the user and the computer interact. There are many different ways in which the HCI of a package may be customised. These include changing the display font, choosing a user dictionary and altering the package's menus.

In a WIMP environment, the file icons may be swapped for a list of file names, which can then be ordered alphabetically, or sorted by the date so that the most recently used file is at the top of the list. The background colour of the screen may be altered, or it may be replaced with a photograph or other graphic. This is sometimes known as 'wallpaper'.

WIMP environment

To try to make computers easy to use, a specialised program has been developed which makes the computer screen more like an ordinary office with a desk. The idea is that you have a 'filing cabinet' (backing storage hard disk), which holds your data, a hand or pointer to use to select and move things, and a bin to throw things out. This system is known as a WIMP environment:

- Window
- Icon
- Menu
- Pointer

An example of a WIMP environment is shown in figure 1.4.

Figure 1.4 *A typical WIMP screen display.*

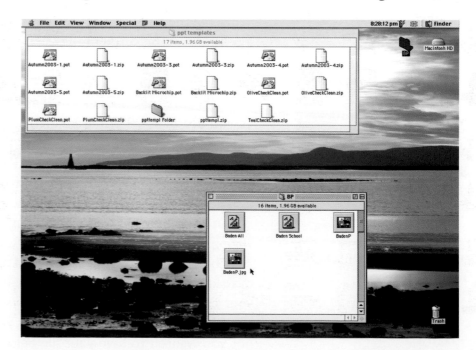

Window

A **window** is an area of the computer screen where you can see the contents of a folder, a document or a program. Some systems allow several windows on the screen at the same time, and windows can overlap each other. To help you keep track of what is going on at any time, the window on top is the one which is 'active' (you can see an example of this in figure 1.5). Most computers allow you to have more than one active window and to have separate documents in each.

Figure 1.5 *Overlapping windows. The window in front is the 'active' window — the one that's being worked on.*

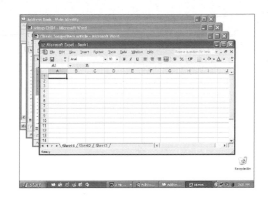

Icon

An **icon** is a small picture that appears on the screen to represent a file, an application program, a directory or a **utility** like the wastebasket or trash. You can see some icons in figure 1.6. Icons may also represent peripherals such as disk drives, printers, servers or other networks. WIMP environments, which use icons to represent different things on the screen, are often called **Graphical User Interfaces** (or **GUIs**).

Figure 1.6 *A selection of icons you might see in a WIMP environment.*

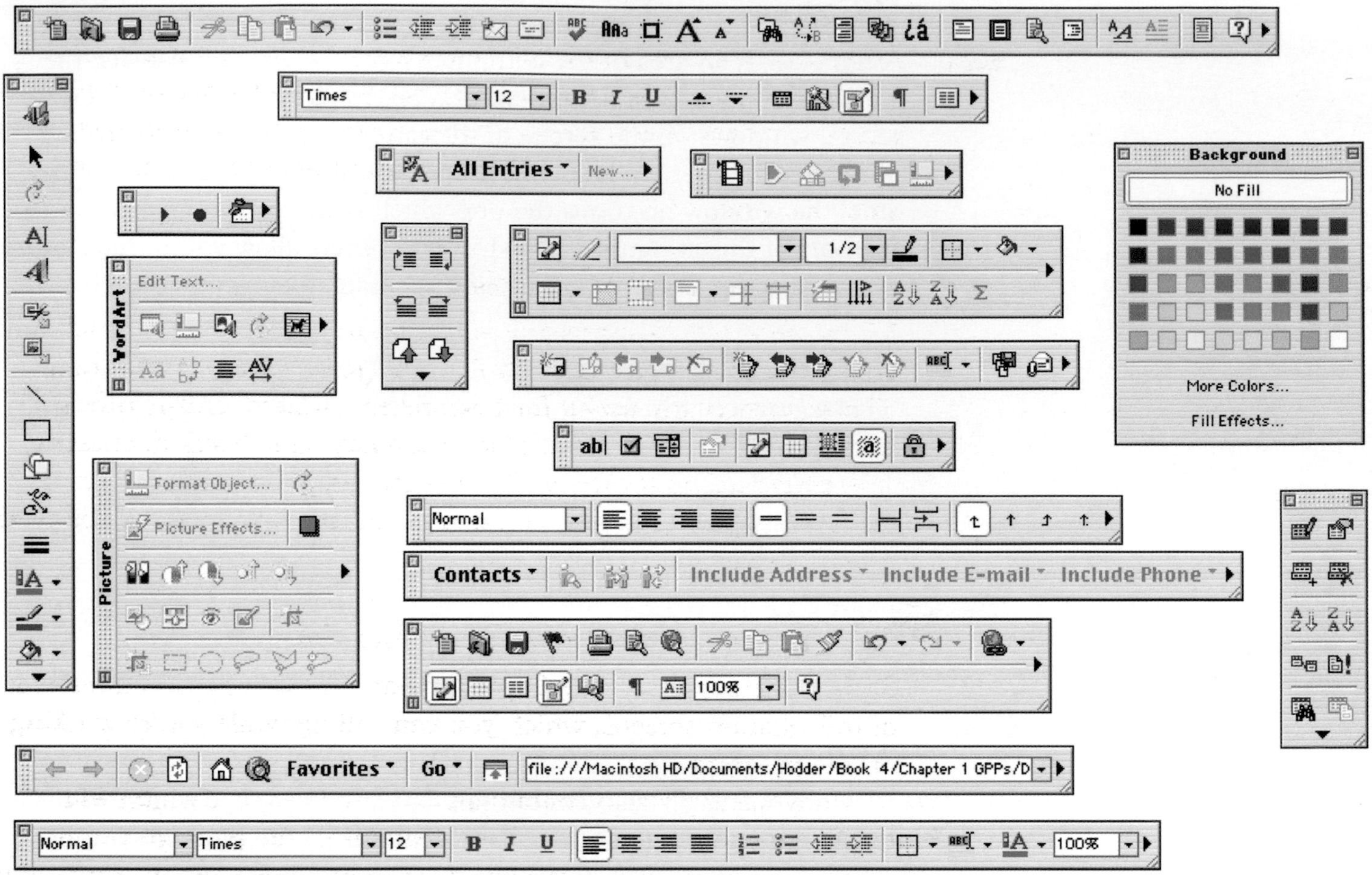

Figure 1.7 *A selection of toolbars from Microsoft Word.*

Credit level

Toolbar

The **toolbar** is a line of screen buttons, which represent the actions or **tools** that are currently available within an applications package. You can see a selection of toolbars in figure 1.7.

Menu

Credit level

A **menu** is another feature that WIMP environments offer. Menus can be 'pop-up' or 'pull-down' depending on the package you are using, but whichever package you use, the menu is operated by pressing or releasing one or more buttons on the mouse. Beginners find menus easy to use because they are given a list of choices, and can pick the most appropriate one for the task.

People who are familiar with a package often prefer to use a sequence of key presses or **keyboard shortcuts** for some operations instead of selecting an option from the menu, because they find it faster than using the mouse. CNTRL-A or CMND-A, for example, is the keyboard shortcut for the SELECT ALL menu choice.

Pointer

You use a pointer on a WIMP environment to select icons or to choose options from a menu. You move the pointer across the screen with the mouse or a trackpad. Some general purpose packages allow you to use the cursor keys on the keyboard instead of a mouse to move the pointer.

Templates and wizards

When creating a document, it is helpful to use a wizard, which is a feature that helps you through the process of document creation. This is particularly useful for beginners. A wizard usually offers a choice of templates. A template is a readymade blank document, with placeholders for items like text and graphics. Using a template can speed up the creation of a document, because much of the page layout has already been done for you.

On-line help and on-line tutorials

Some general purpose packages provide on-line help, in the form of information screens, which you can call up while you're working on the program.

Many packages also contain an on-line tutorial, which will teach you enough about the basic features of the package you're using to get you started. It's like a series of guided lessons on how to use the package.

*It is important to remember here that **on-line** means 'while you are using the program'. It does not mean that the computer must be connected to the Internet to obtain help, although many software companies do provide help on their web sites.*

Software integration

Integrated packages combine two or more general purpose packages (perhaps word processing, spreadsheet and database) in a single package. Integrated packages have a number of advantages over using the general purpose packages separately.

Advantages of using integrated packages

Common HCI

The HCI (human computer interface) is the same for each part of the package. This means that the keys you have to press for an operation in one program in the package will be the same for the same operation in another part. For example CMND–O will open a document whether you're using the word processor or the spreadsheet program.

Links between tasks

Different types of documents can be open at the same time. You can switch between them by pressing a key, choosing from a menu, or clicking the mouse. If you are using a windows system, you can have the different documents open in separate windows.

Ease of transfer of data

It is easy to transfer data between different parts of the package. For example, you can move a table from a spreadsheet to a word-processed document.

Disadvantage of integrated packages

The individual programs that make up the different parts of the integrated package are less powerful or have fewer features than separate general purpose packages, which means that you can't do quite as much with them. For instance, a separate word processing package such as Microsoft Word, may have a grammar checker, but the word processing part of the integrated package such as AppleWorks will not.

Figure 1.8 *Two integrated packages.*

Static/dynamic data linkage

Data in the various parts of the integrated package can be linked together in one of two ways:
1. dynamic data linkage,
2. static data linkage.

Dynamic data linkage means that if the same data is used in different parts of the integrated package, and you change it in one part, the change will be carried over by the computer into all the documents using that data.

Static data linkage means that the data in each part of the package is separate, and changing it in one part will not affect any other files using that data.

EXAMPLE

Look at figure 1.9. When the sales figure for July changes to 23, in dynamic data linkage, changing the number in the spreadsheet automatically changes the figure in the word-processed document. In static linkage, changing the original spreadsheet would have no effect on the copy in the word-processed document, and Mr or Ms Dempster would have to retype the letter.

STATIC

Dear Mr Grimble

You will be pleased to note that our sales figures have increased as shown below:

APRIL	MAY	JUNE	JULY	AUGUST
5	6	10	22	31

I hope that you will reconsider my request for a rise in salary.

Yours sincerely

C. Dempster

DYNAMIC

Dear Mr Grimble

You will be pleased to note that our sales figures have increased as shown below:

APRIL	MAY	JUNE	JULY	AUGUST
5	6	10	23	31

I hope that you will reconsider my request for a rise in salary.

Yours sincerely

C. Dempster

Figure 1.9 *How static and dynamic links work.*

FIRST SPREADSHEET

APRIL	MAY	JUNE	JULY	AUGUST
5	6	10	22	31

STATIC AND DYNAMIC DATA LINKAGE

A spreadsheet table is pasted into a word processed document. Later on, it is realised that a mistake has been made.

The figure in the original spreadsheet is changed from 22 to 23.

In dynamic data linkage, the figure in the word processed document also changes.
In static data linkage, there is no change.

CHANGED SPREADSHEET

APRIL	MAY	JUNE	JULY	AUGUST
5	6	10	23	31

Integration between separate packages in a software suite

A software suite is a collection of separate applications sold as a single package. It is not the same as an integrated package because it is made up of separate programs, which are capable of being run independently.

Here are some examples of software suites and the separate applications which they contain:

- **Microsoft Office Professional**: **Word**, **Excel**, **PowerPoint**, and **Access**
- **IBM/Lotus SmartSuite**: **Word Pro**, **1-2-3**, **Freelance Graphics**, **Organizer**, **Fast Site**, **Screen Cam**, **ViaVoice**

- **Corel WordPerfect Suite Professional**: WordPerfect, Quattro Pro, Paradox, WordPerfect Presentations, InfoCentral, Envoy, Groupwise
- **Sun Star Office**: Star Writer, StarCalc, Star Office Base.

Software suites have the advantage that they are able to share data between the different packages.

Selection of packages

Here are the main purposes of each type of general purpose package:

- **Word processing** — production of text
- **Spreadsheet** — numbers and calculations
- **Database** — storing, sorting, searching and organising data
- **Graphics** — drawing pictures, graphs or charts
- **Desktop publishing** — page layout, like a book or magazine
- **Presentation and multimedia** — production of slides for use with a multimedia projector
- **Web page creation** — making a web page or a web site
- **Expert systems** — classifying data, diagnosing a problem or giving advice.

There are a huge number of packages available — which one should you choose for a particular task?

The answer to this question is further complicated by **the potential of packages to fulfil more than one function**. For example, you may find that a package, which is sold as a word processor, will have features that overlap with other general purpose package functions.

For instance, you may be able to produce a chart from within a spreadsheet or carry out a mail merge operation using only the data contained in your word processor. These extra features are often included by the manufacturer to make their program appear more powerful than a rival package which does the same job. In fact, very few users of modern general purpose packages use all of the features available in the package.

When you are **selecting the most appropriate package to carry out a particular task** you must consider:

- **what hardware and software is available,**
- **the nature of the task.**

EXAMPLE

You have data on a spreadsheet which needs to be charted and printed out in colour. The hardware you have available is:

- Blurb computer, with BlurbSheet (spreadsheet package) and BlurbPlot (charting package), and a colour printer, which only works with the Blurb computer.
- Quack computer with Expel (spreadsheet package) and a black and white laser printer.

Doing the task on the Quack would be very simple, with its easy-to-use HCI and quick plotting facilities, but you could only print it out in black and white.

The Blurb software, although it is less easy to use, because you have to transfer data between packages before you can plot it, may be the only solution since it is running on the system linked to the colour printer.

Data types

Computers store and handle information. Information is handled by a computer in the form of data. Computers control the storage of information and can change the way it is presented to the user. They can control the way data is moved from one place to another and they can change data from one form to another by using the rules that are stored in a computer program.

There are many different types of information stored on a computer as data.

Number

E.g., 0, 1, 2, 3, 4, 5, 6, 7, 999, 0.976, –123 are all numbers.

Text

E.g,. ABCDEFGHIJKLMNOPQRSTUVWXYZ and abcdefghijklmnopqrstuvwxyz are text.

Graphics

The diagrams and other pictures in this book are graphics.

Audio

Music or any other sound produced by a computer is audio.

Photographic

Photographic data is a graphic produced by a digital still camera, webcam or scanner. Photographic data refers only to still images. Most digital still cameras can also record some video data.

Animation

Animation is data made up of moving graphics. Animation is the creation of apparent movement through the presentation of a sequence of slightly different still pictures. One method of producing animation is rapidly changing between two or more still images, like a flick book. Computer animation is used in the film and television industry to mix computer-generated images with 'live' action.

Video

Movies or videos are a type of data produced by a digital video camera and some digital still cameras. Video data is made up of a sequence of moving or 'live' action images. All digital video cameras can also take still photographs, and this is photographic data.

Computers store data as a series of numbers, so any information that can be translated or coded as a series of numbers can be stored as data and processed by a computer. All of the different types of data described above are stored as a series of numbers inside a computer.

Storage of information

Advantages of standard file formats

Software companies know that users can increase their productivity and reduce their workload if it is possible to save files and data so that they may be transferred easily between different packages. For this reason, various standard file formats have been developed. If two general purpose packages are capable of saving or loading files in a standard file format, then it is easy to transfer data between them.

As an example, the word processing package which I am using to write this chapter, has 88 different file formats for saving its files. Each type of application software has its own set of standard file types. The standard file formats, which are dealt with in this section, are text, ASCII and RTF.

Text

Text may be transferred between application packages provided it is stored in a standard file format which both packages can understand. The most common file format used for storing text is ASCII.

ASCII, TXT (text only), text with line breaks

ASCII is the American Standard Code for Information Interchange. An ASCII file consists of plain text, that is individual characters coded in ASCII. Each character in ASCII has its own unique code, which is a number. For instance A=65, B=66 and so on. The representation of text is dealt with later in this book in chapter 21. An ASCII file has no formatting information and so the ASCII file type is readable by most applications. Text with line breaks is a plain text file including RETURN control characters to identify paragraphs.

RTF (Rich Text Format)

RTF is a complex format used to store data from a word processing application. In addition to the text, RTF also holds information about the typefaces, sizes, colour and styles used in the document. RTF can be used to transfer data between most word processing packages without losing the format. This can save a great deal of time because the user does not have to reformat the text after it has been transferred to the new general purpose package.

Why is data stored on computer systems?

Computer systems are being used to store, communicate and retrieve large amounts of information for several reasons:

- The computer can retrieve (or find) the data very quickly, but searching through manual filing systems can take a very long time.
- Manual files take up much more space than computers to store the same amount of information.
- It is difficult to get a complete set of information when using separate manual filing systems.
- They can store large quantities of information on a single disk.
- Computerised filing systems can be constantly updated, so that the information that they contain is always accurate and up to date.
- Databases held by different organisations can be linked in networks, and accessed from anywhere in the world via the Internet. This improves the flow of information between and within organisations.

Because of this, many organisations use computers to store and process records about you and millions of other people. This can help you to get the goods and services you want and can lead to better services, for example, by improving medical care or helping the police to fight crime.

Need for backup

Electronic methods of storage involve using computers to store data on disk or tape. It is important that all the information stored on a computer system is regularly copied to backup disks or tape. If this is not done, one mistake could mean that all of the information is lost.

Calculation of backing storage requirements

It is easy to calculate the amount of backing storage required to hold text in a computer system. Each character requires a storage space of one **byte**, so first work out the number of characters, including spaces, and this gives the answer in bytes. To change the answer into **kilobytes**, remember that 1 kilobyte is 1024 bytes, so divide the total number of bytes by 1024. If the answer is required in **megabytes**, divide the number of kilobytes by 1024, because there are 1024 kilobytes in a megabyte.

Advantages of using general purpose packages

Computers using general purpose packages have a number of advantages over using paper, ink and human brainpower alone:

- **Increased productivity** is possible because:

  - information can be processed more **speedily** and **accurately**,
  - it is **easy to make amendments** to, or change the information,
  - **layout flexibility** — it is easy to change the layout of a document to suit a different purpose.

- **Availability of information** is improved when it is stored in electronic form rather than stored in filing cabinets. For example, it is easier for many people to access the same information when computers are networked.

Security and privacy

The growth of computerised record keeping brings dangers. The information may be entered wrongly, get out of date, or it may be mixed up with information on someone else. The effects can be very serious — people can be refused jobs, housing, benefits or credit, be overcharged for goods or services, or even wrongfully arrested.

If an organisation holds any records about you, you have a **right of access to personal data** in order to **check that it is accurate**. Organisations which hold this type of information are expected to take **precautions to ensure that the data doesn't get lost**, stolen or changed by system failures or mistakes.

An organisation, which holds data, can **control access to the data by using passwords**. Using passwords is one method of **preventing unauthorised access to data**, known as **hacking**.

The **Data Protection Act 1998** covers personal data. Other laws which are concerned with security and privacy include the **Computer Misuse Act 1990**, the **Copyright, Designs and Patents Act 1988** and the **Freedom of Information Act (Scotland) 2002**.

The Data Protection Act allows you:

- to check if any organisation keeps information about you on computer,
- to see a copy of this personal data.

These rights are called subject access rights because people about whom information is held are called data subjects. The person or organisation holding the data is called a data controller (previously the data user). The data controller is responsible to the Information Commissioner, who must be notified about the data that is held.

You can find out more about the role of the UK Information Commissioner at the website:

www.informationcommissioner.gov.uk

Personal data covers both facts and people's opinions. Facts include: name, date of birth, address, examination results, credit rating and medical history. Opinions include political or religious views.

The eight Data Protection principles

1. Personal data should be fairly and lawfully processed.
2. Personal data should only be used or disclosed for the specified purposes.
3. Personal data should be adequate, relevant and not excessive.
4. Personal data should be accurate and kept up to date.
5. Information should not be kept any longer than necessary.
6. Data must be processed in accordance with the rights of the data subjects (see below).
7. Security measures should prevent unauthorised access or alteration of the data.
8. Personal data should not be transferred to countries outside the EC except to countries with adequate data protection legislation.

The rights of data subjects

Data subjects have the right to:

- See data held on themselves, within 40 days, for payment of a fee
- Have any errors in the data corrected.
- Compensation for distress caused if the Act has been broken.
- Prevent processing for direct marketing by writing to the data controller.
- Prevent processing by automated decision making, that is when a computer program makes a decision about you rather than a person.

Exceptions to right of access

There are exceptions to the right of access for government agencies, the police, courts and security services. These exceptions only apply if allowing you to see the data would be likely to, for example, prevent the police from catching a criminal.

You may not see information about yourself if it is kept in order to:

- safeguard national security,
- prevent and detect crime,
- collect taxes.

You do not need to register under the Data Protection Act if:

- the information is used in journalism for historical and statistical purposes,
- the information is personal data relating to your own family or household affairs, for instance, if you have a copy of your family tree on computer.

Computer Misuse Act

The Computer Misuse Act makes it a criminal offence to gain unauthorised access to a computer system, or hacking, or to write and distribute viruses, which can damage data on a computer. Both of these types of crime are now widespread because so many computers may be accessed through networks such as the Internet.

Copyright, Designs and Patents Act

The Copyright, Designs and Patents Act helps to protect copyright owners from having their work copied by others without payment. It is illegal to copy software, for example, without the author's or the software company's permission.

The Freedom of Information (Scotland) Act

'A person who requests information from a Scottish public authority which holds it is entitled to be given it by the authority.' Freedom Of Information (Scotland) Act 2002.

The Freedom Of Information (Scotland) Act came into force on 1 January 2005 and enables any person to obtain information from Scottish public authorities. You can find out more about the act and the role of the Scottish Information Commissioner by looking at the website:
www.itspublicknowledge.info/

Credit level

Social implications

Effects of computers on job types and careers

Computers are used in almost all jobs nowadays and people are expected to be familiar with how to operate them. Some skills, such as touch-typing, are less important for people to have because computers make it easy to correct mistakes. Completely new careers have been brought about because of computers, for instance computer programmers and web site designers.

Retraining

At one time, people used to train as apprentices and had the same job for life. Nowadays this is not the case. Most people expect to retrain several times in their career.

Effects of computers on employment

The development of word processors has reduced the size of the typing pool (see the photos in figure 1.10) because a word processor operator can do the work of at least three typists. Skilled typists are not needed to operate word processors because typing mistakes can be corrected easily. Fewer secretaries are needed in offices because less paper has to be kept and filed.

Figure 1.10 *Offices 50 years ago and today.*

Effects of computers on working conditions

In many offices the working conditions have improved because general purpose packages such as word processing programs have been introduced:

- The office is less noisy because typing on an electronic key board is quieter than a typewriter.
- The office may be cleaner, because the computers can be located separately from a printing works, for example.
- Standards of work can be higher because correction and amendment is easier.

- Tasks can take less time to do, so staff are not overloaded and feel less stressed.
- Links between packages on a computer mean that responses to changes can be very quick — for example if prices change a new price list can be produced easily.
- Some aspects of work have got worse because of computers. A secretary's job used to have quite a lot of variety in it — typing filing, and taking shorthand. But a word processor operator doesn't need to file or take shorthand, and the job can be very boring.

Effects of computers on health

Computer systems themselves can affect your general health, depending on the amount of time that you use them:

- The glare from a computer screen can damage your eyesight if you look at it for long. You can cut down the glare by fitting a screen in front of the computer screen or by wearing specially coated spectacles.
- Radiation from the computer screen is also thought to be unhealthy. Users can wear a special garment to protect them from this radiation.

The EC has developed strict laws about the health and safety of business users of computers. They cover all aspects of the use of computers, from the lighting in the office to the design of the chair that the operator uses.

Mail shots and increased paper

The increase in the use of computers has made it easy to prepare and distribute mail shots to people — you only need to look at your letters each morning to see the amount of correspondence which has originated from a word processor. By combining computerised mailing lists with a standard letter, mail shots become very easy to produce. Most people treat these letters as junk mail and throw them out, often without bothering to read them.

Figure 1.11 *Increased paper!*

This mail shot facility is one reason why computers, which were expected to reduce the amount of paper we use, have actually caused it to increase. A phrase that has been used often is 'the paperless office', which means that all our data would be stored on disk or tape and the amount of paper we use would be less. But this has not happened — paper usage has increased. Vast quantities of paper are being churned out by computer printers and facsimile (fax) machines.

Most people like to have a hard copy of their letters as well as storing it on disk, because they feel that even the poorest quality printout is much easier to read than a document on a computer screen. And there are a few things that you cannot do to an electronic document that you can to one on paper — for example sign it. You can scan your signature and add it to a document, but this is not acceptable legally. Can you think why a scanned signature is not acceptable?

Economic implications

Economic implications mean the cost of owning a computer system, in this case, for businesses. This is sometimes referred to as the *total cost of ownership*. Economic implications include initial costs, replacement costs, running costs and staff costs.

Initial costs

The initial costs are the cost of buying and installing the hardware and software of the computer system.

Replacement costs

Computer hardware and software is constantly changing. Hardware can become out of date in as little as three to six months, which is the interval between the purchase of a new computer system and an updated model being placed on sale. Recognising this fact, many companies change their computer systems every three years or so. The new equipment is always more powerful, although it may not be any cheaper to buy than the equipment it is replacing. The company may have to pay for the disposal of the old equipment, although new laws on recycling place the responsibility for this on the manufacturer.

The same is true for software, although many software companies issue free upgrades for a certain period of time after you have bought the software. Companies may also be forced to upgrade the software to suit new hardware or a new operating system. In any case, the companies' IT department will have to carry out the upgrade, and this will also add to the cost.

Running costs

Electricity, paper, toner/ink and hardware maintenance charges all add to the running costs of computer systems. There may also be software licenses to renew, perhaps annually.

Staff costs

Staff have to be paid to operate the computers, be trained in their use and other staff have to be paid to maintain the computers. Staff also require regular updating of their skills, for instance if new software or hardware is introduced to the workplace.

Foundation level questions

knowledge and understanding

1 Name three types of data stored on a computer system.
2 Give four examples of general purpose packages.
3 Name four common features of general purpose packages.
4 What does HCI stand for?
5 What does the term WIMP stand for?
6 Name three items that can be represented by icons.
7 For any programs you have used, choose one that you think is user-friendly and one that is not. Give reasons to justify your choice in each case.
8 Asfal has lost the manual for his spreadsheet program and cannot remember how to print, but the program has an on-line help system. How will this help him?
9 What is a mail shot?
10 What precautions would you advise an organisation which held personal data on magnetic disk to take?
11 Why is it important that people have a right of access to their personal data?
12 What is an integrated package?
   a. Name one integrated package that is used in your school.
   b. What applications does it contain?
   c. Give two advantages and one disadvantage that an integrated package has over separate general purpose packages.

problem solving

1 Give one example of a how a general purpose package improves the speed or accuracy of processing data.
2 Name a type of package in which you would expect to find:
   a. common features?
   b. a common HCI?
3 What might you find on a document:
   a. header?
   b. footer?
   c. Explain why headers and footers may be useful when printing a book.
4 Which general Purpose package would you use for:
   a. production of text?
   b. calculations?
   c. searching and organising data?
   d. drawing pictures?
   e. page layout?
   f. production of slides?
   g. making a web site?
   h. diagnosing a problem or giving advice?

General level questions

knowledge and understanding

1. What is the difference between an application package and a general purpose package?
2. Why are general purpose packages sometimes described as being 'content free'?
3. Why is increased productivity possible when using a general purpose package?
4. What is meant by the term 'layout flexibility'?
5. What does a general purpose package consist of?
6. Name three files you might expect to find on a CD-ROM containing a general purpose package.
7. What is:
   a. on-line help?
   b. an on-line tutorial?
8. What is a GUI?
9. What is a toolbar?
10. What name is given to unauthorised access to data?
11. Personal data is information about you held on computer.
    a. Make a list of organisations or people who may have information about you.
    b. Compose a letter to one of these organisations, asking to see what information they have.

12. It is important that the information stored on a computer system is accurate, complete and up to date. If the information is not kept in this way, then it can lead to inconvenience, and can have very serious consequences. Give examples of what could happen if information in any of the following systems was not accurate, complete and up to date:
    a. an airline's booking system,
    b. the police national computer,
    c. an employee's tax return.

problem solving

1. What use is an uninstaller program?
2. What is the difference between graphic and photographic data?
3. How could you take audio data into your computer system?
4. How would you print only the third page of a document on your computer system?
5. Does the use of general purpose packages cause an increase or a decrease in the amount of paper being used nowadays? Give a reason for your answer.

Credit level questions

knowledge and understanding

1. What is animation?
2. What is the difference between animation and video?
3. What does 'customising the HCI' mean?
4. What is a keyboard shortcut?
5. What is a:
   a. data subject?
   b. data controller (user)?
6. What rights are given to a data subject by the Data Protection Act?
7. What types of crimes are dealt with under the:
   a. Computer Misuse Act?

b. Copyright, Designs and Patents Act?
8. What is:
   a. static data linkage?
   b. dynamic data linkage?

problem solving

1. How is computer animation used in the film industry?
2. Why is it true to say that all information is numbers?
3. Why is availability of information improved when using a general purpose package?

4   Give one example of how the HCI of a general purpose package may be customised.

5   Is it *always* necessary to be connected to the Internet to receive on-line help?

6   Give one example of static linkage and one example of dynamic linkage in a general purpose package of your choice.

7   Suggest one advantage to be gained by being connected to the Internet when using on-line help.

8   Name one advantage of using keyboard shortcuts when using a general purpose package.

9   Here are some scenarios where you might need to consider which package to use. You do not need to actually design or implement a solution to these problems. Analyse each one, and choose the appropriate hardware and software for this task. Justify your choice in each case.

a. Producing a club newsletter six times a year.

b. Compiling a list of names and addresses for festive greetings cards.

c. Sending the same letter to six different people.

d. Producing a monthly rota for playgroup duty.

e. There is to be a survey of club membership in school. The survey response form has ten check boxes — one for each club in the school — and everyone has to fill in his or her name and class on the response sheet and put a tick in the box for each club they belong to. After you have collected the replies, you must produce a report which lists every person's name and class under every club that they say they belong to.

• Practical work •

1   Ask your teacher to show you a general purpose package such as *Dreamweaver*, *Excel* or *Word*. Have a look at the CD-ROM and any other materials that come with the package, and try to identify the:
    a. manual,
    b. tutorial guide,
    c. quick reference/quick start guide,
    d. software licensing agreement,
    e. software registration document,
    f. system requirements (usually on the box).

2   Find out about the:
    a. film War Games, which showed what could happen when a hacker gained access to the computer controlling the US strategic nuclear missile defences.

b. way your computer system can protect your files from being deleted accidentally or infected by a virus.

c. local postcodes. What is your home postcode? What is the postcode for your school? Look up a local telephone directory which gives a list of all the postcodes in your town or district (like Thomson Local). What do the different parts of your postcode mean? Try to translate the data contained in your postcode into information.

d. Scottish and UK Information Commissioners.

1

• Key points •

- Information (for use by people) is data (for use by computers) with structure.
- Types of data are number, text, graphics, audio, photographic, animation and video.
- Application packages may be single or general purpose.
- General purpose packages need to have information put in before they can be used.
- Examples of general purpose packages are: word processing, spreadsheet, database, graphics, desk top publishing, presentation and multimedia, web page creation, expert systems.
- General purpose packages share common features — like load, run, open, save, print, insert, amend, delete, change text appearance, copy, move, header and footer.
- The human computer interface is the way that the user and the program communicate with each other.
- Changing the HCI of a general purpose package to suit the user is called customising the HCI.
- Programs that are easy to learn to use and help you understand as you are using them are called user-friendly programs.
- On-line help is help in the form of information screens which you can call up while you're working on the program.
- An on-line tutorial is a series of guided lessons on how to use a package.
- WIMP environments use windows, icons, menus and pointers.
- A wizard is a feature that helps you with document creation.
- A template is a readymade blank document.
- Integrated packages combine two or more general purpose packages (like a word processor, a spreadsheet and a database) in a single package.

- Advantages of integrated packages over separate general purpose packages include: common HCI, links between tasks, ease of transfer of data.
- One disadvantage of integrated packages is lack of features.
- Dynamic data linkage means that if the same data is used in different parts of the integrated package and you change it in one part, the change will be carried over by the computer into all the documents using that data.
- Static data linkage means that the data in each part of the package is separate and changing it in one part will not affect any other files using that data.
- The main purposes of each type of general purpose package:
  - Word processing — production of text.
  - Spreadsheet — processing numbers and calculations.
  - Database — storing, sorting, searching and organising data.
  - Graphics — drawing pictures, graphs or charts.
  - Desktop publishing — page layout, like a book or magazine.
  - Presentation and multimedia — production of slides for use with a multimedia projector.
  - Web page creation — making a web page or a web site.
  - Expert systems — classifying data, diagnosing a problem or giving advice.
- When you are selecting the most appropriate package to carry out a particular task you must consider: what hardware and software is available and the nature of the task.
- Manual storage of data usually involves using a filing cabinet or a card index.

- Electronic methods of storage involve using computers to store data on disk or tape.
- If two general purpose packages are capable of saving or loading files in a standard file format, then it is easy to transfer data between them.
- Computers using general purpose packages have a number of advantages:
- Increased productivity is possible because:
  - information can be processed more speedily and accurately,
  - it is easy to make amendments to, or change the information.
  - Layout flexibility — it is easy to change the layout of a document to suit a different purpose.
- Availability of information is improved when it is stored in electronic form.
- All information that is stored on a computer system should be regularly copied to backup disks or tape.
- Personal information stored on a computer system must be accurate, complete and up to date.
- The Data Protection Act 1998 covers personal data. Other laws include the Computer Misuse Act 1990 covering hacking and viruses, and the Copyright, Designs and Patents Act 1988, dealing with the copying of software and other materials.
- Social implications include: job types and careers, retraining, mail shots, effects on employment and working conditions, increased paper.
- Economic implications include: initial costs, replacement costs, running costs and staff costs.

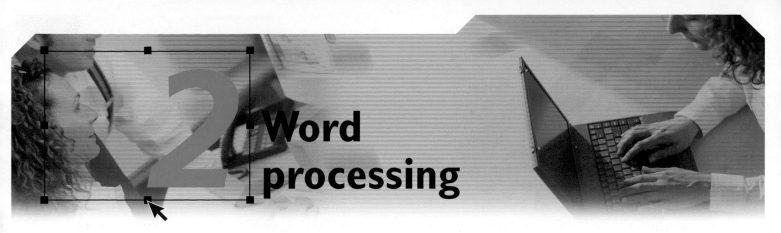

2 Word processing

Most people who use a computer for anything other than playing games use it as a word processor. People use their word processors for many different tasks. At present I am using mine to write this book. Tomorrow I may use it to produce a poster, and the day after for a letter to my local newspaper. If I make a mistake, I can easily change it on the screen before printing the final version. Another name for a printout is a **hard copy**.

What is a word processor?

A **word processor** is a computer that you use for writing, editing and printing text. A dedicated word processor is a system that can only be used for word processing. A **word processing package** is an example of a general purpose package.

Features commonly found on word processors

Word processors have all the features that are found in all general purpose packages. They also have features particular to word processing, such as:

- enter and edit text
- word-wrap
- formatting
  - alter text alignment
  - line spacing
  - alter text style
  - alter page size and layout
  - set margins
  - page breaks
  - tabulation and tables
- search and replace
- spelling check
- grammar check
- standard paragraph

- standard letter and mail merge
- create template.

Let us look at each of these features in a bit more detail.

Enter and edit text

The most common method of entering text into a word processor is by using a **keyboard**. After the text has been entered, it usually has to be **edited**. Editing text may involve **inserting**, **deleting** or **amending**. Insert means to put additional text in. Amend means to change text or correct spelling. Delete means to remove text.

Other possible methods of entering text are by using a **scanner** and **optical character recognition (OCR)** software, or by using a **microphone** and **voice recognition** software. None of these methods gives perfect results each time. For example, the output of **scanned text from OCR** software may need to be **edited**. Figure 2.1 shows an example of the input to, and output from, typical OCR software.

WHY SPAM

Blame Python

How did the name of a meat product come to be associated with unsolicited email? It must have been a source of annoyance for the maker of SPAM, Hormel Foods, that the trademarked name for its product is associated with dubious Web sites.

```
WHY SPAM
Blame Pylhon
How did the name of a moat oroduct come to be associated with
unsoliclted email? It must have been a source of annoyance for
the maker of SPAM, Honmel Foods, that the trademarked name for
its product is associated with dubious Web sites.
```

Figure 2.1 *The input to (left), and output from (right), a typical OCR software package.*

Word-wrap

With a word processor, when you reach the end of a line of text you do not need to press the return key to make a new line. A word processor will make a new line automatically and will move partly completed words at the end of one line to the start of the next line.

Formatting

A word processor allows you to change the way your page is laid out by **formatting** the text.

Alter text alignment

Any text in a document can be **aligned** in four possible ways. When you **centre** text it is placed in the middle of the page, like this:

```
           The quick brown fox jumped
               over the lazy dog.
```
This text is **centred**.

If you **align right**, the text at the right-hand ends will line up, like this:

```
        The quick brown fox jumped
                over the lazy dog.
```
This text is **aligned right**.

Align left makes the left-hand edges even, but the right-hand ends will be uneven.

```
The quick brown fox jumped
over the lazy dog.
```
This text is **aligned left**.

To make both edges even you can **justify** the text. Justifying text means that the software adjusts the spacing between the words in each line to make the ends even. The text of this book is set left aligned.

Line spacing

If you need more space between each line of text, you can set it automatically by choosing double spacing. You can see how different they look in the examples here.

```
The quick brown fox jumped
over the lazy dog.
```
This text is **single spaced**.

```
The quick brown fox jumped

over the lazy dog.
```

This text is **double spaced**.

Alter text style

There are a number of different text styles in common use. These include **bold**, *italic*, <u>underline</u>, shadow, superscript, subscript and ~~strike through~~. It is also possible to use various combinations of these styles. However, if you want your document to be easy for other people to read, it is good advice to limit the use of different styles of text. For instance, which of the following styles is easier to read?

```
The quick brown fox jumped over the lazy dog.
The quick brown fox jumped over the lazy dog.
```

Alter page size and layout

The page size of a document can be altered in a word processor by using the *Page Set-up* menu option. The printer in use determines the *Page Set-up* choice available. Typical page sizes are *A4, A4 small, A5, letter* and *envelope*. The page layout is also known as the *orientation* of the page. Normal page layout (up and down the way) is also called *portrait. Landscape orientation* is the proper name for across the way (or sideways). It is important to set up the page size and layout correctly in order to obtain a printout without wasting paper or ink.

Set margins

You can change the length of each line of the text, making it shorter or longer, by setting the text margins in the document. In most word processors, the text margins are controlled by the settings on a ruler at the top of each page. Figure 2.2 shows a typical word processor screen display with a text ruler.

Figure 2.2 *A word processor screen display with a text ruler.*

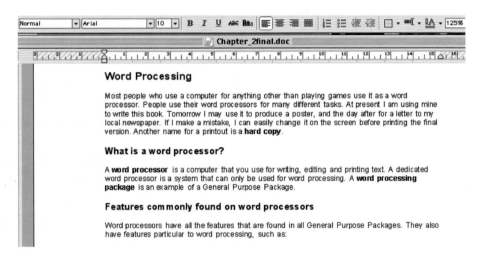

It is also possible to set the margins by typing numbers directly into a dialogue box. Figure 2.3 shows an example of such a dialogue box.

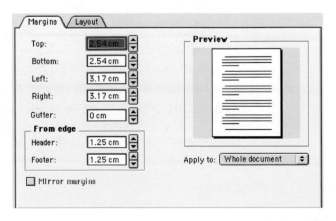

Figure 2.3 *Setting margins using a dialogue box.*

Page breaks

A page break is a point in a word processing document when one page ends and a new page begins. This will happen normally when a page becomes full of text and there is no more room on it. It is also possible to insert a page break at any point in the document. This forces the word processor to take a new page.

Tabulation and tables

By placing tab stops along the text ruler at any position you want you can produce tables. A special key on the keyboard, called the TAB key, is used to move the cursor to each tab stop in turn. There are a number of different tab stops in common use: left, right, centre and decimal. Left, right and centre operate in a similar manner to text alignment, which we discussed earlier. The purpose of the decimal tab is to align columns of figures containing a decimal point. Figure 2.4 shows tab stops in use in a document.

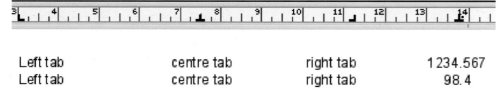

| Left tab | centre tab | right tab | 1 234.567 |
| Left tab | centre tab | right tab | 98.4 |

Figure 2.4 *Tab stops in use in a document.*

Using tab stops is one method of creating tables, but it can take a long time to set the tabs on the ruler and it is not easy to change part of the table without affecting the rest. For this reason, many word processors have a table feature, which makes it easy to draw tables. Table 2.1 is an example of a table.

Quod	Erat	Demons	trandum
Nemo	Me	impune	lacessit
Nihil	Obstat	Imprimatur	Mensa

Table 2.1 *Example of a table.*

In addition to a variety of formatting options within the table, the table feature in some word processors may allow entries to be sorted, or even formulas to be entered, like a spreadsheet.

Search and replace

The search and replace facility means that you can instruct the word processor to replace one word with another wherever it occurs in a document. Some word processors refer to *find and change* instead of search and replace. Word processors carry out search and replace in two ways, globally and selectively.

Selective search and replace

The selective search and replace choice shows you each word before changing it and asks you to confirm that you want it changed by pressing a key before going on to the next word.

Global search and replace

Global search and replace means that every occurrence of the word is replaced throughout the whole document without asking you to confirm that you want each change. This is a very powerful feature but it must be used carefully, otherwise you could make unexpected changes and ruin your document. For example, if you choose to globally change 'is' to 'are' you could end up with Brit*are*h instead of Brit*is*h!

To help avoid mistakes like this, you can search for whole words only, or you can put a space after the word you are looking for (the search string). Some word processors offer extra facilities within their search and replace, such as upper and lower case matching. For example, choosing to replace 'There' with 'Their' would not change 'there' to 'their' because the program is looking specifically for a capital letter at the beginning of the word and will ignore each word that doesn't begin with a capital T.

Spelling check

This book has been written on a word processor with a spelling check facility, so there should be no mistakes in the spelling!

You would normally spell check a document once you have finished entering it into the word processor but before you print out the final version. Spelling checkers have a very large dictionary of correctly spelled words stored on disk. When you run a spelling check it compares all the words in the document with the words stored in the dictionary and highlights any words that it can't find in the dictionary. However, this does not mean that the words you have typed are misspelled – they may be proper names, such as *Harjinder* or *Siobhan*, or simply words it doesn't contain.

When it highlights a word as unknown, the spelling checker will probably offer you alternative words from its dictionary. At this point in the check, you can choose to move to the next word, accept the change the spelling checker has suggested, correct the word by retyping it or have the spelling checker 'learn' the unknown word. If you choose the 'learn' option, then the new word is added to a new user dictionary, not to the main dictionary. This allows you to build up specialised user dictionaries containing for example, technical, medical, legal, or scientific words as required. Specialised dictionaries can often be bought already made up for particular subjects.

CARE!

A spelling checker is not infallible — it can make mistakes. If you use the wrong word in your document (for example, 'their' instead of 'there') but you have spelt it correctly, the spelling checker will ignore it. You could end up with some rather odd phrases.

You must stay alert when spell checking a document. If you hit 'yes' when the program suggests an alternative, but you meant to leave it alone, it will replace your word with the one it wants — again producing some very odd phrases!

Grammar check

A spelling checker program does not check the grammar of your document. For example, 'There is two cows in that field' is incorrect English grammar, but the sentence does not contain any misspelled words, and so would pass a spelling check.

A **grammar checker** works in a similar way to a spelling checker, by highlighting sentences that it thinks contain grammatical errors and suggesting alternative words or phrases. It does not contain a dictionary, but instead is programmed with a set of rules, which it applies to the text in your document. Like a spelling checker, a grammar checker is not always correct. It can improve the grammar in a document, and it is very good for picking up mistakes that you would not otherwise notice. However, some of the suggestions that it makes are just plain wrong, or at best, silly.

Figure 2.5 *The ultimate spelling check?*

A final remark on checkers — spelling and grammar checkers are only useful to users who can spell and write grammatically correct sentences. If the user does not know how to spell, then they will be unable to tell whether or not any suggestion that the checker produces is the correct one.

Word count

This is very useful, particularly if you have to write an essay or an article containing an exact number of words. Some word processing packages will give you a constant readout on the screen of the number of words you have typed. Other packages will give you the total words when you ask them to.

A spelling checker will usually count the number of words in the document, and give you the result when it has finished. This is useful but it means that you must run the spelling checker each time you want to count the words, and this can waste time if you have a long document to go through.

Thesaurus

This is sometimes known as a *word finder*. If you type a word, you can ask the thesaurus program to produce a list of words with the same meaning (synonyms). This can be very useful if you do not want to use the same word twice.

Standard paragraphs

You may find that you want to use the same paragraph in several documents (perhaps you're typing a party invitation). You can save time and typing by making up a standard paragraph and storing it on disk. A standard paragraph is a piece of text which can be combined with others like it to make up a complete document.

Table 2.2 *Examples of standard paragraphs.*

Paragraph number	Paragraph contents
1	Contract for the hire of plant machinery.
2	The period of this loan shall be for no shorter than six months as per our standard contract.
3	The items on loan will be those as specified in appendix D (attached).
4	The party of the first part notwithstanding the use to which the equipment should be put can at any time during the aforesaid period recoup any losses due to malfunction.
5	Any losses which are payable will be honoured on the third of each month preceding the annual claim period.
6	This agreement may be cancelled at any time by giving one month's notice in writing to both parties involved.
7	This contract is invalid unless signed by the Managing Director of Pugloan PLC.

You can then make up a letter by loading a number of such paragraphs from the disk, and placing them into your document. Cut and paste can be used to place each paragraph in the correct order and search and replace may also be used to personalise the document.

Standard paragraphs are typically used in solicitor's offices because legal contracts often have many long and complicated paragraphs, which do not change from one contract to another. To make up a contract, the correct paragraphs are inserted into the new document and the names of the people involved are added. Table 2.2 shows an example of some standard paragraphs which may be used in a contract.

Standard letter and mail merge

There are many instances where standard letters can be used to save typing basically the same letter again and again. Here are just a few examples:

- A letter offering someone a job interview, or even a job.
- Legal documents in a solicitor's office — contracts or deeds of covenant.
- Summonses and notifications of court appearances sent out by the police.

These documents can be produced quickly and easily using a word processor. Each standard letter is typed, and blanks are left for items like name and address, which will be inserted later, and the file is stored on disk. This file can be loaded from disk when needed and the missing details can be added to produce a personalised letter.

Mail merge

If the standard letter has to go to many different people, the list of names and addresses (the mailing list) can be stored on a database. Using a mail merge feature, each name and address on the mailing list will automatically be loaded into the correct places in the standard letters when they are printed. Figure 2.6 shows how this is done. Circular letters (often called 'junk mail') are usually produced using mail merge. When these are sent out or posted, this is known as a mail shot.

The sequence of events is:

1. Create a standard letter using a word processor.
2. Create a database with the required fields.
3. Select the required records.
4. Mail merge (insert fields into standard letter).
5. Print the letters.
6. Post the letters (mail shot).

Mail merge is an example of **dynamic data linkage** between the word processor and the database. Many modern word processing packages include a database feature, which lets the user do a mail merge without having to use a separate database package.

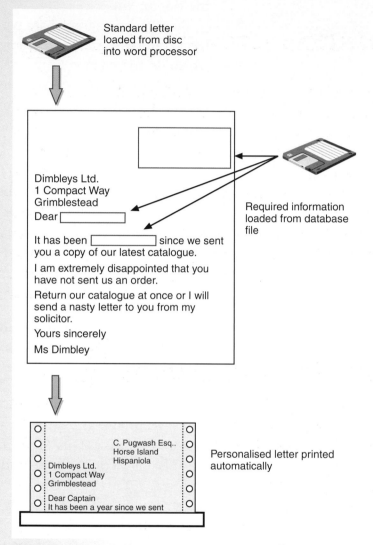

Figure 2.6 *Mail merge using a standard letter.*

Create template

A **template** is a readymade document, with placeholders for items like text and graphics. Using a template can speed up the creation of a document, because much of the page layout has already been done for you.

A template can also contain items such as specific fonts and styles. In order to create a template, you should first set up the document the way you want it, then save the document as a template using the SAVE AS command from the FILE menu.

Foundation level questions

knowledge and understanding

1 Make up a checklist of the features of a word processor that have been described in this chapter. Write a sentence to describe the purpose of each of these features.
2 What is word-wrap?
3 Give examples of the four types of text alignment.
4 State two different common page sizes.
5 State three different text styles.

problem solving

1 What is the difference between a dedicated word processor and a computer system running a word processing package?
2 Apart from the document you are typing, what else has an effect on the page layouts which are possible?
3 Suggest what might happen if you printed a document without bothering to set the margins correctly.
4 Why is it a bad idea to use many different styles in a single document?

General level questions

knowledge and understanding

1 What is a standard paragraph?
2 Name two types of business that could use standard paragraphs.
3 What is a page break?
4 What is a table in a word processed document?
5 State one difference between a spelling check and a grammar check.

problem solving

1 Consider what would happen if a document was to be searched to replace every occurrence of 'he' with 'she'.
  a. Describe how you would do this with the word processing package that you have used.
  b. What might happen to the document if you are not careful?
  c. What type of search and replace should you use to avoid this?
  d. Is there any other way to avoid mistakes like this?
2 Why don't spelling checker programs automatically correct every mistake they find?
  a. Give an example of the type of mistake which would not be highlighted by a spelling checker.
  b. Which feature of a word processor should highlight the type of mistake you described in (a) above?
3 What use is the tabulation feature in a word processor which has a table feature?

Credit level questions

knowledge and understanding

1 What is a standard letter?
2 What is mail merge?
3 What is a mail shot?

problem solving

1 Describe the steps involved in preparing and sending a mail shot to the parents of all the pupils in the first year at your school.

2 If you could have either a spelling check or a grammar check feature in a word processor, which do you think is the most useful? Give a reason for your choice.
3 What is the point in creating a template?
4 Why is it usually necessary to edit text which has been scanned using OCR software?

• Practical work •

1 Look back at table 2.2 of standard paragraphs on page 32.
   a. Enter the text from this table, including the paragraph numbers.
   b. Save the document using the filename Standard1.
   c. Reorder the paragraphs in your document as 1,6,5,7,3,4,2.
   d. Enter your name as Managing Director at the bottom of the page.
   e. Save the document using the filename Standard2.
   f. Print from 1 to 1.

2 Create a standard letter on a word processor on the subject of a party invitation by doing the following:
   a. Create a database with five people's names and a separate 'invite' field.
   b. Enter 'yes' into the invite field on three records.
   c. Carry out a mail merge and produce an invitation for only invited guests.

3 Collect examples of personalised circular letters that have been sent to your home.
   a. Why do businesses take the trouble to send letters like this, rather than sending the same letter to everyone?
   b. Estimate the number of such letters you receive in a year.

• Key points •

- A word processor is a computer used for writing, editing and printing text.
- A dedicated word processor is a system that can only be used for word processing.
- A typical word processor also has the following features:
  - enter and edit text,
  - word-wrap,
  - formatting: alter text alignment, line spacing, alter text style, alter page size and layout, set margins, page breaks, tabulation and tables,
  - search and replace,
  - spelling check,
  - grammar check,
  - standard paragraph,
  - standard letter and mail merge,
  - create template.
- The most common method of entering text into a word processor is by using a keyboard.
- Other methods of entering text are by using a scanner and optical character recognition (OCR) software.
- The output of scanned text from OCR software may need to be edited.

- Word processors allow you to search and replace globally and selectively.
- Spelling checkers work by comparing all the words in the document with the words stored in a dictionary.
- Spelling checkers do not check the grammar in your document.
- A grammar checker works by highlighting sentences that it thinks contain grammatical errors and suggesting alternative words or phrases.
- You can compose a letter by loading a number of standard paragraphs from disk and placing them into a document.
- A standard letter has blanks left for details, such as name and address, to be inserted later.
- Mail merge is the process of automatically loading personal details from a separate mailing list and placing them into the correct places in a standard letter.
- A template is a readymade blank document.
- In order to create a template, you save the document as a template using the SAVE AS command from the FILE menu.

3 Spreadsheet

What is a spreadsheet?

A spreadsheet package is a general purpose package that is mostly used for calculations. A page of a spreadsheet looks like a sheet of paper, which is divided into vertical **columns** and horizontal **rows**. Each column has a letter at the top and each row has a number at the side. Lines between the columns and rows divide the page up into boxes, which are called cells. Cells are identified by their column letter and row number, for example, the cell in the third column and seventh row down is called C7. This is known as the **cell reference**. If you know the reference of a particular cell, then you will know where you are on the page. You can put numbers (**values**), **text** or **formulas** (calculations) into cells, or simply leave them empty. Any text that is in a cell has no effect on the calculations the spreadsheet will carry out, but will be printed along with the figures when you obtain a hard copy. In figure 3.1 you can see a spreadsheet page, with some cell references.

Figure 3.1 *A spreadsheet page showing some cell references.*

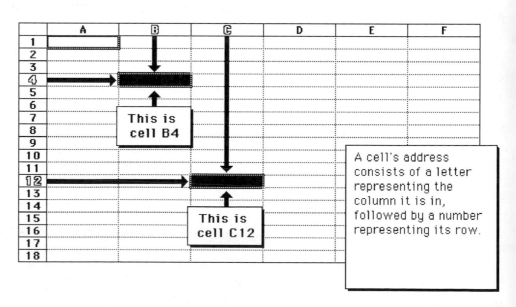

There are usually too many cells in a spreadsheet for them all to be displayed on a screen at once (you can use as many as you want), so the screen acts as a window to look at selected parts of the spreadsheet. You can move round or **scroll** the window when you want.

What are spreadsheets used for?

You can use a spreadsheet for all types of calculations involving numbers — from very simple calculations, like working out the weekly takings from the school tuck-shop, to the complete finances of a multinational company. A typical spreadsheet, with a simple calculation, is shown in figure 3.2.

Row number   Column letter   Text Value   Formula

	A	B	C	D	E
1	School	Tuckshop	Takings		
2					
3		Mars Bars	Coke	Crisps	Kit Kat
4	Monday	32	44	57	89
5	Tuesday	12	22	23	48
6	Wednesday	56	76	73	67
7	Thursday	23	19	34	43
8	Friday	16	20	12	31
9					
10	Total items	139	181	199	278
11					
12	Unit Cost	£ 0.37	£ 0.23	£ 0.19	£ 0.26
13					
14	Cash Total	£ 51.43	£ 41.63	£ 37.81	£ 72.28
15					
16	Weekly Total	£ 203.15			

	A	B	C	D	E
1	School	Tuckshop	Takings		
2					
3		Mars Bars	Coke	Crisps	Kit Kat
4	Monday	32	44	57	89
5	Tuesday	12	22	23	48
6	Wednesday	56	76	73	67
7	Thursday	23	19	34	43
8	Friday	16	20	12	31
9					
10	Total items	=SUM(B4..B8)	=SUM(C4..C8)	=SUM(D4..D8)	=SUM(E4..E8)
11					
12	Unit Cost	£ 0.37	£ 0.23	£ 0.19	£ 0.26
13					
14	Cash Total	=B10*B12	=C10*C12	=D10*D12	=E10*E12
15					
16	Weekly Total	=SUM(B14..E14)			

Figure 3.2 *A typical spreadsheet display. On the left is a simple example and on the right you can see the same spreadsheet with the formulas visible. Note that =SUM(cell1..cell2) in this example is the same as =SUM(cell1:cell2), depending upon the particular spreadsheet application used.*

Spreadsheets are particularly useful for solving problems, planning and making models or simulations of events that happen in real life. By using a spreadsheet you can look at the effects that changing something will have on the final results. This is called looking at a 'what if' situation. Look at figure 3.3. If John Grimes' sales go up in March, then the monthly total will also change.

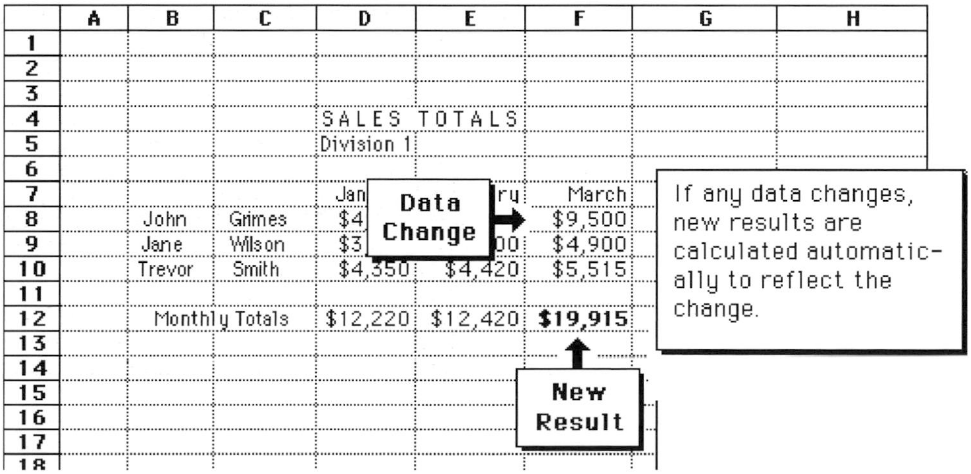

	A	B	C	D	E	F	G	H
1								
2								
3								
4				SALES TOTALS				
5				Division 1				
6								
7				Jan	ry	March		
8		John	Grimes	$4		$9,500		
9		Jane	Wilson	$3	00	$4,900		
10		Trevor	Smith	$4,350	$4,420	$5,515		
11								
12		Monthly Totals		$12,220	$12,420	**$19,915**		

Data Change

New Result

If any data changes, new results are calculated automatically to reflect the change.

Figure 3.3 *Changing data in a spreadsheet.*

EXAMPLE

Figure 3.3 shows a very simple change, but we could look at a much more complex example. A large company uses a spreadsheet with 10,000 cells with many complex formulas to model the company's performance on the stock market. The managing director could find out how changing the annual sales from one branch would affect the overall profits simply by changing a value in one part of the spreadsheet document. This would save her a lot of time and would be very helpful in making management decisions.

Features of spreadsheets

Spreadsheets have all the features common to general purpose packages. The list below gives the features that are special to spreadsheets.

- formulas
- formatting
- cell attributes
- cell protection
- insert rows and columns
- replication
- calculation
- functions
- charting
- conditions
- relative and absolute referencing.

Let us look at these features more closely.

Formulas

Simple formulas*

You can carry out calculations on the spreadsheet by entering formulas into the cells. A **simple formula** is

   = A3 + B9

This formula means 'add the contents of cell A3 to the contents of cell B9 and place the answer in cell …' (here you should give the reference of the cell you want it to go in). Always remember that the formula refers to each cell by its cell reference rather than by its contents.

All spreadsheet packages use the equals (=) sign at the start of a formula. If you enter a formula into a spreadsheet and it doesn't work, the chances are that you have missed out the equals sign at the beginning.

*Note that the Arrangements Document uses the term 'formulae' instead of 'formulas'.

Symbols that are often used in formulas are:

+ (add)
- (subtract)
* (multiply by)
/ (divide by).

Using formulas, you can choose to total, divide, average or express as percentages the figures in rows and columns. If you change the number in a particular cell, the instructions contained in the formulas will change any related figures automatically throughout the whole sheet, so you don't have to go through the whole sheet yourself.

What do these formulas mean?

= A5 + B2
= A10 * P12
= D15 - A3
= K11/E4

Complex formulas

Complex is a fancy name for harder, so **complex formulas** means harder formulas. How about

= ((A9 * 100) - (B9*50) + (H12*H12))/G7?

If you keep reading this chapter until the end, you will see some other examples of more complex formulas.

Formatting

As with word processing, you can format your spreadsheet document to change the way it looks. This is called **altering the cell format**.

Figure 3.4 *In this figure you can see various ways of aligning spreadsheet data in columns.*

	A	B	C	D	E
1			Car Rally Budget		
2	Expenses	May	Percent	June	Percent
3	Basic Food	£ 33420.00	25.71%	£ 10680.00	8.22%
4	Special Food Requests	£ 200.00	0.15%	£ 6000.00	4.62%
5	Lodging	£ 60000.00	46.15%	£ 20000.00	15.38%
6	Cars	£ 20000.00	15.38%	£ 31567.00	24.28%
7	Extras	£ 1200.00	0.92%	£ 1200.00	0.92%
8	Total Expenses	£ 114820.00	88.32%	£ 69447.00	53.42%
9					
10	Total Budget	£ 130000.00		£ 74000.00	
11					
12	Under (Over) Budget	£ 15180.00		£ 4553.00	
13					
14			Centered		
15	Aligned Left				
16					
17		Aligned Right			
18					

Column width

You can make a column as wide or as narrow as you want, so that you can fit in one number or a lot of text into one cell. One reason for increasing the column width is to make sure that there is enough room to display the formulas properly.

Alignment

Again, like a word-processed document, you can choose to align the contents of any cell — left, right or centred. For example, you might want to show a column of numbers centred in their respective cells. You can see what these would look like in figure 3.4.

Cell attributes

You can alter the number of decimal places used when a value is displayed (1, 1.0, 1.00, etc). Some spreadsheets also let you choose from a list of preset configurations for date, currency and so on. For example, if you select 'currency' from the menu, the computer will automatically fix the number of decimal places for any value in that cell at two, because the spreadsheet expects you to enter the value of the currency as pounds and pence. It will also put a currency sign (£) at the start of the number.

If you are trying out some of the examples from this chapter by using a spreadsheet package, be careful not to enter a £ sign. If you do this, then the spreadsheet package will assume that the cell contents are text and not a number, and any formulas that refer to that cell will not work. Always use the cell attributes feature to show currency.

You can apply a different set of attributes to each cell in a spreadsheet. In figure 3.5 you can see some of the cell attributes you can alter.

Figure 3.5 *Here are some of the cell attributes that can be altered in a spreadsheet.*

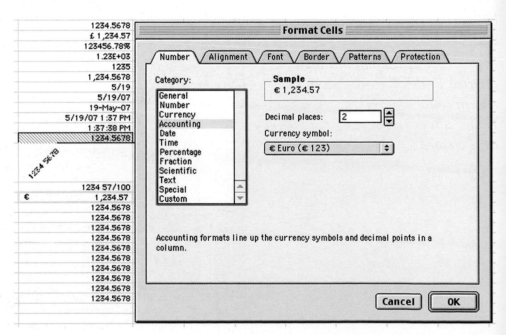

Cell protection

Most spreadsheet packages will allow you to protect or 'lock' the contents of a cell if you don't want them to be changed. This is called cell protection. Cell protection is particularly useful if your spreadsheet is going to be used by someone else, perhaps someone who only wants to enter figures and get the answer without understanding how the spreadsheet works. In this case the programmer of the spreadsheet would set cell protection to cover all of the cells that she doesn't want the user to change.

Insert row and insert column

Most spreadsheets will let you add an extra row or column to your document. If you insert the new column or row between two columns or rows that already have data in them, then the data in those columns (or rows), along with any formulas, will be preserved. Any cell references should also be preserved and reorganised automatically. If the data in your spreadsheet is sorted in order before you insert a new row or column, then always remember to sort the data again after a new row or column has been inserted. In figure 3.6 you can see a spreadsheet window before and after a new column is added.

	D	E	F	G
1				
2				
3				
4	6.5	=D4*2		
5	5	=D5*2		
6	2	=D6*2		
7	100	=D7*2		
8	45	=D8*2		
9	27	=D9*2		
10				
11				
12				

	D	E	F	G
1				
2				
3				
4	6.5		=D4*2	
5	5		=D5*2	
6	2		=D6*2	
7	100		=D7*2	
8	45		=D8*2	
9	27		=D9*2	
10				
11				
12				

Figure 3.6 *A column has been inserted in this spreadsheet. What was in column E is now in column F, and a new column E has been created.*

Replication

Replication simply means copying. This is a particularly useful feature of a spreadsheet, especially for copying formulas from one cell to another. The spreadsheet 'fill down' command is one method of replication.

Look at the spreadsheet in figure 3.7. The formula = H17/I17 has been entered in cell J17. If you want this formula in cells J18, J19, J20 and J21 you can copy it from cell J17 into all the other cells instead of typing it in each time. This saves a great deal of time, and reduces your chances of making a mistake.

Look at figure 3.7 again. Have you noticed that the cell references in column J have changed automatically to match the calculations — H17 has changed to H18, so that when the calculation is carried out the answer in cells J18 to J21 isn't the same as in J17! This happens because the program has a special feature called **referencing**. We will come back to this later.

Figure 3.7 *Relative referencing in a spreadsheet. Note how the numbers in the new cells have changed to keep the calculations correct.*

	H	I	J
15			
16			
17	34	45	=H17/I17
18	56	9	
19	24	8	
20	12	55	
21	43	43	
22			

	H	I	J
15			
16			
17	34	45	=H17/I17
18	56	9	=H18/I18
19	24	8	=H19/I19
20	12	55	=H20/I20
21	43	43	=H21/I21
22			

Calculation

When you change a value in a spreadsheet cell, any other cells in that document whose values are affected by that value, are changed (or updated) automatically. This is known as **automatic calculation**. Some spreadsheets allow you to turn off automatic calculation, preventing this updating until you tell it to. This is called **manual calculation**.

Charting

A printout of the values in a spreadsheet can be very uninteresting to look at but you can make the figures more interesting if you produce them in the form of a chart. One other reason why charts are used is because it is much easier to see trends in a set of figures by looking at a chart than by looking at a set of numbers. Many spreadsheets have built-in charting functions or are linked to other graphics programs that can generate charts. Common types of chart are:

- bar charts
- pie charts
- line graphs.

Spreadsheet packages can produce many kinds of chart, in colour and even in three dimensions. Charts are often used in company reports and can be made into slides for lectures and other presentations. You can see some examples of charts created from the data in the school tuck-shop spreadsheet in figure 3.8.

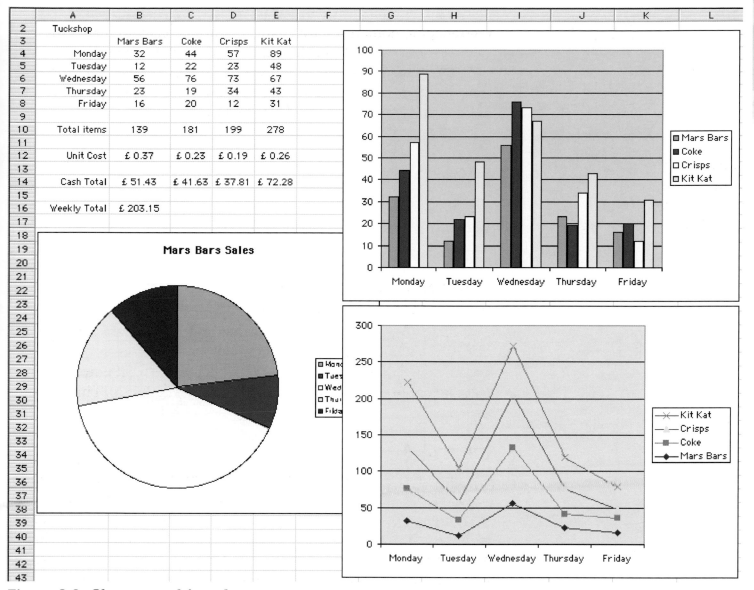

Figure 3.8 *Charts created from the school tuck-shop spreadsheet data.*

Simple charting

Most spreadsheet packages make it very easy for the user to produce charts. The first step is always to select the data that is to be used in the chart. The next step is to choose the chart option from the menu, click on the type of chart that is required, and the chart will be drawn automatically. Some simple charts are shown in figure 3.8.

Fully labelled charting

Depending upon the particular spreadsheet package in use, a chart **wizard** allows the user to choose options related to the chart. Apart from the type of chart that is to be drawn, the user can choose from a range of different options, including labelling the X and Y axes. An example of a fully labelled chart and a chart wizard is shown in figure 3.9.

Figure 3.9 *Fully labelled charting.*

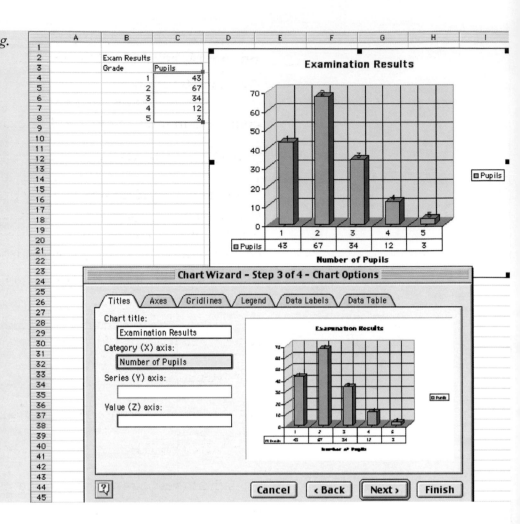

Functions

Spreadsheet packages provide a variety of special functions. Functions are predefined formulas that perform calculations when supplied with the required data. Spreadsheet packages contain many different functions for a variety of applications, but the functions which you should know about for this course are:

SUM, AVERAGE, MAXIMUM, MINIMUM and IF

Sum function

One operation that is commonly done on spreadsheets is totalling a column of figures. To do this, the program uses the sum function. For example, the formula

= SUM (B6:B14)

will tell the program to add together all the values in column B between the cells B6 and B14. Instead of having to write out

= B6 + B7 + B8 + B9 + B10 + B11 + B12 + B13 + B14

we can use a **range** for the numbers. In this example the range is B6 to B14, but it could be any other range of cells, like C1 to C4.

Average function

An **average** function works out the average of a set of numbers contained in a range of cells. For example, the formula:

= AVERAGE (F3:J3)

is the same as adding the contents of the cells F3, G3, H3, I3 and J3 and dividing the total by 5. The advantage of using the AVERAGE function is that you do not need to worry about dividing by the correct number of cells. The spreadsheet will do it automatically.

Maximum and minimum functions

These functions give the **maximum**, or highest number, and **minimum**, or lowest number, in a list. They are used in the same manner as the previous functions:

= MAX (C4:C21)

gives the highest number within the range C4 to C21 and

= MIN (Y6:Z6)

gives the lowest number within the range Y6 to Z6.

IF

The **IF** function is very powerful when you use it in a spreadsheet cell. It allows you to make choices, depending on the values placed in other cells. For example, in cell A10 this formula

= IF (D5>1200,500,200)

means

'if the value of cell D5 is greater than 1200, then place the value 500 in A10, otherwise place 200 in A10'.

You can combine the IF function with the AND and OR logical functions to make the spreadsheet even more versatile. Here are some other examples:

=IF(AND((S62>=26);(Q62="Y"));"Y";" ")
=IF(OR((T85>=20);(U85>=12);(V85>=20));"Y";" ") *

---

* Note that some spreadsheet packages use , (comma) instead of ; (semi-colon)

These functions allow programming of spreadsheets in their own high level language. You could even be using a spreadsheet's language to carry out part of the programming requirement of your Standard Grade course!

Relative and absolute references

As we saw earlier, a cell in a spreadsheet is identified by its cell reference, like A4 or Z19. If you write a formula in another cell, maybe cell B4, you will put

$$= A4 \star 1.75$$

Cell B4 is now said to **refer** to cell A4. Suppose you copy this formula to another cell, somewhere else in the spreadsheet, maybe B5. You will find that the formula in B5 has changed to

$$= B4 \star 1.75$$

The spreadsheet has copied the formula **relative** to the original one. This is normal in a spreadsheet, and will always happen unless you tell the program not to do it. Look at the example in figure 3.7. What happened to the formula as it was copied into cells J18, J19, J20 and J21?

Sometimes you may not want the formula to behave like this. The alternative to relative referencing is called **absolute referencing**. In the previous example concerning cell B5, if the formula had been copied into cell B5 using an absolute cell reference, then it would have remained as

$$= A4 \star 1.75$$

Spreadsheets sometimes use the $ symbol in the cell reference to show that absolute referencing is in operation.

EXAMPLE

You can use absolute referencing in a spreadsheet that calculates the net price of items, to which you must add value added tax (VAT). Suppose you place the current VAT rate in cell B2. Each item, regardless of its position in the spreadsheet, must be multiplied by the contents of cell B2 to give the final price. When you set up the spreadsheet, any formulas will have to refer to cell B2 using an absolute reference. Copy the example in figure 3.10 and try it using a spreadsheet package.

Figure 3.10 *Absolute cell referencing in a spreadsheet. This one helps work out how much things will cost when VAT is added to them.*

	A	B	C	D
1				
2	VAT RATE	17.50%		
3				
4				
5		net price	VAT	gross price
6				
7	balloons	£ 0.50	£ 0.09	£ 0.59
8	lollipops	£ 0.12	£ 0.02	£ 0.14
9	dummys	£ 0.65	£ 0.11	£ 0.76
10				

	A	B	C	D
1				
2	VAT RATE	.175		
3				
4				
5		net price	VAT	gross price
6				
7	balloons	.5	=B7*B2	=B7+C7
8	lollipops	.12	=B8*B2	=B8+C8
9	dummys	.65	=B9*B2	=B9+C9
10				

Foundation level questions

knowledge and understanding

1. Make up a checklist of the features of a spreadsheet described in this chapter. Write a sentence to describe the purpose of each of these features.
2. What types of information can be contained in a spreadsheet?
3. What makes spreadsheets so useful to businesses?
4. What is the difference between automatic calculation and manual calculation in a spreadsheet?

problem solving

1. Use a spreadsheet planning grid to construct at least one of:

   a. the seven times multiplication table,
   b. the school tuck-shop spreadsheet shown in figure 3.2,
   c. your weekly expenses/how you spend your pocket money,
   d. the number of hours of television watched by each of the pupils in your class.
2. Ask your teacher to check your work before testing your spreadsheet, then:

   a. print out the spreadsheet,
   b. produce a pie chart or bar chart of your results.
3. Which function helps you add a column of numbers in a spreadsheet?

General level questions

knowledge and understanding

1. Explain what each of the following spreadsheet formulas do:

   a. = AVERAGE (D5:G5)
   b. = MAX (F4:K4)

2. What happens when a formula in a spreadsheet is replicated?
3. State two ways in which the cell format in a spreadsheet may be altered.

4 State two ways in which the cell attributes in a spreadsheet may be altered.

problem solving

1 What can be done to prevent accidental alteration of the formulas in a spreadsheet?
2 A pupil enters a simple formula in a spreadsheet, but the formula does not work. Suggest one possible mistake that may have been made when the formula was entered.
3 State one advantage of using a chart instead of a table of numbers.
4 A pupil wants to display a number as currency and they put a £ sign before the number.
   a. Suggest what might happen when they do this.
   b. Suggest one method of avoiding this problem.

Credit level questions

knowledge and understanding

1 What features of a spreadsheet are in use in these formulas:
   a. = A5/8?
   b. = IF(G1>=50,"Pass","Fail")?
2 What feature of a spreadsheet can help the user create a fully labelled chart?

problem solving

1 Describe a situation when you would use relative referencing in a spreadsheet and one when you would use absolute referencing.
2 Write a formula which displays the text 'Well done' or 'Average' depending upon whether the value in cell T7 is greater than 4.

• Practical work •

Carry out the following tasks using a spreadsheet package with which you are familiar:

1 *Mr Grimble's sweetie shop*
   a. The sales for Mr Grimble's sweetie shop are shown below:

Sweet	Monday
Humbugs	23
Mint Imperials	12
Gobstoppers	56
Total	

   i. Enter these headings and figures in a spreadsheet and use the spreadsheet to calculate the total for Monday's sales.

Figure 3.11 *Mr Grimble's sweetie shop.*

ii. Save your spreadsheet as *Grimble1*.

iii. Print out your spreadsheet, showing any formulas you have used.

iv. Write a sentence to explain how you got the spreadsheet to do the calculation.

b. One full week's sales were:

Sweet	Mon	Tues	Wed	Thurs	Fri
Humbugs	23	1	5	78	123
Mint imperials	12	34	7	9	49
Gobstoppers	56	26	2	56	12

Daily totals

i. Enter these headings and figures in a spreadsheet and use the spreadsheet to calculate the daily sales total.

ii. Add an extra column to the spreadsheet to show the item totals and weekly total.

iii. Save your spreadsheet as *Grimble2*.

iv. Print out your spreadsheet, showing any formulas you have used.

v. Write down *two* improvements that would make your spreadsheet more useful to Mr Grimble.

c. Make the following changes to the spreadsheet you saved as *Grimble2*:

i. Write formulas to calculate the daily sales totals, the item totals and the average sales of each item.

ii. If humbugs are 1p each, mint imperials 2p and gobstoppers 7p, what would Mr Grimble's weekly takings be? Write suitable formulas to calculate these answers and enter them in appropriate places in your spreadsheet.

iii. Save your spreadsheet as *Grimble3*.

iv. Print out your spreadsheet, showing any formulas you have used.

v. Use the spreadsheet data to produce a pie (or other type of) chart showing the item totals for one week.

vi. Print out a copy of the chart.

2 *Children in Need*

The Cubs have decided to organise a sponsored swim to raise funds for the Children in Need Appeal. The swimming pool can be hired for £30 an hour on a Saturday, and they have decided to hire it for six hours. The *Akela* has also decided that it would be a good idea to get some badges printed as awards to people who take part in the swim.

Peter John is working towards his Computing Hobbies Badge at Cubs. He has estimated some of the cost and has worked out the following figures using a spreadsheet package on his computer.

Figure 3.12 shows the figures if 40 people take part and raise an average of £10 each.

	A	B	C	D	E
1					
2	Children in Need Appeal				
3					
4				Unit Cost	
5	Number of People	40	Badges	£ 0.50	£ 20.00
6	Amount raised per person	£ 10.00	Pool Hire/hr	£ 30.00	£ 180.00
7			Number of hours	6	
8	Income Total	£ 400.00		Costs Total	£ 200.00
9					
10				Profit for Charity	£ 200.00

Figure 3.12 *Children in Need.*

a. Which cells in the spreadsheet contain formulas?

b. Write down what these formulas are, and then type in this spreadsheet and get it working.

c. Save it as *Swim1*.

d. Print out your spreadsheet, showing any formulas you have used.

e. Peter John decides that the Cubs must aim for a higher profit, and that they must aim for at least 50 people, raising £15 each. Which cells will have to be changed to take account of this?

f. Make these changes and save your new spreadsheet as *Swim2*.

g. Use the spreadsheet to find out how much the Cubs would raise if more people took part in the swim, or if the average amount each of the 50 people raised was more than £15. Write your answer on the last printout.

h. How many people would have to be sponsored at £20 if the Cubs wanted to raise £1000? Write your answer on the last printout.

3 *Siobhan's chairs*

Siobhan works in a shop that sells furniture, but the pay is not very good. She has looked around for a way to add to her wages. She has a home computer and she has designed and built a chair to sit on while using it. Siobhan thinks that she could make more chairs and sell them, and she uses a spreadsheet program to work out how much the chairs would cost to make using various materials and how much she would have to charge for them to make a profit.

Figure 3.14 *Siobhan's chair.*

	A	B	C	D	E	F
1						
2	Siobhan's	Chairs	PLC			
3						
4		COST OF		TIME	TOTAL	TOTAL
5		WOOD	PARTS	HOURS	LABOUR	COST
6						
7	Oak	£ 55.00	£ 10.00	6	£ 27.00	£ 92.00
8	Beech	£ 20.00	£ 10.00	6	£ 27.00	£ 57.00
9						
10	Labour /hr	£ 4.50				

Figure 3.13 *Siobhan's chairs.*

The spreadsheet in figure 3.13 shows how much it would cost to make the chair in two types of wood: oak and beech. The PARTS heading covers items like glue, dowels and varnish. Siobhan decides to pay herself £4.50 an hour.

a. Enter the data into a spreadsheet.

b. Save the spreadsheet as *Chair1*.

c. After she has worked out her basic costs, Siobhan realises that she has to deliver any chairs she sells. Her father agrees to deliver the chairs, but insists that Siobhan pays for the petrol. They agree to a price of £10 per chair. Insert a new column called DELIVERY, and insert £10 for each chair.

d. Change the formula in the TOTAL COST column.

e. Save this new version as *Chair2*.

f. Print out your spreadsheet, showing any formulas you have used.

g. Siobhan's boss says that she has a friend in the timber trade who will supply the wood at a lower cost — £40 for the oak and £15 for the beech.

h. Change your spreadsheet to take account of these new figures.

i. Save this version as *Chair3*.

j. Now Siobhan needs to work out how much to charge for the chairs. She decides that she would like a profit of 40%. Add a column to the end of the spreadsheet for SELLING PRICE.

k. Save this version of the spreadsheet as *Chair4*.

l. How much would Siobhan have to sell the chairs for if she decided on a 10% profit?

m. What would the price be if her profit were 50%?

n. With the help of your spreadsheet, work out what Siobhan would make in a year, assuming that she makes and sells 50 chairs.

• Key points •

- A spreadsheet is divided into columns and rows.
- Each box on the sheet is called a cell.
- Each cell is identified by a cell reference — such as B8, Z19.
- Cells can contain numbers, text or formulas, or may simply be left empty.
- Spreadsheets can show the effects of changing events. These are called 'what if' situations.
- Spreadsheets have the features common to all general purpose packages, and, in addition:
  - formulas (= A7 + B6)
  - formatting (column width and alignment)
  - cell attributes (number of decimal places)
  - cell protection (prevents cell contents from being changed)

- insert rows and columns
- replication (copying)
- calculation (automatic and manual)
- functions (SUM, AVERAGE, MAXIMUM, MINIMUM)
- charting
- conditions (IF)
- relative and absolute referencing.
- Relative referencing copies the formula relative to the original one.
- Absolute referencing means the cell references do not change when they are copied.
- The IF function can be used to make decisions in a spreadsheet.

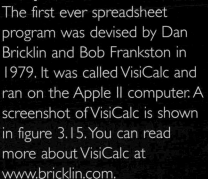

Did you know?

The first ever spreadsheet program was devised by Dan Bricklin and Bob Frankston in 1979. It was called VisiCalc and ran on the Apple II computer. A screenshot of VisiCalc is shown in figure 3.15. You can read more about VisiCalc at www.bricklin.com.

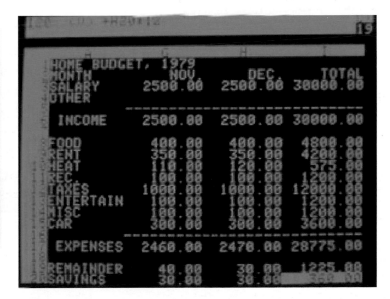

Figure 3.15 *VisiCalc.*

4 Databases

What is a database?

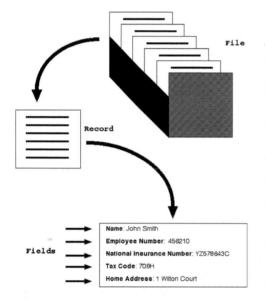

Figure 4.1 *An example of a manual database. Computer databases use the same principles, storing individual items in fields, which together make up a record. A group of records is a file.*

Any large amount of information must be stored in some sort of order so that it can be accessed easily and quickly — a filing system is ideal for the job. Everyone uses filing systems, but they may not always be aware of them — cups, saucers and plates are probably 'filed' in a kitchen cupboard, newspapers might be 'filed' under a coffee table, socks might be 'filed' in a drawer in your bedroom.

A **database** is a structured collection of similar information, which you can search through. Databases can be stored manually (in a filing cabinet, or on index cards) or electronically using a computer system. Keeping your database on computer means that you can access the information much more easily and quickly than if you used the manual system — but the data must be organised in a way that allows speed of access. A program that is used for organising data on a computer system is called a **database package**. A database package is an example of a general purpose package.

Data in a database is organised into **data files**, **records** and **fields**. A **data file** is a collection of structured data on a particular topic. Individual files are made up of records. A **record** is a collection of structured data on a particular person or thing. Each record is made up of one or more fields. A **field** is an area on a record, which contains an individual piece of data. Figure 4.1 shows more clearly how a database is structured.

Figure 4.2 *uk.yell.com*

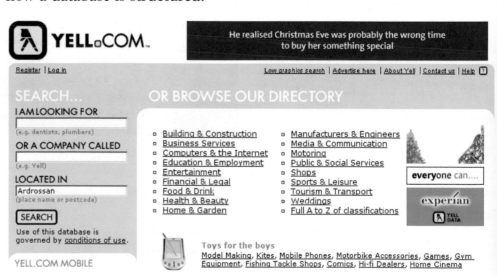

EXAMPLE

Look at a telephone directory. Each separate area in the directory — name, address, town and telephone number — is a field. The set of fields (that is, the whole address and phone number) for one person is a record. The set of records together — the whole directory — is a file. There are now many computer databases which you can access to obtain telephone numbers, for example uk.yell.com (figure 4.2).

What are databases used for?

Databases are used in many applications by many different organisations. Here are a few:

- the telephone directory
- the Police National Computer
- the Inland Revenue
- the Driver and Vehicle Licensing Centre
- a personal Christmas card list
- a magazine's mailing list.

EXAMPLE

The fingerprints of people who have been convicted of an offence or who are awaiting trial are now stored on computer databases. The first fingerprint database to be used in the UK was installed in October 1991 by the Scottish Criminal Records Office in Glasgow at a cost of £1.5 million. It is called The Automatic Fingerprint Recognition System. This system provides a 24 hour electronic fingerprint identification and verification service for the eight Scottish Police Forces. The National Fingerprint Collection currently stands at 321,357 records.

Using computer databases means that records can be processed quickly and accurately, making information available at a speed which is impossible using a manual system.

Database features

Databases, like word processors and spreadsheets, have all of the features common to general purpose packages. The following features are particular to databases:

- create fields
- create, add and alter records
- alter record format
- search, query or find

- search for information on CD-ROM/WWW (Internet)
- sort
- computed field
- alter input and output formats
- keywords.

Let us look at each of these features separately.

Create fields

When you start a database application, the first thing you must do is to create one or more fields to hold the information, which you want to store. Some programs also ask you to choose the size of the field and the type of information that you wish to store.

Types of field

- A numeric field only stores numbers.
- A text field is used to hold letters, numbers and symbols.
- A graphic field holds a picture. Some databases allow a graphic field to hold a multimedia file like a movie.
- Date fields can only contain dates. When the field is created, you can decide how the date is to be displayed, for example 25/12/07 or 25 December 2007.
- Time fields can hold hours, minutes and seconds.

Choosing the size of the field

If you have to decide on the size of the field you want, remember to allow for spaces, because a space is counted as a character and will take up the same amount of room as any other character (letters, numbers, punctuation). It is probably better to choose a field that is bigger than you expect to use, because you may not be able to change it later on without creating a new database.

Create, add and alter records

Once you have created the basic record structure by deciding on the fields, the next step is to use the database package to enter information. At this point the database is empty, and you must add a new record for each item that you are going to enter. After the database has been completed, you may wish to update it if the information changes. In order to do this, you will have to alter a record. Searching a database is dealt with later in this chapter. Once you have located and altered the record, always remember to save the new version of the file.

Alter the record format

Some database packages allow you to alter the record format, that is, you can add new fields or delete existing ones. You can also change the type or size of the fields. You can see a variety of record formats by looking at the various examples in this chapter.

Search

Searching and sorting records are the two main reasons for using a database package. Depending on the database package in use, the commands query or find may be used instead of search. As far as your Standard Grade course is concerned, you can use any of these three terms that you wish. As far as this book is concerned, we will stick with 'search'.

Searching on one field

The search facility allows you to look through the database for information. To do this, you must enter the field that you want to search and the details that you want to find. This is called to search on a field using whatever conditions you require. To give an example, you might be looking for items on your database with 'height in metres greater than 5000' — here the field that you would be searching on is 'height in metres' and the condition you want is 'greater than 5000'. Searching on one field is called a simple search. Figure 4.3 shows how a simple search on one field can be carried out.

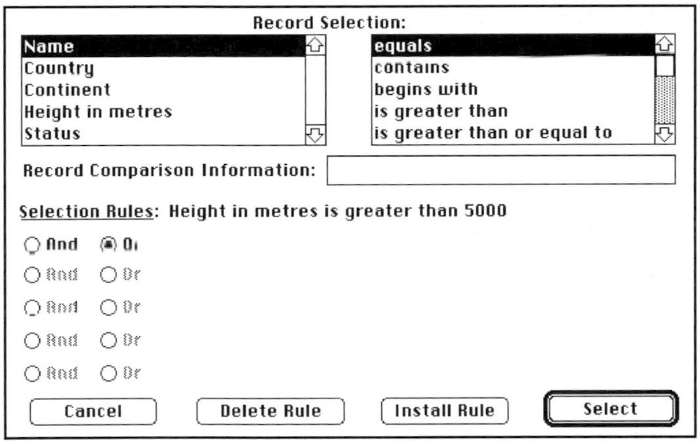

Name	Country	Continent	Height in metres	Status
Cotopaxi	Ecuador	South America	5978	active
Popocatapetl	Mexico	Central America	5452	active
Sangay	Ecuador	South America	5410	active
Tungurahua	Ecuador	South America	5033	active
Kilimanjaro	Tanzania	Africa	5889	dormant
Misti	Peru	South America	5801	dormant
Aconcagua	Argentina/Chile	South America	6960	believed extinct
Chimborazo	Ecuador	South America	6282	believed extinct
Orizaba	Mexico	Central America	5700	believed extinct
Elbrus	USSR	Asia	5647	believed extinct
Demavend	Iran	Middle East	5366	believed extinct

Figure 4.3 *A (simple) search on one field in a database.*

Searching on more than one field

You can link the conditions of search in a field. At the end of the search, all the records which match the set of conditions you have put in will be displayed. If no records match the required conditions, then you can choose to change the conditions or abandon the search. Searching on more than one field is called a complex search.

The conditions which you can use in a complex search are usually linked by the words AND or OR. Linking two conditions with AND means that both of the conditions must be met for a search to be successful. Linking two conditions with OR means that either condition can be met for the search to be successful.

EXAMPLE

In figure 4.4, you can see a search through three fields on a database. The fields are 'occupation', 'sex' and 'age', and the conditions are 'scholar', 'female' and 'greater than 12'. A successful search will give you a list of girls on your database over 12 who are still at school.

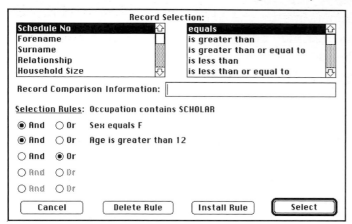

Forename	Surname	Relationship	Family Size	Sex	Age	Occupation	Town of Birth
Charlotte	Page	D	4	F	14	scholar	Datchworth
Louisa	Skeggs	D	7	F	15	scholar	Datchworth
Philadelphia	Colborn	N	3	F	13	scholar	Littlehampton
Lucy M	Chalkley	D	8	F	13	scholar	Aston
Mary J	Shadbolt	D	8	F	13	scholar	Tewin
Dinah	Cutts	D	6	F	13	scholar	Tewin
Jane	Brownsell	D	9	F	13	scholar	Datchworth
Emma M	Collins	D	4	F	14	scholar	Datchworth

Figure 4.4 *A (complex) search on more than one field in a database.*

Here is a simple sentence you can learn which will help you when answering theory questions about searching.

> Search the file _____ on the field _____ for records which match the condition _____ .

You can fill in the blanks with the *file name*, the *field name* and the *condition* to match any search. You can add more fields and conditions. Even if you don't know the correct answer, you should still get some marks, because you have used the terms *search*, *file*, *field* and *record* in the correct manner.

Search for information on CD-ROM/WWW (Internet)

Simple search for information

This is basically the same as the simple search we have just discussed. The main difference is that a general purpose package is not used to carry out the search. In the case of a CD-ROM (or DVD-ROM) such as an encyclopaedia, when you are not using the Internet version, then you must use the encyclopaedia's own program to search. For a simple search you would only enter one word. When searching the Internet, you could use an on-line encyclopaedia or a search engine such as *Google* or *Jeeves* to find the information.

Figure 4.5 *Simple search using Encyclopaedia Britannica.*

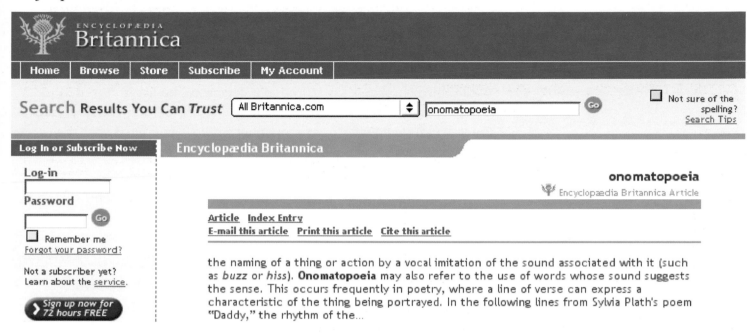

Complex search for information

Instead of entering a single word, for a complex search you should enter more than one word to search for. In the case of the Internet, you should use the advanced search feature of the search engine. Alternatively, you could use a website such as *yell.com* to carry out a search. Figure 4.6 shows the results of such a search.

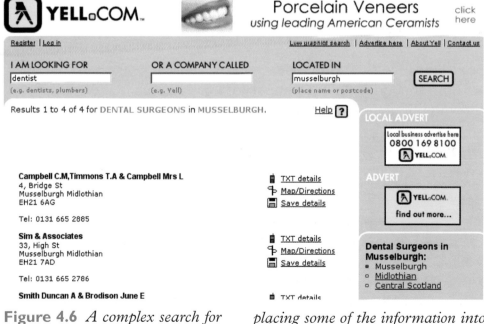

Figure 4.6 *A complex search for information on the Internet.*

Students should note that the reason for the inclusion of these searches is to satisfy the requirements for Core Skills certification. Rather than just obtaining a printout directly from the search results, you should process the information you obtain from these sources, for example, by placing some of the information into a word processing package and formatting it neatly.

Sort

Sorting allows you to arrange the records in a database in **alphabetic** or **numeric** and **ascending** or **descending** order. Ascending numeric order would be 1, 2, 3, 4 …, descending alphabetic order would be Z, Y, X, W … To start the sort you must choose a field (like 'height in metres' in the last example) on which to sort the database, or the records will stay in the order in which you typed them, not the order you want.

You should use sorting whenever you have changed the database by adding or deleting information.

EXAMPLE

A club membership list is stored in a database. The list is stored in alphabetical order by member's name and a new person joins the club. Once you have added the new member's details you must sort the database to make sure that the records are still in alphabetical order.

Sort on one field

In the example shown in figure 4.7, the database has been sorted in order of 'Atomic Number'.

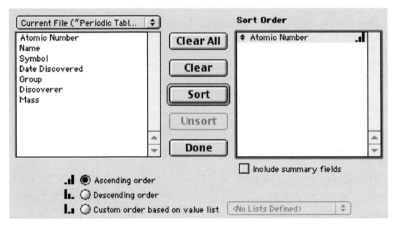

Atomic Number	Name	Symbol	Date Discovered
1	HYDROGEN	H	1766
2	HELIUM	He	1895
3	LITHIUM	Li	1817
4	BERYLLIUM	Be	1798
5	BORON	B	1808
6	CARBON	C	
7	NITROGEN	N	1772
8	OXYGEN	O	1774
9	FLUORINE	F	1771
10	NEON	Ne	1898
11	SODIUM	Na	1807
12	MAGNESIUM	Mg	1755
13	ALUMINIUM	Al	1825
14	SILICON	Si	1823
15	PHOSPHORUS	P	1669

Figure 4.7 *Shows records in a database sorted on one field.*

Sort on more than one field

You can sort on more than one field. For example, the database shown in figure 4.8 is sorted on *surname* and then *age*.

Figure 4.8 *Records in a database sorted on two fields.*

Forename	Surname	Address	Age	Occupation
JOHN	BAIRD	28 KING STREET	1	U
JAMES	BAIRD	36 KING STREET	13	FARM WORKER
JANET	BAIRD	3 NEW BRIDGE	20	HOUSEWIFE
WILLIAM	BAIRD	3 NEW BRIDGE	27	FARM SERVANT
JANET	BAIRD	36 KING STREET	53	HOUSEWIFE
JOHN	BAIRD	36 KING STREET	62	FARM WORKER
MARTHA	BEATTIE	10 NEW BRIDGE	21	GENERAL SERVANT

Here is a simple sentence you can learn which will help you when answering theory questions about sorting.

```
Sort the file _____ on the field _____
in _____ order.
```

You can fill in the blanks with the *file name*, the *field name* and the order such as *alphabetical* or *ascending numerical*. You can add more fields and orders. Even if you don't know the correct answer, you should still get some marks, because you have used the terms *sort*, *file* and *field* in the correct manner.

Computed fields

A computed field (sometimes called a calculated field) can be included in a database. A computed field will carry out a calculation on another field or fields and give you an answer, like a formula in a spreadsheet. To explain this, think of a database that contains two fields, called *total pay* and *total deductions*. You could set up a third field, called *net pay*, with the formula (= *total pay* – *total deductions*). This is a computed field. You can see another example of a computed field in figure 4.9.

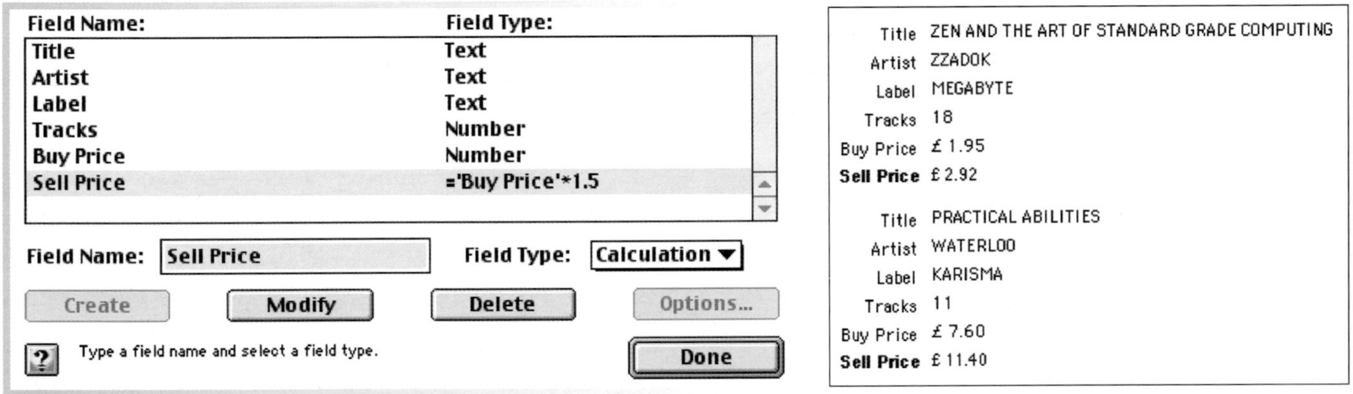

Field Name:	Field Type:
Title	Text
Artist	Text
Label	Text
Tracks	Number
Buy Price	Number
Sell Price	='Buy Price'*1.5

Field Name: **Sell Price** Field Type: **Calculation ▼**

[Create] [Modify] [Delete] [Options...]

[?] Type a field name and select a field type. [**Done**]

Title ZEN AND THE ART OF STANDARD GRADE COMPUTING
Artist ZZADOK
Label MEGABYTE
Tracks 18
Buy Price £ 1.95
Sell Price £ 2.92

Title PRACTICAL ABILITIES
Artist WATERLOO
Label KARISMA
Tracks 11
Buy Price £ 7.60
Sell Price £ 11.40

Figure 4.9 *A computed field in use in a database. The field 'Sell Price' is calculated by multiplying the contents of the field 'Buy Price' by 1.5.*

Altering input and output formats

You can choose how the information in your database is presented to you by altering the format. Some applications allow you to alter both the way the screen looks (the input format) and how the report looks (the output format). In figure 4.10, you can see one of the many possible database input formats. You can set up screen input formats to ease the problems associated with data collection, for example, by making the screen less cluttered or by increasing the size of the text. By using only selected fields in the printout and rearranging the position of the fields you can alter output formats. This means that you can prepare documents, like invoices, on your database, and print them directly from the database without having to retype them onto pre-printed forms.

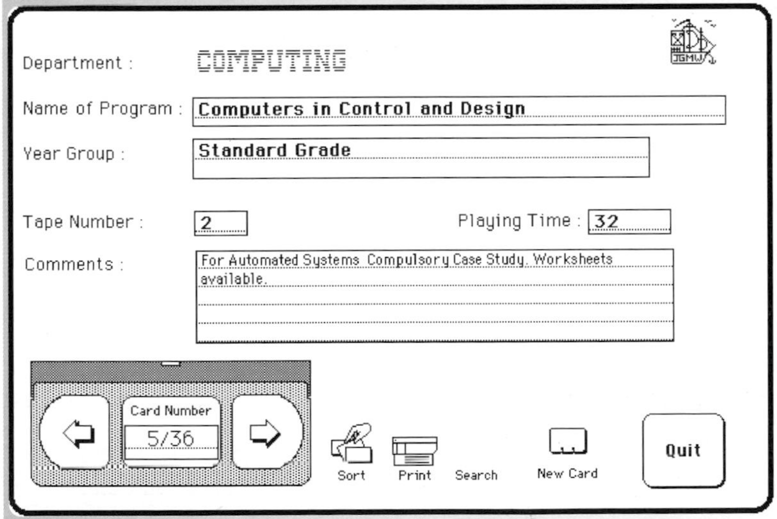

Department : COMPUTING

Name of Program : Computers in Control and Design

Year Group : Standard Grade

Tape Number : 2   Playing Time : 32

Comments : For Automated Systems. Compulsory Case Study. Worksheets available.

Card Number 5/36   Sort Print Search New Card [Quit]

Figure 4.10 *An example of a screen input format on a database.*

Use of keywords

The text that you use to search a file for a particular entry or part of an entry is called a keyword. Some systems use the term search string instead of keyword. By choosing your keywords carefully you can save a lot of time when using databases.

EXAMPLE

You might wish to search a large database such as *yell.com* for someone's phone number or address.

You can narrow down the search by entering the person's full name. However, you must be careful how you enter the name – a search for '*John Harold Greaves*' may be unsuccessful because the database file contains the name only as '*John H. Greaves*'. Unless the name you're searching for is very common (like *Smith*), you would probably be more successful by simply searching for the family name ('*Greaves*' in our example).

If you are not sure how a word in the database is spelt, you may enter only part of it as the keyword and the database will match all items with that set of characters. You can also select 'start of string' or 'whole word', to help your search. In figure 4.11 the user has searched a database using only part of a word, and it has come up with several items to choose from.

Curiously, the approach of using part of a word as a keyword to search the Internet using a search engine may not give you results like those in the list above. If you enter 'comput' into the Google search engine, for example, it will find what it can for 'comput', but also suggest to you 'Did you mean: <u>computer</u>?' If you are interested, try out some other search engines and see what happens.

Figure 4.11 *Using a partial search string on MSN Encarta Dictionary.*

Calculation of backing storage requirements in a database

It is easy to calculate the amount of backing storage required to hold data in a database. Look at each field in one record and count or estimate the maximum number of characters, which are likely to be in each field. Add these together to give the maximum size of a record.

Now multiply the size of one record by the number of records in the database. This will give you the total number of characters in the database. Each character requires a storage space of one byte, so this gives the answer in **bytes**.

To change the answer into **kilobytes**, remember that 1 kilobyte is 1024 bytes, so divide the total number of bytes by 1024. If the answer is required in **megabytes**, divide the number of kilobytes by 1024, because there are 1024 kilobytes in a megabyte.

Foundation level questions

knowledge and understanding

1. Write down the types of information each of the following databases are likely to contain.
   a. Police National Computer.
   b. Inland Revenue (Income Tax) Office.
   c. Driver and Vehicle Licensing Centre.
   d. Your Christmas card list.
   e. The mailing list of a magazine.
2. Explain in your own words what is meant by the terms:
   a. data file
   b. record
   c. field
   d. search
   e. sort.
3. Make up a manual database on at least one of the following:
   a. A list of people and their telephone numbers.
   b. A Christmas card list.
   c. Each person in the class's favourite pop group, DVD, computer game and television programme.
   d. A birthday list.

problem solving

1. Put the following terms in order of size, starting with the smallest: file, field, record.
2. How many fields would you create in a database designed to hold names and addresses? Give a reason for your answer.
3. How many records would you create in a database designed to hold the marks for all of your class tests?
4. When would you need to edit a record?
5. State two things you should do after adding a new record to a database.

General level questions

knowledge and understanding

1. What is the difference between a simple search and a complex search?
2. Name five different field types.
3. State one difference between a simple search on a database and a simple search for information on a CD-ROM.

problem solving

1. What type(s) of field would you use to hold a list of people's names and their birthdays?

Credit level questions

knowledge and understanding

1. What is a keyword?

problem solving

1. State one reason why it may be necessary to alter the:
   a. input screen format,
   b. output format
   of a database?
2. a. Calculate the storage requirements for an address book database containing 300 records. Use your own name and address as a typical entry.
   b. How large would the file be if you included each person's telephone number as well?

1 Using a computer and a database package that you are familiar with, enter the details of the manual database(s) you created earlier. Carry out whichever of the following tasks applies to your database.
   a. Sort the entries in alphabetical order in the name field.
   b. Print out your own record.
   c. Print out the records of the people whose name begins with the same letter as yours.
   d. Search for the people who were born in the same month as you.
   e. What other information could you find out from this database?

• Key points •

- A database is a structured collection of similar information which can be searched.
- Databases can be stored manually on filing cards or electronically using a computer system.
- A database package is a program that is used for organising data in a structured way on a computer system.
- Data in a database is organised into data files, records and fields.
- A data file is a collection of structured data on a particular topic.
- Individual data files are made up of records.
- A record is a collection of structured data on a particular person or thing.
- Each record may consist of one or more fields.
- A field is an area on a record which contains an individual item of data.
- In addition to the features that all general purpose packages have, a database also allows you to create fields, create, add and alter records, alter record format, search, query or find, sort, use computed fields, alter input and output formats, use keywords.

- You can alter the record format of the database to suit a particular purpose.
- Sorting allows the records in a database to be rearranged in a given order such as alphabetical or ascending numerical.
- You can search a database for information which matches the conditions you have entered.
- A simple search is on one field.
- A complex search is on more than one field.
- To search a file for a given entry or part of an entry you can use keywords.
- A computed field will carry out a calculation on another field or fields and give you an answer.
- You can choose how the information in your database is presented to you by altering the input or output format.
- The amount of backing storage required to hold data in a database can be calculated by multiplying the number of records by the number of characters in each record.

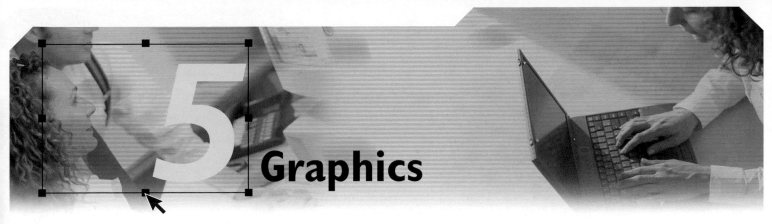

5 Graphics

What is a graphics package?

A **graphics package** is another general purpose package, one that you use to draw pictures (or **graphics**) on the monitor. Like any other general purpose package, the pictures produced can be saved to backing storage or printed out as hard copy.

What is a graphics package used for?

The pictures produced by a graphics package can be used in many ways:

- The pictures may be put with text into a document, like a report or a newsletter — or even a book, like this one.
- They may be used in a computer game, like *The Sims*.
- Computer graphics are used to produce special effects in television programmes and motion pictures.
- Using a graphics package you can alter photographs, for example, from a digital camera, before they are printed.

Like any information displayed on a computer screen, graphics are made up of tiny dots called **pixels**.

Features of graphics packages

In a graphics package you will find all the features possessed by general purpose packages, as well as the following features:

- draw graphic
- enter text
- common tools
- alter tool attributes
- scale graphic
- rotate graphic
- scan and edit graphic
- crop graphic.

Let us look at each of these features more closely.

Draw graphic

You draw graphics — lines, boxes, circles or whatever — on the screen by moving the **cursor** (this is also called the **pointer**). To draw a shape, you must position the cursor on the screen where the shape is to start and then move it in the directions you require to make the shape. Different programs use different methods to control the cursor, and depending on the program, you may find yourself using:

- a mouse
- a trackpad
- a graphics tablet
- the keyboard

to move the cursor around the screen.

Enter text

Graphics packages allow you to enter text anywhere on the screen — so that you can label a diagram, for instance. To do this, move the cursor to the position where you want to place the text and type in the words — just as in the example in figure 5.1.

Common tools

One of the main features of graphics packages is that they have a set of **tools** that you can use for drawing. Each tool in a graphics package has a different function. Here is a list of some common tools:

- **shapes** — circle, ellipse, rectangle, polygon, arc, straight line
- **free hand drawing** — pencil, brush
- **selection** — arrow, rectangle, lasso, magic wand, eyedropper, crop
- **fill** — set fill colour, set line and brush colour
- **eraser**
- **text**
- **zoom**.

Additional special tools are often provided to help with editing digital photographs and scans, for example, redeye, clone, smudge, blur and sharpen.

Usually a menu of the tools available is displayed on the screen. This is called the **toolbar**. A selection of toolbars is shown in figure 5.2. How many of the tools listed above can you spot? Can you see any tool not listed? If so, try to guess its function.

On some graphics packages the cursor will change shape whenever a new tool is selected, so that you can tell which tool you're using. Other packages display a message on the screen or highlight the tool chosen from the menu to remind the user of their choice.

Figure 5.1 *How text can be entered in a graphics package.*

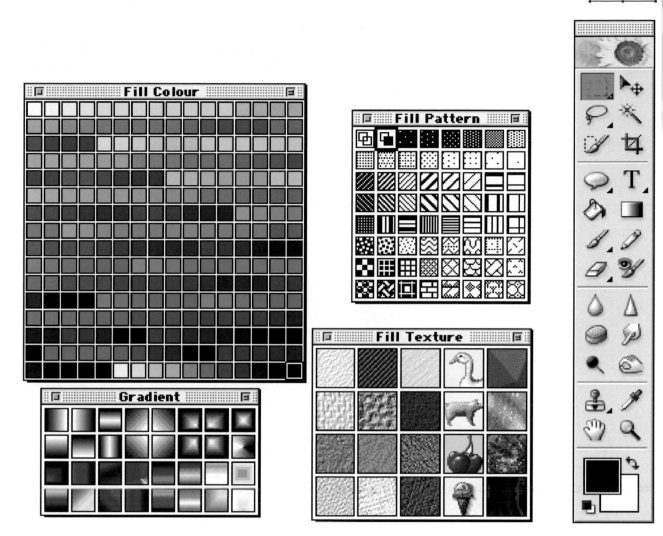

Figure 5.2 *A selection of toolbars and attributes from some graphics packages.*

Alter tool attributes

Whatever method of tool selection the package uses, it will also allow you to change the properties of the tool. This means that you don't have to use different tools to draw lines of different thickness, for example, because you can choose the width of the line that the line tool will produce. Or you could change the type of colour or shading you're using simply by choosing a different type of shading for the shading tool to use. You can see some examples of different attributes in figure 5.2.

Scale graphic

You can change the size of your picture using a graphics package. The changes can be very precise — by putting in a percentage number you can make tiny changes to the graphic. Or you can resize the picture very roughly by stretching or squashing it using the selection tools.

Rotate graphic

Often you will want to rotate a picture or part of a picture. You can rotate a picture in some programs by choosing the area you want to change using the selection tool and simply turning it in any direction. In other programs, the user must enter the exact number of degrees through which he or she wants to rotate the selected area — this will give a very precise rotation. Using this facility to rotate text can be very useful if you are labelling diagrams. In figure 5.3 you can see some examples of graphics and text that have been scaled and rotated.

Figure 5.3 *Scaling and rotating graphics and text.*

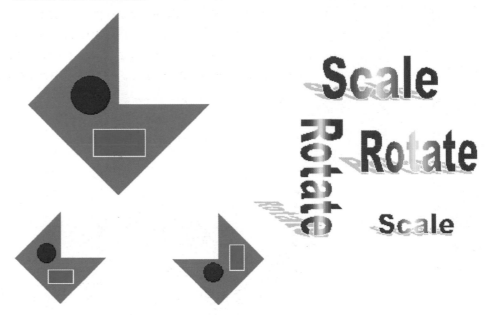

Scan and edit graphic

Scanning a graphic involves using a scanner, which is an input device. Scanning usually involves two steps. The first step is a quick scan, to preview the scanned graphic on the screen, and then the user is able to select the area to be scanned in more detail. At the same time, the user can set the scanning resolution and any other details, such as whether the picture is to be scanned in colour or black and white, or whether it is a photograph or a drawing (line art) which is to be scanned.

After the graphic has been scanned, the scanned picture is displayed on the screen, and may then be saved to disk using a file name of the user's choice. The user should also select the graphics file format, which is to be used to save the picture, for example, JPEG.

Some scanning software automatically saves the scanned picture, without the user having to do anything. Some graphics packages are set up so that the user can operate the scanner from within the graphics package. This makes the process of scanning almost as easy as loading a file.

The next step in the process is to **edit the graphic**. The scanning software allows the user to **crop** the graphic at this stage, but any detailed editing really requires the use of a graphics package. Once the editing is complete, the edited graphic file can be saved to disk and printed or used as required.

Crop graphic

To **crop** a graphic means to reduce its size by cutting parts from the edges of the graphic. A graphic may be cropped to remove an unwanted part of it, or to focus the user's attention on one particular subject within the graphic. Another reason for cropping a graphic is to reduce its file size so that it will take up less room on backing storage. Chapter 21 explains how to calculate the backing storage requirements for bit-mapped graphics.

Figure 5.4 *The effect of cropping a graphic – before and after. Note that the original picture had too wide a subject area, and by cropping the graphic it has focused the user's attention more closely on the subject of the picture.*

Paint and draw

Graphics packages can be classified into two main types: **paint** (or **bit-mapped**) and **draw** (or **vector**). Both types of package are used to make pictures, but they work differently.

Paint packages produce pictures by changing the colour of the tiny dots, called pixels, which make up the screen display. When two shapes overlap on the screen in a paint package, the shape on top rubs out the shape underneath.

Figure 5.5 *Separating overlapping shapes in paint and draw packages. In a draw package the two items are separate, but in a paint package you can see that there's a bit missing from the underneath part.*

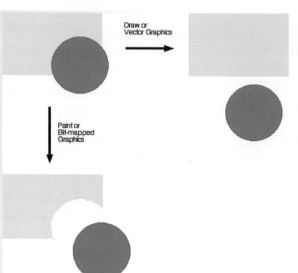

Draw packages work by producing objects on the screen. When you overlap shapes in a draw package, the shapes remain separate. They can be separated again and both shapes stay the same.

You can see these effects in figure 5.5.

Graphics resolution

The quality of the picture you can produce is determined by the **resolution** of the graphics available. The smaller the size of the pixels, the finer the lines that you can display on the screen.

Small pixels mean high resolution. Large pixels mean low resolution.

Figure 5.6 *A high-resolution graphic.*

Figure 5.7 *Teletext graphics are low resolution.*

A high-resolution graphic is shown in figure 5.6. One way of describing the resolution of the screen is to give the number of pixels horizontally and vertically. Teletext graphics have 75 pixels across and 80 pixels down on each screen. This gives a very low resolution picture, as you can see in figure 5.7.

The computer's operating system allows you to choose whether you want high or low-resolution graphics. High-resolution graphics usually need more random access memory than low-resolution graphics, and you will also need more memory if you want to use more colours on the display.

Foundation level questions

knowledge and understanding

1 What is a graphics package used for?
2 Make a checklist of the features of a graphics package described in this chapter. Write a sentence to describe the purpose of each of these features.
3 Which tools have been used in this diagram?

Figure 5.8 *Graphic tools.*

problem solving

1 Why do graphics packages have a selection of tools?

General level questions

knowledge and understanding

1 What is meant by the terms:
  a. scale graphic?
  b. rotate graphic?
  c. tool attribute?
2 Name two tool attributes that may be altered in a graphics package.

problem solving

1 Which tool attribute is being altered here?

Figure 5.9 *Tool attributes.*

Credit level questions

knowledge and understanding

1 What do we mean by the term graphics resolution?

2 Describe the process of scanning and editing a graphic.

problem solving

1 Which type of graphics package — paint or draw — would be suitable to:
   a. draw your self-portrait?
   b. draw a plan of the school?
   c. produce a logo for your club?
   d. edit a digital photograph?
   Give a reason for your choice in each case.

2 How could you tell the difference between a paint graphic and a draw graphic?

• Key points •

- A graphics package is a program that allows the user to draw pictures.
- Graphics, like any information displayed on a computer screen, are made up of tiny dots called pixels.
- A graphics package has the features common to all general purpose packages, and also has the following:
    - draw graphic
    - enter text
    - common tools
    - alter tool attributes
    - scale graphic
    - rotate graphic
    - scan and edit graphic
    - crop graphic.
- Common tools are used for drawing shapes, free hand drawing, selection, fill, eraser, text and zoom.

- Tool attributes may be changed, for example, line width and fill pattern.
- Scaling a graphic alters its size.
- Rotating a graphic turns it around.
- A scanner, scanner software and a graphics package are required to scan and edit a graphic.
- To crop a graphic means to reduce its size by cutting parts from its edges.
- Graphics packages can be classified into two main types: paint and draw.
- Paint packages produce pictures by changing the colour of the pixels that make up the screen display.
- Draw packages work by producing objects on the screen.
- High-resolution graphics are made up from a large number of small pixels.
- Low-resolution graphics are made up from a small number of large pixels.

6 Desktop publishing

What is desktop publishing?

Desktop publishing is producing professional looking reports, newsletters, newspapers, booklets and magazines using a computer system. It is known as desktop publishing or DTP because the whole process takes place within the computer system sitting on the user's desk.

What does a desktop publishing system consist of?

A desktop publishing system usually consists of:

- a computer system
- a desktop publishing application package
- a high-quality printer such as a laser printer
- a scanner and a digital camera to allow photographs and diagrams to be input.

Examples of desktop publishing application packages

- Professional packages include: *Adobe Indesign*, *Adobe PageMaker*, *Corel Ventura*, and *Quark Xpress*.
- Home and small business packages include: *GSP Power Publisher*, *Microsoft Publisher*, *Mindscape Print Shop Deluxe*, and *Serif Pageplus*.

You can see an example of how *Quark Xpress* is used in figure 6.7.

How is a desktop publishing package used?

A desktop publishing package is not designed to be used as a word processor, or as a graphics package — any text or graphics that are used in the final publication should have been prepared in separate application packages. The already prepared material is imported into the desktop publishing package and placed on the page where it is needed. Desktop publishing packages are sometimes called **page layout packages**, because they are used to arrange or lay out each page of a publication.

Many of the terms that were used in traditional publishing are still used in desktop publishing. Let's look at publishing before and after desktop publishing packages were introduced.

The traditional publishing process

In the traditional publishing process: the author types the text of the book (this is called the *copy* or the *typescript*) on a typewriter or word processor and supplies rough drawings and photographs for illustrations. The copy is then typed into a special machine called a typesetting machine, which has all the correct typefaces and styles needed. Once the text has been put into the typesetting machine or *typeset*, the *proof* is printed out and someone has to check it for mistakes. The corrections must be entered on the text held on the typesetting machine. While the text is being typeset, the pages are designed, and any pictures needed are drawn and photographed, so that they can be reproduced. The corrected text and the pictures are then pasted onto the pages to fit the page design, and another proof, this time of the whole page, is printed and must be checked. The pages are corrected again, printed out and checked again. Any more mistakes are corrected. Once everyone involved is happy with the way the pages look they are sent to the printer. An outline of the traditional desktop publishing process is shown in figure 6.1.

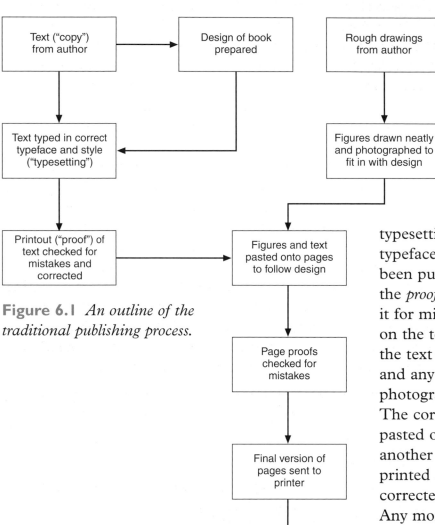

Figure 6.1 *An outline of the traditional publishing process.*

The desktop publishing process

In figure 6.2 you can see the main features of desktop publishing. Here are the typical steps that you would use to create a publication using a desktop publishing application package.

1 The text is typed using a word processor.
2 The graphics are created using a graphics package, or are **imported** using a scanner or digital camera.

3   Templates for the document are designed. The template will include the number of columns of text that will go on a page, where the graphics will be placed and the page numbers. This operation involves the same skills as page design in the traditional process.

4   The text is imported from the word processor and placed on the page where needed. The text should already have been checked for mistakes using the spelling checker in the word processor. If there is too much text to fit on a single page it will run on to the next page, and you can set the text to flow or wrap around the places reserved for graphics.

5   Data from other programs can also be imported — like a table or a chart that you created from data in a spreadsheet package.

6   The graphics are inserted into the places reserved for them. You may have to cut the picture to fit (this is called cropping) or scale it to suit the space available on the page. The completed pages that you have created are then saved to disk.

7   The final document is printed. This can be done on a high-quality laser printer, but if you want a really high-quality printout, or a large number of copies, for example when printing a book (like this one!), a magazine or a newspaper, printing can be done by a professional printer. The disk file containing the pages would then be sent to the printer via electronic mail. You can read more about electronic mail in chapter 10.

Banner headline

Imported graphic

Text wrap around graphic

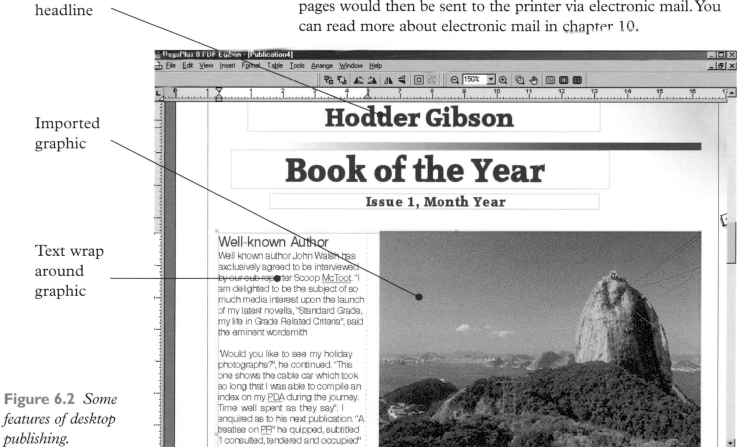

Figure 6.2 *Some features of desktop publishing.*

Toolbar

Non-printing guide

Ruler

Page number

Figure 6.3 *A DTP package in action.*

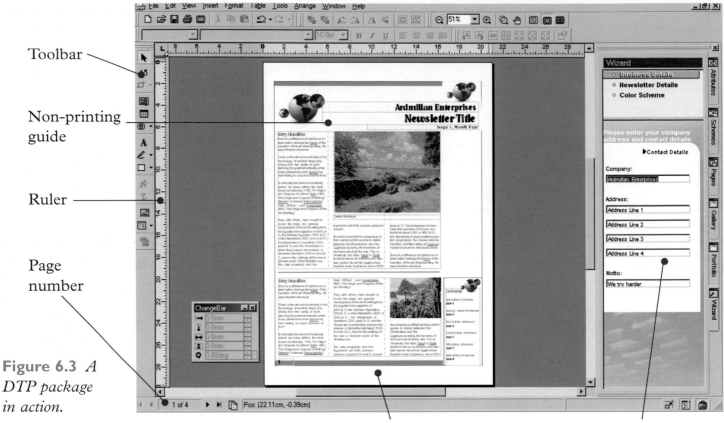

Reduced view of page   Wizard/Template menu

Features of desktop publishing packages

The particular features of desktop publishing packages which we will look at in this chapter are:

- use wizard or template
- enter text
- add clip art

- import graphic
- scale graphic

- change layout
- import text
- text wrap around graphics.

Let's look at these features more closely.

Templates

On a desktop publishing system you can create **templates** or **master pages**. The templates can be used to mark out standard layouts for a number of pages. For example, in a newsletter you might want to use two columns of text on editorial pages, three columns for features pages and four columns for news pages. Using the template you can create as many different master pages as you want — one for each kind of page layout required. Most desktop publishing packages will give you some ready-made templates that you can use for different types of publication. Using these ready-made templates can speed up the process of laying out a page, especially if you haven't used a desktop publishing package before.

Newcomers to a desktop publishing package often use a **wizard** or **assistant**, which leads the user step by step through the creation of a document. Figure 6.4 shows part of the process of choosing a template using a wizard.

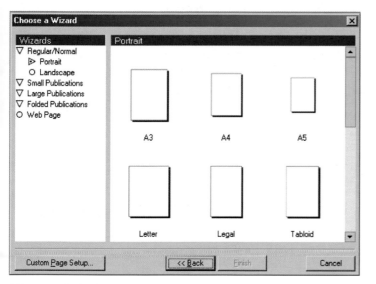

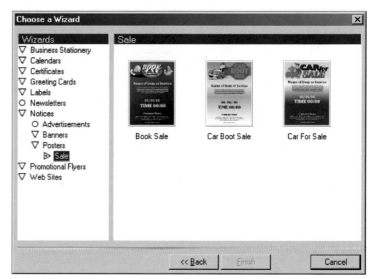

Figure 6.4 *Some desktop publishing templates.*

Enter text

Like all other general purpose packages, a desktop publishing package allows the user to **enter text** into a document. Most of the time, text is input to a desktop publishing package from a separate word-processed file rather than by entering it directly using the keyboard.

Add clip art

While graphics packages allow users to draw their own pictures, many users find it convenient to use **clip art**. Clip art is a collection of professionally drawn images supplied on disk or included as part of an application package. Clip art is so-called because of the way the images are 'clipped' from a file and 'pasted' into a drawing.

Clip art may also be obtained from specific sites on the World Wide Web or by using the image search feature on a search engine such as Google. It is important to check the copyright of images downloaded from the web, although there is usually no problem if they are for personal use in school as part of your coursework. It is a different matter if they are going to be sold or used commercially.

Import graphic

Importing graphics is an alternative way of including images in a document other than adding clip art. One of the features of clip art is that it is designed to be easily included in a document. This is achieved by the clip art having a particular **file format**. The file format is the way the image is saved and the type of file that is created. Typical graphics file formats include GIF, JPEG, BMP, TIFF and EPS.

When writing this book, I have to take care over the graphics file formats used for the book's illustrations, so that they will be compatible with the publisher's chosen desktop publishing package. For instance, when I create a screen shot, it is automatically saved to disk. However, the file format that is used for the screen shot cannot be imported directly into a desktop publishing package, and the file has to be changed or converted into the TIFF format before it can be sent to the publisher.

One other consideration that must be taken into account is picture quality or **resolution**. Some file formats allow higher quality and so they are to be preferred over others. You can read more about resolution in chapter 5.

Scale graphic

Scaling a graphic means changing its size. Scaling allows graphics to be resized to fit into a particular space on a page. Scaling can be very precise — by entering a percentage number you can make tiny changes to a graphic. You can also scale a graphic roughly by using the package's selection tools. One alternative to scaling is to **crop** a graphic. Cropping means cutting off part of the picture to fit the available space. Digital photographs, for example, are often cropped to remove unwanted content around the edges of the photographs.

Change layout

If you turn the pages of a newspaper or a magazine, you will notice that each page is laid out differently. The front page of a newspaper has the name of the newspaper set across the full width of the page as a **banner headline**. The text on each of the pages is set out in columns, and sometimes each story will begin with a **drop capital**. You can see one example of a page layout dialogue box in figure 6.5.

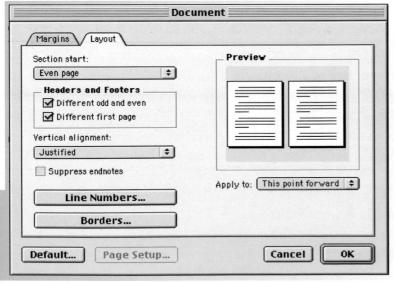

Figure 6.5 *A page layout dialogue box.*

Banner headlines

A banner headline is text set in a large typeface and arranged across the whole page — it is not included in the main body of the text. A banner headline is also often called a *masthead*. An example of a banner headline is shown below.

SQA ABOLISHES EXAMS!

Columns of text

In many publications such as magazines and newspapers, the text is laid out in columns rather than across the whole page. With a desktop publishing package you can set out the text in columns. Some word processors also let you do this, but what you can produce is limited compared with the variety of column layouts available in a desktop publishing package.

Drop capitals

A drop capital is a large initial letter at the beginning of a paragraph of text. Drop capitals are often used to draw the reader's attention to the beginning of an article. You will see these in many newspaper and magazine articles.

Import text

Importing text means entering text from a file rather than directly from the computer keyboard. Text is normally imported into a desktop publishing package, most commonly from a file created using a word processing application. Saving a text file so that it can be loaded into another application is called exporting text. When importing or exporting, you have to be aware of the different text file formats which may be used. Standard file formats include text, ASCII and Rich Text Format (RTF). Using one of these standard formats means that the desktop publishing application should be able to load or import the text easily.

Some text file formats, like RTF, try to preserve as much of the original formatting applied to the text as possible, such as the font, the style and the paragraphs. However, this preservation is not so important when importing text into a desktop publishing application, since the purpose of using such an application is to change the original formatting. You can read more about these standard formats in chapter 1.

Text wrap around graphics

Figure 6.6 *Text wrap around graphics.*

You can choose to wrap the text round a graphic, rather than having to leave, say, half a page for a picture. This can give a very pleasing effect and can save space on the page from being wasted or unused.

If you look back at figures 6.2 and 6.3 you will see some of these features being used.

Additional features of desktop publishing packages

Typefaces

A DTP package allows you to vary the typeface more than a word processor does. A **typeface** is the design of a set of characters (letters or numbers). It is also called a **font**. There are many different fonts. Here are a few:

Times New Roman

Helvetica

♦◲○ᘯ□● (WingDings)

The style of a typeface is the kind of character in a font which is used. Normal type (like most of the text in this book) is called roman or regular — you could also use *italic* or SMALL CAPITALS.

The size of a typeface (how big it is) is measured in points. There are 72 points in an inch. Most of the text of this book is 12 point — it is one-sixth of an inch high.

The weight of the text is the blackness of the characters — for example **bold** text is more black than roman.

Style sheets

In any publication you should be very careful to be consistent in the way you use the typographical style — changing heading style or text size every couple of pages can be very confusing for the reader! Some desktop publishing packages allow you to create a style sheet to specify text attributes such as:

- the size and weight of the typeface
- the line and character spacing
- the tab settings and
- the page length.

Figure 6.7
A style sheet in use in a DTP package.

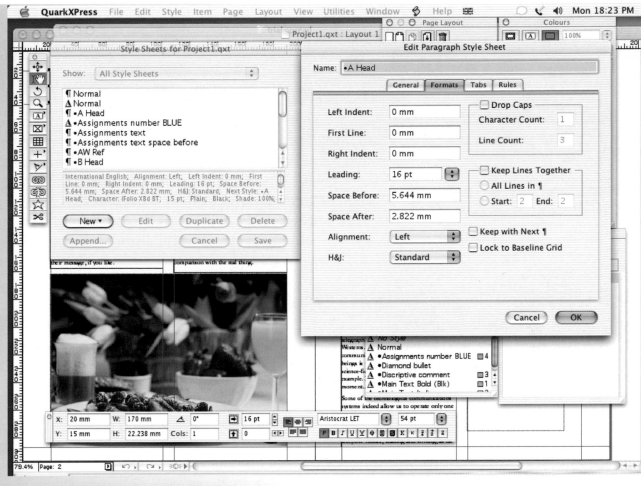

In figure 6.7 you can see a style sheet for a desktop publishing package. Once you have created a style sheet you can apply the same style to many features of a document, without having to set the typeface individually for each one.

Differences between packages

As computer systems become more powerful and software packages offer more features, the differences between packages are becoming less distinct. Many word processing packages now offer most of the features described here for desktop publishing packages. Many graphics drawing packages can now be used for page layout. Many desktop publishing packages now offer word processing and spell checker facilities, so you can create your text directly in the desktop publishing packages rather than typing it into a word processor and importing it.

Where professional desktop publishing packages still have the edge is that they incorporate special pre-press features which help to prepare the document for professional printing such as colour separations and PANTONE® colour matching.

Figure 6.8 *A colour separation.*

A colour photograph in a newspaper is printed in several passes. Cyan, magenta, yellow and then black (known as CMYK) are printed on top of each other to produce the photograph. Figure 6.8 shows a colour separation for a photograph in this book.

The latest colour laser printers can print CMYK images in a single pass through the printer, so maybe even this special feature of desktop publishing packages will become less exclusive in time.

Foundation level questions

knowledge and understanding

1 List the parts of a desktop publishing system.
2 Name one application package which you have used for desktop publishing.
3 Place the following steps in the correct order of the desktop publishing process:
   a. The final document is printed.
   b. Data from other programs is imported.
   c. The completed pages are then saved to disk.
   d. The text is imported.
   e. The graphics are inserted.
   f. The graphics are created.
   g. Templates are designed.
   h. The text is typed.

problem solving

1 You buy a desktop publishing package. What feature of a desktop publishing package could help a new user to speed up document production?
2 Why would you save a desktop publishing document as a template?
3 State one advantage of using clip art in desktop publishing.

General level questions

knowledge and understanding

1 What is meant by the terms:
   a. scale graphic?
   b. import graphic?
2 What's the difference between scaling and cropping a graphic?
3 Why is graphics resolution important?

problem solving

1 You receive a graphic as an attachment to an email message, but the graphic will not load into your desktop publishing package.
   a. Suggest what is wrong.
   b. Suggest what you could do to solve this problem.
   c. You manage to load the file but it is too large to fit into the space available on the page. What can you do to solve this problem?
2 Many newspapers are printed far from the journalist's office where the articles are written. Explain how the journalist could send her article to the printing works.

Credit level questions

knowledge and understanding

1 List three features of a page layout in a desktop publishing package.
2 What is the purpose of a drop capital?
3 What's the difference between a header and a headline?
4 Describe the three features of a typeface.
5 Why is the ability to create a style sheet particularly useful in a desktop publishing package?

problem solving

1 Of what use is the feature text wrap around graphics in a desktop publishing package?
2 What two problems may occur when importing text into a desktop publishing application?

• **Key points** •

- Desktop publishing is a way of producing professional quality printed material on a microcomputer system.
- Desktop publishing leaves less room for mistakes than traditional publishing because there are fewer stages and fewer people involved.
- Desktop publishing packages are used to arrange or layout text and graphics already prepared in separate general purpose packages.
- Features of desktop publishing packages include: wizard and templates, enter text, add clip art, import graphic, scale graphic, change layout, import text, text wrap around graphic.
- A template is used to mark out a standard layout for a document.

- Graphics may be added from clip art or imported from a file.
- The graphics file format affects importing and resolution.
- Scaling and cropping may be used to change the size of a graphic.
- Text which is imported may lose its formatting information.
- Text wrap can help to save space on a page.
- Changing the layout may involve columns, banner headlines and drop capitals.
- The style, size and weight are three features of a typeface.
- Style sheets help to keep a consistent style of text in a document.

7 Presentation and multimedia

What is multimedia?

Multimedia is the presentation of information by a computer system using graphics, animation, sound and text.

What is a presentation package?

A presentation package is an application package used to produce multimedia presentations and displays. It allows the user to create a series of pages or slides which can include sound and video clips as well as text and graphics. Another name for a presentation is a slide show. Presentations may be displayed on a monitor or projected onto a screen in front of an audience.

Many teachers use presentation packages in their lessons. This has a number of advantages for the teacher and for the pupils concerned. Animated diagrams and links to other programs can be included, something that is impossible to do otherwise. Presentations can be kept from one year to the next and are easy to change when the course changes. Students usually find large text on a screen easier to read than a teacher's handwriting. Students can be given printouts if required, saving a great deal of copying out. There is only one disadvantage — see figure 7.1.

Figure 7.1 *PowerPoint poisoning.*

At its simplest level, a presentation may consist of only one slide, although most presentations consist of a number of slides. When these are displayed one after the other in order this is called linear linkage of slides. All presentation packages do this automatically, moving on to the next slide in a sequence when a mouse button is clicked or a key on the keyboard is pressed.

- Examples of presentation packages: *Microsoft PowerPoint*, *Lotus Freelance*, *Corel Presentations*, *Harvard Graphics* and *Apple Keynote*.

Creating a presentation

The first step in creating a presentation is to gather together all of the resources that have to be used, such as text, graphics, audio and video. These are known as the presentation elements, and the process of gathering them together is called assembling the elements of a presentation.

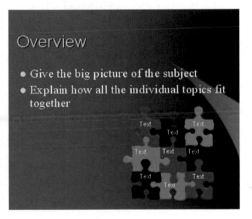

Figure 7.2 *Bullet points.*

Text

A small quantity of text may simply be entered at the keyboard, but a larger amount will usually be entered into a word processing package and then stored on disk before being copied and pasted into a presentation. A word processing package may also be used to create a table to be placed into a slide.

Perhaps the most common method of displaying text in a slide is to use bullet points. A bullet point is a character made up of a large dot, like this (•). See figure 7.2.

Notes may also be created to accompany each slide, either to hand out to the audience, or notes to assist the presenter with the presentation.

Graphics

Presentation packages usually contain a library of clip art images which can be placed into the slides. Alternatively a graphic may be created using a graphics package, or, if it is a chart, then by using the charting facility of the presentation graphics package itself or another general purpose package such as a spreadsheet. Graphics on paper may be scanned. See image capture later in this chapter for more information.

Graphic images may also be obtained from specific sites on the World Wide Web or by using the image search feature on a search engine such as *Google*. It is important to check the copyright of images downloaded from the web, although there is usually no problem if they are for personal use in school as part of your coursework. It is a different matter if they are going to be sold or used commercially.

Audio

Audio may be added from a sound library within the application package, taken from an audio CD, or recorded directly into the presentation by using a microphone. Sound files may also be downloaded from the World Wide Web.

Sound is an important feature of a presentation, but should be used sparingly to add emphasis. If a presentation has too many sounds then users may become distracted and can miss the point that the presenter is trying to make.

Video

Video, or movies may also be added to a presentation. Some presentation packages contain movies as part of their clipart libraries. Video clips may be downloaded from the World Wide Web sites. The regularly updated movie trailers available on *apple.com* are very popular (see figure 7.3). Creating video will be dealt with later in this chapter.

Figure 7.3 *QuickTime Movie Trailers at apple.com.*

Hyperlinks

Hyperlinks are links to the World Wide Web, to another document, or to a particular slide within the presentation. Hyperlinks are non-linear, that is, they do not go to the next slide in sequence. They are activated by clicking on a button or on a particular area of the screen. A common use of hyperlinks is in a menu system. An example is shown in figure 7.4.

One variation of this is an on-screen adventure program which is non-linear. This is shown in figure 7.5.

Another common use of hyperlinks is to take the user out of the presentation package altogether and into a different application such as a web browser. In this case the web address may be programmed into the hyperlink and the result of clicking on the link will launch the browser software and display the relevant web page. A typical (!) hyperlink may look like this one:

http://www.mrwalsh.co.uk

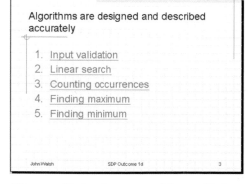

Figure 7.4 *A menu of hyperlinks.*

Figure 7.5 *An adventure program for S1 pupils.*

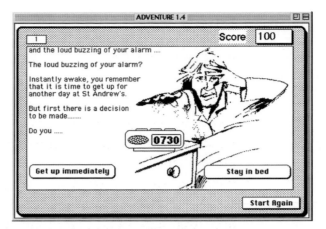

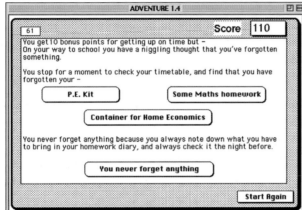

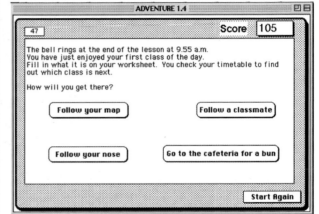

Teachers in Scotland use the Heriot Watt University Scholar system in this way to prepare lessons for their classes. They create presentations for Higher level and Advanced Higher level and can link slides directly to Scholar web pages. This is shown in figure 7.6.

Figure 7.6 *Screenshot of a Scholar web page.*

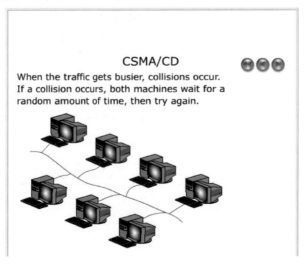

Capturing audio

There are number of different ways in which to capture audio, depending on the source of the sound. The simplest method is to use a microphone attached to the computer. Many computers have built in microphones. The laptop computer which I am using to write this book has a microphone built into the lid above the screen. Sounds input using this type of microphone are low quality, but are suitable for occasional use. An external microphone should be used if high quality sounds are to be recorded. Sounds, which are already in digital form, such as a CD audio track, may be imported directly into a presentation.

Capturing images

Image capture is the way in which images may be changed into digital form (or digitised) in order to display them on a computer screen or in a presentation. If the images are printed as hard copy on paper, then a scanner may be used. The scanner produces an image file, which can be saved and then imported into a presentation. (See figure 16.9 for a picture of a scanner.)

Another method is to use a digital camera and take a photograph. Images may be downloaded from the camera by connecting it directly to a computer or by reading the contents of the camera's flash memory card into an image file. A picture of a digital camera and its memory card are shown in chapter 16.

Transitions

A transition is the name given to the effect shown on the screen when moving between slides. Clever use of transitions can make a presentation more enjoyable to watch. Examples of transitions are: wipe, blinds, cover.

Animation

Animation is the way in which elements of a presentation may be programmed to move around the screen. Animation may be applied to any of the elements which make up a slide. Text may be animated using numerous effects like wipe, fly in or zoom, each accompanied by its own sound effect. In addition, text can be set to appear one character, one line, or one paragraph at a time. Each effect may be separated by a mouse click or appear at a set time after a previous effect. Graphics and video may have the same effects applied. Audio can be set to play when a slide appears or when an on-screen button is pressed.

Did you know?
That one of the first presentation packages was called Transitions and was written in 1983 by Andre Schklowsky.

Credit level

Combining all of these simple effects together can result in a very impressive presentation being produced. Note that including too many effects can spoil a presentation.

Slide masters

Figure 7.7 *A slide master.*

Wouldn't it be a good idea if all the slides in a presentation were based on the same overall style? At the same time wouldn't it be useful to be able to make a change to one slide and have that change apply to all of the other slides?

Presentation packages already have this feature. It's called the slide master. The slide master is a slide, which controls the layout of other slides in the presentation. The slide master controls text characteristics like font type, size and colour, and has place holders for footers, such as the date and slide number. When you want to make an overall change to the look of your slides, you don't have to change each slide individually. If you make the change once on the slide master, the presentation package automatically updates the slides and applies the changes to any new slides you add later. For instance, to have a name or school badge appear on every slide, put it on the slide master. Figure 7.7 shows a slide master.

Creating video

A video camera can be used to create your own video to be included in a presentation. A digital video camera may be connected to a computer system in order to view and edit the video. A separate application package is used to edit the video. Video editing applications include: *iMovie*, *Final Cut Pro*, *Adobe Premiere* and *Pinnacle Studio*.

All of these packages allow the user to input sequences of video, known as **clips**, and rearrange these clips into any order, not just the sequence in which they were originally filmed. This is called **non-linear editing**. Titles and special effects can also be added at any point. The audio part of each video clip may also be edited, or have a new sound track added. Figure 7.8 shows a typical video-editing package.

The edited video film may be output back to the digital video camera and stored on tape. As more and more computer systems are being fitted with DVD writers as standard, the video may also be saved or 'burnt' to a writeable DVD.

Editing digital video is an enjoyable pastime, which is very popular, and it is relatively easy to produce good results with a little practice. One disadvantage of digital video is the large quantity of

Figure 7.8 *A typical video editing package in use (iMovie).*

backing storage taken up by only a short movie. One hour of digital video requires approximately 13 gigabytes of backing storage space. This will become less of a concern as the backing storage capacity of ordinary computer systems increases, and as new types of backing storage media are developed.

Multimedia authoring packages

Multimedia authoring packages can also be used to create presentations. These packages range from easy to learn programs like *Hyperstudio*, to more sophisticated packages like *Supercard*, *iShell* and *Macromedia Director*. They can be programmed to a much greater extent than the presentation packages described throughout this chapter, and may be used to create stand-alone applications, like *Encyclopaedia Britannica* and *Microsoft Encarta*. Figure 7.9 shows these two packages.

7

Figure 7.9 *Multimedia encyclopaedias.*

2004 Encarta Product Family

| Encarta Standard | Encarta Deluxe | Encarta Reference Library on CD | Encarta Reference Library on DVD | Encarta Reference Library Educator's Edition |

Presentation packages cannot be programmed to the same extent as multimedia authoring packages, nor can they be used to create stand-alone applications. The presentations created by these packages always need to be loaded into some kind of application before they can be viewed. For instance, you need to have PowerPoint or a similar application on your computer before you can load a presentation. Even if the presentation is saved as a series of web pages, you still need browser software to be able to load and view it.

Getting help

In common with many other general purpose packages, presentation packages provide the user with help when creating a presentation. A **template** is a ready-made document containing guides or placeholders which can accept objects such as **text** or **graphics**. Another name for a template is a *layout*. Each package provides many different templates for the user to choose from. These may be grouped under headings such as 'business plan' or 'company meeting', or available in a menu when a new slide is being created. Figure 7.10 shows some slide templates.

Figure 7.10 *Slide templates.*

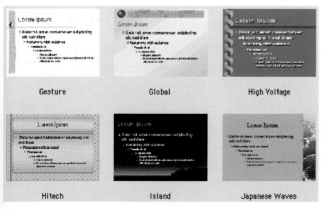

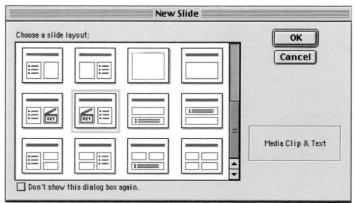

Figure 7.11 *A wizard in action.*

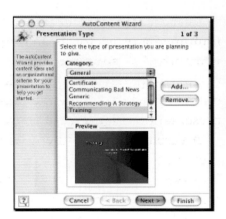

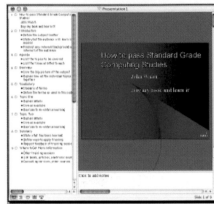

At the same time, a wizard or assistant is a program which leads the user step by step through the creation of a document. This is particularly useful for first time users of a presentation package. Figure 7.11 shoes a wizard in action.

Delivering a presentation

Most presentations are nowadays given using a multimedia projector as an output device connected directly to a computer system. In order to give the presentation, the presenter normally controls the display of the slides using the mouse. Most multimedia projectors also come with a remote control, which may be used to control the presentation from a distance. A multimedia projector is shown in figure 7.12.

Before the advent of multimedia projectors, each separate slide of the presentation was printed as a hard copy onto transparent plastic film (OHT) for use on an ordinary overhead projector (OHP). In order to give the presentation the presenter places each slide on the projector in turn. This is shown in figure 7.13.

Figure 7.12 *A multimedia projector.*

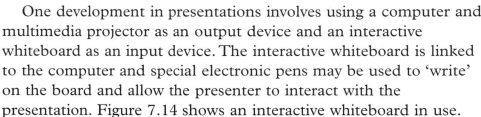

One development in presentations involves using a computer and multimedia projector as an output device and an interactive whiteboard as an input device. The interactive whiteboard is linked to the computer and special electronic pens may be used to 'write' on the board and allow the presenter to interact with the presentation. Figure 7.14 shows an interactive whiteboard in use.

A variation on this theme is for the class to interact with the presentation where each pupil has his or her own remote control. Software has been developed which allows the class to answer multiple-choice questions and other tests by using their remote controls. A typical remote control is shown in figure 7.15.

Figure 7.13 *An overhead projector and transparencies.*

Figure 7.14 *An interactive whiteboard in use.*

Figure 7.15 *Promethean Activote™ – a pupil remote control.*

Presenting without a presenter

Sometimes a presentation is required which will run automatically without a presenter being in attendance. The presentation is created in the normal way, and is set up to run on its own, usually with a preset delay between each slide. This type of presentation is usually set up in a kiosk.

File Formats

Finished presentations may be saved in a variety of file formats, including HTML for web publishing, as a movie or as separate graphics files like JPEG or GIF.

Presenting without a presentation package

Most graphics packages allow you to create simple presentations. One way of doing this is to create a document of several pages and display each page in turn – the slide show option in the drawing module within the AppleWorks integrated package has this feature. The software which accompanies many digital cameras, allows the photographs to be displayed in a slide show on screen.

Foundation level questions

knowledge and understanding

1 What is multimedia?
2 What is a presentation package?
3 Why is a presentation sometimes called a slide show?
4 Name one presentation package.
5 Explain the term 'linear linkage of slides'.
6 State one method used to move to the next slide in a presentation.
7 What is a 'presentation element'?
8 Name the term used to describe the process of gathering presentation elements together.
9 What is a template?
10 What is a wizard?
11 Which output device is normally used with a presentation package?
12 What type of presentation might be run in a kiosk?

problem solving

1 What type of user would find a template helpful?
2 Why is it important to check the copyright of images obtained from the World Wide Web?
3 a. How is it possible to give a presentation without a presenter?
   b. Name a location where such a presentation might be used.

General level questions

knowledge and understanding

1 Name four 'presentation elements'.
2 What is a hyperlink?
3 Name two sources of audio for use in a presentation.

problem solving

1 State one advantage a multimedia projector has over an OHP, and one advantage of using an OHP over a multimedia projector, for delivering a presentation.
2 How can a presentation be given without a presentation package?
3 Why should audio be used sparingly in a presentation?

Credit level questions

knowledge and understanding

1 State two methods of capturing audio to be included in a presentation.
2 State two methods of capturing images to be included in a presentation.
3 Why may a hyperlink be described as non-linear?
4 What is a transition?
5 What is animation?
6 What is a slide master?
7 Compare a presentation package with a multimedia-authoring package. State two differences between these applications.
8 What is non-linear editing?

problem solving

1 Jemima has a computer system and a presentation package but no scanner or digital camera. State two ways Jemima could obtain images to be included in her presentation.
2 Mrs Grofaz, the Head Teacher of St Anselm's Primary, wants the name of the school to appear on every slide of her presentation to the school board. Explain how this could be done.
3 What hardware is required to create a video?
4 State one disadvantage of digital video.
5 Pongo is thinking of buying a computer system to edit digital video. State one important requirement that this new system should have.
6 State one advantage of having a slide master facility within a presentation package.
7 Explain how a presentation package may be used to create an adventure program.

• Practical work •

1 Using a presentation package with which you are familiar, and a suitable template (or wizard):
   a. Create a series of slides which give definitions for some of the terms you have learned in this chapter, for example, *text*, *wizard*, *template*, *linear linkage of slides*. Create a title slide followed by one slide for each term and add a suitable graphic from the presentation package's clip art library.
   b. Choose one slide from your presentation and add a sound effect from the presentation package's library of sound effects or from an audio file supplied by your teacher.
   c. Choose a different slide from your presentation and add a video from the presentation package's library or from a video file supplied by your teacher.
   d. If you have access to a digital camera (or scanner), take (or scan) a photograph and add the photograph to your presentation.
   e. If your computer has a microphone, add your voice (or a suitable sound effect) to the same slide containing the photograph.
   f. Add a hyperlink to your presentation which will take you to a search engine page on the World Wide Web such as *Google*, *Yahoo* or *Teoma*.
   g. Change your presentation so that it runs automatically when the presentation is opened.
2 Make a presentation on your favourite pop group or TV programme.

• Key points •

- Multimedia is the presentation of information by a computer system using graphics, animation, sound and text.
- A presentation package is an application package used to produce multimedia presentations and displays.
- A presentation package allows the user to create a series of pages or slides which can include sound and video clips as well as text and graphics.
- When slides are displayed one after the other, in order, this is called linear linkage of slides.
- Presentation elements include text, graphics, audio and video.
- Gathering the elements together is called assembling the elements of a presentation.
- Text may be entered at the keyboard or imported from a word processing package.
- Graphics may be imported from a clip art image library, or from a graphics package.
- Audio may be added from a sound library or input using a microphone.
- Video images may be imported from a digital video camera and edited using a suitable application.
- Non-linear editing is where clips may be arranged in any order, not just the order in which they were filmed.

- Digital video takes up a large quantity of backing storage space.
- Image capture involves using a digital camera or scanner.
- Hyperlinks are links from a slide to web pages, other documents or programs.
- Hyperlinks are non-linear, that is, they do not go to the next slide in sequence.
- A transition is the name given to the effect shown on the screen when moving between slides.
- Animation is the way in which elements of a presentation may be programmed to move around the screen.
- The slide master is a slide which controls the layout of other slides in the presentation.
- Multimedia authoring packages can also be used to create presentations.
- A template is a ready made up document containing guides or placeholders which can accept objects such as text or graphics.
- A wizard or assistant is a program which leads the user step by step through the creation of a document.
- Presentations are usually delivered using a multimedia projector.
- An interactive whiteboard allows a presenter to interact with the presentation.
- Presentations may be set up to run automatically in a kiosk.

8. Web page creation

What is a web page?

The World Wide Web (WWW) is a collection of information held in multimedia form on the Internet. This information is stored at locations called web sites in the form of web pages. A web page is a single document, although it may be too large to display on the screen without scrolling.

Web pages are permanently available to any user of the Internet. Each organisation, or individual who provides information, organises this information as a web site, often consisting of many pages. Web sites are a very effective way of distributing information.

Fig 8.1 *A web page.*

What software is needed to view web pages?

A browser is a program that allows the user to browse or surf through the World Wide Web. When browsing the World Wide Web, a browser loads web pages from another computer on the Internet and displays them.

Any web page can be accessed directly if its full **web address** or **URL** is known. To make it easier to find information, each web site has its own home page. The home page provides a starting point for the user to explore the site. It's like a main menu, and may also provide **hyperlinks** to other sites. Hyperlinks are links between World Wide Web pages, documents or files. They are activated by clicking on text, or on a particular area of the screen like a graphic. You can read more about URLs and web addresses in chapter 12.

What software is needed to create web pages?

Web pages are usually prepared in a special language called **HTML** or **HyperText Mark-up Language**. You can see an example of some hypertext mark-up language in figure 8.2. You will be pleased to know that you do not need to remember any of this code for your examination!

Using a text editor

One way of creating a web page is to enter HTML code directly in a text editor like *Notepad* or *SimpleText*, save the file and then load it into a browser to see how it will look. This method has the advantage that you do not need to have, or buy any special software, since both the text editor and browser are free.

The disadvantage of this approach is that it is very difficult to tell what the final result of your HTML code will look like while you are writing it. Another disadvantage is, of course, that you must know the correct HTML code to enter.

Using a web page editor

A web page editor is sometimes called a WYSIWYG editor. WYSIWYG stands for 'what you see is what you get'. The advantage of using this type of software is that you can see what the end result will look like (the web page) while you are creating it.

Another advantage is that you do not need to know any HTML code in order to use such a program. All you need to do is enter the text, graphics and whatever else is required, and the web page editor will automatically produce the correct HTML code. Alternatively, if you do know the code, you can enter it directly, and you can see the web page taking shape as you work.

Microsoft Front Page, Adobe PageMill, Softpress Freeway and *Macromedia Dreamweaver* are all web page editors which operate in this manner. Figure 8.2 shows the HTML code together with its associated web page in a WYSIWYG view.

Figure 8.2 *A WYSIWYG web page editor in action.*

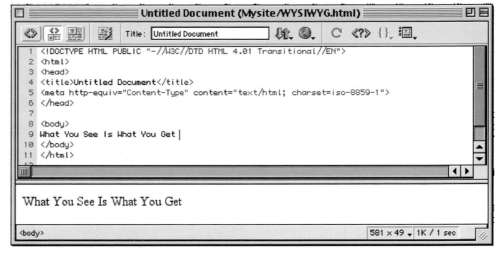

Using a browser

Apart from web page editor programs, which we looked at above, some web browsers help you to create web pages as well as being able to display them. *Netscape Communicator* is one such program. In addition to the usual browser functions, it also has a *Composer* program.

Using a wizard or a template

When creating a web page, it is helpful to use a wizard, which is a feature that helps you to step through the process of web page creation. This is particularly useful for beginners. A wizard usually offers a choice of templates. A template is a readymade blank web page, with placeholders for items like text and graphics. Using a

Figure 8.3 *Web page creation using a template in Dreamweaver.*

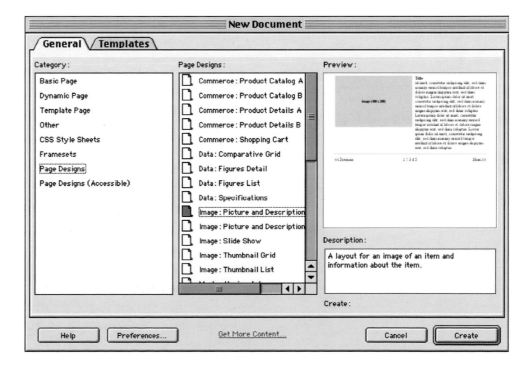

template can speed up the creation of a web page, because much of the page layout has already been done for you. Figure 8.3 shows part of the process of web page creation using a template.

Using another class of general purpose package to create a web page

Many general purpose packages have a 'Save as web page' feature. This allows the user to automatically prepare a web version of an existing document. Figure 8.4 shows part of a presentation which has been converted into a series of web pages.

Figure 8.4 *Using a general purpose package to create web pages.*

Entering text

A small quantity of text may simply be entered at the keyboard but a larger amount will usually be entered into a word processing package and then stored on disk before being imported or perhaps copied and pasted into a web page.

Adding graphics

Web page creation packages may contain a library of clip art images which can be inserted. Alternatively a graphic may be created using a graphics package, or, if it is a chart, then by using the charting facility of another general purpose package such as a spreadsheet. Graphics on paper may be scanned.

Most graphics packages have a 'save as web graphic' or similar menu choice. This feature creates a low resolution graphic which is suitable for display on a web page. Saving graphics in this way also reduces their file size, which makes them faster to load. Web pages, which have a large number of graphics, can take a great deal of time to load, especially when using a slow dial-up connection. This can lead to users becoming frustrated, and they are likely to hit the stop button on their browsers and move away to another site if this happens.

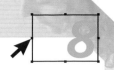

Graphic images may also be obtained from other web pages. It is important to check the copyright of images downloaded from the web although there is usually no problem if they are for personal use in school as part of your coursework. It is a different matter if they are going to be sold, used commercially or published on your own web page. You must always obtain permission from the copyright holder if you plan to copy and use graphics in this way.

Figure 8.5 *A load of old webbish.*

Adding audio

Audio may be added from a sound library within the application package, taken from an audio CD, or recorded directly into the presentation by using a microphone. Sound files may also be downloaded from the World Wide Web.

There are two ways of adding audio to a web page. One method is to create a hyperlink, which will load the audio file. A second method is to embed the file, or make it part of, the web page. If you choose this method, then it gives you more control over the sound. However, the sound will only play if visitors to your web page have the appropriate '**plug-in**' file in their web browser application.

Embedding a large sound file can make your page slow to load. If your sound file is set to play constantly while the web page is displayed, this can be irritating.

Adding video

Video, or movies, may also be added to a web page. Like audio files, video files may be either embedded or linked to a page. Embedding video can increase the file size of the web page and make it slower to download. Once again, a '**plug-in**' may be required to play the embedded video file. Video files may be downloaded from the World Wide Web, or created using a digital video camera and then transferred to disk.

Figure 8.6 shows a simple web page containing some of the features described in this chapter.

Figure 8.6 *A variety of features in a simple web page.*

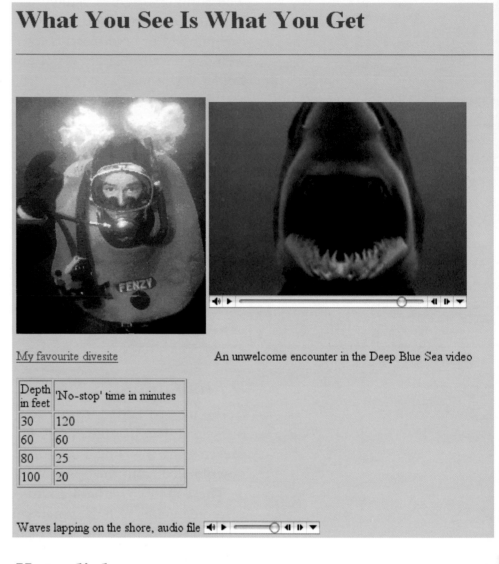

What You See Is What You Get

My favourite divesite

An unwelcome encounter in the Deep Blue Sea video

Depth in feet	'No-stop' time in minutes
30	120
60	60
80	25
100	20

Waves lapping on the shore, audio file

Hyperlinks

Hyperlinks are links to another web page or to another file stored on the World Wide Web or on a local disk. Hyperlinks are activated by clicking on a piece of text, on a button or on a particular area of the screen. You can see an example of a hyperlink to <u>My favourite divesite</u> in figure 8.6.

When the web page is displayed in a browser, and the hyperlink is clicked, then the text changes colour and stays changed. The purpose of the colour change is to show the user that they have already clicked on that particular link.

Adding tables

Tables are often used in web page creation because information can be displayed so that the user can quickly see the overall picture.

Tables are made up of data arranged in columns and rows, like a spreadsheet, and data is placed in cells. Sensible use of tables can improve the design or appearance of a web page. Figure 8.6 shows a table in use on a web page.

Adding hotspots

A hotspot is a special area on a web page, which is normally invisible when viewed in a browser. Hotspots can be identified because the mouse pointer changes in shape when it is moved over one. Graphics or pictures which have hotspots are called image maps.

A hotspot has a hyperlink, or a piece of programming code associated with it, which can react to a user's action, such as moving the pointer over the hotspot or clicking the mouse button. Hotspots are mainly used to display hidden images or highlights on a web page.

You can also see hotspots in action in many general purpose packages by moving the mouse pointer over a button or menu bar. If the pointer is left to rest on top of a button for a few seconds, then a brief description of that button will be displayed.

Figure 8.7 *A hotspot in action (Microsoft Front Page).*

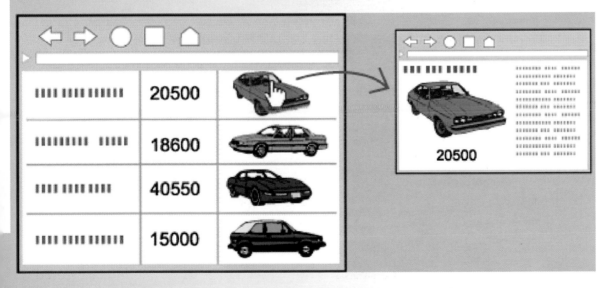

Figure 8.7 shows a hotspot in action. Note that the normal mouse pointer has changed to a hand when placed over the hotspot.

Other features of web page creation

There are many other features of web page creation which you will come across as you browse the World Wide Web. Some web pages use frames to organise their layout. Others contain animations created with *Shockwave* or *Flash*. Animations like these require the user to download and add special 'plug-ins' to their browser software in order to view them. To get the best use out of a radio station's web site, for example, it is often necessary to download the '*Real Audio*' plug-in.

Casual visitors to a web site which uses plug-ins may discover that they cannot access or view these special features, because they have not upgraded their browser software. Users often find this annoying, and may quickly click away from such sites in frustration. On a school network, for instance, most pupils do not have access privileges to install new software and therefore cannot view these sites as their designers intended.

You do not need to know about these other features of web page creation for your Standard Grade course. They are only included here because they are in such widespread use, and anyone who browses the World Wide Web will encounter them.

Foundation level questions

knowledge and understanding

1. Name two types of software that you could use for web page creation.
2. What is a wizard?
3. What is a template?
4. State two methods of entering text into a web page.
5. State two methods of entering a graphic into a web page.
6. What special language is used in web page creation?
7. What is meant by the term WYSIWYG?
8. Why is a web page editor program sometimes called a WYSIWYG editor?
9. Name a browser which allows you to create web pages.

problem solving

1. When would a user use a:
   a. wizard?
   b. template?
2. Your web page editor program has no clip art. How could you obtain graphics to add to your web page?
3. How is it possible to create a web page using only a text editor?
4. State one advantage of using a WYSIWYG web page editor over using a text editor to create a web page.
5. Explain one way in which a web page may be created using a general purpose package.
6. What use is a 'save as web graphic' feature in a graphics package.

General level questions

knowledge and understanding

1. What is a hyperlink?
2. What is an embedded video?

problem solving

1. State two methods of adding audio or video to a web page.
2. State one disadvantage of using embedded video in a web page over using a hyperlink to a video file.

Credit level questions

knowledge and understanding

1 What is a table in a web page?
2 What is a hotspot in a web page and how does it work?
3 Why is a hotspot often called an image map?
4 What is the difference between a web site's home page and a browser's home page?

problem solving

1 Why are tables used in web pages?
2 How can you tell if a web page has any hotspots?
3 Why does each web site have its own home page?

• Practical work •

1 Use a web browser to search the web for a single page which shows some of the features explained in this chapter. Print out a hard copy of the page you have found and draw arrows or use a highlighter to indicate where each feature (or link) is to be found on the printout.

2 Use squared paper to plan a web page about your favourite TV programme. Use a web page editor to create the page. Use a wizard to help you choose a suitable layout for the page and include an appropriate graphic. If possible, download and add some audio and video to your page. Save your work and make a printout of the page.

3 Make up a school web page for use by a new pupil to your class, John Smith or Jemima Wilson. Include some general information about the school, for example, the name of the school, its postal address and telephone number. Add a graphic of the school badge to your page. Assume that they take the same subjects as you do. Create a table on the web page to display their new timetable. Save your work and make a printout of the page.

• Key points •

- The World Wide Web (WWW) is a collection of information held in multimedia form on the Internet.
- A browser is a program that allows the user to browse or surf through the World Wide Web.
- A web page may be accessed directly if its web address is known.
- Web pages are written using a special language called HTML or HyperText Mark-up Language.
- Web pages may be created using a:
  - text editor
  - web page editor
  - browser.
  - another class of general purpose package like presentation software or word processing software.
- The process of creating a web page involves entering text, adding graphics and creating hyperlinks. Sometimes audio and video may be added.
- Audio and video files may be embedded into a web page or linked to by using a hyperlink.
- Hyperlinks are links to another web page or to another file stored on the World Wide Web or on a local disk.
- Hyperlinks are activated by clicking on a piece of text, on a button or on a particular area of the screen.
- Tables are made up of data arranged in columns and rows, like a spreadsheet, and data is placed in cells.
- A hotspot is a special area on a web page which is normally invisible when viewed in a browser.
- Hotspots can be identified because the mouse pointer changes in shape when it is moved over one.

9 Expert systems

Artificial intelligence

The processor of a computer is sometimes described as the 'brain' of a computer system. However, a processor is not like a real human brain because it cannot think or act for itself. The processor can only follow the instructions that are supplied to it in the form of a program.

Ever since the earliest computers, programmers have been writing software to make computers behave as if they had a form of intelligence. This is known as **artificial intelligence**. The earliest artificial intelligence programs concentrated on playing games like Xs and Os and chess, and were applied to relatively simple problems. A chess program may be said to have artificial intelligence if it is capable of learning from its mistakes and plays a better game the next time.

The computer program Eliza was written in 1965 as an experiment to find out if computers could be programmed to make human conversation. Figure 9.1 shows an example dialogue with the Eliza program. Eliza works by recognising patterns in the sentences typed in by the user and responds mechanically with preset adapted responses.

> **Did you know?**
> That in May 1997, Deep Blue, a chess-playing computer developed by IBM, defeated the reigning world champion, Garry Kasparov, by 3.5 to 2.5 games.

Figure 9.1 *Eliza dialogue.*

```
HELLO. MY NAME IS ELIZA. WHAT'S YOURS?
JOHN
ALRIGHT, JOHN, WHAT WOULD YOU LIKE TO TALK ABOUT TODAY?
ARTIFICIAL INTELLIGENCE
ALRIGHT, CAN YOU TELL ME MORE.
COMPUTERS THAT CAN THINK LIKE HUMANS
WHAT DO YOU THINK MACHINES HAVE TO DO WITH YOUR PROBLEM?
DO YOU THINK YOU ARE A HUMAN ?
DO YOU HAVE MANY RESTLESS NIGHTS?
NO
WELL, WHY NOT?
I SLEEP WELL
MANY PEOPLE HAVE MILD INSOMNIA.
DO YOU HAVE A BRAIN ?
NO ONE REALLY KNOWS.
ARE YOU KIDDING ?
APPARENTLY YOU THINK I AM KIDDING.
YES
YOU SEEM QUITE POSITIVE.
I'M POSITIVE
DO YOU THINK IT IS NORMAL TO BE POSITIVE?
IT IS BETTER THAN BEING NEGATIVE
IN YOUR OPINION, HOW FREQUENTLY IS IT BETTER THAN BEING NEGATIVE?
ABOUT 75 PER CENT
WHAT DOES THAT SUGGEST TO YOU?
MOST PEOPLE ARE POSITIVE
I'M NOT SURE I UNDERSTAND YOU FULLY.
ARE YOU ALIVE ?
IT'S HARD TO SAY, JOHN.
DO YOU THINK ABOUT WHAT TO SAY ?
ACTUALLY, I DO THINK ABOUT WHAT TO SAY.
THAT IS VERY INTERESTING
THAT IS VERY INTERESTING?
THANK YOU FOR TALKING TO ME
GLAD TO BE OF ASSISTANCE.
THAT'S ENOUGH FOR TODAY.
GOOD BYE.
```

When we think about intelligent computers, we might recall *Mr Data* from the *Next Generation*, the *Terminator* series of robots, or the programmed world of *The Matrix*.

All of these, just now(!), are science fiction, and computer programs which are capable of world domination or exterminating all human life do not exist.

Figure 9.2 *The Terminator.*

Expert systems

One type of artificial intelligence program which does exist is the **expert system**. An expert system is so-called because it has been programmed with the knowledge of a human expert. For this reason, expert systems are also known as knowledge based systems.

What is an expert system?

An expert system is a program which has access to a large database of knowledge about one particular subject. It can draw conclusions, make decisions and offer advice based on that knowledge. It is called an expert system because in a sense it has the knowledge of a human expert.

An expert system is made up of three parts:

1. The facts and rules, known as the **knowledge base**. This is like a giant database, but is more flexible in that it contains rules as well as facts. It is the job of the **knowledge engineer** to extract these facts and rules from one or more human experts and put them into a form that the computer is able to understand. This process is called **knowledge acquisition**.

9

2. The coding or program. This is known as the **inference engine** or **expert system shell**. The program uses special programming languages like PROLOG to compare the new information with its knowledge base and draw inferences until it reaches a conclusion or can go no further.

3. The screen, or **explanatory interface**, which is used to ask the question of the user. The expert system can also display how the conclusion was arrived at and explain its reasoning to the user, rather than simply presenting an answer.

Consider a medical diagnosis expert system. Patients waiting their turn in the doctor's surgery might type in responses to questions asked by the expert system. The program would be able to analyse these responses using the rules which had been programmed into it. The output from the program could then be used to narrow down the possible illness or condition, which was affecting the patient. The *same program* (the expert system shell) together with a *different knowledge base* could be used to help find out what is wrong with your motorcar.

Figure 9.3 *The computer will see you now …*

Purpose of expert systems

The **purpose of an expert system** is to represent the knowledge of a human expert in a useful way.

The purpose of any particular expert system depends entirely on what knowledge has been programmed into it.

Expert systems can also be grouped according to the way in which they are used, for example medical **diagnosis** or butterfly **classification**.

Applications of expert systems

Medical

MYCIN is the most well known medical expert system. It was developed at Stanford University in 1976 to help doctors treat patients with infectious diseases caused by bacteria in the blood and meningitis. These diseases can be fatal if not recognised and treated quickly.

PUFF is an expert system that diagnoses lung disease by interpreting measurements from respiratory tests.

BTDS — Brain Tumours Diagnostic System helps doctors diagnose brain tumours by looking at pictures. It incorporates a learning system, which allows it to add new rules to its knowledge base.

FocalPoint can examine slides of cell samples for signs of cancer. FocalPoint can teach itself by practising on slides that pathologists have already diagnosed.

5GL Doctor is an expert system designed to provide a preliminary diagnosis of a variety of illnesses. People may use one version of this program at home, although they are encouraged to speak to their doctor to approve any advice that the program may give. A screen shot from this program is shown in figure 9.4.

Figure 9.4 *An expert system interface for medical diagnosis.*

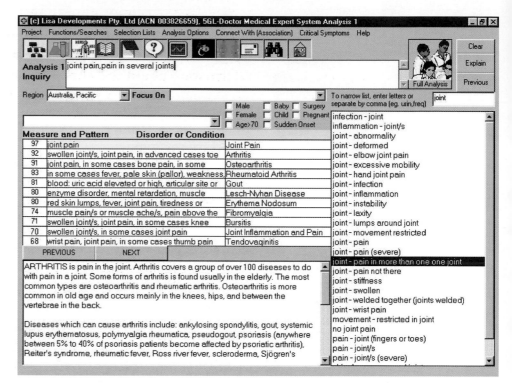

Waste disposal

SewEx is an expert system for sewage treatment works. Here is an example rule from the SewEx expert system:

> IF task is check_flow
>   AND flow is high
>   AND age of pipes is >10
> THEN
>   print the message
>   AND task becomes check_temperature

Geological

PROSPECTOR is a program which helps to find the probable location and type of ore deposits based on geological information about a site.

Dipmeter Advisor helps to interpret the results of oil well drilling.

Archaeological

LITHAN and FAST are two expert systems used to analyse tools from the Stone Age.

Car mechanics

The Service Bay Diagnostic System guides a human technician through the entire service process, from the initial customer interview

at the service desk to the diagnosis and repair of the car in the garage. SBDS gets its information directly from the car's on-board computer. The SBDS works with the technician, who can over-ride the program if he or she thinks that it is ignoring a likely cause for failure.

Chemical analysis

DENDRAL was first developed at Stanford University in the 1960s. DENDRAL was designed to find out the structure of organic molecules from their chemical formulas and mass spectrographic information about the chemical bonds present in the molecules. This program was so successful that many others like it have been written and are now in use worldwide.

Computers

XCON is a system for configuring VAX computers. XCON was developed in 1981, and at one time this software configured every VAX sold by the Digital Equipment Corporation.

DIY

3D Dream House Designer is a house design program that has expert knowledge of wall and ceiling thickness, and stair and roof geometry. A screenshot from this program is shown in figure 9.5.

Figure 9.5 *3D Dream House Designer.*

Some expert system shells

CLIPS

The origins of the C Language Integrated Production System (CLIPS) date back to 1984 at NASA's Johnson Space Centre. CLIPS is now maintained independently from NASA as public domain software.

InterModeller

InterModeller was written by Tom Conlon of Parallel Logic Programming Ltd (www.parlog.com). InterModeller can represent knowledge in a number of different ways, including forward and backward rules, decision trees, classification trees and factor tables. Here is a screenshot from InterModeller showing a classification tree (figure 9.6).

Figure 9.6 *A classification tree in InterModeller.*

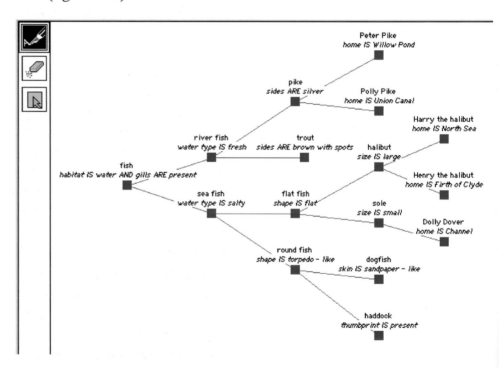

Advantages of expert systems

The advantages of expert systems are:

- Training a human expert is very expensive and time consuming, but expert systems can be copied many times.
- They are always accessible. Computers don't get sick, go on holiday, or move jobs, unlike humans.
- They contain the accumulated knowledge from more than one person about a particular subject.

- They are more consistent than humans. Expert systems always handle transactions in the same way, whereas humans can be influenced, for instance, by recent events.
- They save money by allowing an unskilled and lower paid person to do the job of a highly skilled and higher paid person.
- They allow people who are reluctant to discuss a potentially embarrassing complaint to talk to a computer program rather than a person.

Disadvantages of expert systems

The disadvantages of expert systems are:

- Rule gathering — it is very expensive to have human experts write down a large number of rules, and they may be reluctant to do this. In fact, they may not be able to translate easily their reasoning into IF…THEN rules.
- Human experts often skip steps along the way to a solution. Expert systems cannot do this and need to be given clear rules.
- They lack depth of knowledge of the subject and can only retrace their steps when explaining the reason for reaching a conclusion.
- They are inflexible and can only act within the rules that they have. A human who has a problem to solve can try different methods if they are stuck, but an expert system has a fixed response.
- Expert systems have no common sense. If you look out of the window first thing in the morning and see that the ground is wet, you might reasonably conclude that it had been raining overnight. Expert systems cannot reach conclusions like this without being programmed.
- Like any other computer program, it is impossible to prove that the expert system has no mistakes in it. This could be serious if the expert system is helping to control air traffic, or a nuclear reactor.

Note that this last section is not in the arrangements document but is included here because it is an important aspect of the use of expert systems.

Social, legal and ethical issues

Social

Will society lose skilled people because of expert systems?

Expertise is a fragile asset, which may disappear when staff transfer or retire. Consider one case of a water authority that created an expert system. Of their 3000 employees, 150 people in the company had some specialised knowledge, and 15 were thought expert enough to be worth interviewing. In fact, only 3 people were major contributors of knowledge. The process of knowledge acquisition took almost 5 months of work.

Suppose more and more expert systems are in use and all of the human experts who have learned through their own experience have retired. If trainees use expert systems will they acquire any skills and knowledge of their own?

What would happen if the expert system breaks down? Will the task that the expert system used to perform still be done? Will anyone have the skill to do it?

What would happen if the expert system requires to be given new knowledge? Who will provide it?

Legal

People say that nowadays we live in a 'compensation culture'. They mean that some people who have been injured are looking for someone to blame. When they have identified the person that has caused their suffering then they feel that it is their right to claim compensation.

Will the use of expert systems change or have any effect on this?

If the expert system makes a mistake, then who is to blame? Is it the person who was typing in the answers to the expert system, or is it the knowledge engineer, or is it the human expert or experts whose knowledge is contained in the system? Is it the employer of the person using the system?

Ethical

Is it just or moral to use expert systems?

What level of decision-making should expert systems be in control of? Should all decision-making be left to human experts with the role of the expert system being only to give advice?

What could be replaced with an expert system? A football referee? An assistant referee? A fourth official?

What if a judge in a court of law was replaced by an expert system?

Do you think an accused person would be happy to be judged? and sentenced by a set of rules programmed into a machine?

Which decisions can be left to expert systems and which decisions cannot? For example, when there is a choice between life and death, should an expert system decide which patient is to receive treatment and which is to be left to die?

Social, legal and ethical decision-making

There are more questions raised in this section than there are answers. Expert systems can help in some instances to give advice, but the final decisions should always be taken by people rather than by machines.

Note that there is no detailed content at Foundation (F/G/C) Level in the arrangements document for the Expert Systems Main Aspect.

General level questions

knowledge and understanding

1 Describe the three main parts of an expert system.
2 What is artificial intelligence?
3 How do programs such as Eliza work?
4 What is the purpose of an expert system?
5 State two applications of expert systems.

problem solving

1 How can an expert system shell be used for a different task?
2 Look back at the example rule on page 110. Make up a rule for deciding whether or not you should take a packed lunch to school.

Credit level questions

knowledge and understanding

1 Read the passages below and answer the questions which follow.

At present, the role of the expert system in medicine is that of an assistant in practice management, finding data and providing a second opinion. The main reservation within the profession seems to concern misuse of the assistant, for instance allowing it to make decisions in place of the professionals who properly carry the responsibility. There appear to be mixed feelings about the future effect of expert medical systems. The expert system can draw on a potentially limitless databank of case history and, unlike the doctor, can give an immediate calculation of the probability that its diagnosis is accurate. With the right peripherals, the application might allow someone with lesser qualifications to conduct many examinations. In

time, such developments could limit the general practitioner's role much more to surgical procedures, or to matters of strategy, such as practice management. To the optimists, this would represent only a change in role due to technological innovation, to the pessimists, a threat to jobs.

However, doctors would be quick to agree that proper diagnosis still depends upon a trained mind to trigger new lines of enquiry, without which the science of diagnosis would never advance. This may explain the widely held belief in the medical profession that the expert system can never act as anything more than a passive assistant.

a. According to the passage, what is the present role of the expert system in medicine?
b. What is the main reservation within the profession about expert systems?

c. What can the expert system bring to the diagnosis that the doctor cannot?
d. What could happen in time as more medical expert systems are introduced?
e. What is the view of the:
   i. pessimist?
   ii. optimist?
f. Why do doctors believe a trained mind is necessary?
g. What is likely to be the immediate future role of expert systems in medicine?

problem solving

1 State two advantages and two disadvantages of expert systems.
2 Read the passage and answer the questions which follow:

Figure 9.7 *Alan Turing (1912–1954).*

The British Mathematician Alan Turing wrote about the possibility of an intelligent computing machine in 1950. He proposed the 'Imitation Game', a form of which is now known as the Turing Test. The Turing Test measures the performance of an allegedly intelligent machine against that of a human being. The machine and a human are placed under test in separate rooms and can only communicate with a second human being, known as the interrogator. The interrogator is not able to see or speak directly to either of them, does not know which is the machine, and may communicate with them by use of a text only terminal. The interrogator asks questions over the terminal and tries to find out which is the computer and which is the person. If the interrogator cannot distinguish the machine from the human, then, it is argued, the machine may be assumed to be intelligent.

In 1990 Dr Hugh Loebner established the Loebner Prize of $100,000 and a gold medal to the first computer program whose responses were indistinguishable from a human's. An annual prize of $2000 and a bronze medal are awarded to the most human computer relative to the other entrants in each competition.

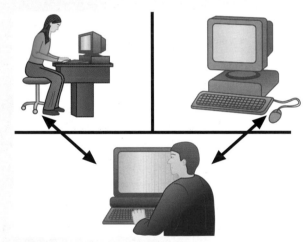

Figure 9.8 *The Turing Test.*

a. Make up a question for the interrogator to ask.
b. Write down what answers you think that the:
   i. person
   ii. computer
   would give in reply to your question.
c. Many people disagree that the Turing Test is a true test of intelligence. What do you think?

• Practical work •

1 Using a suitable expert system shell with which you are familiar, create expert systems which will represent each of the bodies of knowledge described below:

a. Music advice expert system. In the morning chart singles are best. During the day I prefer to listen to albums. In the car I prefer to listen to compilations. At night I like to hear jazz or sometimes classical music.

b. Pet identification. My dog Spot has a black and white coat. Next-door's mongrel, Heinz, is all black with a white tail. My Auntie's dog, Shiner, is all white with one black eye. My cousin's dog, Strangler, is golden brown all over.

c. An expert system to identify people in your computing class.

d. The Widget Manufacturing Company produces a variety of products: cylindrical, spherical, oblong, ring and oval shaped widgets. Create an expert system to classify these products.

e. Make up an expert system to classify vertebrates: fish, amphibians, reptiles, birds and mammals.

2 If you have access to a search engine on the World Wide Web, find out what is known as 'Lady Lovelace's Objection' to intelligent computers. Lady Lovelace is shown in figure 9.9.

Figure 9.9 *Augusta Ada Byron, the Countess of Lovelace (1815–1852).*

3 Find out how a neural net can help an expert system to learn.

4 Find out what is meant by the terms:
a. heuristic
b. certainty factor
when applied to expert systems.

Practical work

1 The answer depends upon the expert system shell or type of knowledge representation used. Here are some possible answers in InterModeller:

a. Music advice

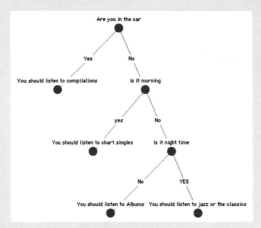

Figure 9.10 *Music advice solution.*

b. Pet identification

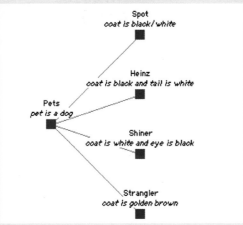

Figure 9.11 *Pet identification solution.*

c. Classmates expert system

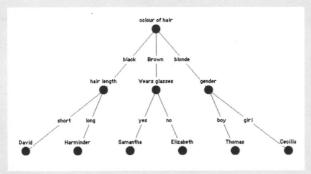

Figure 9.12 *Classmates solution.*

d. Widgets expert system

hollow	shape	hole in centre	sphere	VALUE
yes	*	*	*	cylindrical
no	rectangular	*	*	oblong
no	round	no	yes	spherical
no	round	no	no	oval
no	round	yes	*	ring

Figure 9.13 *Widgets solution.*

e. Vertebrate classification

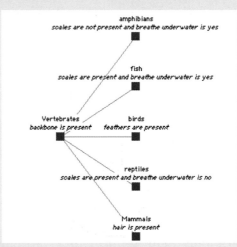

Figure 9.14 *Vertebrates solution.*

2 'Lady Lovelace's Objection', first stated by Ada Lovelace, argues that computers can only do as they are told and consequently cannot perform original (hence, intelligent) actions. "*The analytical engine has no pretensions whatever to originate anything. It can do whatever we know how to order it to perform.*" Ada Byron, *Countess of Lovelace (1842) in a memoir to Charles Babbage.*

3 A neural net is artificial intelligence software that allows a system to learn. A neural net is made up of a network of small junctions or nodes. Each node will 'learn' features according to its input. Once the neural net has learned, then it may be used to recognise features of a similar type to those presented to it.

4 a. A heuristic is a 'rule of thumb' which comes from a human but may be incorporated into an expert system to improve its decision making process.

b. A certainty factor is a measurement that can be applied to a rule in an expert system to take account of the fact that there may be more than one answer to a problem. For instance, the ground is wet therefore CF 99… it had been raining, CF 1… my next door neighbour left his garden hose running all night.

Credit level

• Key points •

- Artificial intelligence is a program which makes a computer behave as if it had a form of intelligence.
- An expert system is a program that has access to a large database of knowledge about one particular subject.
- It can draw conclusions, make decisions and offer advice based on that knowledge.
- It is called an expert system because in a sense it has the knowledge of a human expert.
- The parts of an expert system are the knowledge base, the inference engine and the explanatory interface.
- The knowledge base contains facts and rules.
- The inference engine or expert system shell is the program.
- The explanatory interface is used to ask the question of the user.
- The purpose of an expert system is to contain the knowledge of a human expert and to be able to represent and describe this knowledge in a useful way.
- The applications of experts systems are many and varied. These include medicine, geology, chemistry and engineering.

- The advantages of expert systems are that they:
  - can be copied many times,
  - are always accessible,
  - are consistent in their decision making,
  - contain knowledge from more than one person,
  - can save money by allowing unskilled workers to perform complex tasks,
  - can provide an impersonal source of advice.
- The disadvantages of expert systems are that they:
  - are expensive to create,
  - cannot skip steps or use common sense like humans,
  - may lack depth of knowledge,
  - are inflexible,
  - do not have common sense,
  - may contain mistakes.
- Social issues of expert systems include deskilling.
- Legal issues of expert systems include blame and compensation claims.
- Ethical issues of expert systems examine whether or not vital decisions should be left to machines.

Electronic communication

What is electronic communication?

Electronic communication is the process of sending and receiving electronic messages. Electronic messages include **electronic mail**, **text messaging** and **file transfer**.

What is electronic mail?

Figure 10.1 *Snail mail.*

Electronic mail is a way of sending messages from one computer to another over a transmission medium such as a network cable. For instance, you could type a letter and send it from one computer to another one on a **local area network**. Electronic mail is most useful when the two computers are part of a **wide area network** and a long way apart. Electronic mail is usually shortened to **email**. You can learn more about networks and cabling in chapter 11.

Instead of writing a document or letter on a word processor and posting it, you send it via the network to another computer. You don't need to print your letter on paper, no envelopes or stamps are needed, and no postman delivers the letter. If the person at the other end isn't using the electronic mail system when the message arrives, the electronic mail system stores it until they're ready to read it. This means information can be passed from one place to another straight away. Sending a letter by post is so slow compared to email that it is referred to as '*snail mail*'.

Electronic mail is used a lot for sending letters, but anything which can be saved to disk can be sent by electronic mail – a data file, a computer program, a file containing a newspaper produced by a desktop publishing package or a graphics file. This is called **file transfer** and it is dealt with later in this chapter.

If you prefer to work from home you can communicate with your office using electronic mail. This is known as teleworking. You can read more about teleworking in chapter 11.

> **Did you know?**
> The first email message was sent by Ray Tomlinson in 1971, who also first used the @ symbol. He chose the @ because it doesn't occur naturally in peoples' names and it wasn't a number.

What is required for electronic mail?

- Access to the Internet via an Internet service provider (ISP) or a private network.
- An electronic mail address or mailbox.

- A computer system.
- Software — an email client program or an Internet browser.

Access to the Internet

Most email services are provided by organisations linked to the Internet. This allows email messages to be sent anywhere in the world, provided that the recipient has an email address. Many organisations like businesses, schools and local authorities have internal email systems running on their own private networks.

An electronic mail address or mailbox

An electronic mail address has the format:
username@organisation.country

For example: johnwalsh@freeweb.co.uk, although sometimes country may be replaced with a different suffix such as *com*, *net* or *org*.

If you have a school email address, it might look like:

walshj@yourschool.localauthority.sch.uk

Whatever the email address is, it identifies the user's mailbox. A mailbox is a place on the Internet service provider's computer system where the email is stored until it is read or deleted.

If you want to send an email, you must know the email address of the person to whom the message is being sent. If you want to send a message to eliza@dolittle.net, and make a mistake, typing eliza@dolittl.net, then the email message will *bounce*, which means that a message will be sent back to your mailbox informing you that your email was not delivered correctly.

One other part of an email message is the message subject, which tells the recipient of the message what it is about. A sensible subject line increases the chance of a message being read, especially if the message is being sent to someone you don't know.

Figure 10.2 *How not to choose an email address.*

A computer system for electronic mail

All new computer systems have the capability to send and receive email. Such computers are called **Internet ready computers**. You can find out more about Internet ready computers in chapter 11.

Software — an email client program or an Internet browser

Email client programs

An email client program can be used to send and receive email. Email client programs include *Microsoft Outlook*, *Outlook Express*, *Eudora* and *Apple Mail*. Figures 10.3 and 10.4 show an email client program in use.

All email client programs allow you to:

- See a list of all of the messages in your mailbox by displaying the message headers. The header shows who sent the mail, the subject, the time and date and the size.
- Select a message and read the email.
- Create new messages and send them.
- Reply to a message.
- Forward a message to another email address.
- Delete a message.
- Send a cc (carbon copy) of a message to another email address.
- Send a bcc (blind carbon copy) of a message to another email address.

In addition, email client programs let you:

- Set up folders to manage your email.
- Keep an email address book.
- Add attachments to messages you send and save the attachments from messages you receive.
- Access newsgroups and other services.

When you are connected to the service provider, you are **on-line**. When you're not connected you're **off-line**. One advantage of an email client program is that the program may be used off-line, and you can compose an email message when you are not connected to the Internet. When you're on-line you are charged the cost of the connection to the service provider. If you use a **dial-up connection**, it's cheaper to write a letter off-line, save it and send it later than to write it while you're on-line. If you are replying to letters and the reply is short, it is quicker to reply while you're on-line, but if your reply is more than a few lines long, it is better to type it off-line. Some people or organisations like schools have 'always on' connections to

Credit level

Figure 10.3 *Sending an email message using Microsoft Outlook Express.*

the Internet and/or pay a flat fee to the service provider regardless of the time spent on-line. This advice does not apply to them. Dial-up connections are discussed further in chapter 12.

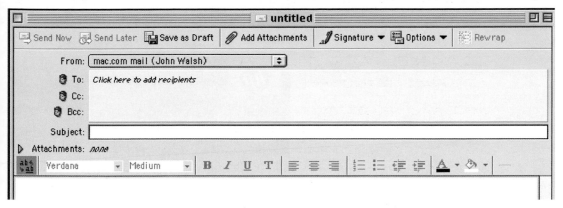

Another advantage of using an email client program is that all your mail is downloaded and stored on your own computer system. One disadvantage is that you need to set up your computer to use the email client program,

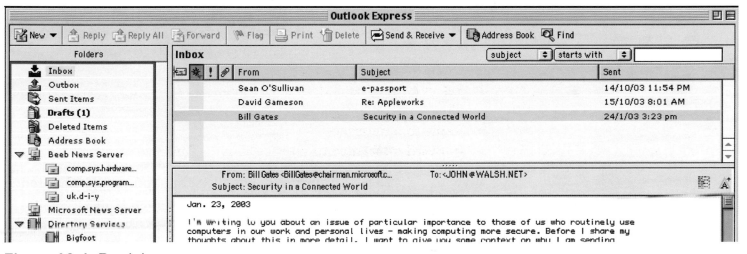

Figure 10.4 *Receiving an email message using Microsoft Outlook Express.*

and you must use the same computer each time you want to send and receive email. If you want to use another computer, it must also be set up first, before you can use it.

Webmail

It would be much more convenient if people could access their email from any computer that has an Internet connection, rather than having to go through a set up procedure first. For this reason, webmail has been developed. *Webmail* is a system which allows you to access email using an Internet browser program, like *Netscape Navigator* or *Microsoft Internet Explorer*.

Instead of setting up an email client program, you open a webmail account with an on-line service. One popular webmail service is *Hotmail* run by *Microsoft*, although many other companies provide similar services. *Hotmail* is shown in figure 10.5. Once you have opened your account, you are given an email address on the system and a password to access it. The facilities provided by webmail are similar to those provided by an email client program described above.

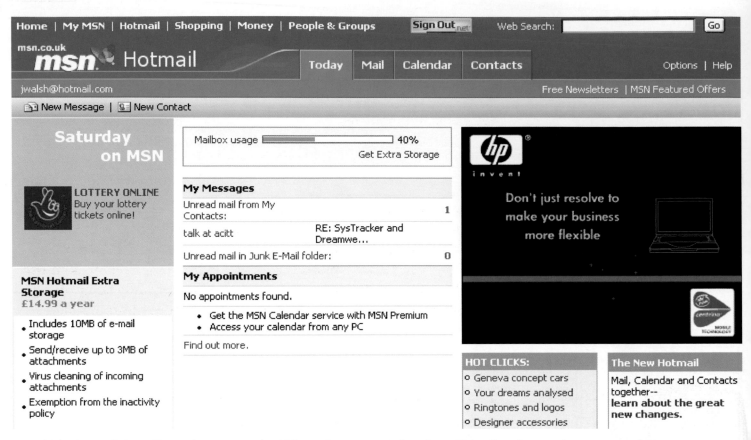

Figure 10.5 *Webmail – using Hotmail.*

The advantage of webmail is that it can be accessed from anywhere that has an Internet connection, but your email is stored on-line, so you must be on-line all the time to read your email and to compose and send messages. This can be expensive if you use the system frequently, depending upon your Internet connection charge.

Belt and braces

Some companies allow users to access their email services using both email client programs and webmail. This can be very useful if you prefer using the facilities and features of an email client program, for example, at home, but you also need to access your home mailbox while you are at your workplace. This system gives you the best of both worlds.

Other methods of sending email messages

Telephone boxes, email telephones and television sets

Some telecommunications companies have set up special email telephones with screens and keyboards which can be used by the general public to send email. It is also possible to buy an email telephone, which can be attached to an ordinary telephone line and used to send email. Similarly, special television sets can be purchased which can be connected to the Internet and used to send email by entering a message using an oversize remote control handset.

Mobile email

Mobile phones can also send and receive email, although they are much more frequently used to send text messages. The intriguing thing about text messages is that this is the one part of this book that I am confident 99% of its users will already know about. So — no excuses candidates!

What is text messaging?

Text messaging is a method of electronic communication using a mobile phone. Text messages are also known as SMS, which stands for Short Message Service. One advantage of SMS is that messages can be sent and received while the mobile phone is in use. One limitation of text messages are that they can only be up to 150 characters in length, plus 11 characters of header information.

What is required for text messaging?

Figure 10.6 *Some mobile phone handsets.*

- A mobile phone.
- An account with a service provider.
- To be in an area of sufficient signal strength to communicate with the service provider.

Sending a text message

In order to send a text message, the message is first composed using the keypad on the mobile phone handset. Most mobile phone handsets are small and have a limited number of keys, so each key has many functions. In order to obtain the letter 'c' for instance, it is necessary to press the 'abc' key three times. This means that a great number of key presses would be required to type a correctly spelled grammatical sentence, but most text messages are not like that. It is normal to use abbreviations, and many of these are based on the sounds of the letters and numbers used. This is known as phonetics.

A typical text message might include the abbreviation 'cul8r', which is 'see you later' or even just 'l8r', which requires even fewer key presses. The basic principle seems to be that you miss out as many letters as you can from a word, as long as you can still make sense of the 'msg'. One benefit of missing out letters is that you can cram more words into a single message, which has a fixed limit. Another more obvious benefit is that it makes messages much faster to type, as you don't have to type each word in full.

Here are some examples of SMS shorthand:

Abbreviation	Meaning
2	To/too
2day	Today
2nite	Tonight
4	For
4eva	Forever
8	Ate
b4	Before
bcnu	Be seeing you
btw	By the way
cul8r	See you later
cya	See ya
d	The
gr8	Great
l8	Late
m8	Mate
msg	Message
pls	Please
r u	Are you
2mrw	Tomorrow
tnx/thx	Thanks
ur	Your
wd	Would
wknd	Weekend
y	Why

Mad About Writing?

Figure 10.7 *A mobile phone with a large keyboard.*

I am sure that you know many other examples.

Writing in capital letters often requires a further key press, so many messages are lower case only. One disadvantage of frequent text messaging is that users may forget how to spell words correctly when required, such as when using a word processing package.

Some handsets offer a predictive text feature, which is designed to speed up the entry of text messages. Predictive text tries to anticipate what the user will type. It is based on a dictionary of correctly spelled words, like a spelling checker. However, if you use a lot of abbreviations, predictive text will slow down your typing and some users find it easier to turn this feature off.

Some handsets contain large keyboards, which are attractive to users used to typing on a traditional 'QWERTY' layout. Figure 10.7 shows one example.

Once the message has been composed, sending the message is just a matter of selecting the recipient mobile telephone number from the stored list on the mobile phone and selecting 'send' from the menu.

Depending on the handset in use, a beep will indicate that the message has been sent. A report may also be fed back to the sender's handset as to whether the message has been 'delivered' or is 'pending'.

A similar beep alerts the recipient to tell them that a text message has been received by their handset.

One other limitation of current mobile phones is that the storage space for text messages is limited, and stored messages often have to be deleted to make room for new messages.

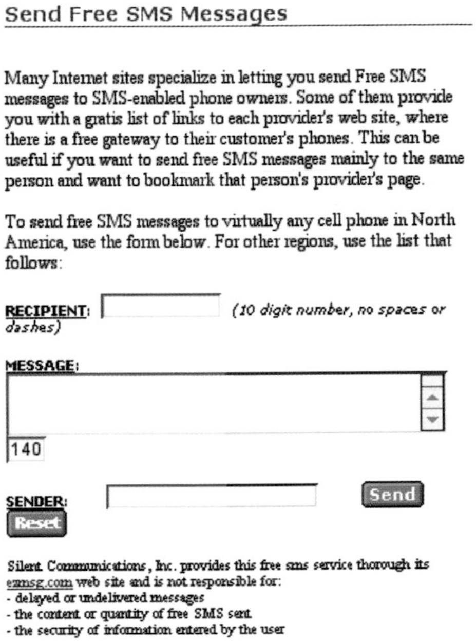

Sending an email

Sending an email is possible from a mobile phone. Some mobile phones have direct access to the Internet and can send an email. Non-Internet enabled mobile phone users can send a text message to certain service providers who will forward their message to a supplied email address, although these users will not be able to receive a reply by email on their mobile phones. You can read more about **mobile Internet technologies** in chapter 12.

Sending a text message from the Internet

Some service providers and websites offer the service where users may enter a mobile phone number and a message into a form on a web page. The message is then sent as a text message. Figure 10.8 shows one example of such a form.

Send Free SMS Messages

Many Internet sites specialize in letting you send Free SMS messages to SMS-enabled phone owners. Some of them provide you with a gratis list of links to each provider's web site, where there is a free gateway to their customer's phones. This can be useful if you want to send free SMS messages mainly to the same person and want to bookmark that person's provider's page.

To send free SMS messages to virtually any cell phone in North America, use the form below. For other regions, use the list that follows:

RECIPIENT: [   ] *(10 digit number, no spaces or dashes)*

MESSAGE:
[   ]
[140]

SENDER: [   ] [Send]
[Reset]

Silent Communications, Inc. provides this free sms service thorough its esmsg.com web site and is not responsible for:
- delayed or undelivered messages
- the content or quantity of free SMS sent
- the security of information entered by the user

Figure 10.8 *Sending a text message from a web page.*

Advantages and disadvantages of electronic mail

Electronic mail systems have good and bad points. Let's look at some of these and compare electronic mail with sending a letter by post or making a telephone call.

Advantages of electronic mail

- Electronic mail is much faster than sending a letter by post, since the message takes only seconds to arrive instead of days.
- Electronic mail is very accessible, since you can check electronic mail from anywhere in the world. If you are travelling around, you can check your mailbox by logging on to the system anywhere where there is Internet access.
- Electronic mail cuts across time zones, for example, between Scotland and Singapore. If the time in Scotland in 10.00 a.m. it is about 7.00 p.m. (later the same day) in Singapore and the offices in Singapore will probably be closed. But your electronic mail will be delivered to the office's mailbox just the same.

Figure 10.9 *Spam*

- There is no need to worry whether the person you're mailing is there to read the message because it will be stored by the system until it is read and deleted. Contacting someone during office hours by telephone can be quite difficult.
- Electronic mail is usually cheaper than sending a letter by post.
- Using electronic mail, you can send the same letter to many different users at once.
- Less paper is usually involved, because messages can be stored on disk. If you need a paper copy you can print it out.

Disadvantages of electronic mail

- You must check your mailbox regularly for the system to work. You'd never think of not looking in your letterbox at home every day, yet some users of electronic mail never check their mailboxes. This is where the system can break down. To make efficient use of the system you should check your mailbox at least once a day.
- The person you're mailing needs a mailbox on the system. If she doesn't have a mailbox, then you can't send electronic mail to her.
- Some official documents will probably always have to be written down or printed on paper and delivered in the traditional way. Electronic mail won't completely remove the need for this.
- Electronic mail can be impersonal because there is much less interaction between callers than there is when you're speaking on the telephone. Sometimes this can lead to problems when email messages are misinterpreted. This is explained further in the Netiquette section later in this chapter.
- Electronic mail is not yet as secure as the postal system. If someone finds out your password he might read your mail. Worse, he could change your password so you can't access the system. He could send out false mail in your name. There are no 'clues' like handwriting or a signature to prove that the message is actually from you or is a forgery. All electronic mail messages do, however, contain the time and date and other technical information contained in the header about when they were sent and where from, so it may be possible to trace a forgery.
- Junk email is a huge problem. Junk email is called unsolicited email because it is sent into your mailbox from strangers or companies whom you have not asked to send you anything. A common name for junk email is spam, so-called because of the Monty Python sketch of the same name.

More about junk email

Apart from the enormous amount of productive time that is lost in deleting spam from a user's mailbox, the huge quantity of spam that

<aside>

Did you know?
That 40% of all email messages are spam. It is estimated that in a person's lifetime, they will spend six months reading junk email.

In the UK since 11 December 2003, spammers face a £5,000 fine from magistrates or an unlimited amount after a jury trial under the Privacy and Electronic Communications Regulations 2003.

</aside>

is sent every day clogs up many Internet Service Provider's computer systems and this results in a slower service for legitimate users.

A number of techniques can help to reduce the amount of spam that is received, but it is difficult if not impossible to eliminate it entirely.

- Create an email address that is hard for spammers to work out. Don't use names or whole words. For instance, faz56rog3@yahoo.com is harder to guess than harry@comal.net.
- Keep your email address as private as possible. One technique that is helpful is to set up two email accounts, one that is private and only given out to trusted friends, the other is more public, and is used to join mailing lists and discussion groups.
- Change your email account when it starts filling up with spam. Once junk email starts it will never stop.
- Never send a reply to spam, especially in order to unsubscribe from the spammer's mailing list. If you do this you are confirming to the spammer that your email address is a valid one.
- Choose an email provider that provides spam filtering features, or use anti-spam software like *Spam Assassin*, *Firetrust Mailwasher Pro* or *McAfee Spamkiller*.
- Don't waste time reading spam – if it appears to come from an address you don't recognise, delete it straight away.
- Don't become a spammer by forwarding chain letters to your friends, delete them straight away.

Netiquette

Netiquette is short for network etiquette. Etiquette is a fancy word for being nice to others and treating them with respect. Netiquette is mainly concerned with the way email messages are written, and how others might interpret them.

Figure 10.10 *'Notiquette'*.

A number of rules have been set up for netiquette. Some are described below. If you look at the rules you will see that they are just common sense combined with polite behaviour.

1 Keep your message short and to the point. The recipient of your message may have another 50 messages to read in their mailbox.

2 Make yourself look good on-line by sharing expert knowledge and being forgiving of other people's mistakes.

3 Be careful about the language you use in a message. Remember that email is impersonal, and the person reading your message cannot see the expression on your face, which would tell them that what you were saying was a joke. To help avoid misunderstandings like this, some people add so-called 'emoticons' to their messages, like this ☺ :-) and :-(☹.

4 Avoid using capital letters in your message. This is the email equivalent of SHOUTING.

5 Never reply to a message in anger. This is known as flaming. Your message may be received in seconds. Once you have sent a message you can't get it back, and it may be stored for years.

6 Never talk about others in a message. The message could end up being forwarded to them!

7 Avoid sending large files as attachments unless the recipient is expecting them. They may have a slow Internet connection and such messages will take hours to download.

File transfer and other features of electronic mail software

File transfer

Besides using email to send written messages, it is also possible to send files along with the email message. Such files are called **attachments**, because they are part of, or 'attached to', the email message.

Both email client software and webmail permit the sending of attachments. If you use a free webmail service, there may be a limit to the size of the attached files that you can send and receive from your account[1].

Figure 10.11 shows part of the process of attaching a file to an email message in *Hotmail*.

[1] It is possible to exchange certain files such as pictures, logos and ring tones using a mobile phone but these are not 'attachments' and are not dealt with in this chapter.

Figure 10.11 *Attaching a file to an email message in Hotmail.*

Home | My MSN | Hotmail | Shopping | Money | People & Groups   Sign Out net   Web Search: [   ] Go
msn.co.uk
msn. Hotmail   Today Mail Calendar Contacts   Options | Help

jwalsh@hotmail.com   **Attach File**

OK | OK and Attach Another

Click **Browse** to select the file, or type the path to the file in the box below.

Find File: [   ] [Browse...]

Current attachments for the message "Test messsage"

Attachments		Size	Delete
	results-COPPER.xls	25 KB	✕
	results-NICHROME.xls	19 KB	✕
		Total 0.1 MB	

Attachment size limit: 1MB
Attachment usage [▮   ] 4%
Increase attachment size limit
Notice: Attachments are automatically scanned for viruses using   **McAfee** SECURITY

Disclaimer: The McAfee.com virus scanner may not be able to detect all known viruses and variants. Please be aware that there is a risk involved

Increase your attachment limit
With Extra Storage, you can send attachments up to 3MB in size. Only £14.99 a year. Plus:
- It includes an increased Inbox limit & virus scanning
- You'll also be exempt from the inactivity policy

File formats

All types of file may be sent as attachments, but it is important to consider the file format to be used. If you want the recipient of your message to be able to read the file, then you must ensure beforehand that the file format that you are sending to them is one that can be read by the software that they already have on their computer. The use of standard file formats can help with this problem.

Unwelcome attachments

Just as the ability to send attachments is an advantage, it is also a potential disadvantage. The files that are attached to some messages that you receive may be unwelcome. One of the most notorious viruses in the past few years, the so-called 'I Love You' virus, was spread via an email attachment. It was called the 'I Love You' virus, because it said 'I Love You' in the message subject.

Across the globe on Thursday, 4 May 2000, millions of Internet users logged on to find friends, relatives and colleagues had emailed them with heart-warming protestations of love. But joy quickly turned to anguish when they realised they had been on the receiving end of one of the most vicious bugs in the history of the Internet, one which cost users an estimated $10bn worldwide. A hacker in the Philippines, 24-year-old Onel de Guzman, created the 'I Love You' virus.

Always treat email messages containing attachments with caution, and do not open them unless you know what they contain. This is sensible advice, but the 'I Love You' virus got around this problem because the email addresses that the virus was sent to were taken from the infected computer's email address book. This meant that people would get a message from someone they knew saying 'I Love You' in the subject line, and most people were naturally curious enough to open the attachment. Once this was done, then their

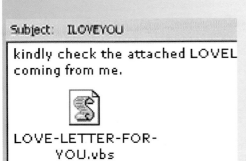

Subject: ILOVEYOU

kindly check the attached LOVEL coming from me.

LOVE-LETTER-FOR-YOU.vbs

Figure 10.12 *Don't open this file!*

computer became infected, and its address book was then used to send copies of the virus to all of the email addresses they had listed.

Organise your email

It is possible to set up folders to manage your email, whether using webmail or email client software. This is useful for filing messages if you wish to store them for any length of time.

You can set up filtering rules that will direct incoming email, such as junk mail, into specific folders. Using filters in this way means that you can avoid most obvious junk mail. You can set the filter to delete what it thinks is junk mail immediately, before you read it. This feature should be used with caution until you are certain that the filter can tell the difference between genuine email and spam. Some filtering software is mentioned earlier in the section on junk mail in this chapter.

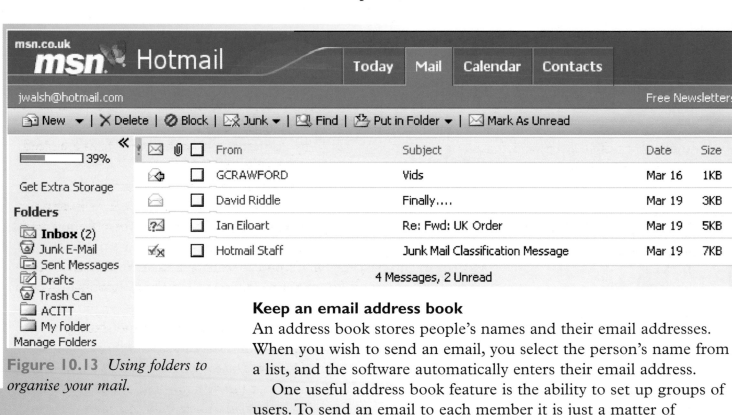

Figure 10.13 *Using folders to organise your mail.*

Keep an email address book

An address book stores people's names and their email addresses. When you wish to send an email, you select the person's name from a list, and the software automatically enters their email address.

One useful address book feature is the ability to set up groups of users. To send an email to each member it is just a matter of entering the name of the group into the To: box.

Newsgroups and other services

Newsgroups and other services are discussed in chapter 12.

Foundation level questions

knowledge and understanding

1 What is electronic communication?
2 What is electronic mail?
3 What is required for electronic mail?
4 Why is it advisable to include a sensible subject line in your message?
5 State two functions of an email client program.
6 Name one email client program you have used.
7 What is text messaging?
8 What does SMS stand for?
9 What is the maximum length of an SMS text message?
10 What is required for text messaging?

problem solving

1 What could cause an email message to *bounce*?
2 How do you know whether or not an email message has bounced?
3 When sending a text message, sometimes the user receives a report '*pending*', which means that the message has yet to be delivered. When will a 'pending' message be delivered?

General level questions

knowledge and understanding

1 Missing out letters from text messages can make them more difficult to read. State one benefit that arises from missing out letters from words in a text message.
2 What is the point of Netiquette?
3 Why is junk mail also known as:
   a. unsolicited email?
   b. Spam?

problem solving

1 State one advantage of using an email client program rather than webmail if you have a dial-up connection.
2 State one advantage that webmail has over an email client program.
3 Look at the list of advantages and disadvantages of electronic mail versus postal and telephone systems. Make up a list of advantages and disadvantages when you compare electronic mail and text messaging.
4 Why do mobile phone handsets have a limited number of keys?
5 a. Translate the following message into an abbreviated version, suitable for sending as a text message. 'The quick brown fox jumped over the lazy dog'.
   b. Given that each character takes up one byte of storage space, how much storage space is required for:
      i. the original version of the message?
      ii. the abbreviated version?
   c. How much storage space has been saved?
6 What steps can you take to reduce spam?
7 Why is it a bad idea to reply to spam?
8 Why should you keep email messages short?

Credit level questions

knowledge and understanding
1 What is file transfer?
2 What is an attachment?
3 What is an email filter?

problem solving
1 Why is it important to consider the file format to be used for file transfer?
2 Explain one possible disadvantage of receiving attachments.

3 Why did the 'I Love You' virus spread so quickly?
4 Suppose you had 50 of your friends email addresses in your address book, and each of your friends who were listed had 10 new email addresses that were not in common with each other. Can you work out how many computers would potentially be infected after:
   a. one generation of the virus?
   b. two generations of the virus?
5 What has phonetics got to do with a mobile phone?

• Key points •

- Electronic communication is the process of sending and receiving electronic messages.
- Electronic messages include electronic mail, text messaging and file transfer.
- Electronic mail is a way of sending messages from one computer to another.
- To access email you need access to the Internet via an Internet service provider or a private network, an electronic mail address or mailbox, a computer system and an email client program or an Internet browser.
- An electronic mail message is stored in the user's mailbox until it is read or deleted.
- Advantages of email include:
  - email is much faster and cheaper than sending a letter by post,
  - you can check email from anywhere,
  - email cuts across time zones,
  - there is no need to worry whether the person you're mailing is there,
  - you can send the same letter to many different users at once,
  - less paper is involved.

- Disadvantages of email include:
  - you must check your mailbox regularly for the system to work,
  - the person you're mailing needs a mailbox,
  - some official documents will have to be written down,
  - email can be impersonal,
  - email is not yet as secure as the postal system,
  - junk email is a huge problem.
- Spam is unsolicited email.
- Techniques to reduce spam include using filtering software and creating an email address which is difficult for spammers to guess.
- Text messaging is a method of electronic communication using a mobile phone.
- SMS stands for short message service.
- Text messaging requires a mobile phone, an account with a service provider and to be in an area of sufficient signal strength to communicate.
- Abbreviations are used to save space since text messages are of limited size.
- Netiquette is concerned with the way email messages are written and interpreted.

- Netiquette rules include:
  - keep your message short,
  - share expert knowledge,
  - be careful about the language you use,
  - avoid using capital letters,
  - never reply to a message in anger,
  - never talk about others in a message,
  - only send messages to interested parties.
- File transfer involves sending attachments by email.

11 Local area networks and wide area networks

What is a network?

Figure 11.1 *Computers in a local area network.*

A **network** is a linked set of computer systems that are capable of sharing programs, data and sending messages between them.

When a computer is not part of a network, it is called a **stand-alone computer**.

There are two types of network, depending on the distance between the computers making up the network.

A **local area network (LAN)** covers a small area such as a room or a building and is usually owned by an individual, a single company or an organisation such as a school. The school or centre in which you are studying Standard Grade Computing is likely to have a local area network. Some computers in a LAN are shown in figure 11.1.

A **wide area network (WAN)** covers a larger geographical area, such as a country or a continent. The **Internet** is the best-known example of a wide area network to which the general public has access.

Local area networks

Each computer on a local area network is called a **station**. Usually one station on the network is set aside as the **file server**. On the file server station all the shared programs and data available are stored, together with a list of names of authorised users.

Logging on and off

Before you can use a network system, you have to identify yourself to the file server — this is called logging on. To log on to any network you usually have to type in your user identity (which might be your name or a code — but it is personal to you) and then a password. When you have done this correctly the file server allows you access to the network — you are now on-line to the network and can load programs or look at your files. When you have finished using the network, you should log off, or go off-line. This means that the network will no longer accept any of your commands until you log on again. Passwords are discussed later in this chapter.

Advantages of local area networks

- You can share data and programs between stations. If you don't have a network connection, you can only share files by copying them to a disk and carrying the disk from one computer to another. This is known as '*sneaker-net*'.
- Everyone on the network can share peripherals such as printers, which makes the system cheaper to set up than if every station had its own printer. This is called resource sharing.
- An electronic mailing service can be operated.
- By using passwords your data can be kept secure.
- Unauthorised interference can be reduced by allowing different users different levels of access.
- Flexible access. A network user may access their files from any computer connected to the network.
- Workgroup computing. Many users can work on the same document simultaneously.

Transmission media for local area networks

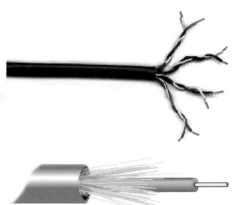

Figure 11.2 *UTP and optical fibre cables.*

Stations on a local area network are relatively close together and can be connected by using cables or wireless technology to transmit data.

Cables

Two types of cable are commonly used. These are unshielded twisted pairs of copper wire (UTP) and optical fibre. Figure 11.2 shows UTP and optical fibre cables.

Copper wire carries data using electrical signals. Optical fibres are very fine strands of glass that can transmit data very rapidly by using beams of light. Many strands are put together into a single cable and each strand is capable of carrying more than one data signal.

Optical fibre cable is more expensive than copper, but does not corrode. Copper cables carry electrical signals that can be subject to interference unlike optical fibre. Copper cables can be tapped but optical fibre cables provide secure data transmission.

Wireless

Figure 11.3 *Bluetooth logo.*

Wireless networking covers a range of possible methods of data transmission. These include infrared communication, *Bluetooth*, *WiFi*, microwave transmission and satellite links. Microwave transmission and satellite links are used in wide area networks and you can read about these in the next section.

Figure 11.4 *WiFi logos.*

Infrared communication uses the same system as a television remote control. It needs a direct line of sight between transmitter and receiver. Infrared is used for short-range communication between devices, and can only link two devices at once. Strong sunlight can interfere with infrared signals.

Bluetooth and *Wifi* both use radio waves at the same frequency. Unlike *infrared*, radio waves can pass through most materials and walls, and devices don't need to be pointing at one another. *Bluetooth* can make temporary short-range links between personal devices, such as mobile phones and headsets, palmtop (PDA) and laptop (notebook) computers. *Bluetooth* is designed as a replacement for *infrared*. Stand-alone *Bluetooth* devices have a range of 10 metres, and are able to transfer information at 1 megabit per second (1 Mbit/sec).

WiFi stands for the Wireless Fidelity Alliance. *WiFi* devices have typical ranges from 12 to 50 metres and typical data transfer rates from 5 to 20 Mbit/sec. Some devices using *WiFi* are shown in figures 11.13, 11.14 and 11.15 later in this chapter.

Wide area networks

Did you know?
That the first *Bluetooth* worm *EPOC.Cabir* was discovered on 14 June 2004.

Wide area networks have most of the advantages of local area networks, but you should remember that they are used differently. For instance, wide area networks are not normally used for sharing peripherals – there would be very little point in printing out your latest masterpiece if you had to travel to the other side of the Atlantic Ocean to collect it! One of the most popular uses of a wide area network is to send electronic mail. You can type a letter at one station and send it instantly to any number of users anywhere in the world. If the person at the other end is not using the network when you send the letter, the computer will store it until they are on line, and are able to read it.

Transmission media for wide area networks

Wide area networks use **telecommunications links** to transmit and receive data. **Telecommunications** is a general term that describes the communication of information over a distance. The telecommunications links used in wide area networks include **microwave transmission**, **satellite links** and **optical fibre**. Some telecommunications links are shown in Figures 11.5, 11.6 and 11.7

Microwave transmission

Microwave transmission is used in the public telephone service. Many organisations use private microwave installations to transmit data between important locations. Microwave systems are highly directional and use dish aerials.

Satellite links

A satellite link is a form of telecommunication link that operates over long distances. Public telephone service providers use satellite links for international communications. Unlike satellite broadcast systems (BSkyB TV), these links use highly directional, narrow beam, two-way transmissions. A single satellite channel is capable of carrying a very large number of separate transmissions. A satellite link is shown in figure 11.5.

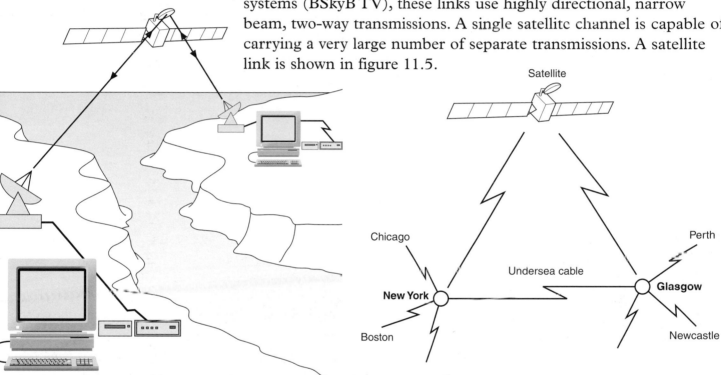

Figure 11.5 *A satellite link.*

Figure 11.6 *Telecommunications links.*

Optical fibre

Optical fibres are described earlier in the cables section. Figure 11.7 shows optical fibre submarine cables also being used as the transmission medium in a wide area network.

Sometimes the data in a telecommunications link is accidentally changed or corrupted by interference. The less chance there is of interference affecting the telecommunications link, the more reliable the data transmission will be. An optical fibre data link is very reliable because it is not affected by electrical interference.

Figure 11.7
Optical fibre submarine cables.

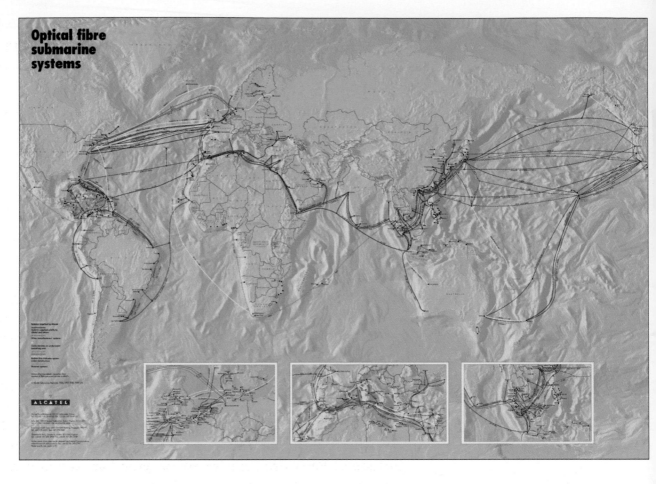

Network security

The information on a network must be guarded carefully so that users can see only the data they're meant to see. Different users on a network are allowed different levels of access so that they can look at, store, or load information, depending on their need. In a school network, the class teacher would have a higher level of access (be allowed to access more data) than a pupil so that she can examine and change the files belonging to any individual in the class. The network manager (administrator) decides each user's level of access or network privileges and gives each user a special user identity and password to allow her or him to log on.

Security methods include **passwords**, **encryption** and **physical** methods.

Passwords

If you use a network, you should change your password regularly so that no one else can discover it, and you shouldn't choose a password that would be easy for someone else to guess — like a family name or your birthday. If someone discovers your password, they could

delete your files or read your private email. Some individuals ('hackers') take great pleasure in trying to outwit network security systems. 'Hacking' usually involves gaining unauthorised access to data belonging to someone else and is illegal.

Figure 11.8 *Passwords.*

Choosing a password

You should always choose a password that will be difficult for others to guess. One school was told by its local authority to assign pupils' dates of birth as their passwords for the school network. This was not a very secure idea, as each pupil had friends who knew their birthdays! Passwords like 'retep' or 'yram' are too obvious. A mixture of random numbers and letters is best, like '6nkf7dod3'.

Encryption

Encryption means putting data into a code to prevent it being seen by unauthorised users. When you type a password to access a network, it is encrypted before it is sent to the fileserver to prevent it from being intercepted and read en route. One common use of

Figure 11.9 *PGP and email.*

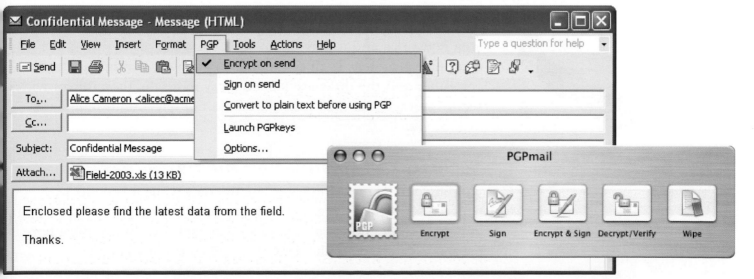

encryption is to protect email messages and files that are sent over a network. Files may be encrypted by using an application package, like PGP (Pretty Good Privacy), or by using a security feature built into the computer's operating system, like File Vault. How PGP is used with some email applications is shown below.

Physical methods

Physical security prevents unauthorised users from getting access to the computer system or data. Locking a computer or disks away will prevent physical access. Methods of preventing physical access include using a magnetic stripe card or a smart card to access a computer room. In order to prevent fraudulent use of these cards, it is becoming common to use a person's fingerprint, iris scan or voiceprint as evidence of their identity. Using a person's physical characteristics in this way is known as *biometrics*. In order to pass a security check, the biometric data stored on the card would be checked against the person's actual fingerprint, for instance. Some examples of biometrics are shown in figure 11.10.

Figure 11.10 *Biometrics.*

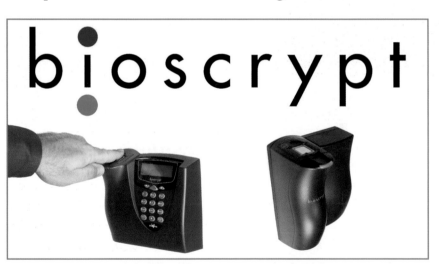

However, many computers are connected to local area and wide area networks, and it may be possible for a hacker to access the computer remotely. If all of the backing storage is removed from the computer and the disks are locked away in a safe, then this provides secure storage, but most computers do not have removable hard disk drives.

Security of transmission media

Tapping of data means intercepting the data while it is on its way between sender and receiver. Using optical fibre cable prevents tapping of data because the signals are carried using light. If the optical fibre is broken in order to tap the data, then the recipient will know immediately. Electrical signals on a copper wire can be tapped by

Figure 11.11 *Physical security has its limits!*

making a connection anywhere along the wire, and data transmissions on a wireless network may be intercepted. Another computer fitted with an aerial can receive data displayed on a CRT monitor.

One popular activity is to travel around with a laptop computer fitted with a wireless network interface card and look for so-called 'hotspots'. A hotspot is an area where wireless network signals may be received, and the laptop may connect to the network. Usually hotspots are located in specific built-up areas close to offices and within public buildings and university campuses. These hotspots may be deliberately put in place for legitimate use, such as university students, or they may be accidentally created if a company's wireless network extends beyond the boundary of the building.

Figure 11.12 *Warchalk symbols.*

A complete sub-culture has grown up around finding and using these hotspots. A code has been developed, which involves placing chalk marks on pavements and buildings where free wireless Internet access may be obtained. These marks are called warchalks, and you can see an example in figure 11.12

Absolute security

Using all of the methods described above will make your data as safe as possible. However, no security method is absolute and cannot be broken into. All that a good security system can do is increase the amount of time it takes for a determined hacker or other unauthorised person to get your data. If you have a secret that you don't want anyone to know, then don't type it into a computer, especially not one that is connected to any kind of network!

A **client and server network** is a method of network organisation in which network stations or **clients** make use of resources available on one or more **servers**.

Desktop computers are the most common type of client on this network. A **network interface card** is required in order to connect to a network. Network interface cards are described later in this chapter.

Different types of server are classified according to their function. Here are some examples:

File server

A **file server** provides central disk storage for users' programs and data on a network. A file server may be similar in appearance to a desktop computer, but usually has a greater amount of RAM and much larger backing storage capacity. It is also likely to have a fast processor, or multiple processors, so that it can serve many users in as fast a time as possible. In addition, the components used to build a file server (like the hard disk drive) should be of a higher quality than an ordinary desktop computer, because the file server is designed to run constantly 24 hours a day, seven days a week. Figure 11.13 shows two file servers.

Some form of backup device is essential for a file server, especially if the clients have no local storage. A **magnetic tape** drive is often used for this. Magnetic tape is discussed in chapter 18.

Figure 11.13 *Two file servers.*

Printer server

A **printer server** allows all of the client stations to use a printer controlled by it. A printer server will also provide a queuing facility that allows users to receive their printouts in turn. A network printer is designed to work quickly, so that users on the network will not have too long to wait for their printouts!

Current network printers are usually large monochrome lasers, although colour laser printers are becoming more common. The network printer will have its own CPU and a decent amount of RAM in order to hold the print data (print jobs) that are sent to it.

Desktop computers on a network without a printer server usually save data temporarily to their own local hard disk drive. This allows background printing.

CD-ROM server

A **CD-ROM server** allows client stations to access data and programs from one or more CD-ROMs held within it. A CD-ROM *jukebox* can hold a number of CD-ROMs at once.

Database server

A database server manages a large database that may be accessed by client stations.

Internet and mail servers

An Internet server allows all the users on a network access to the Internet, and a mail server manages electronic mail.

Network interface card

A network interface card or NIC is a small circuit board that is fitted inside a computer system to allow it to communicate with a computer network. A network interface card is shown in figure 11.14.

The type of computer that is most likely to be connected to a local area network is a desktop computer, although most current laptop computers also have network interface cards fitted.

Some laptop computers also have a wireless network interface card that allows them to communicate with other computers on a local area network from anywhere nearby. One current example of wireless networking is *Apple's Airport* system. You can see two types of wireless network interface card in figures 11.15 and 11.16.

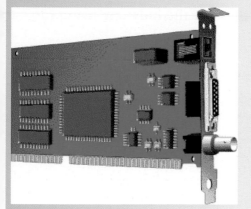

Figure 11.14 *A network interface card.*

Figure 11.15 *Apple's Airport Extreme wireless networking base station and card.*

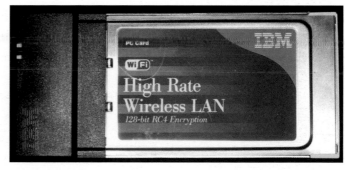

Figure 11.16 *IBM wireless networking card.*

The most common type of local area network in current use is Ethernet.

Network topology

Network topology is the way in which computers in a network are arranged and how they are connected together. Network topology is not covered in this book because it is outside the scope of this course in Standard Grade Computing. You will learn about the different topologies if you study Computing at Higher level.

Figure 11.17 *3Com wireless networking base station.*

Multi-access

Multi-access means that many users may be on-line to a computer system at the same time.

A multi-access system is made up of a large central computer with many terminals linked to it. The central computer constantly checks each of the terminals in turn. If a terminal wants access to the central computer, data is sent very quickly to it and returns from it at the same high speed. This fast response gives the user of each terminal the impression that they are the only one using the system. Multi-access systems like these are used for:

- airline reservations
- the police national computer
- automated telling (cashcard) machines.

A client and server network is also an example of a multi-access system in that many users may be on-line to the file server at once.

Social, legal and ethical issues

Teleworking

Teleworking is the process of using a wide area network to work from home rather than an office or centrally located workplace. Working from home means that you can choose your working hours and that you save time and money because you don't have to travel to work. This also reduces pollution and congestion in public transport and on roads. If you have a young family to look after, you can organise this around your work and you can save money on childcare costs. The employers also benefit, in that they do not have to provide office space or facilities like a canteen. More people may be inclined to work for a company if they provide the option of teleworking.

The Department of Trade and Industry has produced a set of legal guidelines that UK firms must follow if they employ staff who regularly telework from home. Under the terms of the guidelines firms must take responsibility for the 'information security' of remote workers and address health and safety issues, including ensuring all electrical equipment complies with safety regulations. Employers must also provide personal support, to ensure that teleworkers do not become too isolated or lonely. These guidelines are designed to help employees improve the balance between work and home life.

The Flexible Working (Procedural Requirements) Regulations 2002, which took effect on 6 April 2003, require companies to consider allowing parents with young children to change the hours they work, change the times when they are required to work, or to

Did you know?

In the UK in 2003, there were 2.2 million employees working away from central offices using IT. This number is increasing by 400,000 additional teleworkers every year.

work from home. This law could force many companies to allow their employees to work from home, and may increase the market for related services such as broadband network access.

Other social issues

The use of wide area networks can bring social benefits in that it can improve communications in remote areas and reduce social isolation. My family regularly keeps in contact with their relations in the USA via the Internet. Email is exchanged, and family photographs are posted on a website for people to look at. People who have emigrated from the UK enjoy looking at local websites which can keep them up to date with what's happening 'back home'. Sometimes expatriates set up their own website, in order to keep in touch with the UK and with other people who have emigrated.

Some people believe that wide area networks can also increase social isolation. If individuals choose to use a computer as their only means of access to the outside world then they can become remote and detached from other people. One report by researchers at Carnegie Mellon University suggested that even spending an hour a week surfing the Internet could increase depression.

Some people cannot afford the cost of becoming connected to the Internet. Will this lead to a situation where people with a connection to the Internet are seen as being 'information rich' and those who are not connected are 'information poor', and therefore further disadvantaged?

Legal issues

We have already discussed government regulations for teleworking. Other laws which may affect the use of computers include the Computer Misuse Act, the Copyright, Designs and Patents Act, the Data Protection Act and the Privacy and Electronic Communications Regulations 2003.

The Computer Misuse Act makes the activities of hacking and the distribution of viruses into criminal offences. What is the legal situation if these activities are done outside the UK via a network?

The Data Protection Act sets out the rights of data subjects and the responsibilities of data controllers (data users). Unscrupulous companies can send their data abroad to other countries to be processed where the UK law does not apply.

The Copyright, Designs and Patents Act makes unauthorised copying of materials like music and films into a criminal offence, yet these materials may be freely downloaded from file servers in other countries.

The Privacy and Electronic Communications Regulations 2003 state that companies must get permission from an individual before they can send them an email or a text message. This law makes spam a criminal offence and senders of unsolicited emails will face unlimited fines. Business email addresses are not covered.

Ethical Issues

Ethical issues are concerned with people's judgement as to what is right or wrong. Ethical issues of networks include invasion of personal privacy, censorship and freedom of speech.

Invasion of personal privacy

Data that is sent across networks may be intercepted by government agencies like GCHQ in the UK and NSA in the USA. Is this acceptable because it may help to prevent terrorism? Is it unacceptable because all communications should remain private?

Censorship and freedom of speech

Anyone can set up a web site. Should people who are distributing racist hatred material across networks be allowed to? Should a country be able to block access to web sites, such as bomb making, which its government thinks are unsuitable?

Foundation level questions

knowledge and understanding

1 What is a network?
2 What is a stand-alone computer?
3 What is a local area network?
4 What is a wide area network?
5 What term is used for each computer on a local area network?
6 a. What is logging on?
   b. Describe one method of logging on.
7 What is 'sneaker-net'?

problem solving

1 Why is logging on called going on-line?
2 State two advantages of a local area network.
3 Why are wide area networks not normally used for sharing peripherals?

General level questions

knowledge and understanding

1 What is a transmission medium used for?
2 State two types of wireless networking.
3 a. What is meant by the term network privileges?
   b. Who controls a user's network privileges?
4 a. What is a telecommunications link?
   b. What type of network uses telecommunications links?
5 What is the purpose of network security?
6 Name three methods of network security.
7 Why should you change your password regularly?
8 What does encryption mean?

problem solving

1   State one benefit of copper wire over optical fibre as a da transmission medium.

2   Why could it be a waste of time to prevent physical access to a networked computer?

3   Why is optical fibre cable more secure than copper wire?

4   Why is there no such thing as absolute security on a network?

5   Why is REMOH or SNRUBRM a poor choice of password?

Credit level questions

knowledge and understanding

1   Why is it necessary for some users on a network to have different levels of access from one another?

2   Write a sentence to advise someone how to choose a password.

3   What is a client and server network?

4   What is the most common client machine?

5   a. What is the function of a file server?

   b. Why are some components in a file server computer of higher quality than an ordinary desktop computer?

   c. Name two other types of server.

   d. Which type of server might use queuing and what would be in the queue?

6   What is a network interface card?

7   Look at the picture of the card in figure 11.16. Which type of wireless networking does it use?

8   What is multi-access?

9   What is teleworking?

10   Explain the terms 'information-rich' and 'information-poor'.

11   Give one ethical and one legal issue related to networks.

12   Read the article below and answer the questions which follow:

BBC News Wednesday, 29 May 2002, 09:22 GMT
Being wired helps you connect
People who spend time online are not sad, lonely individuals with no social life. Quite the opposite, argues Professor Keith Hampton, an expert in cyber-sociology at the Massachusetts Institute of Technology. "The social impact of new communications technologies is a greater number of social ties, more diverse social ties, more support," he said. "It doesn't cut into your phone communication. It doesn't interfere with your face-to-face contact. It just increases communication," Professor Hampton told the BBC programme, Go Digital.

Various studies have suggested that people who spend time online are more vulnerable to unhappiness and loneliness. One report by researchers at Carnegie Mellon University suggested that even spending an hour a week surfing the Internet could increase depression. But in his research on the relationship between technology, social relationships and the urban environment, Professor Hampton has found that the internet can serve to bind a community together. "It's all garbage," he said of studies labelling net users as depressed or lonely individuals. He argues that the key difference between his research and other studies is that he sees the Internet as part of people's everyday lives. "The internet is just another communication medium that any of us use to communicate with friends and family," he said. "If you look at it as just another technology that provides you with access to people, you see that communication online leads to more communication, in person or on the phone."

Professor Hampton spent two years as a member of the Netville project, a wired neighbourhood in the suburbs of Toronto. The community was built from the ground up with a high-speed computer network — offering fast Internet access — a videophone, an online jukebox, online health services, local discussion forums and entertainment and educational software. Professor Hampton found that living in a wired community encouraged greater community involvement, strengthened relationships with neighbours and family, and helped maintain ties with friends and relatives living farther away. "Netville was a unique situation," he said. "It allowed people to form social relationships when they moved in and solve all sorts of problems they encountered when they moved to the new suburban community. "When you move into a new home, some of the first questions are: where can I find a babysitter, where can I find the best pizzeria? All these questions were answered online with information by existing residents."

Ironically, once the research project was over, the companies that had provided the technology that went into people's homes decided to take it all out. Faced with the loss of their technology infrastructure, the residents pulled together to replace what they had lost. "They now all have cable modem access and they have replicated their neighbourhood email list," said Professor Hampton. "These were the most important technologies to them — broadband access to the internet and simple email technology that allows you to communicate with your neighbours."

a. According to the article, what is the social impact of new technology?
b. Are any contrary views expressed?
c. What is the key difference between this research and other studies?
d. What was the Netville project?
e. What happened when the technology was removed at the end of the research project?
f. What is your opinion of this study? Was the artificial creation of the on-line community too unrealistic to prove anything in real life? How long do you think it will be before every town in Scotland is a Netville?

problem solving

1. What advantage does Bluetooth have over infrared communication?
2. What advantage does WiFi have over Bluetooth?
3. Why do desktop computers on a network without a printer server save the print data temporarily to hard disk?
4. Which type of computer is most likely to use a wireless network interface card?
5. State one argument for and one argument against teleworking.
6. Give *two* reasons why * or o appear on the screen when you are entering a password.
7. When changing your password, why do you have to enter the new password twice?
8. It is an unfortunate consequence of all new technologies that some people will abuse them. Spam is an example of abuse of email. One new technology that is also being abused is *Bluetooth*. So-called '*bluejacking*' involves using a *Bluetooth* device like a mobile phone or a PDA to send anonymous messages to other *Bluetooth* devices. How close would another user have to be in order to 'bluejack'?

• Key points •

- A network is a linked set of computer systems that are capable of sharing programs, data and sending messages between them.
- When a computer is not part of a network, it is called a stand-alone computer.
- A local area network (LAN) covers a small area such as a room or a building.
- A wide area network (WAN) covers a larger geographical area.
- Each computer on a local area network is called a station.

- Usually one station on the network is set aside as the file server.
- Advantages of local area networks:
  - You can share data and programs between stations.
  - Everyone on the network can share peripherals such as printers.
  - An electronic mailing service can be operated.
  - By using passwords your data can be kept secure.

- Unauthorised interference can be reduced, by allowing different users different levels of access.
- A network user may access their files from any computer connected to the network.
- Many users can work on the same document simultaneously.
- Stations on a local area network can be connected by using cables or wireless signals as the transmission medium.
- Two types of cable are unshielded twisted pairs of copper wire (UTP) and optical fibre.
- Wireless networking includes infrared communication, *Bluetooth*, *WiFi* (IEEE802.11), microwave transmission and satellite links.
- Wide area networks use telecommunications links to transmit and receive data.
- Telecommunications is a general term that describes the communication of information over a distance.
- Security methods include passwords, encryption and physical.
- You should change your password regularly so that no one else can discover it.
- You shouldn't choose a password that would be easy for someone else to guess.
- Encryption means putting data into a code to prevent it being seen by unauthorised users.
- Physical security prevents unauthorised users from getting access.

- Locking a computer or disks away will prevent physical access.
- A client and server network is a method of network organisation in which network stations or clients make use of resources available on one or more servers.
- Desktop computers are the most common type of client on this network.
- A network interface card is required in order to connect to a network.
- A file server provides central disk storage for user's programs and data on a network.
- Multi-access means that many users may be on-line to a computer system at the same time.
- Teleworking is the process of using a wide area network to work from home rather than an office.
- Use of wide area networks can bring social benefits in that it can improve communications with remote areas and reduce social isolation.
- Some people believe that wide area networks can also increase social isolation.
- Laws which may affect the use of computers include the Computer Misuse Act, the Copyright, Designs and Patents Act and the Data Protection Act.
- Ethical issues are concerned with people's judgement as to what is right or wrong.
- Ethical issues of networks include invasion of personal privacy, censorship and freedom of speech.

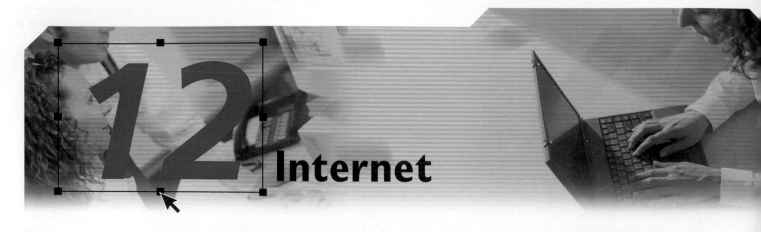

12 Internet

What is the Internet?

The Internet is a wide area network spanning the globe. It can be thought of as many different, smaller networks connected together. This is why the Internet is known as a 'network of networks'. Each connected network may be of any size, use any hardware or be situated anywhere in the world. These networks include very large and well-organised networks like those of governments, universities or multi-national corporations, and small company networks or individuals using Internet service providers (ISPs).

Figure 12.1
An artist's impression of the Internet.

What information is available on the Internet?

A vast quantity of information on any topic you can think of is available on the Internet. A great deal of information is stored on **web pages**, but there are also a huge number of files available for download.

What services are available on the Internet?

The Internet provides three main services:

- The **World Wide Web**, which gives access to remote databases, through **browsing** or **searching**.
- **Electronic mail**, which provides one to one (or one to many) communication and exchange of information.
- **File transfer**, which makes it possible to send and receive large amounts of information.

We covered electronic mail and file transfer in chapters 10 and 11. Other services include:

E-commerce, **on-line banking** and **on-line shopping** are major uses of the Internet. You can read about these services in chapter 13 on Commercial data processing.

Some additional services available on the Internet include:

chat and instant messaging, web logs, bulletin boards, discussion groups, streaming video and video conferencing.
These are discussed later in this chapter.

What is the World Wide Web?

The **World Wide Web (WWW)** is a collection of information held in **multimedia** form on the Internet. This information is stored at locations called **web sites** in the form of **web pages**. A web page is a single document, although it may be too large to display on the screen without scrolling.

Figure 12.2 *A web page.*

Welcome to the New Higher Computing website. This site is designed to support the textbook written by John Walsh for Higher Computing, and is freely available for you to access.

If you would like further details about the New Higher Computing textbook, please click **here**, or on the book cover to your right.

The purpose of the site is to provide program files relating to the exercises described and explained in the textbook. The four programming languages supported here are:

- C
- COMAL
- VisualBasic
- TrueBasic

We have program files for both Mac and PC users - simply click on the relevant button below to find what's available:

 Mac   Windows

 Hodder & Stoughton

Web pages are permanently available to any user of the Internet. Each organisation, or individual who provides information organises this information as a web site, often consisting of many pages. Web sites are a very effective way of distributing information.

Any web page can be accessed directly if its full **web address** or **URL** is known. To make it easier to find information, each web site has its own home page. The home page provides a starting point for the user to explore the site. It's like a main menu, and may also provide **hyperlinks** to other sites. Hyperlinks are links between World Wide Web pages, documents or files. They are activated by clicking on text, which acts as a button, or on a particular area of the screen like a graphic.

Web pages are usually prepared in a special language called **HTML** or **hypertext mark-up language**. You can read some more about HTML in chapter 8 on Web page creation.

A **browser** is a program that allows the user to browse or surf through the World Wide Web. When browsing the World Wide Web, a browser loads web pages from another computer on the Internet and displays them. Related pages may be easily loaded by clicking on hyperlinks, which are shown in a different colour on the web page.

A browser allows pages to be saved or printed, and can move backward and forward through pages already accessed. A browser also stores a history of recently viewed pages, and can remember web page addresses by using **bookmarks** or **favourites**. When you bookmark a page, the web address of the page is stored. Clicking on a bookmark or selecting from a menu will cause the page to be found and displayed.

Figure 12.3 *Internet Explorer menu bar.*

In the same way as a web site has a home page; you can set a browser to access any page on the Internet when it starts up. This is the browser's home page.

More about web addresses

URL stands for uniform resource locator. The URL is a unique address for a specific file available on the Internet. A typical URL looks like this:

http://www.standrewsacademy.sch.uk/departments/Computing/index.htm

The first part (http) is the **protocol**, in this case hypertext transfer protocol. The second part (www.standrewsacademy.sch.uk) is the **domain name**. The last part (departments/Computing/index.htm) is the **pathname**, which leads to the file, in this case the index page.

Note that not all domain names begin with www, for example, http://doit.ort.org.

Accessing the Internet

Internet ready computer

Internet ready computer is a phrase which is used to describe a computer which is in all respects prepared to be connected to the Internet. Some advertisements claim that the user can be online only minutes after unpacking their new computer and switching it on.

An Internet ready computer consists of a computer system, an internal modem and suitable communications software such as a browser and an email client program.

Modem

When a computer uses a telephone line to connect to an Internet service provider's computer, a modem is needed at each end of the link. Computers can only understand digital signals, which are made up of a series of zeroes and ones, but ordinary telephone lines, which are used for voice transmission, can't transmit digital signals. The modem changes the digital signals from the computer at one end of the link to sounds, which can be sent along the telephone line. The modem at the other end of the link changes the sounds back to digital signals, which the receiving computer can understand. An internal modem is contained inside the computer system. An external modem is a peripheral device, which plugs into a computer system.

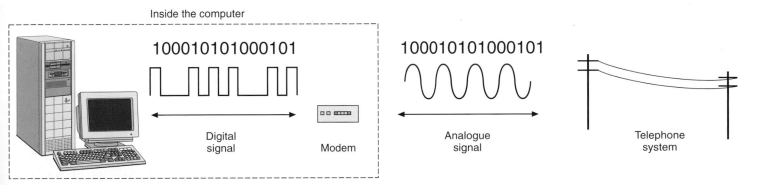

Inside the computer

100010101000101

Digital signal   Modem

100010101000101

Analogue signal

Telephone system

Figure 12.4 *How a modem works.*

Browser

A browser is a program that allows the user to browse or surf through the World Wide Web. Perhaps the two best-known browser applications are *Microsoft Internet Explorer* and *Netscape Communicator*. Other browsers include *Safari* and *Opera*.

Browsers allow the user to find information interactively on the Internet. A browser may be used to access the World Wide Web, or to provide other facilities such as file transfer or email. See chapters 10 and 11 for more information on email and file transfer.

Email client

An email client program is used for sending and receiving email. Email client programs include *Microsoft Outlook, Outlook Express, Eudora, and* Apple Mail. You can read more about email client programs and electronic mail in chapter 10.

Dial-up and broadband connections

When the user has switched on their new computer, a wizard or assistant program will help them set the computer up for connection to the Internet. The most common method is to use a dial-up connection, but more and more home computers are being connected using a broadband connection.

Assuming a dial-up connection is used, a wire will be connected from the computer's modem socket to a telephone socket. The wizard will offer the user a choice of Internet service provider (ISP), and is pre-programmed with a list of telephone numbers and guest passwords. The computer's communications software will dial the ISP's telephone number, and establish a connection to the Internet. Once on-line for the first time, the user will register their details with the ISP, and will choose an email address and a password. Thereafter, all of the connection details will be stored on the user's computer, and the next time they connect to the Internet, the process will be automatic.

Note that the precise details of how broadband operates are outside the scope of this course at Standard Grade. However, it is worth noting some differences between dial-up and broadband connections.

- The main difference between a dial-up connection and a broadband connection is the speed of access to the Internet. A typical dial-up connection operates at a maximum speed of 56 kilobits/sec. A broadband connection operates at 512 kilobits/sec and above, approximately 10 times faster than dial-up. Schools, local authorities and other large organisations will use a higher speed broadband connection to each other and to the Internet. For instance, all schools in my local authority currently share a 100 megabits/sec connection between the schools, although the speed at which each school and therefore each user may access the Internet is much lower.

- Another difference between these two types of connection is that a broadband connection is 'always on', that is, constantly connected or on-line to the Internet. A dial-up connection means that the modem in the computer has to dial the telephone number at the start of each connected session.
- Telephone calls may also be made and received at the same time as connection to the Internet when using a broadband connection.
- You can share a broadband connection by setting up a local area network in your house and having more than one computer connected to the Internet at once.
- A dial-up connection is always made through an Internet service provider (ISP). A broadband connection does not require an ISP, just a telecommunications link.
- While all 'Internet ready computers' contain a dial-up modem, they may not contain the necessary equipment to connect to broadband. An additional modem, adapter or other device such as a router may be needed to connect to broadband. Which type is required will depend upon the method of broadband connection, and again this is outside the scope of this course at Standard Grade.

When the user has finished using the Internet, they can log off, or go off-line. When off-line, the user cannot access any of the Internet services until they log on, or go on-line again.

Internet service provider (ISP)

An Internet service provider is a company that provides a host computer which the user can connect to by dialling in. The host computer manages the communications, and also stores data such as electronic mail, web pages and files for its subscribers. This host computer is connected to the Internet and subscribers can communicate with other computers on the Internet. The Internet service provider charges for these services, and may also provide others.

Searching the Internet

The Internet contains millions of pages of information on every subject. The best way of finding the information you want is to use a search engine. A search engine is a special site on the World Wide Web, which is designed to help you to find information.
Search engines work in various different ways, but they all:

- search the Internet for different words,
- build up an index of these words, and where they can be found,

- allow users to search for particular words in their indexes,
- provide hyperlinks to where these words may be found on the Internet.

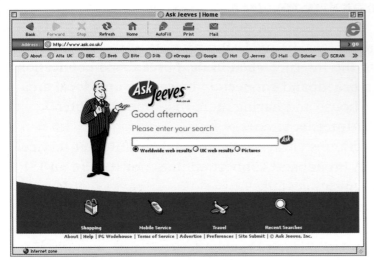

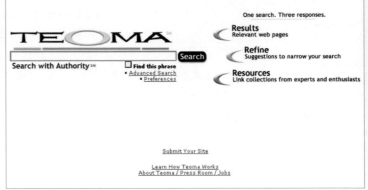

Figure 12.5 *Some search engines.*

Most search engines allow the user to carry out two different types of searches or queries, **basic** and **advanced**. A **simple** search in a **database** involves searching on one field only. A **complex** search in a **database** involves searching for information on two or more fields. For the purposes of this chapter on the Internet, we will consider a **simple search** to be what a search engine calls a basic search, and a **complex search** to be what a search engine calls an advanced search.

Search engine with simple search

A **basic search** allows the user to enter one or more **keywords** into an entry box, and then click a button or press return on the keyboard to start the search. A **keyword** is the text which is used to search a file for a given entry or part of an entry. On some systems the term **search string** is used instead of keyword.

A sensible choice of keywords can save a great deal of time when searching. The more detail you can give in the keywords the better.

Figure 12.6 *A basic search.*

A search for *long nosed bandicoot* (or *Perameles nasuta*) would be more likely to give a precise answer than *bandicoot* on its own.

Using **phrases** is very useful in a search engine. To use phrases they must be enclosed in quotation marks, like this: "St Andrew's Academy", "Ardrossan Highland Games", "Ceud mille failte" and "Seann triubhas". The search engine will only give results that include the exact phrase. Using phrases is very useful, because it can help to narrow down a search, and is more likely to produce the desired results than by using separate key words.

A successful search using a search engine will result in several matches. Each match is called a **hit**. The search engine displays the hits in what it considers to be the most appropriate order or rank.

If you try out the same search using the same keywords on two or more different search engines, you are very likely to get different results, because all search engines have slightly different ways of indexing the information that they find. Sometimes the hits that the search engines find do not work when you click on the associated link. This is usually caused by the site having been moved to a different location, before the search engine has had a chance to update its indexes.

Tip: To get the best results from a particular search engine, you should read its associated help pages and try out various searches in order to familiarise yourself with how it works.

In addition to normal keyword searching for text, it is also possible to search only for sound and graphics data, like music or images.

Some search engines allow you to enter **natural language queries** instead of single keywords. "Where can I buy a DVD rewriteable drive?", "What is the weather like in Grand Junction?". You should avoid making your sentences too long or complicated when using natural language queries.

Search engine with complex search

An **advanced search** allows the user to refine their search in various ways, for example, by restricting the search to only parts of the web, or by choosing different options from a menu.

Most search engines allow the use of AND, OR, NOT. Some search engines allow (+) to represent AND, and (−) instead of NOT.

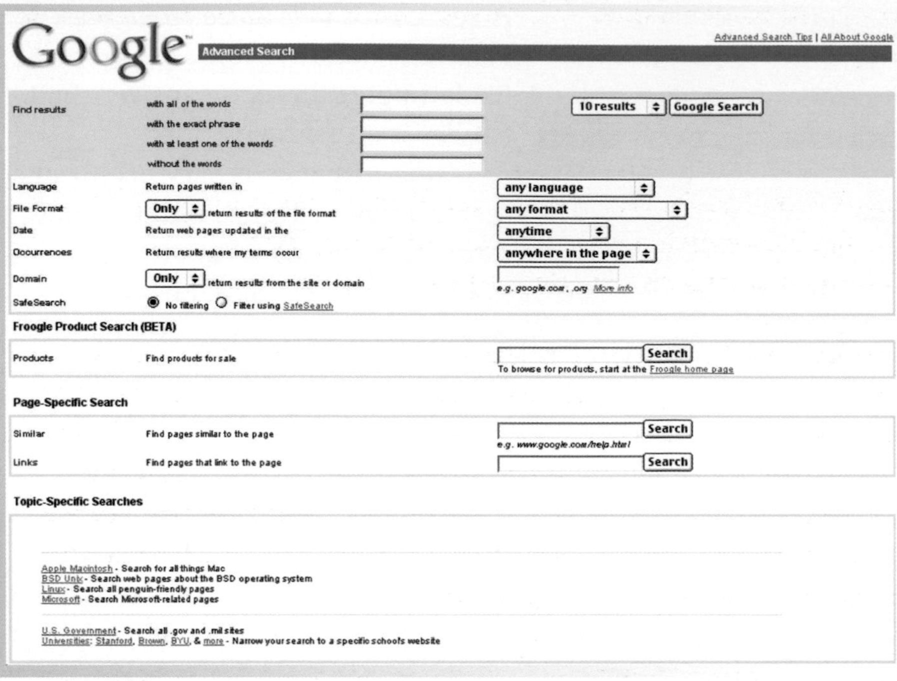

Google™ **Advanced Search**

Advanced Search Tips | All About Google

Find results	with all of the words			10 results ⬍	Google Search
	with the exact phrase				
	with at least one of the words				
	without the words				

Language — Return pages written in — any language ⬍

File Format — Only ⬍ return results of the file format — any format ⬍

Date — Return web pages updated in the — anytime ⬍

Occurrences — Return results where my terms occur — anywhere in the page ⬍

Domain — Only ⬍ return results from the site or domain — *e.g. google.com, .org* More info

SafeSearch — ⦿ No filtering ○ Filter using SafeSearch

Froogle Product Search (BETA)

Products — Find products for sale — [Search]
To browse for products, start at the Froogle home page

Page-Specific Search

Similar — Find pages similar to the page — [Search]
e.g. www.google.com/help.html

Links — Find pages that link to the page — [Search]

Topic-Specific Searches

Apple Macintosh - Search for all things Mac
BSD Unix - Search web pages about the BSD operating system
Linux - Search all penguin-friendly pages
Microsoft - Search Microsoft-related pages

U.S. Government - Search all .gov and .mil sites
Universities: Stanford, Brown, BYU, & more - Narrow your search to a specific schools website

AND means that all the terms linked by AND must appear, for instance: 'standard AND computing', 'mountain AND munro AND Scotland'.

OR means that at least one term must appear, for example: 'chips OR pakora', 'red kola OR irn bru'.

NOT excludes a term, like: 'cd-rom NOT dvd-rom', 'pool NOT swimming'.

Figure 12.7 *Google advanced search.*

Downloading software

Downloading is the process of saving a file from a network onto a computer system. Software is the name for programs that can be run on a computer system. Downloading takes place when a file is being received. Uploading is when a file is being sent.

Most downloadable software is squashed or compressed to reduce its file size. This makes it faster to download than an uncompressed file. Applications called utility programs are used to compress files before they are sent and to decompress files after they have been received. *WinZip* is a compression utility for the PC and *Stuffit* performs the same task on a Macintosh computer.

Three different types of software may be downloaded. These are freeware, shareware and commercial software.

Freeware is totally free software, which you may use on any number of computer systems without paying any money.

Shareware is not free, apart from a short trial period, during which you are allowed to evaluate the software. After the trial period is over, you are expected to either delete the software or pay the shareware fee in order to continue using the software. Shareware is also subject to the same licensing restrictions as commercial software if you wish to use the software on more than one computer system.

Commercial software is not free and should be paid for. There are considerable restrictions upon its use. When you purchase commercial software you are only allowed to use it on one computer system and are not allowed to make copies of it, or distribute it in any way.

If you wish to use a piece of software on more than one computer system, you should purchase one of the following:

- a sufficient number of single copies to match the number of computer systems required, or
- a limited license for the specific number of machines required, or
- a site license, which allows you to use the software on all computer systems at a single location, such as a school.

Some commercial software licenses are sensible enough to allow a user to use a single copy of software on a computer both at work and at home. This means that you do not need to buy two copies. Some school site licenses allow students to have a copy of the licensed software to run on a home machine. However each software license is unique, and you should always check the terms of the license to ensure that you are not breaking the law when using software.

Many companies offer schools and students educational discounts on their software. Considerable savings can be made in this way. Educational versions are usually identical to the full-priced packages, although sometimes they will lack some features. For instance, an educational version of a programming language may not allow the user to create stand alone applications, or write programs using more than a certain number of lines of code.

Copyright

Some of the information on the Internet is free to use but much of it is not.

Suppose you are looking for information for a school project and find a graphic of a laser printer, which you download and save to disk. You then use an application package to paste the image of the printer into your report, print it and hand it in. This type of use of the graphic would be classified as personal study and there should be no financial or legal implications of using the image in this way.

Let's compare the previous example with another one. Imagine you are writing a computing textbook, and you download and save the same graphic of the laser printer for use in your new book. It would be illegal to use the image in the book, which is a commercial publication, without first seeking the permission of, and perhaps paying a fee to, the copyright owner.

MP3

Some web sites allow you to download music in the form of MP3 files to your computer. There is no legal or financial implication with this activity if the copyright owner of the particular piece of music has given permission for their work to be used in this way. In fact, it is a very good way for new musicians and bands to become recognised. However, most MP3 downloads are of copyrighted material, and this activity deprives the copyright owner of any payment, and is therefore illegal.

Instant essays

In order to discourage wholesale copying of other peoples' work, some Universities and Colleges now use special software. Students submit essays to their tutors via email, and the special software is used to compare words and phrases in the student's work with that from various sources, such as other students' essays, or material available on the Internet. If there are too many matches, then the work is judged to have been copied.

Unwelcome downloads

Not all downloads are welcome. You should be sure and check all downloaded software with an anti-virus scanner program before you install the software on any computer system. You can read more about viruses in chapter 10 on Electronic communication.

Mobile Internet technologies

Mobile Internet technologies include laptop (notebook) computers, palmtop (PDA) computers and mobile phones. If a technology is to be mobile then it must be capable of working independently of the mains power supply and without any physical connection to the Internet. Laptops and palmtops can achieve this by using wireless networking interface cards. These cards were discussed in chapter 11.

Figure 12.8 *Some WAP browsers.*

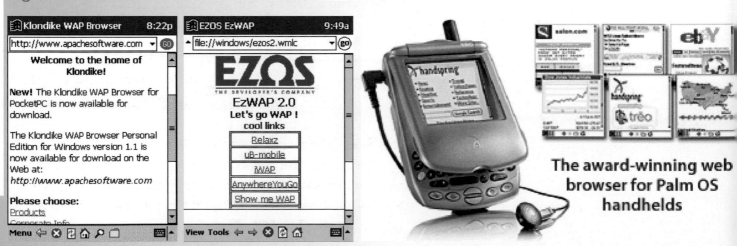

The award-winning web browser for Palm OS handhelds

Laptop computers run the same operating system as the larger desktop computers and can use standard applications in order to connect to the Internet. Palmtop computers and mobile phones use different operating systems and wireless application protocol (WAP) browsers to connect to the World Wide Web.

Video conferencing

Companies who are spread throughout the world need to gather information centrally and also to share information with their employees. Video conferencing is the use of communications links to conduct meetings between people who are geographically separated. A typical video conferencing set up requires a computer system and a webcam in each location, together with a network connection between everyone involved. The video conferencing software allows each participant to see and hear the others on their computer screens, and sometimes to interact with a common document in a screen window.

A webcam is a small digital camera, normally positioned on or beside the computer's monitor in order to capture images for transmission across a network. Video conferencing application software is also required. Examples of video conferencing software include *Microsoft's NetMeeting* and *Apple's iChat AV*.

The quality of video conferencing is determined by the speed of the connection between the users. For example, a videoconference over a broadband connection of 1 megabit/sec is much higher quality than when using a 56 kilobits/sec dial up connection.

Figure 12.9 *Webcam and video conferencing.*

Streaming video

Streaming video is the process of receiving video images over a network and displaying them on a computer screen. Streaming video is different from video conferencing in that streaming video is receive only. The video signal or stream is sent via the Internet to a user's computer. Software used for this application is a web browser such as *Internet Explorer* or *Netscape Communicator*, together with specialised 'plug-in' software such as *Realplayer* or *QuickTime*. Streaming audio is the process of receiving an audio signal over a network. Many radio stations broadcast their output in this way.

Figure 12.10 *Microsoft's NetMeeting software.*

Chat and instant messaging

Chat usually takes place in a chat room, which is a dedicated web site for this purpose. When a user logs in to a chat room, they are given a username. They can then participate in a text discussion on screen with one or more other users.

You should be aware that not all users of a chat room are who they say they are, and young people in particular should never give out any personal information in these situations.

Instant messaging is an application program that keeps track of when a user is on-line to the Internet. Instead of logging on to a special website to chat, the instant messaging software looks for your friends on-line, and informs you that they are available to receive messages.

Weblogging

A weblog or blog is a web page made up of short, frequently updated entries that are arranged in chronological order, like a diary. Weblogs can be used for personal or business purposes. Specialised software makes it easy to create your own weblog and keep it updated.

Bulletin boards and discussion groups

A bulletin board is the electronic equivalent of a notice board, carrying short items that may be of interest to a great number of people. Bulletin boards are sited on a computer, and may be accessed via the Internet. Users can leave or post messages for anyone to read, look at messages left by other users, and download software that has been left on the board. The organiser of the board is called the system operator or sysop.

A discussion group is a group of geographically separated users who have a common interest. The group held or hosted on a website, and users can express their opinions on topics raised or answer questions. Like a bulletin board, the website can hold files and make them available for download. Typically, one of these files is the FAQ, or frequently asked questions. This file contains a list of questions and answers which have been asked and answered by members of the group. It is recommended reading, especially for new members of the group. Each discussion topic on a group is known as a thread, and the website can display messages listed in the order they were posted, or grouped in threads.

Figure 12.11 *Discussion groups.*

Foundation level questions

knowledge and understanding
1. What is the Internet?
2. What information is available on the Internet?
3. List the three main services available on the Internet.
4. What is a browser?
5. What hardware and software would you expect to find in an 'internet ready computer'?
6. What does a modem do?

problem solving
1. What use is a bookmark in a browser?

General level questions

knowledge and understanding
1. What is the World Wide Web?
2. What is a
   a. hyperlink?
   b. web page?
   c. HTML?
3. What is a dial-up connection?
4. What is a broadband connection?
5. List two differences between dial-up and broadband connections.
6. What is meant by the terms:
   a. on-line?
   b. off-line?
7. What is a search engine?
8. How does a search engine work?
9. What is a 'hit'?

problem solving
1. What use is a wizard when connecting to the Internet?
2. How can a web page be accessed directly?
3. Why is it sometimes useful to search using phrases rather than keywords?
4. Why can two search engines produce different results?
5. Why is a broadband connection said to be 'always on'?

Credit level questions

knowledge and understanding
1. What is a URL?
2. Give one example of a URL.
3. What is a natural language query?
4. Give one example of a natural language query.
5. What is:
   a. downloading software?
   b. uploading software?
6. What three types of software may be downloaded?
7. Which of these types is free to use?
8. Which of these types is not free and should be paid for?
9. What is meant by the term 'mobile Internet technologies'?
10. Name two types of computer that may use 'mobile Internet technologies'.
11. What is video conferencing?
12. What hardware and software is needed for video conferencing?
13. What is:
    a. streaming video?
    b. a weblog?

1 Give one example of a complex search other than those in this chapter.

2 Polyglot is a shareware program. What should a school do if it has 20 computers and wants to run Polyglot software on each computer?

3 On which hardware would you be likely to find a WAP browser?

• Key points •

- The Internet is a wide area network spanning the globe.
- A vast quantity of information on any topic you can think of is available on the Internet.
- The Internet provides three main services: the World Wide Web, electronic mail and file transfer.
- E-commerce, on-line banking and on-line shopping are major uses of the Internet.
- The World Wide Web (WWW) is a collection of information held in multimedia form on the Internet.
- This information is stored at locations called web sites in the form of web pages.
- Hyperlinks are links between World Wide Web pages, documents or files.
- Web pages are prepared in HTML.
- A browser is a program that allows the user to browse or surf through the World Wide Web.
- An Internet ready computer consists of a computer system, an internal modem and suitable communications software such as a browser and an email client program.
- When a computer uses a telephone line to connect to an Internet service provider's computer, a modem is needed at each end of the link.
- A wizard or assistant program can help to set up the computer for connection to the Internet.

- Computers may be connected to the Internet by using a dial-up connection or a broadband connection.
- On-line to the Internet means being connected; off-line means being disconnected from the Internet.
- A search engine is a special site on the World Wide Web which is designed to help you to find information.
- A simple or basic search allows the user to enter one or more keywords into an entry box, and then click a button or press return on the keyboard to start the search.
- A complex or advanced search allows the user to refine their search in various ways, for example, by restricting the search to only parts of the web, or by choosing different options from a menu.
- A complex or advanced search uses AND, OR, NOT.
- Downloading is the process of saving a file from a network onto a computer system. Software is the name for programs that can be run on a computer system.
- Downloading takes place when a file is being received. Uploading is when a file is being sent.
- Three different types of software may be downloaded. These are freeware, shareware and commercial software.

- Freeware is totally free software, which you may use on any number of computer systems without paying any money.
- Shareware is not free, apart from a short trial period during which you are allowed to evaluate the software.
- Commercial software is not free and should be paid for.
- An Internet service provider is a company that provides a host computer, which the user can connect to by dialling in.

- Some additional services available on the Internet include: chat and instant messaging, web logs, bulletin boards, discussion groups, streaming video and video conferencing.
- Mobile Internet technologies include laptop (notebook) computers, palmtop (PDA) computers and mobile phones.
- Video conferencing is the use of communications links to conduct meetings between people who are geographically separated.

13 Commercial data processing

This chapter is about how large companies and other organisations use computers in their business. By large companies we mean supermarkets and chain stores with many branches throughout the country, banks, building societies, airlines, mail order companies and organisations like the police, Inland Revenue (income tax) and the Driver and Vehicle Licensing Centre.

Need for computers in commercial data processing

Large companies use computer systems because of the large **volume of documents** they need to deal with to run the company. It is much easier to process a customer's order, or to answer enquiries about a customer's account, with a computer than doing it manually. The computer searches through a large number of records much faster than a human can.

The important point to remember about commercial data processing is the huge amount of data that is being dealt with. Commercial data processing needs large **mainframe computer systems** which can **process data at high speed** and give the user **high speed access** to data. These systems must be able to handle thousands of **repetitive tasks** that may be happening all at once.

Management Information

Another reason why computers are used for commercial data processing is that it is easier to collect **information for managers**. A supermarket manager might want a report of total sales for each month, or breakdown of sales by type, or by area, which would take a very long time to collect by hand. Having a computer to help you speeds up the process.

Advantages of using computers in commercial data processing

Commercial data processing with computers has a number of advantages over a manual system:

- Orders can be processed much more quickly than with a **manual system**.

Credit level

- Errors are less likely because of the checks built into the computer system.
- It is much easier for the company to maintain contact with and hold information about a large number of customers.
- Very large lists of customers can be held on backing storage and easily kept up-to-date.
- Direct mailings to customers can be done automatically using a mail merge.

In a manual system each piece of information, about each customer, for example, would be entered and stored separately by each department that needs it. This means that different departments hold many paper files, all containing much the same information, such as names and addresses of customers. The unnecessary duplication of information in a manual system can be avoided by using a computer to store the information. The information needs to be entered only once and held in a central computer. The different departments within a company can then make use of this information, by viewing it on their own terminals or computers in a local area network. This way of using information is called single entry multiple use.

What is the difference between data and information?

Information has a meaning. For example, '15 August 2007' is information, meaning the fifteenth day of the month of August in the year 2007. Computers store information as a series of numbers. These numbers are data, which don't mean anything on their own. Only if you know how the computer has organised the information as data, does it mean anything to you. For example, 070815 is data.

If you know that the computer puts the last two digits of the year as the first two digits of this data, and the number of the month as the third and fourth digits and the day of the month as the last two digits, then you understand that these numbers mean the same as the information above.

EXAMPLE

When people apply for a driving licence they are given a personal identification number. This is used to help identify a person's details. Part of this number refers to the person's date of birth, but the figures are arranged differently from the way we normally write a date.

For example, if the person were born on 12 October 1998, this would normally be written as 12.10.98 (where 12 is the day of the month; 10 refers to October as the tenth month and 98 is the year 1998).

12.10.98

↓

910128

On the driving licence the computer records the date as 910128. This is simply a string of digits, or a piece of data, unless you know how to 'decode' the data to make the date. When you can do this, the digits become information.

So we can say that

information (for people) = data (for computers) with structure.

Data becomes information when you understand what it means. Computers process data, people use information.

The data processing cycle

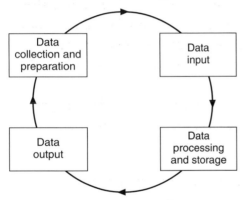

Figure 13.1 *The data processing cycle.*

The **data processing cycle** is the order that data is processed in. The data processing cycle is made up of four stages:

1   data collection and preparation
2   data input
3   data processing and storage
4   data output.

Figure 13.1 shows how these stages are related in the data processing cycle.

Data collection and preparation

The first stage in the data processing cycle is to collect data and prepare it in such a way that the computer can understand it. Data may be collected in many different ways. If the data is written down or printed on a piece of paper, that paper is called a *source document*. An order form for a catalogue, like the one in figure 13.2, is an example of a source document. It is important that a source document is laid out clearly, so that people can fill it in without making mistakes.

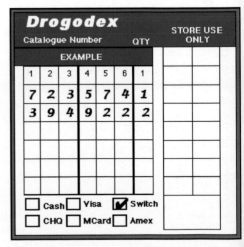

Figure 13.2 *A source document.*

Data input

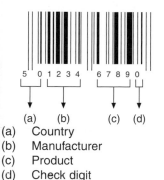

5 0 1 2 3 4   6 7 8 9 0

(a)   (b)   (c)   (d)

(a) Country
(b) Manufacturer
(c) Product
(d) Check digit

Figure 13.3 *The structure of a bar code.*

I think they're trying to sell you...

Figure 13.4

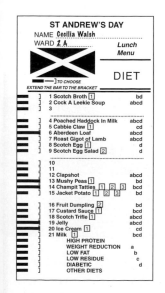

ST ANDREW'S DAY
NAME Cecilia Walsh
WARD 2 A   Lunch Menu

DIET

[ ] TO CHOOSE
EXTEND THE BAR TO THE BRACKET

1 Scotch Broth [1]	bd
2 Cock A Leekie Soup	abcd
3	
4 Poached Haddock In Milk	abcd
5 Cabbie Claw [1]	cd
6 Aberdeen Loaf	abcd
7 Roast Gigot of Lamb	abcd
8 Scotch Egg [1]	d
9 Scotch Egg Salad [2]	d
10	
11	
12 Clapshot	abcd
13 Mushy Peas [1]	bd
14 Champit Tatties [1] [2] [3]	bcd
15 Jacket Potato [1] [2] [3]	bd
16 Fruit Dumpling [2]	bcd
17 Custard Sauce [1]	bcd
18 Scotch Trifle [1]	abcd
19 Jelly	abcd
20 Ice Cream [1]	cd
21 Milk [1]	bcd

HIGH PROTEIN
WEIGHT REDUCTION   a
LOW FAT   b
LOW RESIDUE   c
DIABETIC   d
OTHER DIETS

Figure 13.5 *A mark sense card.*

The data must be input to the computer before it can be processed. Inputting data directly to a computer system means that fewer mistakes are likely to be made (if people are less involved).

Bar codes

You will be familiar with bar codes because they appear on most products, from tins of beans to books and newspapers. A bar code is a set of lines of varying widths which can be read by passing a bar code reader across them. Figure 13.3 shows a bar code. The bar codes on household goods arc made up of 30 lines, which give a unique 13-digit code number to each product. Supermarkets use bar codes to keep track of their stock, as well as to save work in putting the price on every item, and then having to change it if the price changes. When the scanner at the checkout reads the bar code, the computer finds the price of the article from its memory and reduces the stock number by one. Remember: bar codes do NOT contain the price of an item!

A bar code is a series of lines that represent information. If you look at the bar code in figure 13.3 you will see that it also has numbers on it. A typical bar code has 13 digits:

- The first two show the country the product came from.
- The next five digits are the code for the manufacturer.
- The next five digits code for the name and size of the product.
- The last digit is a special number — the **check digit**. The check digit is there to make sure the scanner has read the bar code properly. If the bar code is not scanned correctly, the computer alerts the checkout operator to scan the product again. If the bar code on the item is damaged and the scanner can't read it, the operator can type the number under the bar code directly into the till.

Do you think the situation in figure 13.4 is ever likely to happen?

Mark sense cards

Mark sense cards are cards divided into columns that allow spaces for marking with a pencil line. A machine, a mark sense reader, linked to a computer, can then read these marks by optical scanning. Mark sense cards are useful for collecting data and analysing the responses to multiple-choice type questions. Figure 13.5 shows you a mark sense card used by patients to select their food while in hospital.

Magnetic stripe

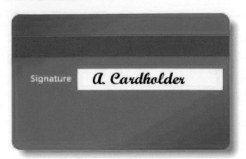

Figure 13.6 *A magnetic stripe card.*

A magnetic stripe is a narrow band of magnetic material on which data is held. You can see a magnetic stripe on the back of a credit card, cheque guarantee card, shop tag or train ticket. This stripe can hold about 64 characters of data. This means that only a few details can be stored — the sorting codes and account numbers on bank cards, or product numbers on shop tags. A magnetic stripe on a bank card is shown in figure 13.6.

Magnetic stripes may also be used on identity cards. Some schools use a card with a magnetic stripe in a system of electronic registration. Every classroom has a magnetic card reader on the wall. Every time a pupil enters the room, they pass their card through the reader. The information from each reader is sent to the school's registration computer, which can produce a period-by-period register for who was present each day.

Smart cards

Figure 13.7 *A cash machine for reloading smart cards.*

A **smart card** has its own processor, and is able to store much more information than fits on a magnetic stripe. Smart cards are also known as **chip cards**. A typical smart card may have around 16 to 64 kilobytes of memory. These cards can be used as cash cards, as credit cards with a preset credit limit, as store loyalty cards, or used as identity (ID) cards with stored passwords. When a smart card is used instead of cash, it is known as an *electronic purse*. Some disposable smart cards are supplied with a quantity of cash already programmed into them. Other smart cards may be reloaded with cash at any time, using a cash machine like the one shown in figure 13.7.

Contact smart cards are easy to identify because they have a gold contact module on one side. However, not all smart cards have this feature. Contactless smart cards have an internal aerial instead of a contact module. A selection of smart cards is shown in figure 13.8.

Figure 13.8 *A selection of smart cards.*

Many bank cards are now smart cards in addition to having a magnetic stripe. One reason for this is the added security provided by a smart card in that it is more difficult to forge. Another reason is that smart cards do not lose the information stored in their

microchips, unlike magnetic strips, which are easily damaged. Your signature or other physical information like your fingerprint, or a retinal scan, could also be stored on a smart card, which could help in defeating fraud. Information like this is known as *biometric* data. Biometric data is also discussed in chapter 11.

Figure 13.9 *Biometric security*

EXAMPLE

Smart cards can be used as a security system to keep track of staff in a building. All the workers are given smart cards with details special to them. A central computer linked to detectors controls the doors in the building. The employee keeps the smart card in his pocket and as soon as he comes within range of a smart card detector, the smart card transmits his identity to the main computer, which logs the employee's location, and opens and closes doors as required. The system can alert security staff if someone tries to enter an area they're not allowed into. It will not open the door. Since the system operates automatically, the employee's hours of working are recorded and linked into the payroll computer. If an employee works overtime, or sneaks off home a little early, then the computer will know about it.

Character recognition

Although computer input devices can read bar codes and magnetic stripes, most people can only easily read characters. You can input characters into a computer by typing them on a keyboard, but it would be much quicker if the computer could read written or printed characters. Two ways that computers can recognise characters that also make sense to people are **magnetic ink character recognition (MICR)** and **optical character recognition (OCR)**.

MICR

In this process characters are printed on forms in magnetic ink. People can easily read the characters, so the forms can be sorted by hand and the characters are also easily recognised by a computer.

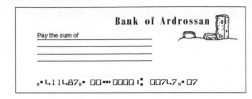

Figure 13.10 *A cheque showing MICR characters.*

Great Gas

MR J WALSH — Customer Ref. No. 216 024 3356

Date	Meter reading Present Previous	Gas supplied 100's cu. ft. Therms	Charges
31 DEC	1878 1502	376 397.432	182.42
STANDING CHARGE			9.40
CREDIT TARIFF		£	191.82

Figure 13.11 *Here is a document with OCR characters at the bottom.*

The numbers along the bottom of a bank cheque are printed in magnetic ink, as shown in figure 13.10. When a cheque is paid in or cashed, a magnetic ink character reader is used to input the information to the computer system. Magnetic ink has another advantage — it is difficult to forge. It certainly can't be copied on a photocopier!

OCR

A device called an optical character reader is able to recognise letters and numbers (like A B C or 1 2 3) and read them directly into a computer. You must be careful if you are filling in forms that are going to be read by an OCR system, because the machine can't recognise letters or numbers that are badly formed. You wouldn't use OCR in situations where someone had to rush to fill in a form. You can use a scanner with suitable OCR software to read in pages of text to a word processor.

Making sure the data is correct

Data entered into a computer *must* be correct. The process of making sure the data is correct is called error checking.

Check digits

One of the easiest ways of checking numbers is to add a check digit at the end of the number. A check digit is an extra digit which is calculated from the original number and put on the end of that number. As the number is entered, the computer calculates the check digit. If it doesn't come up with the same number as the one keyed in, an error message is displayed and the computer won't accept the number.

Calculating a check digit

One system for producing a check digit is that the digits in a number must add up to a number that divides exactly by three.

- Suppose we want to make up a check digit for the number 2954.
- We add up the digits   2 + 9 + 5 + 4 = 20.
- To make the total divide exactly by three, we must add an extra digit, 1, at the end of the number, to make the total 21, since 21 divides exactly by three.
- So the check digit is 1.
- Adding the check digit to the original number gives 29541.

Other checks

Other checks that can be carried out involve checking the number of characters (numbers, letters and spaces) in a field in a database. If the entry has more characters than will fit in the field, then an error message should appear.

A range check can be made on fields that contain numbers, like ages, money or dates, to check that the numbers are sensible. Examples are:

- an age of more than 100 or less than 0
- a total on a bill of £0.00
- a day of greater than 31 or less than 1.

Validation

Checking data to ensure that it is sensible and accurate is called validation. Validity checks do not eliminate mistakes, but they make it difficult for wrong data to get through to the computer or its peripherals. Range checks and check digits are examples of validation.

Verification

The user should type the data in accurately, but everyone can make mistakes. One of the most reliable methods of checking that data is correct is to have the user enter the data twice (or two people can enter the same data). This is called verification. If the second set of data doesn't match the first, the user is alerted to a mistake and has to type it in again. Verification is most often used to confirm a new password.

Data processing and storage

Files, records and fields

The names used for computer files are the same as the ones used for manual filing:

- A file is an organised collection of data arranged according to a particular structure.
- The units of data which make up a file are called records. A record is like a single card in a card index.
- Each record contains a number of separate items of data called fields.
- A file is updated when it is changed, or new data is added to it to bring it up to date.

Backing up

To make sure that valuable data is not lost if a file is damaged, you should always keep a spare copy of the file, a backup, in a safe place. Everyone should have at *least* one backup copy of his or her programs or data, though more than one is recommended.

Interactive processing

Interactive processing is when data is processed or updated as the transaction is entered, and any enquiries are replied to at once.

Reading data files

There are two different ways of reading, or accessing data files:

1 **Sequential access.** Data files stored in sequence can only be accessed in the same way. Magnetic tape is an example of a **sequential access** medium. To read a particular record stored on magnetic tape the users would have to go through all the records in sequence until they find it.
2 **Random/direct access.** Data files stored by random access can be read directly without having to work through from the first one. Magnetic disks, optical disks and chips are three examples of **random access media**.

Because of these different access methods, it takes much longer to find a record on magnetic tape than on disk. Disk storage is normally used when speed is important — for example, during an interactive processing operation like a transaction at an automated telling machine.

Multi-user databases

A **multi-user database** is a database that may be accessed by many users at the same time. To allow multi-user access, the database file is stored centrally, for example, on a mainframe computer or, more commonly, on a computer called a **server** in a local area network. The server may be a **file server**, which holds all types of files, or a dedicated **database server**.

Although many users can access the same file, it is important that two users do not attempt to change the same record in the file at once. If two users do try to access the same record, then the computer will **lock out** one of the users, and prevent access until the other user is finished.

Data output

Paper

Information for customers, like bills or statements, is normally output in printed form. Often businesses print the output on pre-printed stationery. This reduces the amount of printing involved, and so is faster than printing out a complete bill on blank paper. By using pre-printed stationery companies can use different colours of printing and include advertisements.

Screen

After the data has been processed, the information can be output onto a computer screen. Many company's offer their customers the chance to have electronic bills delivered over the Internet, either by electronic mail or on a web page. The customer uses their user identity and password to log in to the companys website, where they can view their bill on screen and pay it. This method saves the company money, compared to sending their bills by using the postal service.

File

Instead of outputting data to a printer or displaying it on the screen it can be saved as a new file. This new file could be held on disk or magnetic tape. The advantage of keeping the data like this is that if it needs to be processed again later, the information can simply be reloaded into the computer without having to be input all over again.

Hardware and software

The basic hardware required for commercial data processing usually consists of a mainframe computer system. A mainframe computer system is made up of several devices. These usually include:

- A central processing unit (or CPU) which carries out the data processing, holds the programs in its memory and coordinates the running of the whole computer system.
- Input devices, such as keyboards and bar code readers.
- Output devices, which can produce various different outputs, for example hard copy from printers, or characters on the screen of a terminal.
- Backing storage. Common types of backing storage are magnetic tape and magnetic disk. Backing storage allows the computer access to large quantities of data, far more than can be stored in the main memory of the CPU at one time.
- Terminals. These are used for data input to the computer. A terminal consists of a keyboard and a screen and is also called a visual display unit or VDU.
- Operator's console. The operator's console is connected directly to the CPU. It has a keyboard and screen like a terminal. The computer operator uses the console to communicate directly with the CPU.

A typical mainframe computer system is big enough to occupy a whole room, like a large classroom, and may cost millions of pounds. You can see a typical mainframe computer in this photograph.

Figure 13.12 *A mainframe computer system.*

A terminal doesn't have to be in the same room, or even in the same building, as the mainframe computer it's attached to. In fact it could be connected to the computer via a wide area network. A terminal connected to a distant mainframe computer is called a *remote terminal*.

Multi-access means that many users may be on-line to a computer system at the same time. The terms multi-access and **multi-user** are interchangeable.

A multi-access system is made up of a large central computer with many terminals linked to it. The central computer constantly checks each of the terminals in turn. If a terminal wants access to the central computer, data is sent very quickly to it and returns from it at the same high speed. This fast response gives the user of each terminal the impression that they are the only one using the system. Multi-access systems like these are used for:

- airline reservations
- the Police National Computer
- automated telling machines (ATMs)
- The National Lottery.

Implications of using computers for commercial data processing: social

Effects on business

The introduction of computers has caused major changes in employment patterns. Computers have replaced many of the people who used to carry out data processing so fewer people are needed to do the same jobs. This has caused great concern about job losses. On the other hand, many people think that not to introduce new technology could make their firm less competitive and even put them out of business.

Companies which introduce computers for data processing need to retrain their workers to operate the computers, and people are still needed to program and maintain the computers. Some of the skills which were needed before the introduction of new technology are still needed today so the operator can see if the new technology is working correctly. For example, a bank employee must still be able to understand the process of cashing a cheque.

Many new businesses have been created because of new technology. **E-commerce**, **on-line banking** and **on-line shopping** are now vast businesses which owe their existence to the introduction of computers and the development of computer networks. These are discussed later in this chapter.

Credit level

Job types and careers

The widespread introduction of computers has meant that many new types of jobs have been created which did not exist before. The jobs include **network manager**, **systems analyst**, **programmer** and **engineer**. We will look at each of these jobs in turn.

Network manager

Network manager

The **network manager** is the person in charge of the network. He or she will be responsible for all of the computer systems attached to the company network. The network manager is concerned with the day to day running of the system. The network manager decides each user's level of access or network privileges and gives each user a special user identity and password to allow her or him to log on to the system. You can read more about network privileges in chapter 11.

Systems analyst

Systems analyst

The job of the **systems analyst** is to plan exactly how computer systems can be used to help the company. The systems analyst will look at all the jobs the company does manually and decide which jobs can be done best by computer. This process is called **systems analysis**. The systems analyst spends a long time talking to the users of a manual system to help them decide what they need the computer system to be able to do. Each step of the task is carefully investigated and described and the systems analyst draws up a diagram of the system.

The systems analyst will also write a report which details the cost of installing and maintaining a computer system. The size of the computer system installed will depend on the size of the company and their plans for expansion. After the computer has been installed and is working, the systems analyst looks for ways to improve the system and make it more efficient.

Programmer

Programmer

The systems analyst will consult a **programmer** about the programs that the company needs and the programmer will write the programs or check whether there are some commercially available software applications to suit the company. Software which has already been written and which can be bought and used straight away without altering it to suit the particular company is called 'off the shelf'. Software written specially to suit a company is called 'bespoke'.

Usually the programmer will have to write completely new software. He might write large programs in several parts. Sometimes each part is written by a different programmer and the parts are combined to make the whole program, and, at the same time, any mistakes are taken out. The process of removing mistakes is called **debugging**.

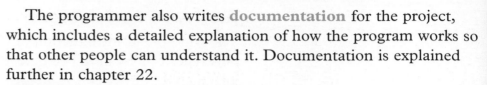

The programmer also writes documentation for the project, which includes a detailed explanation of how the program works so that other people can understand it. Documentation is explained further in chapter 22.

Engineer

Engineer

New computer systems are installed and existing ones maintained by engineers who visit companies to repair and inspect computers. Maintenance is carried out on a regular basis and whenever there is a breakdown. Most companies have a maintenance agreement, which provides a guarantee that repairs will be carried out within a certain time, so that work can continue and their business will not be affected. If a particular computer system is vital to the operation of a company, it is sensible to have a backup machine with a copy of the current data which can be used in the event of a breakdown.

Computer crime

Sometimes a person employed in a data processing department is untrustworthy and uses their position to commit crimes. It can be almost impossible to prevent computer crime, especially if the criminal is very clever.

Fraud

Typical crimes involve damaging the computer system by destroying, corrupting or changing the data files. They may steal money by computer fraud. For example, an employee who knows or can find out the security passwords to a computer system can steal money by transferring it from the company's account into one of their own. There are two very common ways of interfering with computer data — hacking and producing viruses.

Figure 13.13 *Computer crime.*

Hacking

Hacking is gaining access to a computer system, usually illegally, and interfering with the data on it. It is possible for people to hack into a company's computer system from anywhere outside the company via the Internet. So the hacker does not have to be an employee with access to a terminal inside the company. If you are caught hacking you could be prosecuted. Companies can make hacking less easy by changing their security passwords regularly, and keeping them secure. You can read more about security measures in chapter 11.

Computer viruses

A virus is a rogue program that someone has deliberately created. A computer virus is able to make itself invisible to the computer until it passes into the memory of a host computer. Then the virus will reproduce itself on the software being used by that machine

until it is detected and removed. Some viruses can do nothing more serious than display a simple message on the screen, but most viruses can cause a lot of damage by destroying and corrupting files.

In the early days of computing it wasn't easy to share data between computers, and so viruses were not as widespread, but networking and the Internet has changed that. The MyDoom virus, which was active early in 2004, was responsible for 30% of all Internet traffic when it reached its peak. Read the article below.

Article from The Independent on Sunday, 8 February 2004

For most people the MyDoom virus, which last week became the fastest spreading ever to hit the Internet, was just annoying. It filled inboxes with fake, bounced messages, infected attachments and incorrect scoldings from anti-virus companies claiming that you'd tried to infect one of their clients. But unless you were infected (and if you have a PC running Windows, you should check to make sure), it was just the computer equivalent of a traffic jam. But to security experts, MyDoom marked a serious step up in the evolution of the virus because it had all the fingerprints of organised crime. MyDoom did not just email itself to addresses found in the files of any computer it infected. It also installed a "back door" that would let hackers control your machine remotely; it installed "key-logging" software that would silently note every key press, including bank passwords and credit card numbers when you used web pages; and it could direct a deadly attack on a particular website belonging to a company called SCO.

On 1 February, SCO's website disappeared from the Internet under a blizzard of hits. These were known as a DDOS (distributed denial of service) attack from MyDoom infected PCs. SCO's servers were kept so busy answering trivial requests to identify themselves (called "pings") that they had no time to display web pages. "There's a possibility for criminal gangs to threaten blackmail with a virus like [MyDoom]", said Graham Cluley, a senior technology consultant at Sophos. He has been tracking computer viruses for nearly 20 years. "If it was targeted at an on-line bank, it would be extremely costly for them". He notes that the virus is programmed to stop attacking SCO after 12 February. "Maybe that date is there so that whoever's behind it can say to SCO, 'If you don't want it to happen again, then…'"

In 1991, during the first Gulf War, it was rumoured that the United States intelligence agents disabled Iraq's air defence batteries by inserting a virus into the computers which controlled the entire system. The virus was smuggled into Baghdad in a microchip inside a printer, and had the effect of blanking the screen each time the operator tried to open a program.

There are various different classifications of viruses and virus-type programs. The particular details are outside the scope of this course at Standard Grade. You can find out some more about viruses in chapter 10.

Did you know?

The first time someone was convicted of using a virus to sabotage computer records was in the USA in 1988. They were ordered to pay damages of $11,000 to the company that employed them. By then, the Computer Virus Industry Association had documented 250,000 cases of virus sabotage.

The technical implications of commercial data processing involves **e-commerce**, **on-line banking** and **on-line shopping**. **E-commerce** is short for **electronic commerce**. E-commerce is the process of conducting business on-line, such as buying and selling goods and services over the Internet and transferring funds within online banks. E-commerce therefore includes both on-line banking and on-line shopping. These are discussed below.

Figure 13.14 *Amazon is one of the most popular on-line shops.*

On-line shopping

On-line shopping is now a major use of the Internet. In the early days of the Internet, on-line shopping was limited because of users concerns about security of their personal information and bank details, but this has largely been overcome.

The process of on-line shopping

The process of on-line shopping usually begins with a search. If the customer has no idea where to buy a product, then they may use a search engine to find an appropriate supplier. Alternatively, they may already have a supplier in mind and visit their website to find the item(s). Most on-line shopping websites use a *shopping basket* or *cart*, which is a place on the site containing the items that a customer has selected to buy. When they are finished shopping, they can *go to the checkout* which means that they have to pay for their purchases.

Checking out involves entering your personal details such as name and address, bank card number and delivery instructions. If the customer has visited the site before and registered their details, then all that is required is to enter their user identity and password in order to make a purchase. Most sites offer a choice of deliveries, with the cost of delivery depending upon the total amount spent and the urgency with which the item is required.

When the purchase is complete, the website will normally send an email message to the customer to confirm that their order has been placed. A further email may inform the customer that their purchases have been dispatched and are about to be delivered. Some companies offer an on-line tracking feature that allows customers to follow the progress of their orders. It is also possible to request a text message immediately prior to delivery, which ensures that the customer does not miss the package.

Paying for your purchases

There are a variety of different types of bank card, which may be used for different purposes. When you are using on-line shopping, most of the time you will be expected to pay for the goods that you order by using a bank card and electronic funds transfer (EFT). Electronic funds transfer is described later in this chapter. Which card you can use depends upon the purchase you are making, and the particular web site that you are using. Note that on-line shops will only accept some types of card in payment. Some types of bank card are described below.

- **Cheque guarantee cards.** Whenever you write a cheque you give this card to the sales assistant to check your signature. It will guarantee that the bank will pay any cheque up to a certain limit, for instance, £100.
- **Credit cards.** Credit cards (*Visa* and *MasterCard* are two examples) allow you to buy something without exchanging money. The amount is charged to the bank, which will send the customer details of the account every month. The customer can choose to settle the account in full each month, or they can pay in instalments. If you pay by instalments the bank will charge you interest on the outstanding balance.
- **Debit cards.** Debit cards (like *Switch* and *Delta*) let you pay for purchases by electronic funds transfer directly from your bank account — but only if there's enough money in your account to pay for it.
- **Cash cards.** Cash cards (like *Keycard* and *Cashline*) let you withdraw cash from ATMs. Most bank or building society accounts have cash cards and some banks use the cards to

---

Dear Mr Walsh

The following item(s) from your order were sent out on Thursday 19 September 2002.
You should get them tomorrow, or the next working day. The parcel has physically left dabs.com.
Keep this email until the parcel arrives.

Manufacturer: CRUCIAL Product: 512MB Compact Flash Type 1 Quicklinx: 67Y2S1 Quantity : 1

This completes your order. Thank you very much for your business and we hope we can serve you again.

The shipment details are: Courier: Royal Mail Ref: Letter Post Carriage Method : Letter Post

For Parcelforce deliveries, you can also track the parcel on www.parcelforce.co.uk

For delivery to: Mr J Walsh at his house

Please ensure that there is someone at this address to receive the parcel. If no one is present a card will be left so you can contact Royal Mail to arrange re-delivery or collection. Note that normal delivery is between 9am and 6pm. We can't make tracing enquiries until the day after the delivery date. This order cannot now be cancelled. If it arrives please either refuse delivery or accept but do not open/use the product, and use our returns system at http://www.dabs.com/view.asp? Returns - we will refund on return. If the goods are faulty, use the same system. A VAT invoice will be sent to you separately. Please email invoicing@dabs.com if this doesn't arrive within five days.

**** All deliveries will be considered as received in good condition unless you specifically sign as 'damaged' or 'opened' etc. 'Unchecked' will not be accepted as a valid status ****

We listen to our customers and what you think of our service. We always strive to match and beat your expectations of dabs.com as an Etailer. Please take the time to complete our short Online Web Questionnaire and let us know what you think of our service at http://www.dabs.com/contactus/ordsurvey.asp?so=3297645

Thank you very much for your business.

Internet Sales Admin dabs.com plc enquiries@dabs.com

Rank your experience of dabs.com and other dealers at these opinion sites
http://www.romulus2.com - http://www.dooyoo.co.uk - http://uk.ciao.com
----

Figure 13.15 *An email notice of delivery.*

operate deposit accounts. A card reader inside the bank will let you use the cash card instead of a normal passbook.

- **Multifunction cards.** Cards often have more than one function — you can get cards that are combined cash and debit cards which can also be used as a cheque guarantee card.

We looked at smart cards and magnetic stripe cards earlier in this chapter. It is important to note that these are two technologies used in making cards. Any of the types of card described above may be 'smart', have a magnetic stripe, or both.

It is vital that you should NEVER tell anyone else your personal identification number (PIN) for your bank card. No-one, not even bank staff, whether in a bank or on-line, is allowed to ask you to disclose your PIN. If you do give out your PIN, and your card is used without your consent, then you will be liable for its use and you will not get any money back.

One number that you do have to give to an on-line shop in order to buy anything is your bank card number. On-line shops use **encryption** to protect your bank card number while it is stored on their web site. Encryption means changing data into a code so that it is kept private. A message will appear on the computer screen to show that the connection to the shop's web site is **secure** and it is safe to enter your bank card details. Some web browsers display a locked padlock icon to show that a connection is secure.

Types of on-line shopping activities

The most popular activities include finding information about a product's price or features, checking on product selection and deciding where to purchase a product.

The most popular purchases when on-line shopping are:

- computer products (hardware, software, accessories)
- books
- music
- financial services
- entertainment
- home electronics
- clothes
- gifts and flowers
- travel services
- toys
- tickets.

Figure 13.16 *My favourite on-line shop.*

Advantages of on-line shopping

On-line shopping has advantages for companies and for the users of the service.

Advantages for companies

- Lower transaction costs — it is cheaper to sell on-line than off-line. For example, only one shop is needed instead of many shops all over a country. No expensive catalogues need to be printed or distributed.
- Larger purchases per transaction — customers can be tempted to buy other goods related to the particular item they have purchased, such as accessories or related books or music.
- Shops will benefit if they are always open for 'impulse' purchases by customers.

Figure 13.17 *ebay is an on-line auction where you can sell and bid for goods as well as purchase them.*

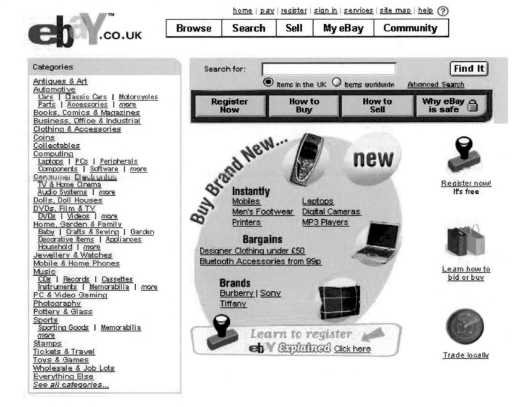

Advantages for customers

- The shop is open 24 hours a day. People can shop from the comfort of their homes at a time that is convenient to them.
- It is easy for customers to:
  - **Search a large catalogue of goods**. An on-line catalogue is much larger than could be printed and contains more goods than may be held in a single shop. You are more likely to be able to find an item in stock on-line than in a single shop.
  - **Compare prices between sellers**. Many websites are set up especially to compare prices.

- **Configure products and see actual prices.** The customer can make changes to the specifications of a product on-line and see how the price is affected. For example, what difference does it make if I want 4 gigabytes or 8 gigabytes of RAM in a computer I'm ordering?
- Improved customer relations — the customer might get an email when the order is confirmed, when the order is shipped, and after the order arrives. Customers can see exactly where their order is at any time with on-line tracking. If the customer is happy, then they are more likely to purchase something else from the company.
- People can shop in different ways, for instance, a *shopping basket* allows customers to build an order over several visits to the website. This gives a customer more time to consider their purchase.

Disadvantages of on-line shopping

There are also some disadvantages.

- Bank card fraud can occur when goods are obtained by using a stolen card number, perhaps taken from a discarded receipt. This type of fraud is known as 'card holder not present', where the owner of the card is not in the shop in person to carry out the transaction. To combat this type of fraud, banks have introduced an additional security code number, which is printed on the card's signature strip. This number is not embossed on the card, and unlike the card number, does not appear on a receipt.

Figure 13.18 *Searching for the perfect gift on-line.*

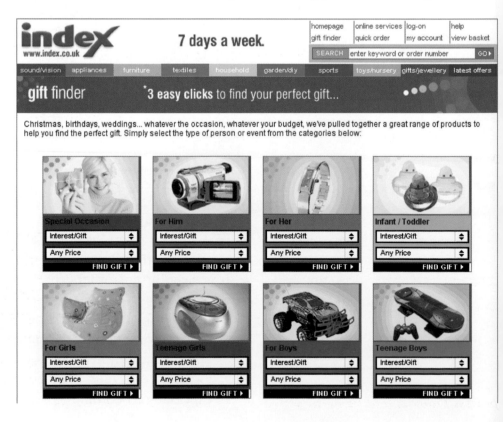

- Receiving goods. Most deliveries occur during the working day and you may not always be at home to receive your goods. You may have to make alternative delivery arrangements. Recognising this, companies offer a number of services to make deliveries more convenient — see advantages for customers.
- Returning goods. All reputable on-line shops have an efficient returns service. If the goods are damaged, or are not exactly what was ordered, or even if the customer has changed his or her mind, they should be able to send the goods back to the on-line shop easily. However simple this process, and even if the goods are picked up and replaced, some people consider that this is too much trouble to go to and cannot be bothered.

On-line shopping has many advantages, but it is not going to make ordinary shops close down. Many people enjoy the social and entertainment aspects of shopping. In a shop you can touch and examine the product, try it on, and buy it there and then. On-line shopping does not offer any of these features. Shops are here to stay.

On-line banking

The process of on-line banking

Part of the process of on-line banking is outlined in the screenshots below. These show some demonstration pages from a bank's website.

Figure 13.22 shows a customer's statement, which allows him or her to keep track of all transactions on the account. The menu on the left of the screenshot shows the services that are available. These include money transfer and payments, standing orders and direct debits. Figure 12.23 shows the process of making a payment.

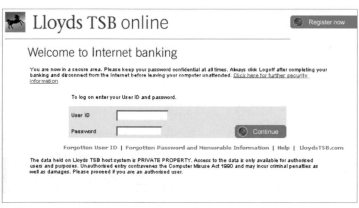

Figure 13.19 *On-line banking — logging in with your user identity and password.*

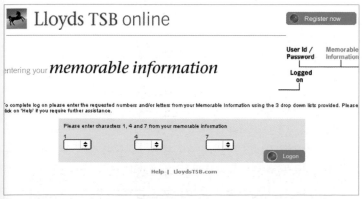

Figure 13.20 *On-line banking — a second login process provides additional security.*

Figure 13.21 *On-line banking — a list of bank accounts.*

Figure 13.22 *On-line banking — an account statement.*

Figure 13.23 *On-line banking — making a payment.*

Advantages of on-line banking for banks

On-line banking shares some of the advantages of on-line shopping. For instance, an on-line bank does not need to have any premises or branches for people to visit. The development of on-line banking has been helped by the increase in use of bank cards and the decrease in use of cash. On-line banks which do not have any branches do not need to handle any cash at all. The only physical payments which they may have to deal with are cheques when accounts are opened or closed. This saves the bank a great deal of money in the cost of staff and buildings.

Advantages of on-line banking for customers

The main advantage is that the customer does not need to travel to a branch to do any of their banking. The customer can stay at home and carry out all of their business on-line, and at a time which is convenient to them. On-line banks are available 24 hours a day.

A consequence of on-line banking

Most banks which have branches in the high street now encourage their customers to move to on-line banking, because of the savings which can be made in staff costs. This means that those customers who choose to use the services of a branch, may have to put up with long queues for service. Banks justify this by saying that if on-line banking is available, then it is the customer's choice if they wish to use the most expensive service that the bank provides, that is, personal service in a branch.

Electronic funds transfer

Electronic funds transfer (or EFT) is a way you can pay for goods without using cash. When you decide to buy something, the amount of money that you owe the shop is transferred automatically from your bank account into the shop's bank account. To pay for your goods this way you must have a bank card that supports this system.

The place in a shop where the goods change hands is called the point of sale (POS) — when you pay at the checkout, the item becomes yours. Most shops have computers at the POS so any

Figure 13.24 *Examples of bar codes.*

Figure 13.25 *EPOS at the checkout.*

Figure 13.26 *Itemised receipts printed at the POS.*

record, such as the amount of goods in stock, can be changed as it happens. A POS terminal will be directly connected to a mainframe computer. POS terminals usually have a bar code reader built in to them. As the assistant passes the goods through, the information from the bar code is read into the terminal, which will add up the total bill — and keep track of what's been sold for stock control.

The idea of electronic funds transfer can be combined with the POS terminal to give an **electronic funds transfer** at **point of sale (EFTPOS)** system.

Electronic point of sale

Computers already play an important part in shopping. Big shops, especially chain stores with branches all over the country, have to deal with huge amounts of information, which would take humans a lot of time and effort to cope with.

- They have to keep the shelves well stocked with goods for customers to buy.
- They need to reorder stock that is low.
- Someone must decide which things are selling well so they can decide whether to do a special promotion.
- The price has to be right.

Computers are very good at keeping track of this type of information. This is why many shops have installed **electronic point of sale (EPOS)** systems.

What is an electronic point of sale system?

EPOS is the name given to a computerised system that collects data automatically from the checkout, or point of sale, as the customer buys the goods.

Shopping with an EPOS system

In a shop that uses EPOS, each item is marked with a bar code unique to it. You can see some labels with bar codes in Figure 13.24. The manufacturer puts on the bar code, so the retailer does not have to employ someone to go around putting prices on each item. The prices only need to be displayed on the edge of the shelves where the goods are stacked so the customer can see them.

Customers choose their goods and take them to the checkout. At the checkout, a scanner reads the bar code. The scanner reads the data from the bar code and sends the product code to the till. The computer connected to the till is programmed to recognise the product codes for all of the items on sale in the shop. The till displays the name and price of each item as it is scanned and prints this information on an itemised receipt.

Advantages of EPOS systems

- Using an EPOS system can make shopping quicker and easier, because shoppers can go through the checkout more quickly. The operator doesn't have to type prices into the till, and you don't have to wait for someone to go and find the price of something because the price label has fallen off.
- The customer is given an itemised receipt, which gives the name of each item, the price and the date of purchase. This makes it easy for you to check that your bill is correct. It also means that if someone brings an item back the retailer will know if it was bought recently.
- The shop's computer keeps a record of exactly how much of each item is sold. The retailer can therefore see which goods sell fast, and which ones are not popular. He can tell how much to reorder at the end of each day so the shop is always well stocked. He can decide to advertise slow selling goods or give them a special price to encourage people to buy them.
- Retailers can easily organise special prices for some goods, or arrange a price cut if you buy several of the same item (you've probably all seen advertisements like 'buy two, get one free') or goods that could go together (like tea and biscuits). Instead of changing the price label on each item, they only have to tell the computer what the special price is for the bar codes on those goods, and change the price label on the shelf edge.
- Because none of the items have price labels on them, fewer staff are needed. This means the retailer has to pay out less in wages and can keep their prices down.
- The checkout operator doesn't need to type in prices and doesn't need to remember the prices of items.
- Management can check up on how fast the checkout operators are working.

Disadvantages of EPOS systems

- If the computer in the shop has been programmed with the wrong price then you could be overcharged without knowing it. When each item had its own price ticket, the shopper could keep an eye on the checkout operator as he typed in each price and could have any mistakes corrected straight away. But with an EPOS system, the price is only displayed on the shelf. To prove a mistake has been made you'd have to go back to the shelf to find out the displayed price and compare it with your receipt.
- Each item has its own bar code, and a multi-pack of items must have a separate bar code to make sure the scanner can recognise them as new items. If this isn't done properly, the individual bar code may be scanned by mistake and the customer could be

charged only for one item instead of a six-pack, for example. You might not think this is a disadvantage but the retailer would!

Electronic funds transfer at point of sale

Electronic funds transfer at point of sale or **EFTPOS** is when money is authorised to be debited from a customer's bank account at the checkout terminal. At the terminal, the assistant passes, or *swipes*, the customer's card through a card reader, which reads the information on the magnetic stripe on the card. This is shown in figure 13.27. If it is a smart card, then it will be placed in a slot during the transaction. The terminal first checks that the card is not on file as a stolen card — if it is, it rejects the card and warns the operator. If the total amount is below a set limit, known as the *floor limit*, the computer authorises the transaction. If the total amount is above the floor limit the checkout operator has to contact the bank before the sale can go ahead. Usually the terminal dials the bank's computer and gets automatic *authorisation* for a sale. If a smart card with an electronic purse is used, then there is no need for authorisation, the cash is debited directly from the card and transferred to the shop's bank account.

Figure 13.27 *EFTPOS — swiping a bank card.*

Advantages and disadvantages of EFTPOS

These systems are very popular for several reasons, including:

- Payment into the shop's bank is guaranteed by the system as long as the transactions are properly authorised or are below the floor limit.
- There is less paperwork, and no cheques or cash to process, when goods are paid for using EFTPOS, so fewer staff are needed and the shop collects less cash, so there is less chance of theft.

But EFTPOS has some disadvantages too:

- The systems are expensive to install.
- The customer's account is debited within two days, so you have to keep careful track of your spending.
- When you spend cash, you can tell when it has run out, but when using a card, it is easy to overspend.

Implications of using computers for commercial data processing: economic

Initial costs

The costs of setting up a system are high — it costs a lot of money to buy the equipment needed to computerise a large business. You need to buy both hardware and software and the software may be more expensive than the hardware because of its complexity.

Mass market

Businesses introduce computer systems in order to increase their productivity, to sell to as many people as possible and to develop a mass market for their products. On-line shopping companies like *Amazon* are a good example of how businesses can use computer systems to sell to a huge number of people all over the world.

Running costs

The larger a program is, the longer it takes to write. Hardware needs to be checked regularly and the software programs need to be checked and maintained. Maintaining hardware and software contributes to the running costs of a data processing department. Electricity, paper, toner/ink and hardware maintenance charges all add to the running costs of computer systems. There may also be software licenses to renew, perhaps annually.

Implications of using computers for commercial data processing: security and privacy

Accuracy of information and privacy

All large companies hold data about their employees and customers on computer. Any information which a company holds must be registered under the terms of the Data Protection Act, and must be accurate and up to date. Companies must tell their customers if their details are to be stored on a computer system and must show the customers any information they hold about them if they ask for it. The Data Protection Act is explained in more detail in chapter 1.

Information held on computer files must be kept private. Information about how much credit someone was allowed, or details about how much they earn, must not be shown to anyone who doesn't need to know about it.

Physical and software security

Information must also be kept secure. Files can be held in a safe place to which only certain members of staff have access, files can be protected by passwords or be encrypted, and the system can allow different levels of access for different users. You can read more about physical and software security in chapter 11.

An advantage of computer files

A problem that many companies face is customers who don't pay their bills on time. How can a computer system help? A computer system can gather the records together on all the customers whose payments are overdue and display or print out a list. This will save someone having to search through all the records by hand. A reminder letter can be sent automatically to these customers.

Sale of customer lists

In order to get back some of the money that they have had to spend in building up a data processing computer system, some companies sell their lists of customer's names and addresses to other companies. This is why we get so much 'junk mail' nowadays. People disagree whether it is right to sell lists like this.

Businesses have been set up around selling mailing lists. Some companies carefully study the area you live in, and group housing estates and roads into 'social classes'. Mail order companies can buy lists of names and addresses arranged like this. They then target a mail shot at people they think will buy particular products.

Customer lists and the law

The Advertising Standards Authority has imposed strict regulations on the sale and transfer of mailing lists between companies, since 1 January 1992:

- The person must be told when their data is collected that it might be used for direct mail.
- The person must have the right to stop their name being used in this way.
- If anyone asks an advertiser to remove his or her name from this list, then the advertiser must do so.

Foundation level questions

knowledge and understanding

1 Give two reasons why computers are used for commercial data processing.
2 Name the stages of the data processing cycle.
3 What is a bar code?
4 What is a mark sense card?
5 What is a magnetic stripe?
6 What is a file?
7 What is a record?
8 What is a field?
9 Name two forms of data output.
10 What is the basic hardware for commercial data processing?

11 What is e-commerce?
12 What is on-line banking?
13 What is on-line shopping?

problem solving

1 Why is the price of an item not contained in its bar code?
2 Why is it a good idea to keep a backup copy of your data?
3 Why do customers like on-line shopping?
4 Why do banks like customers to carry out their banking transactions on-line?

General level questions

knowledge and understanding

1 What is the difference between data and information?

2 What is meant by the term MICR?

3 What is a check digit?

4 Describe one type of check used to ensure that data is correct (other than a check digit).

5 What is meant by the term, interactive processing?

6 What do the following people do?
   a. programmer
   b. systems analyst
   c. engineer
   d. network manager.

7 What is electronic funds transfer (EFT)?

8 What is the point of sale (POS)?

9 What is meant by the term 'running costs'?

10 State one method of physical security and one method of software security for data.

11 Read this article and answer the questions which follow.

> The SellQuick supermarket chain recently announced record profits and a big performance lead over its rivals. Use of computerised stock control linked to laser reading checkouts was attributed to its success. SellQuick's technology lead looks set to continue with the announcement they are to start EFTPOS trials. In conjunction with Mainland Bank, two branches in Musselburgh and Buckie will have EFTPOS terminals, enabling electronic payment of grocery bills.

   a. What has caused SellQuick's 'record profits'?
   b. What does a 'laser reading checkout' read?
   c. What is EFTPOS?
   d. Explain how you can use EFTPOS to pay for your groceries at SellQuick.

problem solving

1 Here are the parts of four people's driving licence identification numbers which refer to their dates of birth. What are the dates of birth of these people?
   a. Alex Jones   712119
   b. Mary Campbell   511254
   c. Miriam Horowitz   408309
   d. Joseph Timmons   704192.

2 What would the code numbers be for:
   a. 15 October 1976?
   b. 27 June 1959?
   c. 7 March 1936?
   d. 11 February 1908?
   e. Your own birthday?

3 By using the number 201203 as an example, show how this number could be treated as either data or information.

4 Why are customer lists often sold between companies?

5 What is likely to happen to customers if their names and addresses are sold to another company?

6 Why do banks use magnetic ink rather than ordinary ink on cheques?

7 What type of check would you use for making sure that a person was old enough to start school?

8 Why does a bar code have a check digit?

9 What does a customer need to have before they can use EFT?

10 Give two advantages and two disadvantages of:
   a. an EPOS system
   b. an EFTPOS system.

11 One of the advantages of EPOS to the shop's management is that they can check up on the work rate of the till operators. How would you feel about this if you were:
   a. the employer?
   b. an employee?

Credit level questions

knowledge and understanding

1. Give two examples of management information that may be provided by a shop's computer system.
2. What is optical character recognition?
3. What is validation?
4. What is verification?
5. What is the difference between sequential and random/direct file access?
6. What is a multi-user database?
7. Give one example of a computer crime.
8. What is meant by the term single entry multiple use?

problem solving

1. What could happen if a company doesn't bother to take security measures with its data?
2. Give one example of a data processing situation in which sequential access would be inappropriate. Give a reason for your answer.
3. If the bar code doesn't have the price of goods on it, explain how the till can display the price when a bar code is scanned at the checkout.
4. How does an EPOS system keep track of stock?
5. Suppose an unscrupulous retailer used an EFTPOS system to make a database about his customers that linked their names with the items they buy in his store.
   a. What could he do with this information?
   b. What prevents this from happening today?
6. When electronic funds transfer was first introduced, some people thought that it would lead to a 'cashless society'. Has the 'cashless society' arrived?

• **Key points** •

- Commercial data processing involves very large amounts of data, which are processed by mainframe computers.
- Information (for use by people) is data (for use by computers) with structure.
- The data processing cycle consists of:
  - data collection and preparation,
  - data input,
  - data processing and storage,
  - data output.
- Data must be collected and prepared in a form that the computer can understand.
- Examples of direct data input are bar codes, magnetic stripes, mark sense cards and smart cards.

- A magnetic ink character reader is used to input the special characters on the bottom of cheques into a computer system.
- An optical character reader can recognise normal characters and read them directly into a computer.
- All data input into a computer must be checked for errors.
- Two ways of error checking are to use check digits and range checks.
- Validation is checking that data is sensible and accurate, for example, a range check.
- Verifying data is checking it has been entered correctly.

- A file is updated when it is changed or has new data added to it.
- Interactive processing is when data is processed or updated as the transaction is entered, and any enquiries are replied to at once.
- Data files can be accessed by sequential access or random/direct access.
- Data may be output in several ways — onto paper, on screen or to a file.
- A multi-user database is a database that may be accessed by many users at the same time.
- The basic hardware required for commercial data processing usually consists of a mainframe computer system and terminals.
- Multi-access means that many users may be on-line to a computer system at the same time.
- Staff who work in a data processing department include:
  - Systems analyst — a systems analyst looks at all the jobs a company does manually and decides which jobs can be done best by computer.
  - Programmer — a programmer writes programs.
  - Engineer — an engineer installs new computers and maintains existing ones.
  - Network manager — a network manager is the person in charge of the network. He or she is responsible for all of the computer systems attached to the company network.
- Social implications of commercial data processing include effects on business, job types and careers, computer crime and fraud.
- Deliberately damaging a computer system, corrupting files or committing fraud are all examples of computer crime.
- A virus is a rogue program which reproduces itself automatically and may cause damage or loss of valuable data.
- The technical implications of commercial data processing involve e-commerce, on-line banking and on-line shopping.
- E-commerce is the process of conducting business on-line, such as buying and selling goods and services over the Internet and transferring funds within online banks.
- On-line shopping has advantages for companies:
  - lower transaction costs
  - larger purchases per transaction
  - shops always open for 'impulse' purchases.
- On-line shopping has advantages for customers:
  - shops never close
  - easy to search and find items
  - easy to compare prices
  - easy to configure products
  - improved customer relations
  - can take as long as you like.
- Disadvantages of on-line shopping:
  - bank card fraud
  - receiving goods — you have to be there
  - returning goods — may be too much trouble.
- Advantages of on-line banking for banks:
  - save money on staff and buildings
- Advantages of on-line banking for customers:
  - do not need to travel to a branch
  - always open.
- Banks may issue various types of card to allow customers to make use of their services.
- Keeping your personal identification number secure can prevent your card being misused.
- Smart cards are bank cards which contain a microprocessor.
- Smart cards can store much more information than a card with a magnetic stripe.
- Electronic funds transfer is a way of paying for goods without using money.
- The point of sale is the place in the shop where goods change hands.
- Electronic point of sale (EPOS) is a system which collects sales data automatically as a customer buys goods.

- In a shop which uses EPOS, all the items are marked with a bar code.
- EPOS systems help the shopper and the retailer:
  - Shopping can be quicker for shoppers to go through the checkout.
  - The shopper is given an itemised receipt.
  - The retailer can reorder fresh supplies quickly and accurately.
  - The shop's computer keeps records of exactly how much of each item is sold.
  - It is easier for retailers to organise special prices for certain goods.
  - There is less chance of fraud.
  - Fewer staff are needed since it is not necessary to attach a price to each item.
  - The checkout operator needs less skill.
- Management can check up on the rate of work of the checkout operators.
- Electronic funds transfer at point of sale (EFTPOS) is when a customer's bank account is authorised to be debited at the checkout terminal.
- Advantages of using EFTPOS:
  - payment is guaranteed by the system
  - there is less paperwork
  - transactions are quicker than writing a cheque
  - there is less chance of theft because there is less cash in the shop
  - fewer staff are required for administration in the shop.
- Information held on a computer system must be accurate, secure and private.

14 Industrial applications/ automated systems

What is an automated system?

An automated system is a system where you provide the **input**, and the machine or computer carries out the **process** and provides you with the **output**. See if you can identify the input, process and output for each of the examples given in the next few pages.

Automated systems in everyday life

Figure 14.1 *An automatic washing machine, an automatic camera and a video handset.*

You see and use automated systems in your everyday life, but you might not know them. Here are a few examples.

- A washing machine is an example of an automated system. Water is put in, together with washing powder and dirty clothes. The machine contains a number of stored programs. By setting the controls of the washing machine, you can select the program you want for the clothes you've put in. You don't have to do anything else.
- Using an automatic camera you get perfect(!) photographs every time. A window in the front of the camera senses the amount of light around and the computer inside the camera sets the shutter speed, aperture and flash automatically to give the right exposure. All you have to do is point the camera and press the button.
- You can use a central heating programmer for heating or hot water continuously or at any time of the day.
- You can program a video recorder to record a series of television programmes. Each programme is called an event. A small computer in the video recorder takes in the start and stop times, the data and channel for each event. Once you have programmed it correctly, the recorder will switch itself on at the right time and off again when the programme is finished. Some video recorders use special numbers called Videoplus codes, which are published along with the TV listings, to make video recorders easier to program. Other video recording systems take the programme details automatically from the television signal transmission. Some systems are capable of 'learning' programmes that have been recorded previously and will automatically record the same or similar programmes each time they are transmitted.

- A vending machine can make up a selection of hot and cold drinks, supply you with a can of drink or a packet of crisps, depending on the buttons you press.

Can you think of any more examples of automated systems in your home?

Automated systems in industry

Figure 14.2 *Welding on a car assembly line. The robot's arm has an arc welder as its tool.*

Industrial processes use automated systems — here are some examples.

- Car manufacture is almost completely automated. A few years ago a television advert for a family car claimed that its product was 'Designed by computer, built by robots, driven by the intelligent'. The centre of every car manufacturing plant is the assembly line, where the cars are put together. The assembly line uses a conveyor belt to move the parts from one part of the factory to the next. A fully automated production line is controlled by a mainframe computer, which is linked to individual robots and machines that assemble the components. A typical robot on an assembly line will have a movable, jointed arm with a specialist tool (like a spray gun) attached to it. Figure 14.2 shows how a computer controlled robot is used to weld a car. The assembly line control program is designed so that the components from other parts of the factory are sent to the right place at the right time — for example so that the right colour of paint goes to the automated paint shop in time for the body panels reaching it to be painted.

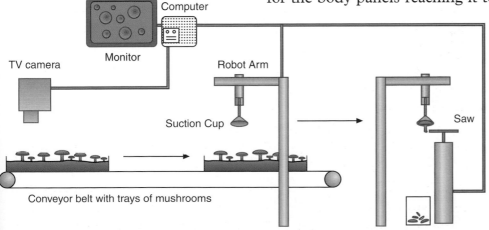

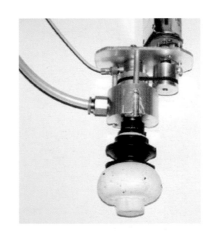

Figure 14.3 *Automatic harvesting of mushrooms.*

- Mushrooms grow very quickly, and will double in size in 24 hours. Figure 14.3 shows you how an automated system can help the mushroom grower to make sure that only mushrooms of the right size are picked to be sold. The system uses a television camera linked to a computer. The grower programs the computer with the size of mushroom that she wants to be picked. The trays holding the mushrooms pass along the conveyor belt, where they are scanned by the camera, which sends information about the size and position of all the mushrooms in the tray to the computer. When the tray moves into a particular position the robot arm lifts each correctly sized mushroom out using a suction cup and passes the mushroom over a circular saw blade. This cuts off the end of the stalk. The prepared mushroom is then packed for sale. The tray containing the rest of the mushrooms is left to grow for another day, and the process is repeated. By using this system, the grower can be confident that the mushrooms are picked at the best time, the time which will give them the biggest profit.

- In a large bakery, bread making is completely automated although it is monitored by a human operator. The carefully measured ingredients (flour, water, salt, yeast, conditioner) are mixed in a huge bowl. The operator watches the display on a computer screen, which shows a diagram of the measuring and mixing process (like the one in figure 14.4). This type of display is called a **mimic controller**, because it shows the exact details of the process on the screen. The display keeps the operator informed of the weights and temperatures of the ingredients so they can adjust the process if they need to by using the control panel.

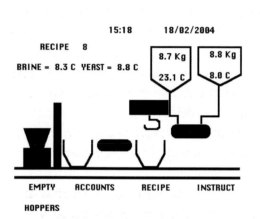

Figure 14.4 *An example of a mimic display during bread making.*

Why do we use automated systems?

Automated systems are used because:

- They can carry out the process much **faster** than a human can.
- The tasks that they are programmed to do are often boring or **repetitive**.
- They can be used in **hazardous environments** where it would be harmful or dangerous for people.
- They are more **efficient** than people because they can work all day without a break.
- They are more **accurate** than people and can do finely detailed work without getting tired and making mistakes.
- They are **adaptable** because they can be programmed to carry out different tasks.

Implications of using automated systems

Automated systems have taken over many of the jobs that people used to do, and they have had effects on many aspects of our lives. Let us look at the main effects.

Social implications

Automating operations at work affects people in many ways:

- Quite a few workers will lose their jobs because a computer can do it quicker and cheaper.
- Some of these people will be retrained to do other jobs — like maintain the automated systems.
- This means the skills which these people have will have to change, and so will the nature of their jobs.
- The people who used to do boring, repetitive and dangerous jobs will have increased leisure time because computers have taken over these jobs. Hopefully these people will use their extra free time to develop their talents and improve their quality of life. The time allowed for holidays will increase, and the time you have to spend working during a single day will decrease.
- This promise of more leisure time hasn't always worked out — some people have found that the technology has made life more hectic than it was before!
- Nowadays you can do certain jobs from a computer terminal at home. Fewer people working in potentially dangerous factory conditions means there will be fewer industrial accidents.

Technical implications

Safety precautions must be taken when using industrial automation:

- The moving parts of a machine must be covered so that no one can be hurt when they're operating the machine.
- People who work alongside robots must take care that the robot doesn't injure them when it moves.
- Robot vehicles are programmed to move slowly so that people can get out of their way.
- Robot vehicles are also fitted with sensors to detect collisions. If the robot bumps into something, it should instantly stop moving, preventing any damage from being done. This is an example of feedback from a sensor being relayed to a computer, which then makes a decision. Feedback is discussed later in this chapter.
- Robot arms, which carry out tasks like paint spraying on an assembly line, should only operate when a component is in position.

Quality control

Using automated systems the quality of a product can be kept consistent. For instance, the automated system in a bakery is continuously checking loaves from each batch to make sure that their weight is within a set range of values. It will produce a printout of the results, which the bakery manager can use to monitor the efficiency of the production process. He or she can then change the process as they need to.

Economic implications

Automated systems are expensive to install. There is a high initial cost. A completely automated production line can cost many millions of pounds to set up. Many businesses have changed to automated systems in spite of the costs involved — why?

Unlike people, automated systems don't demand wage rises or costly facilities, like a canteen, while they are working, or go on holiday, so the employers hope that by reducing the number of employees they will save money in a few years time. These are long term savings. If the automated system works properly, the employers will also gain because more goods will be manufactured in the same time and for the same cost. This is known as increased productivity, and this will also help to produce savings in the longer term.

After a few years, the automated systems will eventually become less efficient. Machines may break down, or their speed of operation or their accuracy is no longer sufficient to keep up with the competition. If this is the case, new automated systems will have to be installed. The money that will have to be paid for this is known as the replacement costs.

EXAMPLE: WHEN AUTOMATED SYSTEMS GO WRONG
This automated system didn't work in the way it was supposed to …

In 1987 a computer-controlled traffic system in Melbourne turned into a headache for Australian police. The system had minimum speed signs which instructed motorists to drive at speeds which would take them through traffic lights while they were green. When the system was first installed, the signs in Melbourne were flashing a minimum speed of 75 kilometres per hour — until the local police realised that the city's maximum speed limit is 60 kilometres per hour!

Systems analysis

Before designing a new automated factory or introducing new technology to a manual system, a systems analysis needs to be carried out. A systems analyst looks at how various jobs are done manually, and sees if any of these jobs could be done by computer. If a company decides to introduce a computer, the systems analyst may have to design the computer system that will be used. Once the computer has been installed, the systems analyst will monitor the process and try to find ways to improve its performance.

Modern factory

Automated systems have changed the way the workplace is designed. Since many large factories now have very few people working in them, architects have designed these factories to suit the way the machines operate. Automated warehouses have products stacked on very high shelves on forklift pallets — no one could lift or move these pallets without using a machine.

Design of the workplace

There are some things that human workers would need in the workplace which robots wouldn't:

- The workplace would have to be at the right temperature — if it was too cold or too hot the workers would be uncomfortable and wouldn't work as well. Robots can work all day without being affected by the cold.
- Humans also require frequent breaks, canteens and rest rooms.
- If there were no human workers on the assembly line the amount of noise in the factory wouldn't matter.
- In an automated factory, the few human technicians could be confined to the control room, which could be well sound proofed and at a comfortable temperature.

Robotics

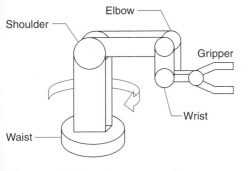

Figure 14.5 *Anatomy of a jointed arm robot. You can see how the various parts resemble (and are named after) parts of the human body.*

Robot anatomy

Some robots have parts that resemble human limbs. It is not surprising therefore that these parts are called after the human parts they resemble. A jointed arm robot (like the one in figure 14.5) has a **waist**, **shoulder**, **elbow** and **wrist**. The part on the end of the arm, the **tool**, is specialised to suit whatever task the robot is programmed to do. This could be a gripper, a screwdriver, a suction cup, a paint spray or a welding electrode. Figure 14.6 shows a few of these tools.

A **motor** powers each movable part of the robot arm. Robots may have one or more motors, either inside them or connected to them.

Robots are connected to a computer by a device called an **interface**. The job of the interface is to make sure that the correct signals are sent between the computer and the robot.

Sensors and feedback

A **sensor** is a device which detects a physical quantity, like light, heat (temperature), movement, bump, strain (weight) or sound

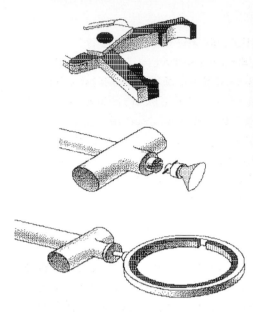

Figure 14.6 *Types of tools —
you can see a gripper for thin
cylindrical objects, a paint spray
and a circular collar which can
be inflated to grip objects inside
it. The robot arm on the right is
using a polishing tool.*

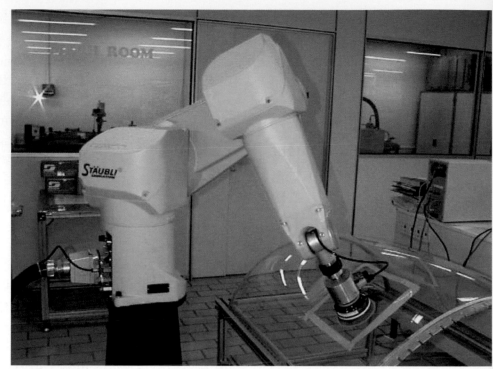

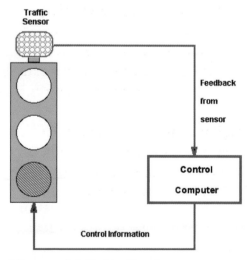

Figure 14.7 *Feedback.*

Figure 14.8 *Analogue signal.*

(microphone). Robots and other automated systems are often fitted
with sensors so that they can detect what is going on around them. A
sensor is connected to the control computer by an interface. The
signal which a sensor sends back to the computer is called feedback.
Feedback is very important to automated systems because it allows
the control computer to make a decision based on what type of
feedback it receives.

EXAMPLES

Traffic lights

Most traffic lights are fitted with sensors which detect if there are any
cars waiting. The traffic sensor sends feedback to the control computer,
which can change the lights as required.

Automatic lifts

Automatic lifts are fitted with strain sensors which detect the weight of
the people or goods, which are placed in them. If the sensor detects a
weight above the lift's safe operating limit, then the doors will stay open
until the weight is reduced.

Stationary and mobile robots

Robots which stay in one place all the time, for example at a fixed
point on an assembly line, are called stationary robots. Robots
which move are called mobile robots. Throughout this chapter you
can see various different examples of stationary and mobile robots.
How many of each type can you spot?

Analogue input/output (I/O)

Most electrical signals, like the output from a microphone, are analogue signals. Analogue signals can vary continuously between two limits. If you could see an analogue signal it would look roughly like the shape a skipping rope makes when you hold the ends and shake it up and down (something like figure 14.8). An example of analogue input is recording sound on an audio cassette using a microphone. The microphone picks up the sound, which is an analogue signal, and the signal is recorded on the tape. When the tape is played back, the analogue sound is output through the loudspeaker.

Digital signals

Computers can only work with digital signals, which have only two values — on or off. A digital signal therefore consists of a series of 'ons' and 'offs'. An 'on' signal is represented by a 1 and an 'off' by a 0. When used like this, 0 and 1 are binary numbers, and a series of 0s and 1s are called bits. A sequence of these bits sent to the computer gives the required instruction. Figure 14.9 shows what a digital signal would look like if you could see it.

0 1 1 0 1 1 1 0 0 1 0 0

Figure 14.9 *Digital signal.*

Analogue to digital (A to D) and digital to analogue (D to A) converters

A computer is connected to another device (a printer, a disk drive, a robot or another peripheral) by a circuit called an interface. Usually this interface has to be able to change the digital signals from the computer to an analogue signal that the other device can understand. This is done by a digital to analogue converter. Signals can be changed in the other direction by an analogue to digital converter. Digital to analogue and analogue to digital conversion is shown in figure 14.10. An analogue to digital converter samples the incoming analogue signal at regular intervals, changes the continuously varying voltage to binary numbers, and sends the bits to the computer.

EXAMPLES

Audio CD player

An audio CD player contains a digital to analogue converter to change the digital data on the CD into analogue data, music, so that we can hear it.

Scanner

A **scanner** converts an image from a photograph or drawing into digital form that a computer can process. This is an example of analogue to digital conversion.

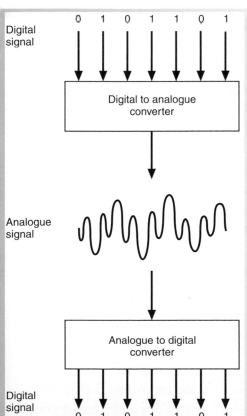

Digital signal

0 1 0 1 1 0 1

Digital to analogue converter

Analogue signal

Analogue to digital converter

Digital signal

0 1 0 1 1 0 1

Figure 14.10 *Conversion from digital to analogue signals and back again.*

Programmable robots

Robots are normally controlled by a computer program, which is made up of **instructions** written in a **high level language**.

Robots that work on different assembly lines sometimes need to be reprogrammed to carry out different tasks. Writing a new program for the new task could do this, but some robots can be 'taught' exactly what movements you want them to make.

Teaching robots

To teach a robot to do paint spraying, a human operator will spray one item using the end of the robot's arm. The positional sensors in the arm tell the control computer about the sequence of movements of each joint involved in the process, and the control computer stores this information. The motors in the robot arm can then repeat the stored sequence of movements to spray an item. This is called **programming by example** or **lead-through programming**.

If the robot arm is too large or heavy for the operator to move like this he will use a device called a teach pendant. He controls the arm with the buttons or a joystick on the pendant and sets the computer up to learn or copy each movement of the arm.

ROM software and embedded systems

Stationary robots, which are linked directly to a computer, store their control programs on magnetic tape or disk, especially those which can be 'taught'. Mobile robots, on the factory floor or in outer space, have control programs that are fixed and are not changed easily. Their programs are stored on **read only memory (ROM)** chips. ROM chips are a more expensive way of storing software than disks, but they retain their information if the power is switched off, and a program contained in ROM can be loaded many times faster than from a disk.

Embedded systems all use software stored in ROM. An **embedded system** is a tiny computer inside another, larger piece of equipment, like a washing machine, a car or a mobile phone. Most people are not aware that embedded systems even exist, but they are very common. The embedded system has the computer's operating system and application functions combined into a single program. Embedded systems are often used to control critically important systems, like a car's ignition. Embedded systems process data in **real-time**.

Autonomous guided vehicles (AGVs)

In a modern, fully automated factory, using a different type of robot, called an **autonomous guided vehicle**, can solve the problem of keeping the production line supplied with parts. The term autonomous means that the vehicle can, to a certain extent, work on its own. Sometimes these vehicles are called automated guided vehicles. One of these is shown in figure 14.11.

Autonomous guided vehicles do all the fetching and carrying of parts from the warehouse to the assembly line. They are controlled by computer during their journey, and can find their way from one place to another by following wires buried in the factory floor. This is an example of a **magnetic guidance system**.

In some factories the vehicle follows a painted line on the factory floor. This system is called a **light guidance system** and is more flexible than magnetic guidance, since it is much easier to paint a new line than it is to dig up the floor and bury a wire. However, the light guidance system can be affected by dirt on the floor covering the paint.

The latest autonomous guided vehicles use a special form of light guidance. This system uses a rotating laser on the vehicle and reflective targets fixed to the walls of the factory. No matter where the vehicle goes in the factory, the laser beam can hit at least three targets. The computer on the autonomous guided vehicle can then calculate its position using simple trigonometry. This system allows the auto-nomous guided vehicle to know where it is to an accuracy of ±1 cm.

All autonomous guided vehicles are fitted with front and rear sensors to detect unexpected objects in their path (like people or other vehicles which have broken down). If anything touches these sensors, the vehicle will stop instantly so that it doesn't hurt someone or break something. The control program on the autonomous guided vehicle has to interact with the computer and receive the output immediately — it must use **real time processing**. This means that the program must be constantly operating and ready to take action. If the vehicle doesn't stop immediately when it meets an obstruction, people could be hurt or costly equipment damaged.

Advantages of using autonomous guided vehicles over manual labour:

- **Reduced labour costs**. One AGV operating three shifts a day can replace the salary of three manual forklift operators.
- **Increased dependability and productivity**. AGVs can operate 24 hours a day, 7 days a week without taking a break or days off. This reduces replacement labour costs.

Figure 14.11 *An autonomous guided vehicle. Note the front and rear bumpers which are used to detect objects in the vehicle's path. A sensor underneath the vehicle lets it follow a pre-programmed path.*

Figure 14.12 *A remotely operated vehicle for use in bomb disposal.*

- **Less product handling damage**. AGVs have controlled vehicle motion with a repetitive stopping accuracy of ±1 cm. This reduces product damage caused by manual forklift handling.
- **Increased safety**. Accidents and injuries are reduced because the vehicles always act according to pre-programmed instructions. This reduces time wasted from collisions and prevents damage to equipment.
- **Flexibility**. Unlike fixed conveyor belts, the route that an AGV takes can be reprogrammed to reflect changes in factory layout.

Remotely operated vehicles (ROVs)

Remotely operated vehicles are used in **hazardous environments** where it is not safe for people to go.

Figure 14.12 shows a remotely operated vehicle being used by a bomb disposal expert to examine a suspicious device on the underside of a car. The vehicle is equipped with a television camera, which relays a picture to the operator controlling it at a safe distance. The tool on the vehicle is a grab that the operator can use to remove the bomb from the car.

Educational robots

Floor turtle

The turtle was one of the first educational robots to be developed. It is made of a plastic dome which covers two large wheels. Each wheel has a motor attached. The turtle has a device that raises and lowers a pen through an opening underneath. Some turtles also have a small hooter which can make sounds. You can connect the turtle directly to the computer via a cable, or operate it by infrared remote control (like the remote controller on a television set).

Floor turtles can draw shapes by moving in a pattern over a piece of paper with the pen held down. They are programmed using a language called Logo.

Figure 14.13 *Remotely operated vehicles for undersea exploration.*

Figure 14.14 *Turtles.*

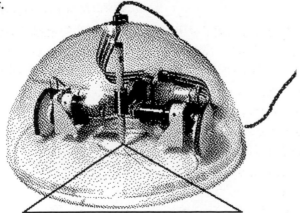

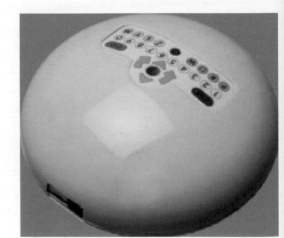

Control languages

Computer programs are always written in a programming language. There are many programming languages. Here are a few:

- BASIC
- C++
- COMAL
- Java.

Some languages, called high level languages, are similar to English and therefore are easy for us to read and understand. The higher the level of the language, the closer it is to English and therefore the easier it is for someone to read a program listing and understand what task it is performing.

Some robots are programmed in languages like the four we just mentioned, others are programmed in languages specially designed for robot control. These are called control languages, and the commands they use (like GRASP, MOVE, WAIT, TURN, SPEED) are related directly to the robot world.

Control Logo is a language that allows programmes to define their own high level commands. To do this the programmer uses simple routines such as TURNON, TURNOFF, WAIT and PULSE, and incorporates them into higher level procedures such as MOVE_BUGGY. Here is an example of a Control Logo command:

```
TO MOVE_BUGGY
TURNON 1
WAIT 100
TURNOFF 1
END
```

Intelligent robots

An expert system is a special computer program which can apply hundreds of rules that it has learnt from a human expert within a particular field of knowledge. Expert system programs can diagnose your health problems, give you legal advice or help you to find out what is wrong with your car when the engine won't start!

Expert systems can apply human-generated rules more consistently than humans do, and can explain how they came to any conclusions. This means that any mistakes they make can be corrected easily. You can read more about expert systems in chapter 9.

In order to produce an intelligent robot, it would need to be programmed with its own expert system. Remotely operated vehicles

Figure 14.15 *ASIMO*

used in space or on the seabed could be replaced by intelligent robots with expert systems to control their navigation and the work that they are doing.

EXAMPLE — ASIMO

Frankfurt, September 9, 2003 — Honda President and CEO Takeo Fukui today unveiled ASIMO — the company's advanced humanoid robot — at the Frankfurt Motor Show.

Developed by Honda, ASIMO (which stands for Advanced Step In Innovative Mobility) is regarded as one of the most advanced walking robots in the world. ASIMO was widely acclaimed by members of the European scientific community at a symposium entitled 'From High-Tech to Intelligence — The Challenge of Humanoid Robots' held at the Technical University of Darmstadt on 30 June 2003.

Using new advanced motion technology, ASIMO not only walks forwards and backwards, but also turns sideways, climbs up and down stairs and turns corners. ASIMO is the closest robot yet to replicating the natural walking motion of humans.

"The mission of Honda is to harness the potential of advanced technology to improve the lives of our customers", said Mr Fukui, speaking at the show. "To fulfil this vision, we have not limited ourselves to the mobility concepts of today. We continue to dream."

Honda stressed that there is a long way to go before specific roles can be assigned to humanoid robots. Honda is already renting out ASIMO to corporations and organisations in Japan for promotional roles such as welcoming visitors. Commenting further on ASIMO, Mr Fukui said "I see my role as providing the freedom to dream and will to challenge as a motivating force for Honda associates throughout the world. ASIMO is a new technology that we have developed independently, and we hope that one day it will play a role in assisting humans in all sorts of ways".

Computer aided design/computer aided manufacture (CAD/CAM)

What is computer aided design?

Computer aided design (usually shortened to CAD) is a way of using a computer to design the structure or appearance of an item on the screen. The operator of a CAD system can create and manipulate images on a high-resolution screen. A designer often uses a graphics tablet as an input device to a CAD workstation. A graphics tablet allows the designer to draw in the usual way, using an electronic pen. Figure 14.16 shows you what a graphics tablet looks like. The menu for the graphics tablet may be displayed on the screen or on the surface of the tablet itself. Sometimes the design is output in a form suitable for transfer to a computer-controlled machine, ready to start the manufacturing process. If a high-quality printout is required a plotter may be used as the output device.

Using a CAD system can greatly reduce the amount of work a designer has to do by making all the necessary calculations and by allowing her to change the design many times on the computer screen before it is printed. Using CAD, a picture on a computer screen can be turned around and viewed from any angle. The operator can input any changes to the design to the computer and see its effect straight away on the screen. Also, the computer can enlarge any part of the picture so that very small details are visible.

Figure 14.16 *A graphics tablet in use/A CAD station.*

CAD packages

A professional CAD system consists of:

- a computer,
- one or more terminals with large high-resolution colour monitors,
- high-quality colour plotters, and
- a range of specialised software packages to drive the system.

In a commercial CAD system, a graphics tablet is often used as the input device (like the one in the photograph). A graphics tablet allows the operator to draw in a natural way and also to choose from a menu using an electronic pen.

The hardware and software used for CAD ranges from large systems costing several hundreds of thousands of pounds (like the systems used in the car and aircraft industries) to relatively inexpensive systems, which are designed specifically for personal computers.

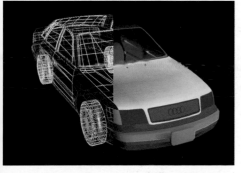

Figure 14.17 *A car designed by a professional CAD package, such as AutoCAD.*

Uses of CAD

The use of CAD is growing rapidly and computers are now being used to help design anything from postage stamps to motorways. Here are a few examples.

Car design

CAD may be used to design the shape of a car body. The designer tries to produce a shape which looks good and people will want to buy. At the same time she must make sure that the shape of the car is streamlined so that it will have a low petrol consumption and so on. You can see a car designed by computer in figure 14.18.

Kitchen units

Many DIY stores sell kitchen units. Some of these stores offer a free kitchen planning service. The customer measures the dimensions of their kitchen and draws it out on squared paper. The figures are input

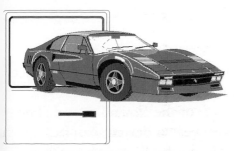

Figure 14.18 *A car designed by CAD.*

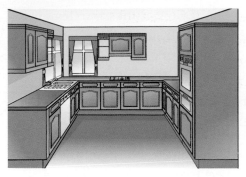

Figure 14.19 *A kitchen planned by computer.*

Figure 14.20 *A computer-generated retail development (Bradley Shanks Rotch Travelling Scholarship 2003).*

to a special computer program together with details of any doors and windows in the room. The operator uses the computer program to plan the kitchen by placing kitchen units (held on memory) onto the plan. A hard copy of the plan is printed out for the customer. A kitchen planned by computer is shown in figure 14.19. The computer can also be used to calculate the cost of the kitchen by adding together all the prices for the units which have been selected. A list of the separate kitchen units may be printed to simplify ordering.

Road design

Road designers use CAD. A new road must be safe to drive along. A driver must have a good view of the road at every bend and junction. The designer can use the computer to plan the route the road will take and to show how the road will appear as you drive along it even before it has been built. By using CAD, mistakes can be corrected before any money is spent on the road.

Housing

A computer can be used to design a housing estate. The appearance and location of each house can be adjusted to give the best appearance and the most economical use of the available land. The local authority planners, who must approve the design, can be shown how each street on the proposed estate will appear — to pedestrians, to drivers or from the air. Prospective house buyers don't need to imagine the view from the windows of their new house — they can see it on the computer screen.

What is computer aided manufacture?

Computer aided manufacture (usually shortened to CAM) is using a computer to control the production process — like making a part for a car or cutting cloth to make an item of clothing. The details about a particular product are stored, and can be changed or added to later. Using CAM means that products can be consistently made very accurately.

Uses of CAM

Like CAD, CAM systems are being used more and more, in many different situations. Here is an example.

Postage stamp manufacture

One method of making postage stamps involves taking a photograph of the original stamp design and using a process known as chemical etching to transfer the design to a copper cylinder which is then used in the printing press.

A computer-controlled process has replaced this chemical etching of the printing cylinder:

1. First, the original design of the stamp is scanned and a digitised image is produced and stored on the computer.
2. Next, the cylinder is laced in a special lathe, called a computer numerically controlled (CNC) lathe.
3. Using the digitised image the computer tells the lathe to engrave the design on to the cylinder. This process uses a very high resolution — 117 lines per centimetre (or 300 lines per inch).

Fig 14.21 *A CNC lathe in action.*

This new process means that corrosive chemicals are no longer needed, and the copper removed from the cylinder during engraving can be recycled. The whole process is therefore much friendlier to the environment than the old method.

Effects of computer-controlled systems

The introduction of new technology has caused major changes in employment patterns. Machines have replaced people on the production line so fewer people are needed. This has caused great concern about job losses. On the other hand, many people think that not to introduce new technology could make their firm less competitive and even put them out of business.

Companies which introduce new technology need to retrain their workers to operate it and people are still needed to program and maintain the computers. Some of the skills which were needed before the introduction of new technology are still needed today so the operator can see if the new technology is working correctly. For example, a person who operates a CNC lathe needs the same basic skills as a manual lathe operator does, but must also understand what part the computer plays in the operation.

Studies into the effect that new technology has had on the work force have shown that generally people enjoy using the new systems. Some workers were even more enthusiastic about the technology than the management who introduced it.

Advantages of computer aided design and manufacturing

- It is a faster, more accurate process than older methods.
- The amount of waste can be minimised.
- A single operator can see a complete job through from start to finish.
- It is simpler to operate and demands less skill of the operator.

Simulation

Designers are not just concerned with the way things look — a new car must look good but it must also be safe and efficient. When a new car is produced, dummies are strapped into the seats and the car is crashed against a wall to test how well protected the people inside would be in a car crash. This is very expensive and time consuming because the design has to be changed, a new car built and the whole process repeated if the design has any faults.

Using a computer, the car can be designed and tested without spending any time or money on production. Once all the data about the new car has been input, the computer is programmed to 'crash' the car. The effects of this pretend crash are measured and the design is changed as needed. Because all of this happens inside the computer, no real cars need to be produced and the design can be changed very quickly. This way of using computers to model something that happens in real life is called simulation.

Using computer simulation we try to predict what will happen in a real life situation from a model of that situation on the computer. A computer simulation program is a useful tool in providing answers to questions like these:

- An engineer would like to know the effects of various loading conditions on a bridge he's designing without actually having to build the bridge.
- An aircraft designer would like to know how changing the shape of the wings or the tail would affect the way the plane flies without having to build an aircraft specially.

Figure 14.22 *An aircraft simulator.*

There are also programs that will simulate the timing of traffic lights, or the effect that hunting will have on wildlife populations. In all of these (and lots of other) problems, computer simulations give you useful information which would have been difficult to obtain otherwise. Remember that the results depend heavily on the computer program used to model what will happen. The closer the computer program is to real life, the more reliable the results will be.

Training aircraft pilots

Computer simulation is used extensively for training. Perhaps one of the most well known applications of simulation is in training pilots to fly aircraft. Using simulators saves time and money when training pilots. Because a trainee isn't using a real plane, no fuel is wasted — and if he or she makes a mistake and crashes the plane no one gets hurt! Aircraft simulators are more than just computer programs. They usually consist of a working model of the aircraft cockpit, with all the controls and indicators operating just as they would be in real life.

The main differences between a simulator and a real aircraft are:

- The windshield consists of computer monitors rather than being a view of the outside world.
- The controls are linked to a computer running the simulation program, not to real wings or engines.
- The model cockpit is mounted on a moveable base which can simulate the movement of the aircraft during flight.

Normally a simulator is controlled by a human operator who monitors the trainee pilot's performance under different conditions, including emergency situations that are too dangerous to practice in a real aircraft. Simulations like this one are a form of virtual reality.

Figure 14.23 *A virtual reality headset and gloves.*

Virtual reality

Virtual reality is a method of reproducing the outside world digitally within a computer system and displaying it to the user in such a way that it allows them to interact with a wide range of situations. To take part in virtual reality, the user wears a **headset** with earphones and goggles, together with special **data gloves** rather than use a keyboard and monitor. In this way, the computer controls three of the five senses. In addition to feeding sensory input to the user, the devices also monitor the user's actions. The headset, for example, tracks how the eyes move and responds accordingly by sending new video input.

Virtual reality allows a user to project him or herself into the computer-generated world and move freely within it. While inside this digital environment, the user is represented as a computer graphic called an **avatar**. Avatars may be either two or three-dimensional. They may also be created either entirely as computer graphics, or else by mapping digital photographs of a real person onto a virtual three-dimensional model.

Figure 14.24 *Virtual reality.*

Foundation level questions

knowledge and understanding

1 What is an automated system?

2 Give two examples of automated systems in:
  a. your home
  b. industry.

3 Give one example of a hazardous environment where automated systems may be used.

4 a. Give two examples of occupations or jobs which have been changed because automated systems have been installed.
  b. Will these people need to be re-trained?
  c. What new skills will they need?

5 What is:
  a. a sensor?
  b. feedback?
  c. CAD?
  d. CAM?

6 Name four different parts of a robot.

7 What part of a robot arm carries out a task?

8 What part of a robot allows it to move?

9 Draw up a table with two columns. Head the columns 'stationary' and 'mobile'. Look at the pictures of the robots in this chapter and write the name of each robot in the correct column.

problem solving

1. What may need to happen to employees when a new automated system is introduced to the family?
2. Why is it useful for robots to be programmable?
3. What is the difference between a stationary and a mobile robot?
4. Identify the feedback in:
   a. A set of traffic lights.
   b. The water cistern in figure 14.25.
5. What advantages does CAD/CAM bring
   a. to a company?
   b. to an employee?

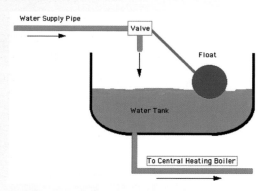

Figure 14.25

General level questions

knowledge and understanding

1. Why is it true to say that robots are more efficient than human workers?
2. Why is an interface needed?
3. What is an AGV?
4. Describe one way in which an AGV may be guided.
5. What is:
   a. simulation?
   b. virtual reality?
   c. real-time processing?
6. State two safety precautions which should be taken when robots are used beside human workers.
7. Describe how the nature of a factory worker's job is likely to change if automated systems are introduced into the workplace.
8. Give your opinion on whether or not the introduction of automated systems has brought increased leisure time to workers.

problem solving

1. Why would dirt on a factory floor have no effect on a magnetic guidance system on an autonomous guided vehicle?
2. What advantage does laser guidance have over light guidance?

3. If automated systems are expensive to install, why are so many businesses using them?
4. Give one reason why robots are more accurate than human workers.
5. Explain how a programmer could teach a robot to weld two parts of a car door together.
6. Study the mushroom harvesting example shown in figure 14.3.
   a. Why must the grower tell the computer what size of mushrooms to pick?
   b. Why does the grower not have to tell the computer where the mushrooms are in the tray?
   c. What would happen if none of the mushrooms in a tray were the correct size?
   d. Why is there a connection on the diagram between the computer and the circular saw?
7. A pupil once described an advantage of using a simulation to train aircraft pilots using these words:

   "If you crash and are killed, then you are not really dead."

   Give one other advantage of using a simulation to train aircraft pilots.

Credit level questions

knowledge and understanding

1 What is meant by the term adaptability?
2 What is a control language?
3 What advantages do control languages have over other high level languages?
4 Why does an interface contain an analogue to digital converter?
5 Why is some robot control software stored on ROM?
6 What is an avatar?
7 What is an embedded system?
8 Name two places where you would expect to find embedded systems.
9 Look at the picture of the Mars Explorer robotic vehicle in figure 14.26.
   a. Identify one sensor which provides feedback to the vehicle.
   b. What type of software is likely to be on board the vehicle?
   c. Identify one tool on the vehicle.

problem solving

1 Describe a situation where an
   a. A to D converter
   b. D to A converter
   would be required.

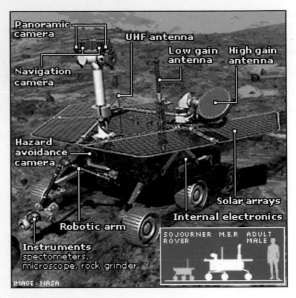

Figure 14.26 *Mars Explorer robotic vehicle.*

2 Why is it important to carry out a systems analysis in the workplace?
3 State one disadvantage of having software stored in ROM.
4 A pelican crossing is operated by pedestrians pushing a button beside the traffic lights. Draw a diagram similar to the one in figure 14.7 to show a pelican crossing including the button, and explain how the automated system operates.

• Practical work •

1 Use a CAD package to:
   a. Draw a plan of one of the rooms in your house. Fill it with furniture.
   b. Design a kitchen, gym or workshop. Save your work to disk and obtain a hard copy.

• Key points •

- In an automated system you provide the input, and the machine or computer carries out the process and provides you with the output.
- Automated systems can work much faster than humans.
- Automated systems may be programmed to do repetitious tasks, or work in places that are harmful or dangerous for people.
- Automated systems are more efficient and more accurate than humans.
- Automated systems are adaptable because they can be reprogrammed to carry out different tasks.
- An automated system uses sensors to detect what is going on around it.
- An automated system can change its action depending on feedback from the sensors.
- A jointed arm robot is said to have a waist, shoulder, elbow and wrist, like the parts of the human body.
- Robots that stay in one place all the time are called stationary robots.
- Robots that move are called mobile robots.
- Robots are connected to a computer by an interface.
- Many of the signals that robot sensors output are analogue signals.
- Analogue signals can vary continuously between two limits.
- Computers can only work with digital signals, which have only two values – on or off.
- An interface between a computer and a robot arm may need a digital to analogue converter.
- Robots are normally under the control of a program written in a high level language.
- An embedded system is a tiny computer inside another, larger piece of equipment, like a washing machine.
- A control program for a mobile robot must work in real time.

- Robots may be programmed by using a control language.
- The control program for a ROV is often held in ROM.
- An intelligent robot would need to be programmed with its own expert system.
- The tool on a robot arm may be changed to carry out a different task.
- Autonomous guided vehicles in a factory may use magnetic guidance or light guidance systems.
- Before designing a new automated factory or introducing new technology to a manual system, a systems analysis needs to be carried out.
- In computer aided design a computer is used to design the structure or appearance of an item on the screen.
- A graphics tablet is often used as an input device in a commercial computer aided design system because it allows the operator to draw in a natural way.
- Computer aided manufacture is when a computer is used to control the production process.
- Computer aided manufacturing involves storing information about a product which can be changed or added to later.
- Components produced using computer aided manufacture can be consistently produced very accurately.
- Advantages of computer aided design and manufacturing:
  - It is a faster, more accurate process than older methods.
  - The amount of waste can be minimised.
  - A single operator can see a complete job through from start to finish.
  - It is simpler to operate and demands less skill of the operator.

- Computer simulation involves trying to predict what will happen in a real life situations from a model of that situation.
- Computer simulation is used for training and in design work.
- Virtual reality is a method of reproducing the outside world digitally within a computer system and displaying it to the user in such a way that it allows them to interact with a wide range of situations.
- To take part in virtual reality, the user wears a headset with earphones and goggles, together with gloves.

15 Hardware

What is hardware?

Figure 15.1 *A typical desktop computer system.*

All the physical parts of a computer system (the bits you can see and touch, not the programs) are called the hardware. A single item of hardware is called a device. A computer system is made up of a processor and main memory together with input, output and backing storage devices.

A typical computer system might include a processor, a monitor, a keyboard, a printer and one or more disk drives.

The processor

This is the part of the computer where all the sorting, searching, calculating and decision-making goes on. In a lot of computers nowadays all these processes are carried out by a single chip. A chip is a specially treated piece of silicon and is very small, only a few millimetres across. You can see a processor chip in figure 15.5

Figure 15.2 *A block diagram of a computer system.*

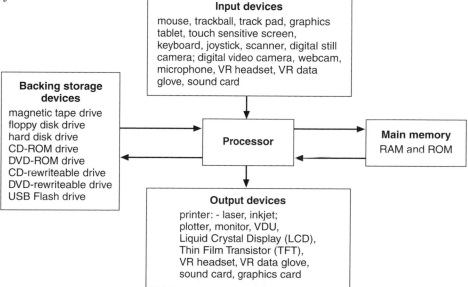

Input devices
mouse, trackball, track pad, graphics tablet, touch sensitive screen, keyboard, joystick, scanner, digital still camera; digital video camera, webcam, microphone, VR headset, VR data glove, sound card

Backing storage devices
magnetic tape drive
floppy disk drive
hard disk drive
CD-ROM drive
DVD-ROM drive
CD-rewriteable drive
DVD-rewriteable drive
USB Flash drive

Processor

Main memory
RAM and ROM

Output devices
printer: - laser, inkjet;
plotter, monitor, VDU,
Liquid Crystal Display (LCD),
Thin Film Transistor (TFT),
VR headset, VR data glove,
sound card, graphics card

A computer can carry out any process if it is given a set of instructions to tell it what to do. The set of instructions that control how a computer works is called a **program**. Another name for computer programs is **software**. It may help you to think of the processor as the 'brain' of the computer system — but it isn't like a real brain because a computer can't think or act for itself. It can only carry out the instructions programmed into it. Computers can carry out instructions very quickly because the processor can process billions of instructions every second.

Main memory

The **main memory** or **main store** of a computer is used to store programs and data. A computer *must* have a memory. The processor can't store a whole program at one time so the computer needs its memory to store the parts of a program and data it's not using at any particular moment.

The amount of information that can be stored in the memory of a computer depends on the number of **storage locations** that are available. A single storage location can hold one byte of information. One byte is the amount of space needed to store one character, for example the letter B takes up one **byte** of storage.

The main memory of a computer system is made up of a set of memory chips. There are two types of memory chip. Each type of memory chip is used for a different purpose in a computer system.

Figure 15.3 *Random access memory (RAM) chips.*

Random access memory (RAM) chips

RAM is also called read/write memory. RAM is used to store programs and data temporarily because anything stored in RAM is *lost* when the computer is switched off.

Read only memory (ROM) chips

ROM can be used to store programs and data permanently. The contents of a ROM chip are *not* lost when you switch the computer off.

ROM chips are used on some computers to store the programs that control how the computer works from the moment it is switched on. These programs are called operating system programs. Operating systems are explained further in chapter 20. ROM chips are also used to store many other types of programs such as games.

Figure 15.4 *A read only memory (ROM) chip.*

More about chips

Look back at the photographs of silicon chips. The chips inside a computer are held on a printed circuit board and they are connected to the other parts of the system (like the screen and the keyboard). A circuit board is a thin board on which chips and other components are fixed by solder. The chip is made up of thousands of tiny components and circuits all squeezed into a space only a few millimetres square.

Types of chip

There are many different types of chip, not just microprocessors and memory chips. Different chips are designed to do different things. A telephone might have three chips — one to turn the incoming analogue signals into digital data, a control chip to carry out functions like automatic dialling and a memory chip to store telephone numbers. Chips are programmed to perform these tasks when they are made and can't change what they do — so you couldn't take the control chip out of a dishwasher and make it work a computer. These are all embedded systems. You can read some more about embedded systems in chapter 14.

Figure 15.5 *Microprocessor chips.*

Effect of changes in technology

Each year, the number of storage locations and circuits (connections) that can be placed on a single chip gets bigger. This has affected computer systems because:

- The price of memory chips is continuing to go down.
- The memory size of computers (ROM and RAM) has gone up.
- Chips work faster and can handle more data in a single operation.
- Complete computers can be produced on a single chip.
- Computers are now tiny, for instance palmtop computers.

Manufacturers have to work very hard to keep pace with the advances in chip technology and computer design. The computer user now expects more and more features from her machine. The latest, fastest and most powerful computer system is now outdated in a few months as competition forces manufacturers to make new models with extra features to keep up with the opposition.

Desktop computer

A desktop computer is so-called because it is normally used whilst sitting at a desk and is mains operated.

A desktop computer usually has a colour monitor, although many are supplied with liquid crystal display/thin film transistor (LCD/TFT) screens at additional cost. Large LCD/TFT panels are very expensive.

Figure 15.6 *Various designs of desktop computer.*

The keyboard is a full size model, usually with cursor keys, function keys and a numeric keypad.

The normal pointing device is a mouse, with one or more buttons. Some mice have a handy scroll wheel, which makes it easy to navigate windows. All desktop computers have a hard disk drive, typically between 20 and 100 gigabytes. Many desktop computers also incorporate a floppy disk drive, although several manufacturers no longer include these. All desktop computers have at the very least a CD-ROM drive, and many have a CD rewriter and a DVD-ROM or DVD rewriter drive. Almost all current standalone desktop computers have a modem.

All desktop computers have one or more loudspeakers and may also have a microphone for sound input. Other peripheral devices which are usually attached to a desktop computer system are a printer, scanner and web/video camera.

Palmtop, laptop and tablet computers

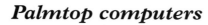

Palmtop, laptop and tablet computers are battery operated and may be used without being plugged into mains electricity, for example, whilst travelling.

Palmtop computers

A **palmtop computer** is so-called because it is small enough to be held in one hand while it is being operated. For this reason a palmtop computer is also called a **handheld computer** or a **personal digital assistant** (PDA).

A palmtop computer has an LCD screen as an output device. Some types of palmtop computer have a very small keyboard as an input device. One type of palmtop computer even has a full size folding keyboard, but most types use the LCD screen as a touch sensitive input device operated with a plastic pen or stylus.

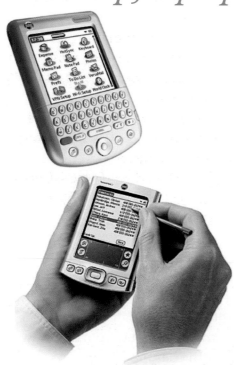

Figure 15.7 *Palmtop computers.*

Palmtop computers are battery operated, usually with normal penlight cells. Figure 15.7 shows two designs of palmtop computer. Palmtop computers are frequently used for keeping schedule calendars, address book storage and retrieval, note taking, doing calculations and, with a modem, exchanging e-mail and retrieving information from the Internet. A microphone is often provided for voice recording.

Palmtop computers may be connected to a desktop computer using a cable, or they may use wireless technology, such as *Bluetooth* or *WiFi*. Some palmtop computers are **dedicated** to particular tasks such as stock control in shops and warehouses.

Figure 15.8 *A palmtop computer?*

Figure 15.9 *Some laptop computers.*

Laptop/notebook computers

A **laptop computer** is so-called because it is possible to use it resting on your lap while seated. Laptop computers are also commonly known as **notebook** computers. Some laptop computers have the same processing capacity as desktop computers and are known as **desktop replacement** machines.

Laptop computers use an LCD/TFT screen as an output device, but with a much larger keyboard than a palmtop computer, which can be used comfortably for word processing. Most designs are 'clamshell', with the screen built into the lid and the keyboard and all other devices in the base. Laptop computers typically use a track pad or a raised button to control the pointer on the screen. Laptop computers are battery operated, with rechargeable power packs. A laptop computer normally has a hard disk, floppy disk and a CD-ROM drive. Some have a CD rewriter and DVD-ROM or DVD rewriter drive. Figure 15.9 shows various designs of laptop computer.

Tablet computers

A tablet computer has a large, touch sensitive screen which is used with a special pen for drawing and handwriting. Some tablet computers also have a keyboard for data entry. When the keyboard is attached to the tablet, the tablet computer becomes very similar to a laptop computer in appearance. A tablet computer is shown in Figure 15.10

Figure 15.10 *A tablet computer*

Tablet computers were developed because people find it more natural to write with a pen rather than to type using a keyboard. Early tablet computers used handwriting recognition software to change a person's writing into text, but this could not cope with the sketches that people do while they are taking notes. Current tablet computers allow handwritten notes and sketches to remain on the screen as 'digital ink', which can be saved to a file in the normal way without being changed into text.

Mainframe computers

Figure 15.11 *A mainframe computer system occupies a whole room.*

A **mainframe** computer is a very large computer system which can process a very large amount of data at high speed. It occupies a whole room and may be connected to hundreds of user **terminals**. It is common to have many simultaneous users on a mainframe computer. This is why a mainframe is a **multi-user** or **multi-access** system. The users of a multi-access system each appear to have individual control of the computer at the same time, although only one program is actually being run at any one time. The mainframe computer also allows **multi-tasking** or **multi-programming** which allows several different tasks or applications to be available at the same time.

A mainframe computer has a number of processors — it is a **multi-processor** machine. There is usually a vast amount of RAM, and many extra peripherals such as tape and disk drives.

A **dumb terminal** has no processor and no local storage devices. All that is required is a screen and a keyboard since all of the processing and storage will be done within the mainframe computer.

Supercomputers

Did you know?
Some universities, research establishments and companies have created their own design of 'supercomputer' by linking together hundreds of ordinary microcomputers to provide a huge amount of processing power

A mainframe computer is not necessarily the fastest and most powerful type of computer. Instead, this term is reserved for the **supercomputer**. Supercomputers are used for intensive mathematical calculations such as weather and climate forecasting, car design, aerospace engineering, molecular modelling or the production of high resolution graphics such as digital animation in motion pictures.

Current input devices, **current output devices** and **current backing storage devices** are dealt with in chapters 16, 17 and 18.

Backing storage

Backing storage is used to store permanently programs and data. Computers need backing storage because data in the main memory is lost when the computer is switched off. Magnetic tape, floppy disks, hard disks and all types of CD and DVD are all examples of backing storage media. The hardware that uses or holds the media is known as a backing storage device.

Capacity of backing storage

The capacity of backing storage is the quantity of data that can be held in a particular medium. The capacity of a floppy disk depends upon how it is formatted.

Examples of backing storage media which are covered in this course include: magnetic tape, floppy disk, hard disk, CD, DVD and USB Flash ROM. The table 15.1 shows some typical backing storage capacities for these media.

Backing storage medium	Typical capacity	Type of access
Magnetic tape	20 to 100 gigabytes	Sequential
Floppy disk	1.44 megabytes	Direct
Hard disk	20 to 500 gigabytes	Direct
CD-ROM, CD-R, CD-RW	650 or 700 megabytes	Direct
DVD-ROM, DVD-R, DVD-RW	4.7 to 17 gigabytes	Direct
USB Flash ROM	16 megabytes to 1 gigabyte	Direct

Table 15.1

You can also read a comparison of backing storage in terms of: speed (data transfer), cost and capacity in chapter 18.

Sequential and random/direct access devices

Suppose you have a music centre at home with a cassette tape recorder and a compact disc player. If you want to find a particular song on the tape, you have to play the tape from the beginning and listen to all the songs until you find the one you want. You can speed things up by fast forwarding or rewinding the tape to the position where you think the song will be, but it is still quite slow.

It is much quicker to find a song on a disk than on a tape. You can send the player directly to any track and it will start playing the song immediately.

Finding data on a tape is slow because you can only get the data back in the same order you recorded it onto the tape. Tape gives sequential access to data because the data can only be read back in sequence. A tape recorder is a **sequential access device** because it reads and writes data in sequence.

Disks can access data **directly** because the read/write head on the disk drive can go straight to the track where the data is stored without having to read all the data in between. Direct access is also called **random access** because you can read the data on the disk in any order, not just the order it was written in. A disk drive is called a **random access device** because the disk drive head can read data in any order.

Foundation level questions

knowledge and understanding

1 What is:
   a. hardware?
   b. software?
2 What is a:
   a. desktop computer?
   b. laptop computer?
   c. palmtop computer?
3 Name two current:
   a. input devices
   b. output devices
   c. backing storage devices.
4 In addition to a keyboard, what input device would you expect to find on a:
   a. desktop computer?
   b. laptop computer?
5 Draw a labelled diagram of a desktop computer system.
6 Where are programs and data held inside a computer system while they are being processed?
7 What is a microprocessor?

8 What is a chip made of?

problem solving

1 Why do computer systems need a main memory when programs and data can be loaded from disk?
2 What can you do to stop a program stored in RAM from being lost when you switch your computer off?
3 Mary has been given a pocket computer game for her birthday. She has two different games which are stored on plug-in cartridges. Her sister Sarah is doing Computing Studies at school. Sarah says the cartridge that plugs into Mary's game is a ROM cartridge.
   a. What is ROM?
   b. Why are the games stored on ROM cartridges and not RAM cartridges?
4 What device on a palmtop computer acts as both an input and an output device?
5 State two ways in which a palmtop computer may communicate with other computers.

General level questions

knowledge and understanding

1 How much information can a single storage location hold?
2 What is a mainframe computer?
3 What does the term 'capacity of backing storage' mean?

problem solving

1 A computer is sometimes described as 'a very fast idiot'. Why is this a good description?
2 Where would you expect to find a storage location?
3 What would you expect to find in a storage location?

Credit level questions

knowledge and understanding

1 What determines the capacity of a magnetic floppy disk?
2 What is sequential access?
3 What is direct access?
4 What storage medium has only sequential access?
5 Why is direct access also called random access?

problem solving

1 Why is a sequential access medium slower than a direct access medium?
2 What effects are advances in technology having on the microprocessor chip?

• **Key points** •

- All the physical parts that make up a computer system are known as the hardware.
- A single item of hardware is called a device.
- A computer system is made up of a processor and main memory together with input, output and backing storage devices.
- A typical computer system has a processor, a monitor, a keyboard, a printer and one or more disk drives.
- The types of computer are:
  - desktop
  - laptop/notebook
  - palmtop (PDA)
  - mainframe.
- Chips used in computers are made of silicon and are only a few millimetres across.
- A set of instructions that control the operation of a computer is called a program.
- The main memory or main store of a computer is used to store programs and data.
- A single storage location can hold one byte of information.

- One byte is the space on a disk needed to store one character.
- There are two types of memory chip: random access memory (RAM) chips and read-only memory (ROM) chips.
- The contents of random access memory are lost when the computer is switched off.
- The contents of a read-only memory chip are not lost when the computer is switched off.
- Backing storage is used as permanent storage for programs and data.
- Magnetic tape gives sequential access to data because the data can only be read in the order it was written.
- Disks give you direct access because the data on a disk can be read in any order, not just the order in which it was written.
- The capacity of backing storage is the quantity of data that can be held in a particular medium.
- The capacity of a floppy disk (how much data it can hold) depends on how it is formatted.

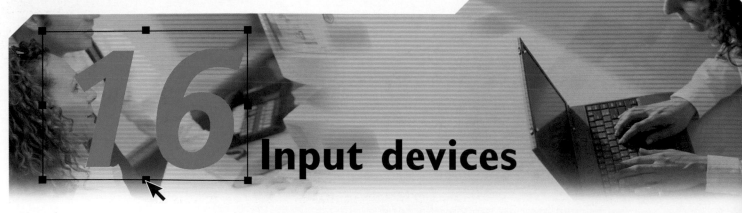

16 Input devices

What is an input device?

The physical parts of a computer system are known as **hardware**. A single item of hardware is called a **device**. An **input device** is a device which allows data to be entered into a computer system.

We will look at the following types of input device in this chapter:

- keyboard
- graphics tablet
- touch sensitive screen
- mouse
- trackball
- trackpad
- joystick

- scanner
- microphone
- digital still camera
- digital video camera
- webcam

- sound card
- specialised input devices for disabled users and virtual reality
- input devices for multimedia.

Credit level

Keyboard

The input device used most often with a computer system is a **keyboard**. Each key on a keyboard has a switch under it. When you press the key, the switch beneath it is closed and a signal is sent to the computer. The keyboard is wired so that each key switch sends a different code number into the computer. This code is called the **American Standard Code for Information Interchange** (shortened to **ASCII**). You will find more about ASCII in chapter 21. The keys on a computer keyboard are normally arranged in the same way as they are on a typewriter, so a standard computer keyboard is sometimes called a QWERTY keyboard (from the top row of a typewriter, where the keys are QWERTYUIOP).

Did you know?
In France, keyboards have AZERTY instead of QWERTY.

Many computer keyboards also have function keys, and on some computers you can program these keys. Other keys have built-in functions (like 'print' or 'clear screen'). A software package which uses the function keys will often have an overlay that you put over the function keys to label the keys. This is called a function key strip. Some keyboards also have a small keypad to the side of the main keyboard which has numbers on it (it is the numeric keypad). This can speed up your work if you have to enter a lot of numbers.

Figure 16.1 *A computer keyboard.*

Figure 16.2 A 'concept' keyboard.

A 'concept' keyboard is a flat board which contains a grid of key switches. You can program each switch or group of switches like you would program a function key. By placing a paper overlay on the concept keyboard and loading the appropriate software you can operate the program from the concept keyboard. This is especially useful for very young children or for people who find using an ordinary keyboard difficult. It is a specialised input device.

Graphics tablet

Figure 16.3 *Graphics tablets.*

A graphics tablet is a flat pressure-sensitive board with a pen or pointer connected to it. By pressing on the graphics tablet with the pen, the pen's position is sent to a computer. Often the pointer has a small window with a fine cross hair marked on it. This helps the user to position the pointer accurately on the board. By using a graphics tablet the user can draw or trace a shape which will appear on the computer screen. A graphics tablet is often used for computer aided design (CAD) applications.

Touch-sensitive screen

There are two main types of screen in use in computer systems. These are a CRT (cathode ray tube) and an LCD/TFT (liquid crystal display/thin film transistor — flat) screen. On a CRT touch sensitive screen there is an invisible infrared grid across the front of an ordinary glass screen. When you touch the screen with your finger you 'break' the grid, and a message is sent to the computer to give the position of the finger. On an LCD/TFT touch sensitive screen the sensitive part is built into the screen itself, which has a slightly flexible plastic surface. LCD/TFT touch sensitive screens are operated with a plastic stylus, rather than using your finger. LCD/TFT touch sensitive screens are used as the main input device on palmtop and tablet computers.

Handwriting recognition

In handwriting recognition, the user writes in his or her normal handwriting and the computer reads the shape of the writing and decodes it into text that goes into a word processor. When starting off, the user has to 'teach' the computer to recognise his or her writing.

A touch-sensitive screen can be used in many ways:

- For handwriting recognition on a portable computer.
- To help very young children or people who have a disability to use a computer.
- In dedicated systems like a holiday resort guide in a tourist information office.
- As a guide in a museum or exhibition where it is easier to make choices by touching a screen than using a keyboard.

Mouse

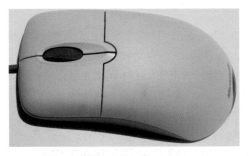

Figure 16.4 *Microsoft optical mouse.*

There are two types of mouse in current use. The traditional type has a ball underneath it. The ball rolls along when the mouse is moved, and this operates a mechanism inside the mouse. An optical mouse has a light underneath it instead of a ball. Any movement is detected by a sensor which picks up the reflected light from the surface under the mouse. All mice have at least one button to allow objects on the screen to be selected. Some mice have a small wheel on top to help with scrolling.

Whatever type of mouse you're using, when you move the mouse on your desk a signal is sent back to the computer, giving the position of the mouse and indicating whether you've pressed a button. The computer uses this information to move a pointer and to select items on the screen.

Trackball

Figure 16.5 *A trackball — Kensington Orbit.*

A trackball (sometimes called a **tracker ball**) works exactly the same way as a mouse, except that the ball is on top. You can see one of these in figure 16.5. The user rolls the ball around with her hand to operate it, and can select objects by pressing a switch. If you use a trackball you don't need any extra space on your desk to move it around (like you do with a mouse). Large trackballs are also used on some video games machines where it wouldn't be practical to operate a mouse. Most small trackballs on laptop and notebook computers have now been replaced with **trackpads** or **stick pointers**, because a trackball requires regular cleaning to keep it in good working order.

Trackpad

Figure 16.6 *A trackpad.*

A trackpad is a touch sensitive plate. Movements of the user's finger over the plate control the movement of the pointer on the screen. Like a trackball, if you use a trackpad you don't need any extra space on your desk to move it around. Trackpads are used mainly on notebook and laptop computers.

Figure 16.7 *A stick pointer — IBM Trackpoint.*

Stick pointer

A stick pointer is a small button which is touch sensitive. Movements of the user's finger over the stick control the movement of the pointer on the screen. Stick pointers are used on some laptop and notebook computers instead of a trackpad.

Joystick

Figure 16.8 *A joystick.*

A joystick is another input device you can connect to a computer system. The joystick is able to move in eight directions. Joysticks are mostly used in computer games to control the way a picture on the screen moves. Joysticks have one or more buttons which may be programmed for various actions within the game. Sometimes two joysticks are connected to a computer so that two people can play the game at once. You can see a joystick in figure 16.8.

Scanner

Figure 16.9 *A scanner.*

Using a scanner you can input printed drawings, photographs or text directly into a computer. A scanner works like a photocopier — a light is shone on the material and the scanner detects the reflected light. You can use a scanner with optical character recognition (OCR) software to input the scanned text into a word processing package. A scanner may be fitted with a transparency adapter, which allows slide films and negatives to be scanned.

Microphone

A microphone is used to allow sound to be input to a computer system. Most computer systems have microphones built in, usually above the screen, or have an interface where a microphone may be plugged in. The sound quality captured by a built in microphone is low, and this would not normally be used for recording music.

Voice recognition

One application which uses a microphone is **voice recognition**. To use this system, the computer must have **voice recognition software**. To use voice recognition the user must speak slowly and clearly and the system usually understands only a limited number of words. The user usually has to 'teach' the computer to recognise her voice by repeating certain words or phrases. Users who may have difficulty using a mouse or a keyboard to control a computer system also use voice recognition.

Digital still camera

Figure 16.10 *A digital still camera.*

Digital still cameras are similar to ordinary film cameras, in that they both use a lens which focuses reflected light from the subject onto a sensor and the image is then stored for later processing. In a film camera, the film itself is both sensor and storage medium. In a digital still camera, the sensor is a postage-stamp sized electronic chip. The surface of the chip is packed full of light sensitive elements. The greater the number of these elements, then the greater the level of detail, or **resolution**, that may be obtained. The resolution of a digital still camera is measured in *megapixels*. Once the chip has been exposed to light, the information from these elements is turned into digital data, or **digitised**, and stored in the camera's memory. Unlike film, the stored picture does not need to be developed, and the memory can be reused over and over again. Perhaps the greatest benefit of digital photography is the fact that you can see the pictures that you have just taken, decide whether or not to keep them, copy them to the computer's backing storage, then delete all of the pictures from the camera and start over.

Most digital still cameras store their pictures on removable **memory cards**, but these have a limited capacity. While you can erase and reuse the memory cards, you really need something to copy the pictures onto first. A computer system's hard disk is ideal, but if you are away from your computer, this can pose a problem. One solution adopted by digital photographers is to take a portable computer such as a laptop along with the camera in order to

download the pictures and allow the memory card to be erased. Some cameras allow saving to floppy disk instead of memory cards. One type even has a CD writer built in and saves the images to CD-R.

In order to edit pictures, it is necessary to transfer them to a computer system. This can be achieved by using a cable to connect the camera to one of the computer's interfaces. Alternatively, a device called a **card reader** may be attached directly to a computer system.

Some cameras may also be connected directly to a TV set to allow the images to be viewed.

Most digital cameras incorporate a colour LCD screen, which may be used to view an image and check it.

If you own a digital still camera, you really need a computer system and printer in order to store, edit and print out the images. However, printers are now available which contain card slots to accommodate the memory cards used by digital cameras. Such printers allow the user to print images directly from the card.

Many mobile phones now have built in digital still cameras. The pictures which these cameras take are small and relatively low resolution.

Digital video camera

Figure 16.11 *A digital video camera.*

A **digital video camera** is used for taking movies. It works on the same principal as a digital still camera, but records the moving pictures to videotape instead of memory cards. Most digital video cameras incorporate a small colour LCD screen, which may be used as a viewfinder when filming, and also as a monitor when playing back movies.

A digital video camera may be connected to a computer system in order to download the movie and edit it on screen. A great deal of storage space is required to hold a movie taken with a digital video camera. For instance, a movie lasting one hour requires 13 gigabytes of backing storage.

Webcam

Figure 16.12 *A webcam — Logitech.*

A **webcam** is a small digital camera, which is normally positioned on or beside the computer's monitor in order to capture images which may be transmitted across a network. Webcams make applications like **video conferencing** possible. A webcam is shown in figure 16.12.

Video conferencing

Video conferencing is the use of communications links to conduct meetings between people who are geographically separated. A typical video conferencing set up requires a computer system and a webcam in each location, together with a network connection between everyone involved. The video conferencing software allows each participant to see and hear the others on their computer screens, and sometimes to interact with a common document in a screen window.

Sound card

Credit level

Figure 16.13 *A sound card — SoundBlaster.*

Sound cards improve the quality of sound output from games and multimedia applications. Additional bundled software allows users to compose, edit and print music, record and edit digital audio, and play audio and multimedia CDs.

Sound is analogue in nature, it is a continuously varying quantity. Computers work in digital quantities. In order to input sound into a computer the sound must be changed from analogue into digital. This process is called **analogue to digital conversion**. A microphone or another sound source is connected to the computer's sound card in order to capture the sound. The sound card carries out the ADC in a process called sampling.

Specialised input devices for disabled users and virtual reality

A **specialised input device** is an input device which is adapted for a particular purpose, such as use by a person who is disabled or for virtual reality.

Devices for disabled users

Users who have a visual impairment can use spreadsheets and word processors linked to voice output devices and Braille keyboards.

Figure 16.14 *Debbie McMullan and her 'Touch Talker'.*

This web site was designed by Susan, vice-president of In Touch Systems, using the Magic Wand Keyboard.

Figure 16.15 *A 'Magic Wand' keyboard in use.*

The photograph in Figure 16.15 shows a 'touch talker' — this is a device that Debbie uses to communicate with her parents and fellow pupils at school. Debbie can communicate by touching a picture on the 'touch talker', which contains a speech synthesiser.

Devices for virtual reality

Virtual reality is a method of reproducing the outside world digitally within a computer system and displaying it to the user in such a way that it allows them to interact with a wide range of situations. To take part in virtual reality, the user wears a **headset** with earphones and goggles, together with special **data gloves** rather than use a keyboard and monitor. In this way, the computer controls three of the five senses. In addition to feeding sensory input to the user, the devices also monitor the user's actions. The goggles, for example, track how the eyes move and respond accordingly by sending new video input. The data glove sends input back to the system from the user's hand movements.

The virtual reality headset acts as both an output and an input device, in that the headset contains one or more viewing screens for output and that it can feedback the user's head movements to the computer.

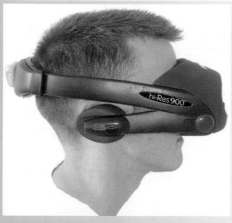

Figure 16.16 *Virtual reality headset and data gloves.*

Use of a variety of input devices for multimedia

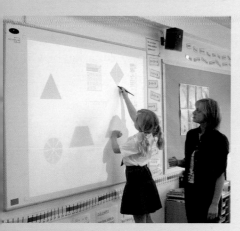

Figure 16.17 *An interactive whiteboard in use.*

Multimedia is the presentation of information by a computer system using graphics, animation, sound and text. Many of the input devices described in this chapter may be used for multimedia. Some manufacturers produce special multimedia keyboards which have function keys dedicated to performing specific actions. The keyboard in figure 16.1 is one example. Digital video cameras can create movies that may be edited directly on a computer system and used to produce multimedia. A microphone may be used to record sound for multimedia.

One development in presentations involves using a computer and multimedia projector as an output device and an **interactive whiteboard** as an input device. The interactive whiteboard is linked to the computer and special electronic pens may be used to 'write' on the board and allow the presenter to interact with the presentation. You can read more about multimedia in chapter 7.

Foundation level questions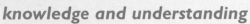

knowledge and understanding

1 What is an input device?
2 List the input devices that are part of the computer system that you use in class.
3 What is a:
   a. keyboard?
   b. graphics tablet?
   c. touch sensitive screen?
   d. mouse?
   e. trackball?
   f. trackpad?
   g. joystick?

4 Which input device would you use to:
   a. enter text?
   b. select an icon on the screen?
   c. play a game?
   d. draw a computer aided design (CAD) diagram?
   e. control a pointer on a laptop computer?
   f. recognise your handwriting?
5 Why is a keyboard called a QWERTY keyboard?

problem solving

1 Why do laptop computers not have a mouse?
2 Why do laptop computers use trackpads instead of trackballs?

General level questions

knowledge and understanding

1 What is a:
   a. scanner?
   b. microphone?
   c. digital still camera?
   d. digital video camera?
   e. webcam
2 Name two items that a scanner can be used to scan.
3 What storage medium is used in a:
   a. digital still camera?
   b. digital video camera?

4 Which device is used for sound input?
5 Which units are used to measure the resolution of a digital still camera?

problem solving

1 Suggest how a webcam could be used by:
   a. a security company,
   b. a family with relatives in Canada.
2 How is it possible for each key on a keyboard to produce a different character?

Credit level questions

knowledge and understanding

1 What is multimedia?
2 What is a sound card?
3 What is virtual reality?
4 What is a specialised input device?
5 Give one example of a specialised input device for:
   a. use by a person who is disabled,
   b. virtual reality.
6 Which input devices may be used for multimedia?

problem solving

1 What is voice recognition?
2 What use is a concept keyboard?
3 a. Name two input devices which require the use of an application package to make the best use of them.
   b. Name the application packages and explain how they would be used with the input devices.
4 a. Which senses are NOT given any input when using virtual reality?
   b. Why is this?

• Key points •

- All the physical parts that make up a computer system are known as the hardware.
- A single item of hardware is called a device.
- Examples of input devices are:
  - keyboard
  - graphics tablet
  - touch-sensitive screen
  - mouse
  - trackball
  - trackpad
  - joystick
  - scanner
  - microphone
  - digital still camera
  - digital video camera
  - webcam
  - virtual reality headset and data glove
  - sound card.
- Using specialised input and output devices with a computer system can often help people who are disabled in some way.
- A variety of input devices are used for multimedia.

17 Output devices

What is an output device?

The physical parts of a computer system are known as hardware. A single item of hardware is called a device. An output device is a device which allows data to be displayed or passed out of a computer system.

We will look at the following types of output device in this chapter:

- printers: laser printers and inkjet printers
- plotter
- monitor
- VDU

- liquid crystal display (LCD)
- thin film transistor (TFT)

- sound card
- graphics card
- specialised output devices for disabled users and virtual reality
- output devices for multimedia

Credit level

Printers

Figure 17.1 *An inkjet printer — Canon i850 and a laser printer — Brother HL1870.*

A printer is a device which is used to produce a printout or a hard copy of the output from a computer. Both laser and inkjet printers are able to produce monochrome (black and white) and colour images.

Laser printers

Laser printers use a special powder called toner to produce the image on the paper. A laser beam is used to project the image of the page to be printed onto a cylinder known as a drum. The toner sticks to the parts of the drum which have the image on them. The paper is passed over the drum and the toner is transferred to the paper. The paper, now with the toner on it, is then passed between heated rollers, to melt and seal the toner onto the paper. If you have used a laser printer, you will notice that the printouts are warm to the touch.

Figure 17.2 *Black and colour laser toner cartridges.*

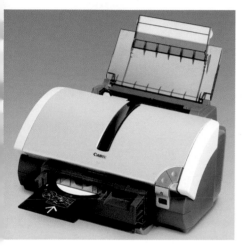

Figure 17.3 *Printing on CD.*

Figure 17.4 *Black and colour ink cartridges.*

A monochrome laser printer uses only black toner. A colour laser printer uses four different colours of toner: cyan, magenta, yellow and black, to produce the different printable colours.

Inkjet printers

Inkjet printers are quiet in operation and can produce a high quality printout of both graphics and text. They are particularly good at producing photographic printouts and can print on different surfaces, even on CDs.

An inkjet printer works by squirting small droplets of ink onto paper through tiny holes in the print head. The number of holes in the print head determines the printer's **resolution**. Most modern inkjet printers hold two ink cartridges, one with black ink and one containing three different colours, cyan, magenta and yellow.

Photo printing

Apart from printing text, inkjet printers are used mostly to print hard copies of photographs taken by a digital camera and stored in its memory card. To make this task easier, some inkjet printers have memory card slots so that photographs stored on a card may be printed out without needing to first load the photographs into a computer system.

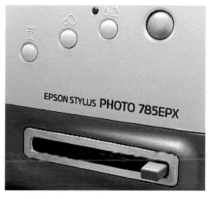

Figure 17.5 *A card slot on an inkjet printer.*

Alternatively, it is possible to connect a digital camera directly to a printer. Some printers have small LCD screens to help with printing photographs.

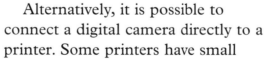

Figure 17.6 *Printing directly from a digital still camera and an LCD screen on a printer.*

Comparison of printers

In this comparison the numbers used have all been obtained from printers that have a standard A4 paper size. Numbers for A3 or larger printers have not been used.

Resolution

A printer's accuracy is known as its **resolution**. Resolution is measured in **dots per inch (dpi)**.

A typical laser printer will print at resolutions from 300 x 300 dpi up to 2400 x 1200 dots per inch. A typical inkjet printer will print at resolutions of 360 x 360 dpi up to 2880 x 720 dpi.

Speed

The speed of a printer is measured in **pages per minute (ppm)**. Typical speeds for laser printers are from 4 to 32 pages per minute. Inkjet printers typically have print speeds between 2 and 15 pages per minute.

Cost

The **capital cost** of a printer is how much it costs to buy the printer. The capital cost of a printer depends upon the **resolution** and the **speed**. A fast printer capable of printing at a high resolution will cost more. The **running cost** is how much it costs to use the printer. The running cost depends upon the cost of the electricity, the paper and the ink or toner and any maintenance required.

Capital costs

The capital cost of laser printers can range in price from under £100 to £2000 or more. Inkjet printers range in price from £30 to £300 or more.

Running costs

Black ink cartridges for inkjet printers can be quite expensive at around £10–£15, and colour at around £15–£25. Many companies recycle and refill old cartridges, which can reduce the cost by half or more. Some inkjet cartridges have an embedded microchip which monitors the ink level.

The number of pages obtainable from a black ink cartridge ranges from 500 to 900. The number of pages obtainable from a three-colour ink cartridge ranges from 200 to 500.

Toner for a laser printer costs between £30 and £200 per cartridge. This typically allows between 3000 and 8000 pages to be printed, depending upon the page coverage. If you are refilling a colour laser printer, you may have to buy four toner cartridges (one

Figure 17.7 *Inkjet cartridges with a built-in microchip.*

for each colour), although it is unlikely that they will all run out at the same time. Like inkjet printer cartridges, laser toner cartridges can be refilled. This can reduce the running costs.

The cost of electricity used to run an inkjet printer is relatively low. Laser printers use more electricity than inkjet printers because they have to heat the paper in order to melt the toner. Some laser printers also have a cooling fan inside. Laser printers can reduce their use of electricity by going into standby mode if they are switched on but not actually printing.

The cost of paper is the same for both printers only if they are using the same paper. Most users use photocopier paper as standard. The running costs can increase dramatically if sticky labels, envelopes, special photo quality glossy paper or colour transparency film is being used.

More about the running costs of inkjet printers

One disadvantage of a single three-colour cartridge system is that only rarely are the three different inks all used up at the same rate. If the printer detects that one of the colours has run out, it will send a signal to inform the user that the colour cartridge needs to be replaced.

Unfortunately the printer will then refuse to print until the colour cartridge is replaced, even if the required printout will use only black ink. Recognising this as a concern, many inkjet printers are now fitted with separate colour ink cartridges which can be replaced individually.

If you price a black inkjet cartridge at £15, and a colour inkjet cartridge at £20, then would you be surprised to learn that a new inkjet printer can be bought for £30? Printer manufacturers do this because they know that users will be obliged to pay for ink. Users have countered this by refilling the cartridges themselves. Manufacturers have tried to stop users from refilling by introducing cartridges with a microchip, which tells the printer that the cartridge is empty even if it has been refilled. Manufacturers state that using other makes of ink can invalidate any warranty on the printer. The consequence of all of this is that a lot of money is being made by manufacturers, plus many specialist cartridge refill companies who provide refilled cartridges at half or less than the price of manufacturers originals.

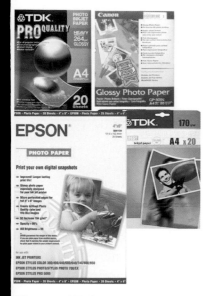

Figure 17.8 *High quality inkjet printer paper.*

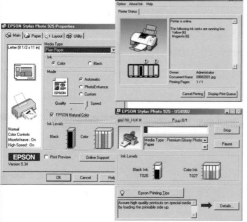

Figure 17.9 *Printer ink status.*

Did you know?

That one consumer organisation has calculated the cost of printer ink at around £1.70 per millilitre. Vintage champagne costs 23 pence per millilitre. Compare some other liquids. Milk costs around 50p a litre. Petrol costs around 80p a litre. Printer ink costs around £1,700 a litre.

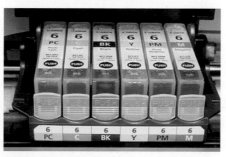

Figure 17.10 *Separate colour inkjet cartridges.*

Plotters

Figure 17.11 *A flat bed plotter.*

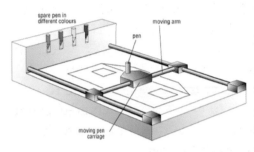

A **plotter** is another device for producing hard copy of the output from a computer. The difference between a printer and a plotter is that a plotter uses a pen to draw the computer output onto paper. There are two main types of plotter, **flatbed** and **drum**.

On a **flat bed plotter**, like the one in figure 17.11, the paper is fixed and the pen moves in two dimensions (up and across — XY).

On a **drum plotter** the pen moves in one dimension and the paper is moved in the other dimension by the rotation of the drum. Figure 17.12 shows a drum plotter.

By using several different coloured pens you can get colour output from plotters. Plotters are capable of producing very accurate drawings and are most often used in computer aided design (CAD).

Although many pen plotters are still in use for CAD applications, many current plotters use the same inkjet technology as ordinary inkjet printers instead of coloured pens.

Figure 17.12 *A drum plotter.*

Monitors and VDUs

A **monitor** is an output device, which accepts a video signal directly from a computer and displays the output on a **screen**. A **visual display unit** (or **VDU**) is made up of a monitor and a keyboard. The **screen** is the part of a monitor or VDU, which displays the output.

A monitor gives a higher quality output than would be obtained by connecting the computer to a television set. Monitors are available in monochrome (black and white) and colour as well as in different **resolutions**. A high resolution monitor will be able to show very fine detail on the screen compared to a low resolution monitor. It is important to choose a monitor of a suitable resolution to avoid eye strain, especially when using an application such as a word processor which displays a lot of text on the screen.

Figure 17.13 *CRT and TFT monitors.*

Another difference between a monitor and a television set is that a monitor does not usually have a tuner, so on its own it cannot receive television broadcasts. A monitor may have one or more loudspeakers which can output sound.

The two types of monitor that we will look at are cathode ray tube (CRT) and liquid crystal display (LCD).

CRT monitors

The most common type of monitor is the cathode ray tube or CRT. A CRT looks just like a large electric light bulb with a flat end where the image is displayed. The inside of the flat end of a colour CRT is coated with substances which glow when they are hit by electrons. The coating is arranged in sets of three dots, one red, one green and one blue. Three separate beams of electrons are focused on the dots, making each dot glow to a greater or lesser extent in order to produce a picture element or pixel of the required colour and brightness. A large number of these pixels taken together is used to make up a complete image on the screen.

The quality of the display depends upon the screen resolution, which is the *number of horizontal pixels* in a row x the *number of vertical rows*, together with the dot pitch. The dot pitch is the distance between adjacent dots of the same colour, usually between 0.22 mm and 0.3 mm.

LCD monitors

A basic liquid crystal display consists of a thin layer of fluid sandwiched between two sheets of plastic. Complicated wiring is used to apply voltages to different points, changing the ability of the liquid to reflect or transmit light. So a liquid crystal display is built up of light and dark dots (pixels) of varying intensity. A colour display has three layers of different coloured liquid and each layer has its own wiring. The pixels in a liquid crystal display have to be switched on and off individually. There can be as many as 2.3 million red, blue and green pixels in a 1024 x 768 display.

Passive matrix addressing is one method of switching these pixels on and off, but it is a slow process and can lead to smearing or ghosting on the display when the picture changes. Passive matrix LCDs are used for small, low resolution devices like calculators and watches.

Active matrix thin film transistor (TFT) displays avoid these problems by using a separate transistor to control each pixel, which is a much faster process, and also results in a display with improved clarity and colour. Active matrix TFT displays are used for high quality colour displays on notebook and laptop computers and increasingly as replacements for CRT monitors connected to desktop computers. By 2003, at least one computer manufacturer had stopped the production and supply of CRT monitors in favour of TFT monitors.

TFT screens have several advantages over CRT monitors:

- They are much smaller and lighter than a CRT and they use much less power (15-20 watts as opposed to 100-150 watts for a CRT). This makes them ideal for use on portable systems which have to rely on battery power.
- TFTs do not flicker like CRT monitors, nor do they give out static electricity or any other form of radiation.
- TFTs do not suffer from the reduction in viewable size that CRT monitors do. A 17 inch CRT has only around 15.8 inches viewable. A 17 inch TFT has the full 17 inches viewable.

TFT monitors do have some disadvantages:

- A limited viewing angle (although for certain applications this could be seen as a security advantage).
- They are difficult to produce without defects, which makes them expensive compared to CRT monitors.
- A TFT monitor cannot cope with as wide a range of resolutions as a CRT monitor can.

Loudspeakers

Figure 17.14 *Loudspeakers.*

A **loudspeaker** is a sound output device. Most computers have a built-in loudspeaker or can be connected to one or more loudspeakers. Computer systems sold as multimedia computers usually include so-called **active speakers** which are mains powered and have a built-in amplifier. Loudspeakers on a computer system are useful if there is only one computer in use, but not otherwise. When sound output is required from a classroom full of computers, then it is much more sensible to use **headphones**. If the computer is being used for developing a multimedia program or sound editing, then headphones will give a better sound quality than loudspeakers.

Sound card

Sound cards improve the quality of sound output from games and multimedia applications. Additional bundled software allows users to compose, edit and print music, record and edit digital audio, and play audio and multimedia CDs.

Sound is analogue in nature, it is a continuously varying quantity. Computers work in digital quantities. In order to output sound from

Figure 17.15
A sound card.

a computer the sound must be changed from digital to analogue. This process is called digital to analogue conversion. This is exactly the same process which is used when an audio CD is played in the CD-ROM drive of a computer or in a music CD player. Sound cards are capable of outputting a number of sound channels in high quality formats such as *Dolby Digital*.

Graphics card

Figure 17.16 *A graphics card — ATI All in wonder.*

A graphics card is a device which controls the quality of output on a monitor. Another name for a graphics card is a display adapter. Graphics cards often contain a large quantity of RAM and can support different types of screen displays at a variety of resolutions, for example VGA, SVGA and XGA.

Specialised user interfaces

People who are disabled in some way can often be helped to use a computer by having a specialised user interface with a computer system. For example, visually impaired users can use spreadsheets and word processors linked to voice output devices and magnified screens.

Voice output

When a computer produces speech (speech synthesis) on its own it is easily recognisable. By saving real speech onto backing store and telling the computer to play it back at the appropriate time you can get real speech output. Voice output is especially useful for users who have a disability such as visual impairment. Look back at the picture of the 'touch talker' device in chapter 16 (figure 16.14).

Combat aircraft — the use of a specialised output device

Computers can be used to prevent the pilot of a military aircraft from being overloaded with information during combat. Using a specialised output device built into the helmet's visor, the computer can alert the pilot to situations that require immediate attention without being distracted by irrelevant details.

Devices for virtual reality

Virtual reality is a method of reproducing the outside world digitally within a computer system and displaying it to the user in such a way that it allows them to interact with a wide range of situations. To take part in virtual reality, the user wears a headset with earphones and goggles, together with special data gloves rather than use a keyboard and monitor. You can read about the use of specialised input and output devices for virtual reality in chapter 16.

Use of a variety of output devices for multimedia

Figure 17.17 *A multimedia projector.*

Multimedia is the presentation of information by a computer system using graphics, animation, sound and text. Many of the output devices described in this chapter may be used for multimedia. A monitor may be used to output a multimedia presentation. A loudspeaker may be used to output sound for multimedia.

One development in presentations involves using a computer and multimedia projector as an output device. A multimedia projector is often combined with an interactive whiteboard, but many users prefer to use a multimedia projector on its own. A multimedia projector combined with a set of loudspeakers and a video recorder, satellite receiver or DVD player makes a very effective wide-screen television.

You can find out more about interactive whiteboards and multimedia in chapters 7 and 16.

Foundation level questions

knowledge and understanding

1. What is a hard copy?
2. State one difference and one similarity between a printer and a plotter.
3. State one difference between a monitor and a visual display unit.
4. How does:
   a. an inkjet printer work?
   b. a laser printer work?
5. What type of printer uses toner?

problem solving

1. Which type of printer can print on a CD?

General level questions

knowledge and understanding

1. What is mean by the terms:
   a. capital cost?
   b. running cost?
2. What units is the:
   a. speed
   b. resolution
   of a printer measured in?
3. Which three colours are used in colour printing?
4. What does CRT stand for?
5. What does LCD stand for?
6. What does TFT stand for?

problem solving

1. What factors influence the:
   a. capital cost
   b. running cost
   of a printer?
2. Why are individual colour cartridges replacing some three-colour cartridges on inkjet printers?
3. What use is the small LCD screen found on some inkjet printers?
4. Why are some inkjet printers fitted with memory card slots?
5. What advantages do TFT monitors have over CRT monitors?

Credit level questions

knowledge and understanding

1. How is the resolution of a CRT monitor measured?
2. What does the term dot pitch mean?
3. What is a sound card?
4. What is a graphics card?
5. What is speech synthesis?
6. What output device is used in virtual reality?
7. What would you use a multimedia projector for?

problem solving

1. State one problem associated with passive matrix displays.

• Key points •

- All the physical parts that make up a computer system are known as the hardware.
- A single item of hardware is called a device.
- Examples of output devices are:
  - printer: laser printer, inkjet printer
  - plotter
  - monitor
  - VDU
  - liquid crystal display (LCD)
  - thin film transistor (TFT)
  - sound card
  - graphics card
  - specialised output devices for disabled users and virtual reality
  - output devices for multimedia
- Using specialised input and output devices with a computer system can often help people who are disabled in some way.
- A variety of output devices are used for multimedia.

18 Backing storage

What is backing storage?

The physical parts of a computer system are known as **hardware.** A single item of hardware is called a **device. Backing storage** is used to store permanently programs and data. Computers need backing storage because data in the main memory is lost when the computer is switched off. Magnetic tape, floppy disks, hard disks, CD-ROMs and DVD-ROMs are all examples of backing storage **media** and the hardware that uses or holds the media is known as a **backing storage device**. Be careful not to confuse the terms media and software.

Remember: software means programs or data not disks!

We will look at the types of backing storage devices and media given in table 18.1 in this chapter.

In addition, we will carry out a comparison of backing storage, in terms of speed (data transfer), cost and capacity.

We will also look at backing storage requirements for different applications.

Backing storage devices	Backing storage media
Tape drive	Magnetic tape
Floppy disk drive	Floppy disk
Hard disk drive	Hard disk
CD-ROM drive	CD-ROM
DVD-ROM drive	DVD-ROM
CD Rewriter drive	CD-Recordable
CD Rewriter drive	CD-Rewriteable
DVD Rewriter drive	DVD-Recordable
DVD Rewriter drive	DVD-Rewriteable
USB Flash Drive	Flash ROM

Table 18.1

Magnetic tape

Figure 18.1
A DAT and a DAT drive.

Magnetic tape is a backing storage medium which uses plastic tape coated on one side with magnetic material. It is many years since audiotape cassettes were the only backing storage medium on home computers, but magnetic tape is now widely used as a backup system for computer data. The system, which is most commonly used for this, is **digital audio tape (DAT)**. DAT was originally designed to hold high quality audio as a replacement for audio cassettes. DAT is the standard used in professional recording environments for creating audio CD masters.

DAT is a sequential access medium, which makes it ideal for routine backups and long term archiving of data. Loading and saving individual programs on magnetic tape takes much longer than from floppy or hard disks, so magnetic tape isn't used where speed of access to data is important.

Capacity depends upon the length of tape being used. Because the backing storage capacity of hard disks is now measured in gigabytes, tape is one of the few types of media that allows a complete hard disk to be backed up on a single tape. Tape is also relatively inexpensive in terms of capacity compared to other media. Backups made on DAT are often compressed to allow more data to fit on a single tape. Restoring a compressed file from a backup means that it must be uncompressed before use.

Floppy disks

Figure 18.2 *A floppy disk and a floppy disk drive.*

A floppy disk is a plastic disk coated with magnetic material and enclosed in a rectangular cover of hard plastic. Disks have a metal flap which covers the read/write area. The inside of the cover is coated with tissue paper, which cleans the disk as it spins around in the disk drive. Floppy disks are called 'floppy' because the disk is made of a thin flexible material. They are easily damaged and you must be careful when using them. If the disk is damaged you could lose all the data it contains. This is one good reason why you should always keep a backup copy of anything you have on a floppy disk.

Formatting floppy disks

Before you can use a floppy disk in your computer it must be prepared in a special way. This process if called formatting. Formatting produces invisible circles, called tracks of magnetism on the surface of the disk. You can see these in figure 18.3. A disk doesn't look any different after it has been formatted — you can't see the tracks or tell by looking at it. But if you try to use an unformatted disk you won't be able to save any data. By the same token, if you format or initialise a disk which already contains data, then all the data will be lost.

There are many different types of disk formats. If you format a disk on one type of computer system, it may not be readable on another. For example, Macintoshes and PCs have a number of different disk formats. One tip to remember, if you want to make your disks compatible with both of these systems, then format the disks on a PC and they will be readable by both systems. If you want to make your files interchangeable, then use the same application to create or read your files.

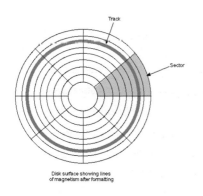

Figure 18.3 *Formatting a floppy disk. You can't see the tracks on the disk, because they're circles of magnetism.*

Figure 18.4 *An Iomega ZIP drive and disk.*

Write protection

If you format a disk that already has data on it you will lose all that data. To stop accidents like this from happening, floppy disks have a 'write protect' notch. The hard plastic case has a slider in it which you can use to open or close the notch as you want. When the notch is open the disk is write protected. When the notch is covered, the disk is write protected or read only — you can't write anything to that disk.

A floppy disk has a capacity of 1.44 megabytes. Floppy disks are useful for saving small amounts of data but they are now being used less often because of their low capacity. Most software is now distributed on CD-ROM rather than floppy disk, and many files are now easily downloadable via the Internet in a few minutes. Several manufacturers no longer produce computer systems containing floppy disk drives.

'Super disks'

In the past few years, new types of magnetic disk have been developed. These disks have a much higher storage capacity than ordinary floppy disks. These removable disks can only be used in special disk drives. This may be a disadvantage to a user who wishes to share files with someone else — the other person would need to have the same type of disk drive in order to read the disk. One of the most popular 'super disks' in current use is the Iomega ZIP disk, which has capacities ranging from 100 to 750 megabytes.

Hard disks

Figure 18.5 *Inside a hard disk drive.*

A hard disk is a circular metal disk coated with magnetic material. Hard disks are usually sealed inside a hard disk drive and cannot be removed, though you can buy external hard drives which can be easily transported between computers. Hard disks are used because you can store much more data on them and access the data more quickly than with floppy disks.

How a hard disk works

A hard disk drive normally contains several disks stacked on top of each other with a gap between them — you can see how in figure 18.6. The gaps are needed so the read/write heads on the disk drive can move across the disk surface and reach the tracks nearest the centre of the disk.

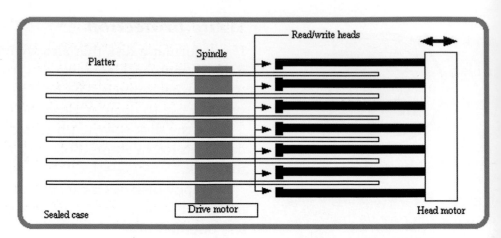

Figure 18.6 *A hard disk drive.*

Hard disks rotate very fast and the gap between the read/write heads and the surface of the metal disk is tiny. If you bump or drop the hard disk drive while it is switched on, or switch it off without shutting it down properly, the heads could collide with the surface of the disk. This is called **crashing** and it usually results in all the data on the disk being lost. The disk itself could also be permanently damaged. If you treat a hard disk properly it is much more reliable than a floppy disk.

Hard disks can load and save programs faster than floppy disks. It takes a second or two for the disk drive to start spinning the floppy disk around before the read/write head can move to the right track but a hard disk drive is spinning all the time and much faster than a floppy disk, so there is only a fraction of a seconds delay before the read/write head can reach the correct track.

Hard disks can store more data than magnetic floppy disks. You can store more on a hard disk than on a floppy disk because the read/write head in a hard disk drive is very small and the tracks can be packed together closely when the disk is formatted.

CD-ROM (Compact Disk Read Only Memory)

A CD-ROM looks just like an audio compact disk. CD-ROMs can store nearly five hundred times the amount that you can get onto a floppy disk. A CD-ROM disk comes with information already stored on it so it doesn't need to be formatted. A CD-ROM disk is read only, so you can't erase the data on it. Many software companies distribute their programs on CD-ROM.

A CD-ROM is 120 mm in diameter and 1.2 mm thick. When a CD-ROM is made, the data is moulded into tiny holes called **pits** on the clear plastic disk. The plastic disk is then coated with a reflective metal layer and then a protective lacquer. The pits are arranged in a spiral starting in the centre of the disk. If it were

possible to unwind the spiral of data on a CD-ROM and lay it in a straight line, it would stretch for three and a half miles.

The data is read from a CD-ROM by focusing a laser beam through the clear plastic onto the tracks. When the laser light strikes the area between the pits, (these areas are called lands) it is reflected into a photo-detector, and light which hits a pit is scattered and absorbed. The result is that the series of pits and lands in the surface of the disk are interpreted as a series of corresponding 0s and 1s which makes up the data.

CD-ROMs should be treated with care, because scratches on the label side can enable air to penetrate and cause the metal layer to oxidise, making the disk unusable. On the other surface, the laser focuses on a layer within the clear base and small scratches have no effect.

CD-ROM drives must have extensive error correction features. This is not as important in an audio CD where a single bit being read incorrectly will be unlikely to be noticed. However, a single bit wrong in a computer program or a data file could have disastrous results.

Read/write heads on a CD-ROM drive are faster than ordinary CD players. One important difference between an audio CD player and a CD-ROM drive is that the read/write head in a CD-ROM drive *must* move faster than in an audio CD player because the CD-ROM drive must be able to access the different tracks on the CD-ROM in a random fashion. It's not so important when you're playing music to be able to leap randomly from track to track.

All new desktop and laptop computer systems have at the very least a CD-ROM drive. The current trend is to include either a 'combo' drive, which is a combination of a DVD-ROM drive and a rewriteable CD drive, or a rewriteable DVD drive, which can also read and write CD-Rs and CD-RWs. Some desktop computer systems have two such drives.

CD-Recordable and CD-Rewriteable

CD-R and CD-RW disks are the same size and have the same outward appearance as CD-ROMs. Writing data to a CD-R or CD-RW is called *burning* and a drive capable of writing to a CD-R or CD-RW is often called a *CD burner*.

CD-Recordable (CD-R)

The part of a CD-R which stores the data (the recording layer) is a layer of dye. A microscopic reflective layer, either a special silver alloy or gold, is coated over the dye. The colour of the disk depends on the particular combination of metal and dye used. Like a CD-ROM, a

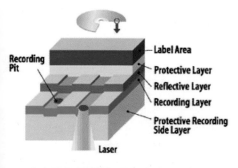

CD-R Structural Cross Section

Figure 18.7 *Recording on a CD-Recordable disk.*

CD-R writes data in a spiral pattern, which is formed on the disk when it is manufactured.

Data is written to a CD-R by using a high-powered laser beam which is focused on the layer of dye in the disk. When the laser shines on a tiny area of the dye, the dye is heated and a chemical change takes place. A CD-R's data is represented by changed and unchanged areas, in a similar manner to a CD-ROM's pits and lands. A low powered laser beam, which does not affect the dye, is used to read the data back from the CD-R. After a CD-R disk has been written to, it can be used in an ordinary CD drive as if it were a CD-ROM. One feature of a CD-R is that the whole disk does not need to be written to at once, instead data may be written in stages called *sessions*. However, once all of the available space on the recording surface has been used up, a CD-R behaves like a CD-ROM.

CD-R drives are classified according to their speed of recording. CD-R drives are now available which write data at around 50x normal speed. Given that a 74-minute CD-R disk takes 74 minutes to completely fill with data at single speed (1x), these fast recorders are a considerable advance.

CD-Rewriteable (CD-RW)

The fact that CD-R disks cannot be erased and rewritten has given rise to the development of CD-RW. CD-RW allows a user to record over data or to delete individual files.

Like recording data on a CD-R disk, a CD-RW disk works by using a laser beam to change the state of a recording medium. In the case of the CD-R disk, this recording medium is a dye which is permanently changed by a high-powered laser beam. In the case of a CD-RW disk, if it is to be erasable, then the recording medium must be able to have its change of state reversed. In simple terms, an example of a change of state is when ice (solid state) melts to form water (liquid state), and this may be reversed to form ice again. CD-RW disks use special chemicals for this purpose.

When a CD-RW drive is operating it uses a laser beam set at three different powers: high, medium and low. The high or *write power* is used to record data by changing the state of the recording layer to absorptive. The medium or *erase power* is used to change the state of the recording layer back to reflective. The low or *read power* is not powerful enough to affect the state of the recording layer, so it is used to read the data.

One disadvantage of CD-RW disks is that there is a limit to the number of times CD-RW disks may be rewritten, but this is several thousand times, so this restriction is unlikely to become a problem in normal use. CD-RW drives are dual function, capable of handling

Figure 18.8 *CD-Rewriteable disks.*

both CD-R and CD-RW recording, so the user can choose which recordable medium is going to be the best for a particular job.

CD rewriter drives are usually described as having three speeds, such as 48x10x32x. The first speed is the speed at which a CD-R may be written to. The second speed is the speed at which a CD-RW may be written to. The third speed is the speed at which any type of CD may be read. Blank CD-R and CD-RW disks are also rated for different speeds. The drive described above would be able to write to a 52x CD-R at its maximum speed of 48x. However, writing at 48x to a CD-R rated at only 32x may not work and the CD you create may be unreliable, or may only work on your drive and not on another one.

Figure 18.9 *Various types of DVD.*

DVD-ROM is a high capacity data storage medium, with the same overall size as a standard CD-ROM. DVD disks can provide from 4.7 up to 17 gigabytes of storage.

A DVD-ROM can easily be mistaken for a CD-ROM: both are plastic disks 120 mm in diameter and 1.2 mm thick and both use lasers to read data stored in pits in a spiral track. How is it possible that a DVD can hold so much more data than a CD-ROM?

There are several reasons:

- The tracks on a DVD-ROM are placed closer together and the pits are also a lot smaller than a CD-ROM.
- DVD-ROMs can have two layers on each side of a disk and DVD-ROMs can also be double-sided, but they need to be taken out of the drive and turned over to read the data on the other side.
- A DVD-ROM has more efficient error correction than a CD-ROM, and this means that more space on the disk is available to hold data.

DVD-Recordable (DVD-R)

DVD-R is a write once medium that can contain any type of information normally stored on DVD, such as video, audio, images, data files and multimedia programs. DVD-R disks may be used on DVD-ROM drives and DVD video players. DVD-R operates in a similar manner to CD-R, with recordable disks containing a layer of dye.

DVD-Rewriteable (DVD-RW)

DVD-RW uses more complex methods of recording data than the purely optical methods used for CD-R and DVD-R. A special format also allows data to be recorded on both the grooves formed on the disk and in the lands between the grooves. There are currently several different DVD-rewriteable standards available, each with a variety of capacities.

USB Flash Drives

USB stands for Universal Serial Bus. USB is a type of computer interface. Many different devices now use the USB interface, such as printers, scanners, external hard disk drives, mice and keyboards. USB Flash Drives are now becoming common. They are *solid-state* devices, because they have no moving parts. The media contained inside the USB Flash Drive is called flash ROM. Although flash drives contain computer memory chips, they are not used instead of RAM, but more as a substitute for a disk drive.

They are available in USB1 and USB2 formats, and are sometimes held on a key ring or a lanyard. One type of USB Flash Drive has even been incorporated into a wristwatch. They are much easier to use than a disk drive. Most computers recognise the devices and display the icon on the desktop the moment they are plugged in. The USB connection means that the device is compatible with many different computer systems and is easy to connect. Their range of capacities from 16 megabytes to 1 gigabyte makes them suitable for a large number of applications, from storing digital photographs to transporting multimedia presentations.

Figure 18.10
A USB Flash Drive, showing the USB2 logo.

Figure 18.11
A watch incorporating a USB flash drive.

All new computer systems are now fitted with USB interfaces, and fewer manufacturers are fitting floppy disk drives. While the cost of USB Flash Drives continues to fall and their capacity increases, it would be a reasonable expectation in the future that USB Flash Drives would take over the role of floppy disks and even so-called 'super disks'.

Comparison of backing storage

In this section, backing storage is compared in terms of speed (data transfer), cost and capacity. The speed of data transfer to and from backing storage is dependent upon the type of media in use and the hardware of the computer system. One of the main

factors is the type of interface between the backing storage device and the computer. For instance, an external hard disk drive with a USB1 interface has a much slower rate of data transfer than the same device with a USB2 interface.

Note that the costs given here are approximate. Note also that the general tendency with cost of media and capacity of media is for cost to go down and capacity to increase.

The comparisons are given in table 18.2.

Table 18.2

Media	Speed (data transfer)	Cost (approximate)	Capacity (range)	Read/write
Magnetic tape	Slow to find a program (faster for sequential backup)	£20 to £100	10 to 100Gb	Read/write
Floppy disk	Slow	£0.10	1.44 Mb	Read/write
Hard disk	Fast	£50 to £500	20 Gb to 1Tb	Read/write
CD-ROM	Medium	Depends on contents	650 or 700Mb (74 or 80 minutes of audio)	Read only
DVD-ROM	Medium	Depends on contents	4.7 to 17Gb	Read only
CD-Recordable	Medium	£0.25	650 or 700Mb	Write until full then read only
CD-Rewriteable	Medium	£1	650 or 700Mb	Read/write
DVD-Recordable	Medium	£5	4.7Gb	Write until full then read only
DVD-Rewriteable	Medium	£10	4.7 to 9.4Gb	Read/write
USB Flash ROM	Medium/fast	£10 to £200	16Mb to 1Gb	Read/write

Sequential and random/direct access devices

Suppose you have a music centre at home with a cassette tape recorder and a compact disk player. If you want to find a particular song on the tape, you have to play the tape from the beginning and listen to all the songs until you find the one you want. You can speed things up by fast forwarding or rewinding the tape to the position where you think the song will be, but it is still quite slow.

It is much quicker to find a song on a disk than on a tape. You can send the player directly to any track and it will start playing the song immediately.

Finding data on a tape is slow because you can only get the data back in the same order you recorded it onto the tape. Tape gives sequential access to data because the data can only be read back in sequence. A tape recorder is a sequential access device because it reads and writes data in sequence.

Disks can access data directly because the read/write head on the disk drive can go straight to the track where the data is stored without having to read all the data in between. Direct access is also called random access because you can read the data on the disk in any order, not just the order it was written in. A disk drive is called a random access device because the disk drive head can read data in any order.

Backing storage requirements for different applications

As you might expect, different application packages require different amounts of backing storage space on a computer system. There are two factors to be taken into account when considering the amount required. These are the space taken up by the application package itself and the space taken up by any files produced by the package.

The space taken up by the application package itself

The space taken up by the application package is more or less fixed when the package is installed on a computer system. The program files do not tend to 'grow' significantly, although some packages may have extra features added to them, for instance 'plug-ins' to programs like web browsers and graphics packages, as the user requires them. One other instance where the application package may increase significantly in size is when an update or a new version is released and installed.

Many packages offer several installation options. A *basic installation* loads enough of the package for the majority of users, and saves some backing storage space over a full installation. A *full installation* contains all of the features of the package, and may take up a considerable amount of backing storage space. A *custom installation* allows the user to choose which features of the package they require.

One choice, which users often have when installing a package from a CD-ROM, is whether or not they wish to insert the CD-ROM each time they want to use the program. If they choose to run the program from the CD-ROM, then only a small amount of backing storage is required.

The space taken up by any files produced by the package

Again, this depends upon the type of package. Any type of multimedia files such as music, high quality graphics or movies normally requires

a great deal of backing storage space. For example, one hour of digital video takes up 13 gigabytes of backing storage space.

Many files are compressed to save space. Common file types, which use compression to save space, include GIF and JPEG for graphics, MP3 for music and MPEG for movies. MP3 files are normally compressed by around 10 times. Make sure that you do not confuse backing storage requirements with RAM requirements.

Foundation level questions

knowledge and understanding

1 Name two types of backing storage media.
2 Name two backing storage devices.
3 What does DAT stand for?
4 What is the main use of DAT with computers?
5 Why are floppy disks called 'floppy'?
6 State one difference between a CD-ROM and a DVD-ROM.

problem solving

1 What two advantages do hard disks have over floppy disks?
2 Why are backing storage devices needed in a computer system?
3 What is the difference between backing storage and backup?

General level questions

knowledge and understanding

1 What is formatting?
2 What happens when a disk is formatted?
3 What happens when a hard disk 'crashes'?
4 What is a 'combo' drive?
5 What type of substance forms the recording layer on a CD-R?
6 In a CD-R, what are 'sessions'?
7 What is USB?
8 What is a USB flash drive?
9 Which backing storage medium would you choose if you needed:
   a. less than 1 megabyte of storage space?
   b. fast access to large quantities of data?
   c. compatibility with the maximum number of computers?

problem solving

1 Give two reasons why floppy disks are now used less often than they used to be.
2 State one advantage and one disadvantage of 'super disks' compared to ordinary floppy disks.
3 Why are CDs and DVDs sometimes called optical disks?
4 Why does a CD-R drive need to use two different powers of laser?
5 What is the main difference between a CD-R and a CD-RW?
6 If a DVD-ROM and a CD-ROM are the same size, how is it possible for a DVD-ROM to hold so much more data than a CD-ROM?
7 What can you NOT do to a write protected floppy disk? (Two answers please.)

Credit level questions

knowledge and understanding

1 Explain how data is stored on a CD-ROM.
2 Give two ways that a CD-ROM drive and an audio CD player are different, and one way they're the same.
3 What effect do scratches have on a CD-ROM?
4 Why is a sequential access medium slower than a direct access medium?

problem solving

1 What feature of magnetic tape makes it ideal for backup?
2 Why are different installation options an advantage for the user?
3 Why is data sometimes compressed?
4 Why is it important to know how a disk is formatted?
5 Why is it important to know the speed rating of CD-R media?
6 Why might a loudspeaker damage a floppy disk but not have any effect on a CD-ROM?

• Key points •

- All the physical parts that make up a computer system are known as the hardware.
- A single item of hardware is called a device.
- A disk drive is used for storing information on a disk. It is a backing storage device.
- Magnetic tape, floppy disks, hard disks, CDs, DVDs and USB Flash ROM are all examples of backing storage media.
- Backing storage is used as permanent storage for programs and data when the computer is switched off.
- DAT is used for backing up a hard disk.
- Disks must be formatted before they can be used to store programs.
- Formatting produces invisible tracks and sectors on the surface of the disk.
- A CD-ROM disk doesn't need to be formatted and it can't be accidentally erased since it is a read-only disk.
- Data may be written onto a CD-R or CD-RW using a CD rewriter drive.
- CD-ROMs use pits and lands to represent the data.

- CD-R/CD-RW disks use dye to record data in place of pits and lands.
- CD-RW allows a user to record over data or to delete individual files.
- Magnetic tape gives sequential access to data because the data can only be read in the order it was written.
- Disks give you direct access because the data on a disk can be read in any order, not just the order in which it was written.
- Hard disks are used because you can store much more data on them and access the data more quickly than with floppy disks.
- A DVD can hold more data than a CD-ROM because:
  - the tracks on a DVD-ROM are placed closer together and the pits are smaller
  - DVD-ROMs can have two layers on each side of a disk and can also be double-sided
  - a DVD-ROM has more efficient error correction than a CD-ROM.
- USB flash drives are solid state devices and the media is called Flash ROM.

- Different application packages require different amounts of backing storage space. There are two factors to be taken into account, the space taken up by the application package and the space taken up by any files.

19 Systems software

The **systems software** is a collection of programs that help the computer hardware to work properly. The systems software includes:

- the **operating system**
- the **filing system**
- **translator programs**.

This chapter is mostly about **translator programs**. We will look at the operating system and the filing system in the next chapter.

A set of instructions that a computer can understand is called a **program**. Programs are written in **computer languages**. Here are two programs, each written in a different computer language:

Program 1	Program 2
PRINT 'HELLO'	1000 1101
PRINT 'PLEASE TELL ME YOUR NAME'	1110 0011
INPUT YOUR NAME	1000 1101

Which one is easier for you to understand? Program 1 is written in a language very like English. A computer language that uses normal or everyday language is called a **high level language**.

The second example is not at all easy for most people to understand. This is because it is written in the computer's own language. The computer's own language is called **machine code**.

Need for translation

When you give an instruction to a computer in a high level language (like this: PRINT 'Hi There!') the computer changes the high level language into machine code so it can understand it before it can carry out the instruction. The instruction 'PRINT' in the example becomes '11110001' inside the computer. Only once the computer changes the instruction into machine code will it be able to carry out the instructions.

Like changing a sentence from Gaelic into English, changing a program from one computer language into another computer language

is called translation. Programs that carry out translations are called translator programs.

Purpose of high level languages

It is possible to classify high level programming languages according to the purposes for which they were developed.

The computer language BASIC is a high level language. The name BASIC is made up from the initial letters of the words **B**eginner's **A**ll-purpose **S**ymbolic **I**nstruction **C**ode. Thomas Kurtz and John Kemeny invented BASIC at Dartmouth College in the United States in 1964. BASIC was originally designed as a computer language to help beginners learn to program. BASIC is a very popular language and there are many different versions of the BASIC language. *TrueBASIC*, *REAL BASIC* and *Visual BASIC* are just a few examples.

Table 19.1 gives some high level languages and their purposes.

Table 19.1

High level language	Purpose for which the language was developed
ADA	Real time systems
ALGOL	General purpose
BASIC	Learning programming
COBOL	Commercial data processing
COMAL	Learning programming
C++	Creating applications, operating systems and games
FORTRAN	Scientific and mathematical
HTML	Creating web pages
JAVA	Internet programming
LOGO	Learning programming
PASCAL	Learning programming
PROLOG	Artificial intelligence/expert systems

Common features of high level languages

High level languages have a number of features in common:

- High level language programs are much easier to read and to write than programs in machine code because the program's instructions are like instructions written in everyday language.
- Programs written in a high level language must be translated into machine code before they can be run.

- High level languages should help the programmer solve problems. In the same way as someone who drives a car doesn't care about how every part of the car works while they're driving, a person who programs in a high level language doesn't care about what happens inside the computer when she tells it PRINT 'HELLO'. She is more worried about the result — whether the machine does what she wants it to do.

Types of translator

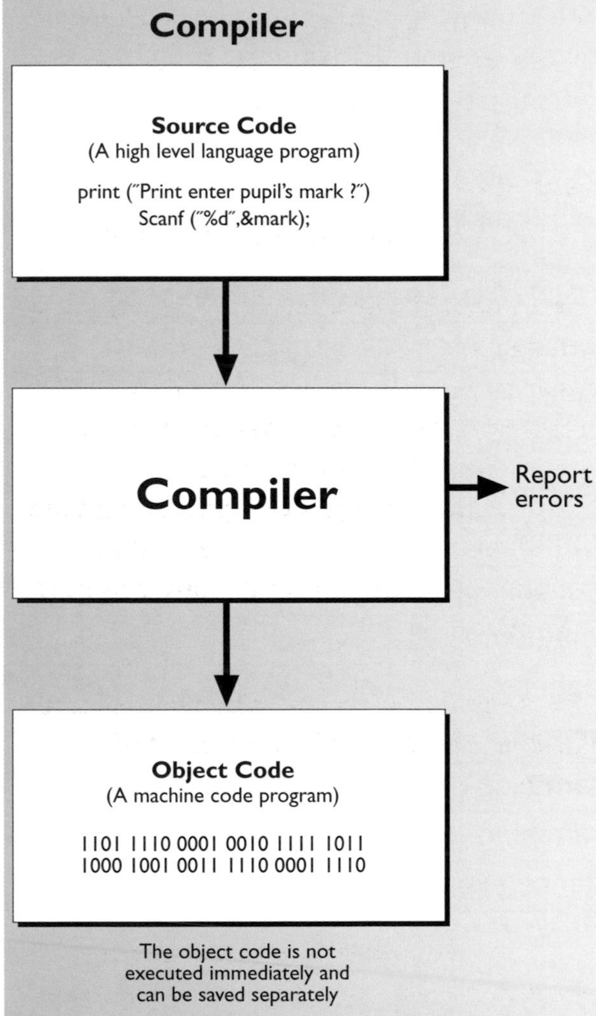

Compiler

Source Code
(A high level language program)

print ("Print enter pupil's mark ?")
Scanf ("%d",&mark);

Compiler → Report errors

Object Code
(A machine code program)

1101 1110 0001 0010 1111 1011
1000 1001 0011 1110 0001 1110

The object code is not executed immediately and can be saved separately

Figure 19.1 *A compiler.*

A translator program changes program instructions into machine code. Translator programs are used because writing programs directly in machine code is very difficult. It is much easier for the programmer to write the program in a high level language and then have it changed into machine code by the translator program in the computer.

Translator programs are part of the systems software of the computer.

You need to know about two types of translator programs for your Standard Grade course. They are called compilers and interpreters.

Compilers

A compiler is a program that can translate a high level language program into machine code in a single operation. The original high level language program is called the source code and the machine code program produced by the translation is called the object code.

The compiler changes each high level language instruction into several machine code instructions. The object code runs very fast because it is in the computer's own language, machine code.

The source code in the high level language isn't needed once it has been compiled and the object code can be saved and run on its own. However, you should keep the source code in case you want to change or update the program in the future.

The programming language PASCAL is a language which is normally compiled before it can be run. You can see a diagram showing how a compiler works in figure 19.1.

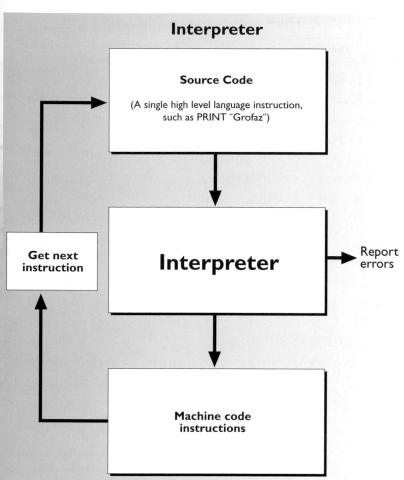

Interpreter

Source Code

(A single high level language instruction, such as PRINT "Grofaz")

Interpreter → Report errors

Get next instruction

Machine code instructions

Figure 19.2 *An interpreter.*

Interpreters

An **interpreter** is a translator program which changes a high level language into machine code one instruction at a time and then the instruction is carried out. Interpreted programs run much more slowly than compiled programs because the interpreter must translate each instruction every time the program is run. Unlike compilers, there is no object code produced by an interpreter. You can see how an interpreter works in figure 19.2. The programming language COMAL normally uses an interpreter.

Which translator?

Each translator has good and bad points:

- A program written in an interpreted language will run more slowly than a similar program which is compiled.
- Interpreted languages make it easier to find any mistakes in the code.
- A programmer using a compiled language has to wait until the compilation stage before the system will report any errors in the program.

Always remember that it is the compiled program which runs faster than the interpreted program. It is the speed of the translated programs that we are comparing.

Portability of software

The **portability of software** is whether or not you can run a computer program that you write on one computer system on a different computer system without altering it. The more easily it can be used on different systems, the more portable the program is. For example, if this BASIC program was typed into a number of different computers which had a BASIC interpreter, it would probably work without any changes.

```
CLS
PRINT "This program is portable"
END
```

Programs written in machine code are related directly to the processor and aren't portable.

Portability is very important for software companies. Imagine a company which has spent a long time and a lot of money to develop a game for a PC. If they could easily change their game to run on an Apple Macintosh computer as well as on the PC, the sales of the program would go up.

Portability is also important to individuals or organisations who own a number of different computers because a portable program would be able to run on all of their systems.

(Note that there is no detailed content at Foundation (F/G/C) Level in the arrangements document for the Systems Software Main Aspect.)

General level questions

knowledge and understanding

1   What is a high level language?
2   Give two features that the various high level languages have in common.

problem solving

1   Why must programs written in high level languages be translated before they can be run?

Credit level questions

knowledge and understanding

1   What is:
   a.   an interpreter?
   b.   a compiler?
   c.   source code?
   d.   object code?
2   What is meant by the term portability of software?

problem solving

1   A programmer has to write a program that will run fast. Which type of translator software should she choose?
2   Why is portability of software important?
3   Why should a programmer keep the source code for a program, even after it has been translated into object code?

• Practical work •

1   Choose one programming language from the list on page 265 and answer the questions below:
   a.   When was it invented?
   b.   Who invented it?
   c.   What was it invented to do?
   d.   How did it get its name?
     i.   Was it named after a famous person?
    ii.   Is its name short for something else?

• Key points •

- A set of instructions which a computer can understand is called a program.
- Programs are written in computer languages.
- The computer's own language is called machine code.
- Changing a program from one computer language to another is called translation.
- Translation is done by a translator program.
- The computer language BASIC is a high level language.
- High level languages:
  - are like everyday language
  - must be translated
  - are intended to help the programmer to solve problems.

- A translator program is used to change program instructions into machine code.
- Translator programs are part of the systems software of the computer.
- Two types of translator program are compilers and interpreters.
- A compiler translates a complete high level language program into machine code.
- An interpreter translates a high level language program into machine code one instruction at a time.
- Portability means whether or not a computer program can be run on different computer systems without being altered.

20 Operating systems

The operating system as a program

Most people probably don't realise that there is a program running in a computer from the moment it is switched on. This **program** is called the **operating system**. The operating system is part of the **systems software** of the computer. An operating system program is needed to control how the computer works and to control any **devices** attached to the computer.

The processor of a computer works much faster than the devices (such as a keyboard or a printer) attached to it. The operating system coordinates the activities of the other parts of the computer system so the processor is used efficiently.

What does the operating system do?

- It checks input devices like the keyboard and mouse.
- It manages the sending of data to output devices like the screen and the printer.
- It controls where programs and data are placed in the main memory of the computer.
- It manages the filing system.
- It controls the security of the system.
- It provides a human computer interface (HCI) for the user.
- It lets the user know if any mistakes have occurred.

EXAMPLE

Let's look at how the operating system helps a user who is using a word processing application program on a computer system.

- The operating system retrieves the word processing program from backing storage and puts it in the right place in the computer's memory.
- Each time the user presses a key on the keyboard, the operating system checks to see which key he has pressed and displays that character on the screen.
- When the document is finished, the operating system asks the user to name the file and then saves the document to backing storage.

- If the user wants to print the document, the operating system sends the data to the printer.

If you are using a computer on a network, you may have to type in your user identity and password before you're allowed on to the system. This process, called logging in, is also controlled by the operating system.

Memory management

The operating system controls where programs and data are placed in the main memory of the computer. For example, when a spreadsheet file is being edited, the computer's memory will contain the spreadsheet program, the spreadsheet data, and the operating system. If any of these three items is placed in the wrong place in the memory, then the program could stop working, the data could be lost, or the computer could crash.

Error reporting

The operating system lets the user know if any mistakes have occurred. For instance, if there is no paper in the printer while you are trying to print, then the operating system will display a suitable message.

File management

The filing system deals with how files are held on backing storage. It controls the processes involved in saving or loading a particular file from disk. You can read more about the filing system later in this chapter.

Human computer interface

The operating system provides a human computer interface (HCI) for the user. Most modern computers use a graphical user interface (GUI). One type of graphical user interface is a WIMP system. The way in which the WIMP system works is controlled by the operating system. The user may choose to tailor or customise the WIMP system to suit their own preference, for example, by displaying a different desktop picture or by choosing to look at a list of file names rather than icons in a directory.

It is helpful to separate out the different parts of the operating system so that each part can be described in more detail. However, you should remember that all of the parts of the operating system work together and not in isolation.

Interactive system

Most microcomputers operate using an **interactive system**. In an interactive system the user and the computer communicate, they **interact**, and the computer program responds directly to commands.

For example, in an interactive system, the user can type in a program and ask the computer to run it, or can load and run a program from backing store. If she finds any mistakes in the program or in the data she has entered, then she can make changes at once, and so interact with the program while it is being processed.

If you are using a word processing program, like I am just now, then you are interacting with the computer system. The characters appear on the screen as you type, and when the document is complete, it may be saved to disk.

When you are playing a game, then you are interacting with the computer system. As you press the keys or operate the joystick, the computer program is responding to your instructions.

Real-time systems

If you are booking a seat on an aircraft, the reservations program must give you an accurate, up to date picture of the seats available on a particular flight at any time. If the information isn't up to date, more than one person could book the same seat on the aircraft. To stop mistakes like this happening, the program must reserve your seat by updating the passenger list at the moment your booking is made. It must work in **real time**. Systems like this are called **real-time systems**.

Figure 20.1 *Interactive and real-time computer games.*

A program that controls a robot vehicle moving around a factory floor is working in real time. If the vehicle bumps into an obstruction it must be able to stop instantly. Real-time systems are also used in military applications such as missile guidance systems.

The difference between a real-time system and an interactive system is that *the speed of response in a real-time system is vital.* The speed of response in an interactive system is not vital. Look at figure 20.1

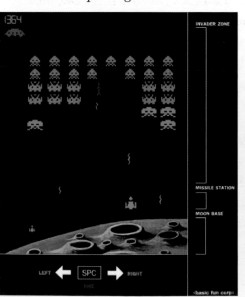

which shows screenshots of two games from the BBC website. The noughts and crosses quiz game is interactive because you have to give the correct answer to get a nought in your square, but you can take as long as you like to answer the questions. The space invaders game works in real time. If you don't shoot the invaders quickly enough, then you lose!

Interactive systems with background job capability

Suppose you are using a word processing program on a computer, and have just finished typing a document. You save your document to disk and print it out. You've now got another document to type, but have to wait for the printer to finish printing before you can get on with it.

It would be much more useful if the operating system of your computer allowed you to print the first document while you were typing the second document, because you wouldn't have to waste time waiting for the printer before you could continue with your work.

In fact, computers do allow you to do this. They have interactive operating systems, which let tasks like printing go on in the background while you're working. The tasks that go on like this are called background jobs, and the word processing, or whatever task the user is working on, is the foreground job.

This is an example of the way the operating system always tries to use the processor's time efficiently. A fast processor in an interactive processing situation, such as word processing, spends a lot of time (for the computer) waiting for the user to press a key — even the fastest typist can't type as fast as the computer can accept the data. The operating system uses these gaps to share out the processor time between word processing and background printing. Because the processor is operating so quickly, the user thinks the tasks are happening at the same time.

Device drivers

A device driver is a program which is an add-on to the operating system in a computer, to allow the computer to operate a particular device which is attached to it. For example, if you buy a new printer or scanner for your computer system, you may need to load a new device driver so that the device will operate correctly. The device driver is usually supplied on CD-ROM and must be loaded when the new device is installed for the first time.

Most modern operating systems can recognise when a new device has been connected to a computer system. If you use the Windows

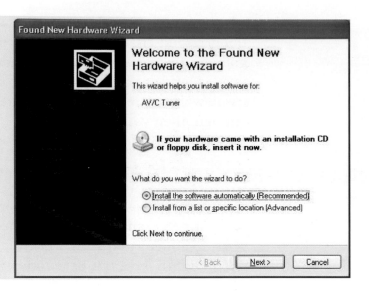

Figure 20.2 *Installing a new device driver.*

operating system, you will be familiar with the '*Windows has found new hardware*' wizard.

Printer drivers

Figure 20.3 *Printer drivers.*

Printers can produce many different printing styles, such as <u>underline</u>, **bold**, *italic*, and different typefaces, such as:

Times New Roman, Helvetica, Courier, Comic Sans, Arial

Before a printer can produce these styles, it must have the correct code sent to it from the computer. The code which is required for any given style is different depending on the type of printer that is in use. For example one code may produce **bold** print on a SAMSUNG laser printer and the same code may produce *italic* print on an EPSON inkjet printer.

To overcome this problem, **printer driver** programs have been developed. A printer driver takes the codes used in the document and translates them into the appropriate code for the type of printer in use. If the user has access to a monochrome laser printer via the office network, and a stand alone colour inkjet printer attached to their own computer, then all they need do is to select the correct printer driver. Some printer drivers are shown in figure 20.3.

Filing systems

A very important function of the operating system is managing your files on backing storage. The part of the operating system which deals with files on backing storage is called the **filing system**.

Types of file

Think about what happens when you are using a database of your friends' names and telephone numbers. You make up the database by entering the data into the program and then save your work to disk. To store the file on disk you must give it a name. Suppose you call your file '*Telephone*'. The file '*Telephone*' is called a **data file** because it contains the list of names and numbers which you entered. The database package itself, such as *Access* or *Filemaker*, is a **program file**, not a data file.

When you write a program in a high level language like COMAL or Visual Basic, you are creating a **program file** because it is made up of a list of instructions.

Hierarchical filing systems

The filing system used by modern computers is called a **hierarchical filing system**. An area where files are stored is called a **directory** or a **folder**. In a hierarchical filing system, each directory may contain other directories. These are called **sub-directories**. Each sub-directory may have other sub-directories in it, and so on. In figure 20.4 you can see a diagram of a hierarchical filing system.

Figure 20.4 *A hierarchical filing system.*

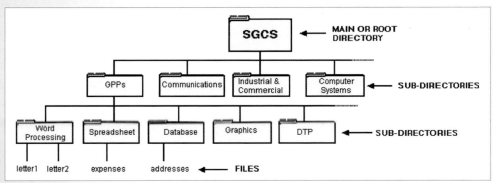

Imagine that a filing system is like the roots of a tree. The directory at the top level is called the **root directory** and all the other directories in the filing system are sub-directories of the root.

Advantages of a hierarchical filing system

- A hierarchical filing system allows you to create your own sub-directories to keep groups of related files. It is sensible to group related files like this, because it's much easier to find a file — especially when a single disk can hold hundreds of files.
- In a hierarchical filing system you are much less likely to give two files in a directory the same name. Each directory will also have fewer files in it, so it's easy to see all of the files in a single directory.

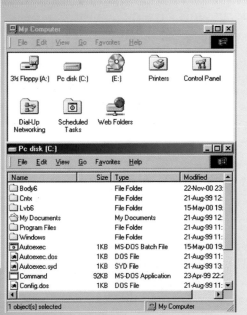

Figure 20.5 *A hierarchical filing system in use.*

Sequential and random/direct access to data

Suppose you have a music centre at home with a cassette tape recorder and a compact disk player. If you want to find a particular song on the tape you have to play the tape from the beginning and listen to all the songs until you find the one you want. You can speed things up by fast forwarding or rewinding the tape to the position where you think the song will be, but it is still quite slow. Finding data on a tape is slow because you can only get the data back in the same order you recorded it onto the tape. Tape gives sequential access to data because the data can only be read back in sequence.

It is much quicker to find a song on a disk than on a tape. You can send the player directly to any track and it will start playing the song immediately. Disks can access data directly because the read/write head on the disk drive can go straight to the track where the data is stored without having to read all the data in between. Direct access is also called random access because you can read the data on the disk in any order, not just the order it was written in.

Foundation level questions

knowledge and understanding

1   What is an operating system?
2   What is the name for an area in which files are stored?

problem solving

1   When does the operating system program:
    a. start running?
    b. finish running?
2   You have ten BASIC programs and five word processing documents on a disk. What could you do to organise these files?

General level questions

knowledge and understanding

1   What is meant by the terms:
    a. real-time system?
    b. interactive system?
2   Explain the difference between a data file and a program file.
3   Name the part of the operating system which deals with files on backing storage.

problem solving

1   Here is a list of applications. For each one, state whether it would use an interactive or a real-time system.
    a. Airline reservations.
    b. Word processing.
    c. Air traffic control.
    d. Entering a BASIC program into a computer.

Credit level questions

knowledge and understanding

1 What is:
   a. file management?
   b. memory management?
   c. error reporting?
2 What is a hierarchical filing system?
3 What is a device driver?
4 Name one type of device driver and explain what function it performs.

problem solving

1 The ability to process a background task is one way of improving the efficiency of the use of the processor of a computer.
   a. In what way does the operating system do this?
   b. Why does it improve the efficiency of the processor?
2 Why is it quicker to find a program stored on disk than a program stored on tape?
3 A disk is a direct access medium used in a computer system. Name one other direct access medium.
4 Clare installs extra RAM in her computer. Which part of the operating system makes sure that the RAM is used efficiently?

• Key points •

- The operating system is a program which is running in the computer from the moment it is switched on.
- The operating system controls the operation of the computer and any devices attached to it.
- The operating system does the following things:
  - checks input devices
  - manages the sending of data to output devices
  - controls where programs and data are placed in memory
  - manages the filing system
  - controls the security of the system
  - provides a human computer interface for the user
  - reports any errors.
- Most microcomputers use an interactive operating system.

- In an interactive system the user and the computer communicate and the computer program responds directly to commands.
- Interactive systems can process jobs in the background.
- Systems which are constantly updated are called real-time systems.
- Real-time systems are used for airline reservations.
- A device driver is a program which allows the computer to operate a particular device which is attached to it.
- A printer driver takes the codes used in the document and translates them into the appropriate code for the type of printer in use.
- The part of the operating system which deals with files on backing storage is the filing system.
- An area where files are stored is called a directory or a folder.

- Two types of files are data files and program files.
- In a hierarchical filing system, entries in a directory may be other directories.
- Magnetic tape gives sequential access to data because the data can only be read back in the order it was written.
- Disks give you direct access because the data on a disk can be read in any order, not just the order in which it was written.

21 Low level machine

Input, process and output

Most jobs that you do can be split up into three main stages:

- input
- process
- output.

This system is usually shortened to **IPO**. Here are some examples of how different tasks can be broken into these three stages:

- **Boiling a kettle**
  input — electricity and cold water
  process — heating
  output — boiling water.

- **Washing clothes**
  input — dirty clothes and soap and clean water
  process — washing
  output — clean clothes and dirty water.

- **Making toast**
  input — bread and electricity
  process — toasting
  output — toast.

- **Playing a CD**
  input — compact disk and electricity
  process — playing
  output — music.

You find the words **input**, **process** and **output** used all through this book because computer systems also work in this way. Like a washing machine a computer accepts input (which might be a list of names), processes the input (the list could be sorted), and gives output (a new list in alphabetical order).

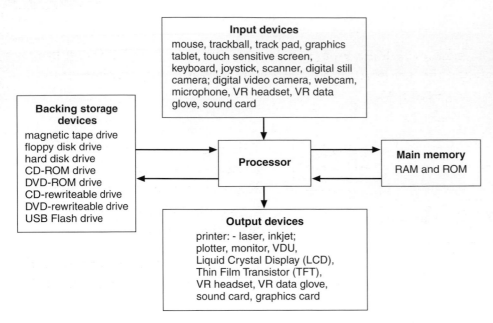

Input devices
mouse, trackball, track pad, graphics tablet, touch sensitive screen, keyboard, joystick, scanner, digital still camera; digital video camera, webcam, microphone, VR headset, VR data glove, sound card

Backing storage devices
magnetic tape drive
floppy disk drive
hard disk drive
CD-ROM drive
DVD-ROM drive
CD-rewriteable drive
DVD-rewriteable drive
USB Flash drive

Processor

Main memory
RAM and ROM

Output devices
printer: - laser, inkjet; plotter, monitor, VDU, Liquid Crystal Display (LCD), Thin Film Transistor (TFT), VR headset, VR data glove, sound card, graphics card

Figure 21.1 *Input and output devices used in a computer system.*

Input and output devices

To work through the stages of IPO, the computer system needs input and output devices. For example, to get the names into the computer in the first place, you could type them in using an input device like a keyboard. The new list, which is the output, can be displayed on a monitor or printed on a printer (these are both output devices). We looked at input and output devices in chapters 16 and 17. Some of the input and output devices used in a computer system are shown in figure 21.1.

Processing

The part of the computer which carries out the actual process is known as the **processor**. The processor can carry out a process only when it is given a set of instructions called a **program**. By changing the program, which is **stored** or held in the computer's memory, a computer can carry out a completely different process.

In order to give instructions to a computer, we must give them in a language which the computer can understand. The computer's own language is called **machine code**. You can read more about machine code in chapter 19.

You could think of the processor as the 'brain' or 'nerve centre' of the computer system. But the processor isn't like a real brain because a computer can't think or act for itself — it can only carry out the instructions it's given. Computers can carry out instructions very quickly because the processor can process millions of instructions every second.

Processor structure

The processor has three main parts. These are the:

- **Control unit**
  The control unit makes the computer carry out instruction of a program in the right order and controls the other parts of the processor.

- **Arithmetic/logic unit**
  The arithmetic/logic unit (usually shortened to **ALU**) does all the calculating (arithmetic) and performs the logical operations (it makes decisions).

Figure 21.2 *Processor structure.*

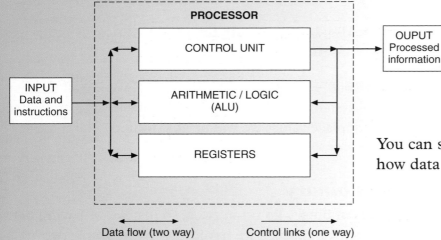

- **Registers**
  The registers are memory locations inside the processor. Registers are used to hold the programs and data while they are being processed.

You can see the main parts of the processor and how data is passed between them in figure 21.2.

How data is stored in a computer

Figure 21.3 *Some examples of two-state systems.*

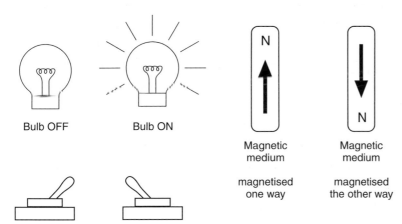

The processing and storage devices of a computer system have one feature in common — they can exist in one of two states, 'on' and 'off'. They are called two-state systems. You can see some examples of other two-state systems in figure 21.3. All of the codes which represent data in a computer system use only two numbers, 0 and 1. This number system is called **binary** because the word binary means 'two states'. Just as a light bulb can have two states ('on' or 'off'), a **binary number** has two values, 1 or 0 ('on' or 'off').

Representing numbers

Computers need some way to store data. In the binary system the two states 'on' and 'off' inside a computer represent the number 1 (for 'on') or 0 (for 'off'). A single unit in binary is called a bit. The word **bit** is made up from the two words **b**inary dig**it**.

Counting in decimal

Humans usually count in units, followed by tens, hundreds (ten × ten), thousands (ten × ten × ten) and so on. This is called the decimal system, from the Latin word for 'ten'.

For example, the number 5430 is made up like this:

```
1000   100   10   1 — these are the place values
   5     4    3   0 — these are the digits.
```

This means $5 \times 1000 + 4 \times 100 + 3 \times 10 + 0 \times 1$. We are all familiar with the decimal system and find counting like this easy to understand. By thinking about place values we will be able to understand the binary system.

Counting in binary

The place values in binary go up in twos, so instead of having place values of units, tens, hundreds we have units twos, fours (two × two), eights (two × two × two) and so on.

Let's look at a binary number made up of four bits:

```
8   4   2   1 — these are the place values
1   1   0   1 — these are the bits.
```

This binary number is 1101. This means $1 \times 8 + 1 \times 4 + 0 \times 2 + 1 \times 1$, which is 13 in decimal.

Practice with binary

Work out the decimal values of these binary numbers:

(a) 1001
(b) 1000
(c) 1010
(d) 0011
(e) 0000.

Now change these decimal numbers into binary numbers:

(a) 4
(b) 6
(c) 15
(d) 11.

Bytes

A binary number which is made up of eight bits (for instance 1101 0110) is called a **byte**. What is the largest number a byte can be?

Let's work it out. A byte is made of eight bits, and the biggest value of each bit is 1. If every bit in a byte had the value 1, you would get 1111 1111.

Now let's look at the place values for eight bits.

Place values	128	64	32	16	8	4	2	1
Bits	1	1	1	1	1	1	1	1

The value of this byte is 128 + 64 + 32 + 16 + 8 + 4 + 2 + 1, which is 255 in decimal.

Of course, a byte can have the value zero, so the smallest number a byte will have is zero (0000 0000). So a byte can hold a range of values from zero (0000 0000) to 255 (1111 1111), making a total of 256 different numbers.

Adding more bytes

In the decimal system we use the prefix *kilo* to mean 1000 ($10 \times 10 \times 10$, or 10^3). We use *kilo* in computing as well, but it doesn't mean 1000. One **kilobyte** is 1024 bytes. The reason why it is 1024 and not 1000 is because 1 kilobyte is 2^{10} (or $2 \times 2 \times 2 \times 2 \times 2 \times 2 \times 2 \times 2 \times 2 \times 2 = 1024$) — remember computers work in binary. We usually write one kilobyte as 1 **Kb**. A **megabyte** (which we write as 1 **Mb**) is 1024 kilobytes. One **gigabyte** (we write this as 1 **Gb**) is 1024 megabytes. One **terabyte** (we write this as 1 **Tb**) is 1024 gigabytes.

Main memory size

We measure the **main memory size** of a computer in megabytes or gigabytes because it is large. In most cases the main memory size of a computer is not fixed. You can buy extra memory and add it to a computer system, so you can use larger programs and keep more data in memory.

Representing text

A computer stores characters in its memory in bytes — one byte for each character. What do we mean by 'character'? A character is a symbol or letter on the computer keyboard. Characters include the digits 0 to 9 (these are the **numeric** characters), letters (these are the **alphabetic** characters) and punctuation marks (these are the **special** characters). The numeric and alphabetic characters together are called **alphanumeric** characters. a, b, c, A, B, C, 0, 1, 2, 9, &, £,

* are all characters. We worked out earlier that bytes have a range of values. Each value could stand for one character. How many different characters can we represent by using one byte?

The computer must be able to represent all the characters we might want to use. A list of all the characters which a computer can process and store (or which can be produced by a keyboard) is called the computer's character set. Different types of computer have slightly different character sets. So that a computer can represent all the characters it needs to, every character has a different code number in binary.

ASCII

The code that is most used is called the American Standard Code for Information Interchange — this is shortened to ASCII. Each ASCII character takes up one byte of storage. Many different computers use ASCII to represent text. This makes it easier for text to be transferred between different computer systems. You can read more about ASCII and other standard file formats in chapter 1. In table 21.1 you can see how some characters are represented in ASCII.

Table 21.1

Character	Binary	Decimal	Character	Binary	Decimal
Space	0010 0000	32	K	0100 1011	75
!	0010 0001	33	L	0100 1100	76
'	0010 0010	34	M	0100 1101	77
0	0011 0000	48	N	0100 1110	78
1	0011 0001	49	O	0100 1111	79
2	0011 0010	50	P	0101 0000	80
3	0011 0011	51	Q	0101 0001	81
?	0011 1111	63	R	0101 0010	82
@	0100 0000	64	S	0101 0011	83
A	0100 0001	65	T	0101 0100	84
B	0100 0010	66	U	0101 0101	85
C	0100 0011	67	V	0101 0110	86
D	0100 0100	68	W	0101 0111	87
E	0100 0101	69	X	0101 1000	88
F	0100 0110	70	Y	0101 1001	89
G	0100 0111	71	Z	0101 1010	90
H	0100 1000	72	a	0110 0001	97
I	0100 1001	73	b	0110 0010	98
J	0100 1010	74			

Representing graphics

Graphics or pictures on the computer screen are made up from tiny dots called **pixels**. The whole of the computer screen is made up of thousands of *pixels*. Each pixel may be 'on' or 'off' depending on whether the value of the pixel in memory is 1 (on – so you can see it) or 0 (off — so you can't see it). These graphics are called **bit-mapped graphics** because there is a direct relationship between the bits in the computer's memory and the picture displayed on the computer screen. You can read more about bit-mapped and other types of graphics in chapter 5.

Calculation of storage requirement of bit-mapped graphics

It is easy to calculate the **storage requirements of black and white bit-mapped graphics**. You begin by working out the total number of pixels in the graphic. Multiplying the height in pixels by the width in pixels gives the total number. Each pixel requires one bit of storage, so your answer is given in bits. To change bits into bytes, divide by eight, because there are eight bits in a byte. To change bytes into kilobytes, divide by 1024 and so on.

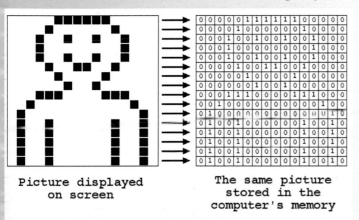

Picture displayed on screen

The same picture stored in the computer's memory

Figure 21.4 *How graphics are stored.*

Look at figure 21.4, which shows how graphics are stored in the computer's memory. The picture is drawn on a grid 16 pixels across and 16 down. A 1 represents grid squares, which are 'on', and a 0 represents grid squares, which are 'off'. The amount of memory needed to store this picture would be 16 × 16 bits — which is 256 bits or 32 bytes.

The picture would be more clearly defined or less rough if we used more and smaller pixels to make it up. You can see how reducing the size and increasing the number of pixels affects a picture by looking at the two graphics shown in figure 21.5. By doing this we can put more detail into the picture. This is called increasing the **resolution** of the graphics.

Think about the amount of memory used to store the picture on the right in figure 21.5.

It is 2666 pixels wide by 1764 pixels high.

The total number of pixels is therefore 2666 × 1764

= 4702824 pixels
= 4702824 bits (in black and white)
= 4702824 / 8 bytes
= 587853 bytes
= 574.075 **kilobytes**.

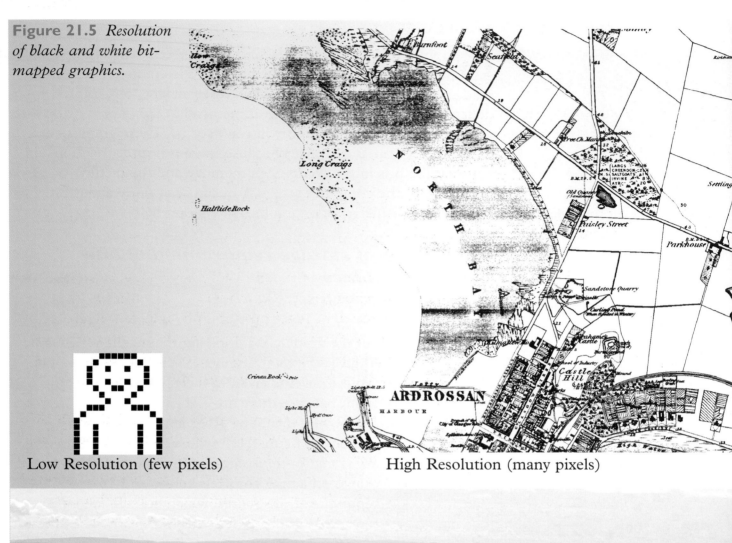

Figure 21.5 *Resolution of black and white bit-mapped graphics.*

Low Resolution (few pixels)

High Resolution (many pixels)

Figure 21.6 *A high resolution colour graphic.*

Credit level

Colour graphics

Calculation of the memory requirements for the storage of colour graphics is not required for this Standard Grade course. However, you may be interested to know that each pixel requires more than one bit in order to represent more than two colours or shades.

More about storage in memory

Do you have a good memory? Having a poor memory may be inconvenient or embarrassing for a person, but for a computer a poor memory would be a disaster. If it doesn't have a perfect memory the computer can't work properly, since it needs its memory to store programs and data before and after processing. A single error in memory would mean that a program wouldn't work.

The place where each item is stored in a computer's memory is important because the computer has to be able to find any given item of data. An item is stored in memory in a **storage location**.

Just as your home has an address, each storage location has its own unique **address** in the computer's main memory. If you look at figure 21.7, you will see how a computer can use an address to find a particular storage location. The method it uses to identify storage locations is called its **addressability**.

Suppose you were only allowed one digit to identify every house in the street where you live. In the decimal system you could have numbers from zero to nine — you could only identify ten houses. If you were allowed to use two digits you could have a hundred houses (0–99), or three digits, a thousand houses (0-999) and so on.

The number of storage locations in the computer's memory that a processor can identify depends on the number of bits in the address (in binary). A **one-bit address only** has two values, 0 and 1, so a one-bit address could only identify two storage locations, one at address 0 and one at address 1. With a **two-bit address** you could identify four locations (00, 01, 10 and 11). A three bit address could identify eight locations (000,001,010,011,100,101,110,111), and so on.

Table 21.2 gives some more examples.

Each storage location in a computer's memory can hold a single unit of storage which is called a word. A **word** is the number of bits that the processor can process in a single operation. A word can store one or more characters, or numbers, or an instruction to the computer.

Some computers process data in groups of 32 bits, so the word size is 32 bits. This is why computers are sometimes called 16-bit, 32-bit or 64-bit machines.

Figure 21.7 *Addressing memory.*

Address identifies house

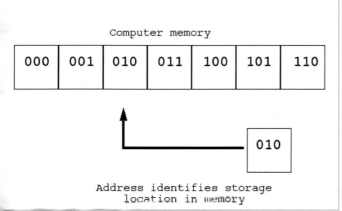

Address identifies storage location in memory

Number of bits in address	Number of storage locations that can be identified
1	2
2	4
3	8
4	16
5	32
10	1024
16	65536
20	1048576
30	1073741824

Table 21.2

Foundation level questions

knowledge and understanding

1 What is a:
   a. bit
   b. byte
   c. kilobyte
   d. megabyte
   e. gigabyte
   f. terabyte.
2 What is a program?
3 What is meant by the term stored program?
4 Arrange these terms in order of size, from smallest to largest: byte, gigabyte, bit, megabyte, kilobyte, terabyte.

problem solving

1 Where is a program stored in a computer system?
2 What units are used to measure the main memory size of a computer?
3 What is the function of the processor in a computer system?
4 Outline the IPO involved in formatting a disk.

General level questions

knowledge and understanding

1 What is machine code?
2 How are numbers represented in a computer system?
3 What range of values can be held in a byte?
4 What is meant by the term bit-mapped graphics?
5 What is a:
   a. character?
   b. character set?
   c. pixel?
6 What is ASCII?
7 Explain how ASCII is used.

problem solving

1 Why isn't the processor of a computer like your brain?

2 Why may it be an advantage if your computer uses ASCII to store text?
3 If someone sent you this message in ASCII, what would you send in reply?
   72, 69, 76, 76, 79, 32, 72, 79, 87, 32, 65, 82, 69, 32, 89, 79, 85, 63
4 Draw an 8 x 8 grid on squared paper. Use it to decode the following bit patterns:
   a. 11111111 01000010 00100100 00011000
      00011000 00100100 01000010 11111111
   b. 00111100 01000010 01000010 01000010
      00111100 00100100 01000010 10000001
   (Looking back at figure 21.4 might help you work it out.)

Credit level questions

knowledge and understanding

1 Name three parts of the processor.
2 Draw a diagram of the processor.
3 What is the function of the ALU?
4 What is the function of the control unit?
5 What is the function of the registers?

6 What is meant by the term word?
7 What is a storage location?
8 What is meant by the term addressability?

problem solving

1 How do we find a particular storage location in the memory of a computer?

2 How many bits are needed to identify 128 storage locations?

3 Prabhu says that his 64-bit computer system is faster than his friend Ravinder's 32-bit computer. Ravinder says that his is faster because it has an extra 256 megabytes of memory.
  a. What is a 32-bit computer?
  b. What advantage does Ravinder's extra 256 megabytes provide?
  c. Who do you think is correct?

4 Calculate the storage requirements of the following graphics:
  a. an icon 16 x 24 pixels
  b. a photograph 600 x 400 pixels
  c. a poster 2350 x 1876 pixels.

5 How many bits are used to represent a single pixel in black or white?

6 How many storage locations are there in a computer system with 1 gigabyte of main memory?

7 Why do computers use the binary system and not the decimal system to represent numbers?

• Key points •

- Most tasks can be split up into three stages — input, process and output.
- The part of the computer which carries out the process is known as the processor.
- A program is a set of instructions which controls the operation of the processor.
- By changing the program, which is stored in the computer's memory, a computer can carry out a completely different process.
- The processor is made up of three main parts — the control unit, the arithmetic/logic unit (ALU) and the registers.
- The processing and storage devices in a computer have only two states — on or off.
- All the codes which represent data on a computer use only two digits, 0 and 1. This is the binary system.
- A single unit in binary is called a bit.
- A binary number which is made up of eight bits is a byte.
- A byte can hold 256 different values.
- A byte is the space in memory which is used to hold one character.

- One kilobyte (Kb) is 1024 bytes.
- One megabyte (Mb) is 1024 kilobytes.
- One gigabyte (Gb) is 1024 megabytes.
- One terabyte (Tb) is 1024 gigabytes.
- The main memory size of a computer is measured in megabytes or gigabytes.
- A list of all the characters a computer uses is its character set.
- Bit-mapped graphics on the computer screen are made up of tiny dots called pixels.
- Bit-mapped graphics have a direct relationship between the bits in the computer's memory and the picture displayed on the computer screen.
- The graphics resolution may be increased by having a large number of small pixels.
- The place in memory where an item of data is stored is a storage location.
- Addressability is the method used by a computer to identify storage locations.
- A word is the number of bits which can be processed by the processor in a single operation.

Programming

This chapter is not a programming manual! It is an outline of how to solve problems by writing programs that are readable, easy to develop and easy to maintain. The information in this chapter applies to any programming language, although the examples given may not match exactly the programming language which you are using for your Standard Grade course. Your teacher will provide suitable examples for your own programming language.

The software development process

The software development process may be divided into seven stages. These are: analysis, design, implementation, testing, documentation, evaluation and maintenance. We will now look at an example problem, and at the same time describe each of the stages of the software development process as we work through the problem.

Example problem
Problem statement

```
The computer must take in a list of ten words, one
word at a time and count the number of words with
seven letters. The result should be displayed on the
screen.
```

Analysis

The analysis stage involves reading and understanding a problem.

The first thing you must do is think carefully about the problem. Here are some suggestions to help you. Decide what the problem is. Read the question carefully. Sometimes writing the problem in your own words helps you to understand it. Ask yourself if using a computer is the best way to solve this problem. Can it be solved more easily in any other way?

If you decide to use a computer to solve the problem, what information does the problem contain which you must enter into the computer? What must the computer do to this information? What must the output from the computer be? Write down the

headings INPUT, PROCESS and OUTPUT and write the answer to these questions under the appropriate headings.

INPUT
ten words

PROCESS
count the number of letters in each word
keep a count of any seven letter words

OUTPUT
the number of words with seven letters

What software do you have to help you solve the problem? Can a general purpose package like a spreadsheet or database help? If you decide to use a package instead of writing your own program, does the package have the features you need already built in? Can you program the package (for example using its special language) to solve the problem?

If you think you can use a general purpose package to solve the problem, you must decide what properties you need the package to have. The package must be able to handle text, to count and should be able to tell you about the length of each word. One type of package that might be able to do this is a spreadsheet. In figure 22.1 you can see a sample solution for this problem using Microsoft Excel (a spreadsheet).

Setting up the spreadsheet

	A	B	C	D
1				
2				
3	Spreadsheet	Solution for	Seven Letters	Problem
4				
5	Please enter	word 1		=IF(LEN(C5)=7,1,0)
6	Please enter	word 2		=IF(LEN(C6)=7,1,0)
7	Please enter	word 3		=IF(LEN(C7)=7,1,0)
8	Please enter	word 4		=IF(LEN(C8)=7,1,0)
9	Please enter	word 5		=IF(LEN(C9)=7,1,0)
10	Please enter	word 6		=IF(LEN(C10)=7,1,0)
11	Please enter	word 7		=IF(LEN(C11)=7,1,0)
12	Please enter	word 8		=IF(LEN(C12)=7,1,0)
13	Please enter	word 9		=IF(LEN(C13)=7,1,0)
14	Please enter	word 10		=IF(LEN(C14)=7,1,0)
15				
16	Total number	of words with	7 letters is	=SUM(D5:D14)

Sample run using test data

	A	B	C	D
1				
2				
3	Spreadsheet	Solution for	Seven Letters	Problem
4				
5	Please enter	word 1	Hello	0
6	Please enter	word 2	there	0
7	Please enter	word 3	I	0
8	Please enter	word 4	am	0
9	Please enter	word 5	looking	1
10	Please enter	word 6	for	0
11	Please enter	word 7	text	0
12	Please enter	word 8	with	0
13	Please enter	word 9	seven	0
14	Please enter	word 10	letters	1
15				
16	Total number	of words with	7 letters is	2

Figure 22.1 *Using a spreadsheet to solve the seven letters problem.*

Let's assume for the moment that you don't have access to a suitable spreadsheet. So what now? If none of the application packages have the features you need, you may have to write a program in a high level programming language like Visual BASIC, TrueBasic or COMAL.

Can you use any of the programs (or parts of programs) you've already written to help solve the problem?

Design

Design involves the careful planning of a solution to the problem using a recognised design methodology, for example top-down design. There are several ways of representing the design of a problem. Two methods are shown here.

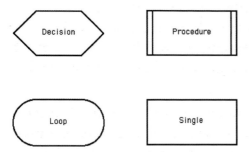

Figure 22.2 *Common symbols used in structure diagrams.*

Method 1: structure diagrams

Computer programs used in business and industry are often thousands of lines long. You're not likely to understand one of these programs just by looking at the printed listing. The programmer needs some way of describing the overall way the program looks (its structure) so it's easier to understand. One way of describing the structure of a program is to use a **structure diagram**. Structure diagrams use specially shaped boxes to show loops, decisions, procedures or single steps. Common symbols used in structure diagrams are shown in figure 22.2. These boxes are usually joined together by lines to form a diagram. The example in figure 22.3 shows how a programmer can link these boxes to describe the structure of a program.

Method 2: pseudocode

Break the problem down into its main steps and write them out in a list, using plain language that you can understand, instead of programming keywords.

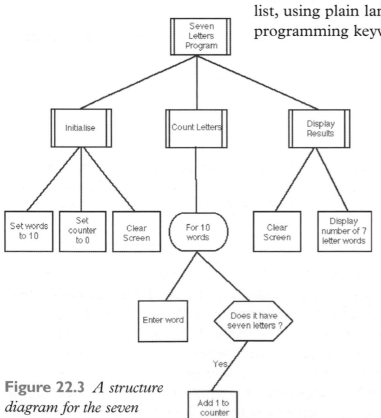

Figure 22.3 *A structure diagram for the seven letters problem.*

List of main steps for seven letters problem
1 Initialise
2 Count letters
3 Display results

Keep breaking down these steps into smaller ones — **refinements**.

Refinements
1.1 Set number of words to ten
1.2 Set counter to zero
1.3 Clear the screen

2.1 Start loop for number of words
2.2 Take in a word
2.3 If it has seven letters then add one to counter
2.4 End loop

3.1 Clear the screen
3.2 Display the total number of seven-letter words

When you can't break the steps down any further, you need to change each step into instructions in your chosen programming language. This is called coding.

User interface

A program's user interface is the way your program looks to the person who is using it. The user interface is part of the human computer interface (HCI) of the program. The screen layout, the prompts or instructions which appear, and the way it checks the input are all parts of the user interface. Let's examine these in more detail.

Screen layout

The way your program looks on the screen is important. If it is clearly laid out the user will find it easier to follow. A problem statement may well include a description of the way your screen must look to the user during input or output or while the program is running.

Prompts to user

A sensible programmer will always make sure they tell the user about what keys to press to operate the program, or what type of input to give.

EXAMPLE

```
PROC input      PROC input
CLS             CLS
INPUT cost      PRINT 'Please type the cost and press
                RETURN'
......           PRINT 'Use whole numbers from 1 to 20
                only'
                INPUT cost
                ......
```

If you run the program on the left in the example, you will see a blank screen and a question mark and you won't be told what you should type. The program on the right gives you the information you need to put in the right numbers.

Input validation

In any situation where the user can choose what they input, the program must check the input to see that it is what it needs (like text or a number). If a number has been put in, the program has to check the number is in the right range. These checks are called validating the data. If they are not done, even the most carefully written program will fail to work as it should, or might stop altogether (this is called 'crashing'). A well-written program will either not respond if the wrong keys are pressed or it will print a message on the screen and give the user a second chance to enter the data.

Implementation

Implementation is changing the program design into instructions that the computer can understand and the production of internal documentation.

Readability and programming style

Which of these program listings do you find easier to understand?

```
INPUT a
INPUT b
c = a * b
PRINT c
END
// Area 1 — a program to calculate the area of a
rectangle
// By Cecilia
// 07.07.07
//
PRINT "Please enter the length of the rectangle
(Type a whole number between 1 and 50)"
INPUT length
PRINT "Please enter the breadth of the rectangle
(Type a whole number between 1 & 50)"
INPUT breadth
area: = length * breadth
PRINT "The area of the rectangle is "; area
END
```

You probably find the second program listing easier to understand because:

- It uses ordinary words, like 'length' and 'breadth', instead of 'a' and 'b' for the names of the variables. When writing your code, *always* use ordinary words rather than single letters as far as possible. This is called using **meaningful variable and procedure names**.
- It makes use of **internal commentary**. In this language these are shown by //. We use comment lines to give information about a program, but they don't have an effect when the program is run. Including comments in your program listings helps to show anyone reading it what each part of your program is doing. Put comment lines at the top of the program to identify it: you should put the name of the program, your name and the date.
- It contains questions or **prompts to the user**, which make it clear what keys should be pressed.

- If you can, give the user an example of what they should enter. Telling them:

  `'Please enter a whole number between 1 and 20'`

  is much more helpful than:

  `'Please enter a number'`

- If you follow these three points when you're writing a program they will be more readable and easier to maintain.

Any programs you write should:

- be easy for yourself and for others to read,
- have a clear purpose and structure,
- be easy to maintain (change or expand later on).

Identifying and fixing errors

Types of error

There are three types of error:

- system errors
- syntax errors
- logic errors.

Let's have a look at them.

System errors

System errors affect the computer or its peripherals. You might have written a program which needs access to a printer. If there is no printer present when you run the program the computer will produce a system error message. Sometimes a system error makes the computer stop working altogether and you will have to restart the computer.

A sensible way of avoiding system errors like this is to write code to check that a printer is present *before* any data is sent to it. Then the computer would warn you by a simple message on the screen, like 'printer is not ready or available', so you can turn the printer on before you try to do any more.

Syntax errors

A syntax error is a mistake in the programming language (like typing PRNIT instead of PRINT). Programs which have syntax errors won't run.

High level language interpreters and compilers normally have a syntax checker built in to them. Some languages also contain special

Figure 22.4 *A system error.*

commands such as 'debug', which will report structural errors in a program (like forgetting to put ENDPROC at the end of a procedure definition). The programming manual for the particular language you're using will give details of error messages and what each message means.

Logic errors

A logic error is more difficult to detect than a syntax error. This is because a program containing logic errors will run, but won't work properly. For example, you might write a program to clear the screen and then print 'Hello'. Here is the code for this:

```
// Message
PRINT "Hello"
CLS // clear the screen
END
```

EXAMPLES

This code has a logic error in it, but the syntax is right so it will run. Can you see what the error is? What do you think will happen if you run this program?

PROGRAM 1

```
// Logic error 1
FOR times := 2 TO 10 DO
IF times=1 THEN PRINT "HELLO"
NEXT times
END
```

In this program the value of times never reaches 1 so 'HELLO' will never be printed.

PROGRAM 2

```
// Logic error 2
total := 0
REPEAT
total := total+1
UNTIL total=0
END
```

In this program the value of total will *always* be more than 0 and so the program will go on forever. This is called an infinite loop.

You can get rid of logic errors from simple programs by hand testing them, which means working through each line of the program on paper to make sure it does what you want it to do. You should do this long before you type in the code. Testing your program on paper first is also known as doing a *dry run*.

Here is the final program, which has been written in COMAL.

Program for seven letters problem
```
// Filename: Seven
// Seven Letters Program
// By Elizabeth Mary
// June 2007
//
initialise
count_letters
display_results
END
//
PROC initialise
number_of_words := 10
// counter counts up the number of seven letter
words
counter := 0
CLS
END PROC initialise
//
PROC count_letters
FOR times := 1 TO number_of_words DO
INPUT "Please type in a word ":word$
// If the word has seven characters, then add 1 to
counter
IF LEN (word$) = 7 THEN counter := counter+1
NEXT times
END PROC count_letters
//
PROC display_results
CLS
PRINT "You typed in ";counter;" seven letter words"
END PROC display_results
```

After you have typed your program into the computer, correct any mistakes and get the program working. Save your program.

Testing

The testing stage involves making sure that your program actually solves the problem it is supposed to. To carry out a proper test on a program you need to use a set of data, called **test data**.

The best way to use test data is to calculate what the answers will be if your program works properly, *before* you run the program. Then run the program with the test data. If the results from the program match the answers you got from your first calculation, the program's probably correct.

Testing a program

There are three different types of test data:

- normal
- extreme
- exceptional.

Let's look at part of a program which will help us to understand what we mean by normal, extreme and exceptional test data.

```
// date3 - a program to check that a date has been
entered correctly
// by Siobhan
// 08.08.08
//
REPEAT
CLS
PRINT "Please enter the day (1-31)"
INPUT day
PRINT "Please enter the month (1-12)"
INPUT month
PRINT "Please input the year (1954-2019)"
INPUT year
check_date
UNTIL correct
PRINT "Your date is correct - Thank You"
END
```

This program allows you to enter a date. It then uses the check_date procedure to check if you have put the date in correctly. The check_date procedure makes sure that:

- The number of days entered is within the range for the month (February 29 is only allowed in a leap year).
- The month number is in the range 1–12.
- The year is in the range 1954–2019.

Using test data

Here are appropriate test data for this program:

Normal — the program should accept this data

2.2.1989	(2 February 1989)
3.3.1954	(3 March 1954)
24.7.1980	(24 July 1980)

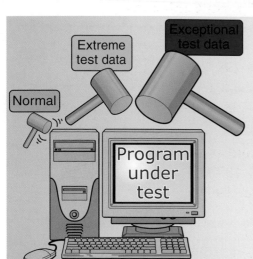

Figure 22.5 *Testing a program.*

Normal data is data which is well within the limits that your program should be able to deal with.

Extreme — the program should accept this data

1.1.1954	(1 January 1954)
31.12.1999	(31 December 1999)
29.2.1996	(29 February 1996)
31.12.2019	(31 December 2019)

Extreme data is data which is at the ends of this range — on the limit.

Exceptional — the program should reject this data

29.2.1993	(29 February 1993)
31.11.1994	(31 November 1994)
1.4.2000	(1 April 2000)
24.7.2020	(24 July 2020)

Exceptional data is data which is invalid. A well-written program should be able to detect exceptional data, warn the user of the error, and give them a chance to enter the data again.

Some commercial programs are so large and complicated that it is impossible to test them and be sure that you've got rid of all the errors. The programs used in some aircraft which have computerised controls are also so big they can't be tested properly. Any mistakes in this program could be very dangerous.

Figure 22.6 *Some programs are so large that it is impossible to test them completely.*

Any programs you'll be asked to write in your Computing course will be quite short and should pass all the tests that you can think up. You should try to write programs that are as free from errors as you can make them.

Depending on the problem you've been asked to solve, you might be given a set of test data to use, or might make up your own. If you have to make up your own test data, you should try to choose a set of data, which includes normal, extreme and exceptional data.

If your program doesn't produce the results you expect, you'll have to check through each line of the code. Sometimes it is useful to put extra statements into the program which will print out the values of certain variables at different stages of the run. This is called '*printing a snapshot of selected variables*'. It can help you find out where the program goes wrong.

Now you have coded your program, and it is time to make up test data. You should use several sets of test data to thoroughly test your program.

```
Hello, there, I, am, looking, for, text, with,
seven, letters
```

You would expect the output using this test data to be:

```
You typed in 2 seven letter words
```

Run the program a number of times using different test data as input. Check that your program produces the expected results when you enter the test data.

Print a **listing** of your program code. If you can, print a *sample run* or *test run* of your program using your test data as well.

Documentation

Documentation can be of two types:

- **User documentation**
  User documentation (this is often called the user guide) gives the instructions on how to use a program.
- **Technical documentation**
  Technical documentation explains what each part of the program code does. This would be useful to another programmer or to the person who wrote the program, if they decide to make changes to it later (maintenance). Comment lines are part of the technical documentation. The technical documentation also includes system requirements and installation instructions.

You might be asked to write a set of instructions to tell someone else how to use your program. This is the **user documentation** or **user guide**. Write some **technical documentation** for your program for somcone who wants to know how your program code works.

User documentation
Load the program and chose Run from the Program menu.
Follow the instructions on the screen. The program
will print out the number of words with seven
characters that you have entered. To run the program
again when it is finished, type RUN.

Technical documentation
The program is written in COMAL.
It was written on a Macintosh computer.
The number of words that can be taken in is set in
the line that has number_of_words := 10
The variable 'counter' is used to count the number of
words with seven letters.
The value '7' in line **IF LEN (word\$) = 7 THEN counter
:= counter+1** controls the length of the words which
are counted by the program.

Evaluation

Evaluation involves reviewing your solution against suitable
criteria.

Now, evaluate your solution. Does your program solve the
problem as you wrote it out in the analysis stage at the start? Is it
easy for others to use? Make a list of anything that could make your
program better. List any problems you had in doing the task.

Evaluation of seven letters problem
When the program is run, it works as expected and
gives the correct output from the test data.
The program has clear instructions and is easy to
use.
I could have improved the program by:
● allowing the user to enter the number of words
● allowing the user to enter the length of the word
  to be counted
● adding colour to produce a more attractive screen
  display.

Problems
When I started I didn't know how to find the length
of a word.
I solved this problem by looking up the keyword 'LEN'
in the COMAL programming manual.

Depending on the problem, you might not have to complete all of these stages to produce a fully documented solution. If you are doing a coursework task or a programming project, you will usually have to produce a solution with all of these stages in it.

Maintenance

Maintenance is the last step in the software development process. Maintenance starts as soon as a program is written. Maintenance involves changing a program, for example, to improve it by making it work better, or adding extra features. Making sure that it is easy for others to read the code that you have written helps to make it straightforward to maintain a program. You do not have to maintain any of the programs that you write for your Standard Grade course.

Summary of the steps involved in producing a solution to a problem

- Read the question carefully.
- Is using a computer the best way to solve this problem?
- What information does the problem contain which must be input?
- What must the computer do to this information?
- What must the output be?
- Can you use a general purpose package or must you write a program?
- Can any of the programs you have already written help?
- Break the problem down into its main steps.
- Keep breaking down the steps into smaller steps until you can't break them down any more.
- Write out your program code.
- Make up test data.
- Write the documentation.
- Type your program into the computer, correct any mistakes, and get the program working.
- Save your program.
- Run the program several times using your test data as input.
- Print a listing of your program code.
- Print a sample run of your program using your test data.
- Evaluate your solution.
- If necessary, maintain your solution.

Depending on the type of the problem you might not have to do all of these steps, or you might have to do some of them more than once. You should at least consider all of the steps for each problem.

Foundation level questions

knowledge and understanding

1 Describe two ways you can make your program code easier for other people to read.

2 Why should a program be tested?
3 What is the purpose of user documentation?

General level questions

knowledge and understanding

1 Name one way of describing the structure of a program.
2 What does the term 'prompts to user' mean?

problem solving

1 Draw a structure diagram to describe the design of the Area 1 program earlier in this chapter.
2 What can the programmer do to avoid system errors occurring when the program is run?

Credit level questions

knowledge and understanding

1 Name the steps in the software development process.
2 Name and describe the three categories of test data.
3 What is pseudocode?
4 What is the purpose of technical documentation?

problem solving

1 Why are logical errors in program code much more difficult to find than syntax errors?
2 Why do you need to validate input?

• Practical work •

Here are some programming ideas for you to try. Begin by thinking about how to solve the problem using the approach we have described in this chapter.

1 Write a quiz program which asks ten questions and gives a score at the end. The program should ask for the user's name at the start, and display a suitable message depending on the score.
2 Write a program to calculate the number of days between any two dates in a single year. Use the day and month only as input.
3 Write a program which will ask the user for two numbers and give their sum, product and quotient.
4 Write a program which will take in a list of words until the word 'stop' is entered and print the list in the reverse order to the way it was entered.
5 Write a program which will count the number of words in any sentence that is input (up to a maximum of twenty words).
6 Write a program that will calculate how fast a runner is moving (in kilometres per hour)

if you input the time they take to run 100 metres.

7   Write a program which will take in a word of up to fifteen letters and display it on the screen backwards.

8   Write a program to test a person's reaction time from the time a word appears on the screen until they press the space bar. The word should appear at random intervals each time the program is run.

• Key points •

- The software development process may be divided into seven stages. These are analysis, design, implementation, testing, documentation, evaluation and maintenance.
- The analysis stage involves reading and understanding a problem.
- Design involves the careful planning of a solution to the problem using a recognised design methodology, for example top-down design.
- One way of describing the structure of a program is to use a structure diagram.
- Another way of describing a program's structure is to use plain language or pseudocode.
- The user interface is the way a program appears to the person using it.
- All user input to a program should be validated as far as possible.
- Implementation is changing the program design into instructions that the computer can understand and the production of internal documentation.
- Program errors may be of three types:
  - system errors, which affect the computer or its peripherals,
  - syntax errors, where mistakes have been made in the programming language,

- logic errors, where the programs seem to run, but don't work the way you meant them to.
- The testing stage involves making sure that your program actually solves the problem it is supposed to.
- Testing a program makes sure that the program solves the problem which was set.
- Test data may be of three types:
  - normal
  - extreme
  - exceptional.
- Documentation can be of two types:
  - user documentation
  - technical documentation.
- Evaluation involves reviewing your solution against suitable criteria.
- Maintenance starts as soon as a program is written.
- Maintenance involves changing a program, for example, to improve it by making it work better, or adding extra features.
- Making sure that it is easy for others to read the code that you have written helps to make it straightforward to maintain a program.
- Programs can be made more readable and easier to maintain by using:
  - meaningful variable and procedure names
  - comment lines in the code

- prompts for the user.
- There are 18 steps involved in producing a solution to a problem:
  - Read the question carefully.
  - Is using a computer the best way to solve this problem?
  - What information does the problem contain which must be entered into the computer?
  - What must the computer do to this information?
  - What must the output from the computer be?
  - Can you use a general purpose package or must you write a program?
  - Can any of the programs you already have written help?
  - Break the problem down into its main steps.
  - Keep breaking down these steps into smaller ones until you can't break them down further.
  - Write out your program code.
  - Make up test data.
  - Write documentation.
  - Type your program into the computer, correct any mistakes and get the program working.
  - Save your program.
  - Run the program a number of times using your test data as input.
  - Print a listing of your program code.
  - Print a sample run of your program using your test data.
  - Evaluate your solution.

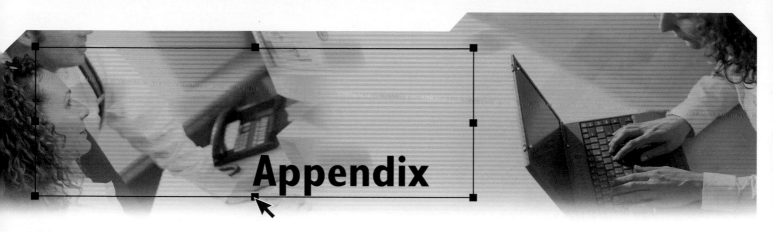

Appendix

Glossary of terms used in the book

absolute reference A cell reference in a spreadsheet which remains the same when copied (replicated) to another cell

access To gain entry to a computer system

accuracy of information Whether or not information is correct - this is essential

adaptability The ability of an automated system to be able to carry out a variety of different tasks

addressability a way of identifying storage locations in main memory using a number called an address

alignment The way text is set out, for example, right, left, centred or justified

amend To change

analogue I/O A signal which changes continuously rather than in steps, such as temperature and speed

analogue to digital converter Equipment (usually a chip) which can accept an analogue signal and changes it into a digital signal (usually binary)

analysis The analysis stage involves reading and understanding a problem

anatomy Anatomy – parts of a robot which resemble human anatomy – waist, shoulder, elbow, wrist

animation Data made up of moving graphics

applications package A piece of software (together with its accompanying disks and manuals) which performs a particular task

Arithmetic/Logic Unit (ALU) Part of the processor of a computer system which does the calculations and makes the decisions

ASCII American Standard Code for Information Interchange

audio A type of data made up of music or any sound produced by a computer

AVERAGE(..) A function used to find the average value in a range

background job A secondary task or program which runs in a computer system at the same time as an interactive program being run by the user

backing storage A system for permanently holding data on media such as disk or tape

backing storage medium An object upon which software and data may be held, such as a CD-ROM

backup A copy of a program or data made in case the original is lost or destroyed

bar code A bar code is a set of lines of varying widths, which can be read by passing a bar code reader across them. Used to identify goods in a shop

basic hardware for Commercial Data Processing Basic hardware for Commercial Data Processing is a mainframe computer and terminals (VDUs)

basic hardware for General Purpose Packages Basic hardware for General Purpose Packages includes a processor, monitor, keyboard, mouse, disk drive and printer

batch processing Collecting together all the data to be processed and inputting it to the computer in one set or 'batch'

batch system A system which carries out batch processing, for example cheque clearing, gas and electricity billing

binary Having only two states, counting using only two digits, 1 and 0

biometrics Using physical characteristics to identify a person, e.g. fingerprint, retinal scan or voiceprint

bit A binary digit, either one (1) or zero (0)

broadband connection A high speed connection to the Internet, for example, at least 512 Kilobits/second

byte A group of eight bits

cable A medium for the transmission of data, including copper wires or optical fibre

CAD/CAM Computer Aided Design / Computer Aided Manufacture

capacity of backing storage The quantity of data that can be held on a backing storage medium, such as CD-ROM

capital costs The cost of buying or setting up a computerised system. Also called initial costs

CD- Rewriteable (CD-RW) A CD which can be written to and erased over and over again

CD-Recordable (CD-R) A CD which can be written to until it is full

CD-ROM Compact Disk Read Only Memory. An optical disk which can hold 600 or 700 Mb of data

cell A box on a spreadsheet that can contain text, numbers or a formula

cell attributes The way the spreadsheet cell displays data such as numbers or dates

cell format The way the spreadsheet cell looks, for example, changing the column width or alignment

cell protection Locking the contents of a cell to prevent them from being changed

Central Processing Unit (CPU) The part of a mainframe computer which processes the information

character set A list of all the characters, symbols and numbers which can be produced by a keyboard

charting Drawing a graph from a set of numerical data, usually from a spreadsheet program

check digit A figure that's calculated from the digits of a number and placed at the end of a number. Used to check that the number has been input correctly

chip A small piece of silicon used to make an integrated circuit

circuit board A thin board on which chips and other components are fixed by solder

client and server network A method of network organisation in which network stations or clients make use of resources available on one or more servers

clip art Images on backing storage or on the World Wide Web which may be added to a document

closed loop system A control system which uses feedback

columns Vertical parts of a spreadsheet

command driven software Software that needs commands typed in by the user to work

commercial software Software which is not free and must be paid for. It is also subject to considerable restrictions as to how it may be used

common HCI The similarity of the human computer interface across the different parts of an integrated package - makes it easy to learn how to use the package

comparison operators Equals (=), greater than (>), less than (<), does not equal (<>)

compiler A translator program which is part of the systems software of a computer. A compiler translates a high level language into machine code in a single operation

complex formulae Complicated formulas used in a spreadsheet

complex search A search on more than one field in a database

complex search for information on CD-ROM/WWW (Internet) A search using more than one condition or keyword - an advanced search on a search engine

computed field A field containing a calculation involving one or more other fields

Computer Aided Design (CAD) Using a computer system to help design something

Computer Aided Manufacture (CAM) Using a computer system to help manufacture something

computer crime Using a computer for criminal purposes. Hacking is a computer crime

Computer Misuse Act A law which allows computer criminals like hackers and the creators of viruses to be prosecuted

Computer Numerical Control (CNC) Automatically controlling a machine like a lathe according to instructions

computer operator A person who oversees the day to day operation of a mainframe computer system using a terminal

control language A special language designed to control a device such as a robot or a robot arm

control unit Part of the processor which controls the running of a program

corrupt To corrupt a file means to damage it so that it cannot be read. This why you should always keep a backup copy!

crop graphic To reduce the size of a graphic by cutting parts from the edges of the graphic

customising HCI Changing the HCI of a General Purpose Package or an Operating System to suit the user

data A general term for numbers, characters, symbols, graphics and sound which are accepted and processed by a computer system

data collection Part of the data processing cycle which involves the gathering of data. May involve source documents

data controller The person or organisation holding the data (previously known as the data user)

data file A file containing data on backing storage or in memory. May be organised as a set of records

data glove An input device used in virtual reality

data input Part of the data processing cycle when data is input to the computer system. May be direct or indirect

data output Part of the data processing cycle where data is sent out

data preparation Part of the data processing cycle where data is made ready for input

data preparation operator Person who inputs data into the computer system

data processing Processing data as part of the data processing cycle

data processing cycle A cycle of events beginning with data collection and preparation and ending with data output

Data Protection Act A law which regulates how personal data about individuals should be kept on computer.

data storage Part of the data processing cycle which involves the transfer of data to backing storage

data subject A person about whom data is held

data user The person or organisation holding the data (now known as the data controller)

database A structured collection of similar information which can be searched

dedicated A computer or machine which can only perform one particular task

degrees of freedom The number of independent axes (or planes) of movement

delete To remove data

design (of a program) Design involves the careful planning of a solution to the problem using a recognised design methodology, for example top-down design.

desktop computer A microcomputer consisting of a processor, keyboard, mouse and monitor which is normally operated sitting at a desk

desktop publishing (DTP) Producing professional looking publications by using a computer, peripherals and software

device A single item of computer hardware

device drivers A program which is an add-on to the operating system in a computer, to allow the computer to operate a particular device which is attached to it

dial-up connection A method of connecting to the internet using a modem and a telephone line

digital A signal which changes in steps and not continuously like an analogue signal

digital still camera A digital camera mainly used for taking still photographs

digital to analogue converter Equipment (usually a chip) which can accept a digital signal (usually binary) and change it into an analogue signal

digital video camera A digital camera mainly used for taking movies

Digital Video Disk (DVD) An optical storage medium, similar to CD-ROM, which can hold video (TV programmes or films)

digitise Converting an analogue quantity into a digital one. Digitising a picture breaks it into dots and each dot (or pixel) is given a digital value for brightness and colour e.g. using a scanner or a digital still camera

directory An area on backing storage where files may be stored (also called a folder on some systems)

documentation A detailed explanation of how a program works -made up of a user guide and a technical guide

download software - freeware, shareware, commercial A file which is received via a network, such as a software update

DVD-Recordable (DVD-R) DVD-R is a write once medium. DVD-R operates in a similar manner to CD-R, with recordable disks containing a layer of dye.

DVD-Rewriteable (DVD-RW) DVD-Rewriteable is similar to DVD-R, but can be written to and erased many times over

DVD-ROM An optical storage medium, similar to CD-ROM, but of a much higher backing storage capacity, which can hold video data

dynamic data linkage A change to the data in one file is automatically carried over to the same data in another file

e-commerce A method of doing business over a network such as the Internet

EFTPOS Electronic Funds Transfer at Point Of Sale - a way of paying for goods using a bank card instead of cash

electronic funds transfer (EFT) Automatically moving money from one account to another using a computer system where no cash changes hands

electronic mail Is sending messages from one computer to another over a network

e-mail Electronic mail is sending messages from one computer to another over a network

embedded systems An embedded system is a tiny computer inside another, larger piece of equipment, like a washing machine, a car or a mobile phone.

encryption Processing a message so that it can't be understood by anyone who is not authorised to use it - putting data into a code or scrambling data

end effector The part on the end of a robot arm which is specialised to carry out a particular task, like spraying paint. Also called a tool.

engineer A person who maintains and repairs a computer system

error reporting A message from the operating system of a computer to the user to let them know if an error has occurred

evaluation Evaluation involves reviewing your solution against suitable criteria, such as, does your program solve the problem?

facsimile (fax) machine A machine that scans a document and changes it into a signal that can be sent along a telephone line. The document is printed on another fax machine somewhere else

facsimile (fax) modem A modem that can send messages to a fax machine or another computer with a fax modem

feedback The signal which a sensor sends back to the computer. The computer to makes a decision based on the feedback

field A single item of data stored in a record

field types (numeric, text, graphic, date, time) The type of data which is to be stored in a field. You may need to set up the field types when you create a new database

file Information held on backing storage or in memory. Files may hold data or programs

file ancestry A system for keeping backups of files using generations of files like grandparent, parent and child

file management A part of the operating system. The filing system deals with how files are held on backing storage. It controls the processes involved in saving or loading a particular file from disk.

file server A computer on a local area network which holds files which can be accessed by the users

File transfer – attachments Sending a file over the Internet alongside an e-mail message

file A set of records

floppy disk A plastic disk coated with magnetic material used as a backing storage medium

folder An area on backing storage where files may be stored (also called a directory on some systems)

footer An area at the bottom of every page of a document. The footer usually contains the page number

formatting (a disk) Laying down tracks and sectors on a disk. It is also called initialising

formula A calculation involving one or more cell references in a spreadsheet

freeware Freeware is totally free software, which you may use on any number of computer systems without paying any money.

Gigabyte (Gb) One thousand and twenty four Megabytes (1024 x 1024 x 1024 bytes)

GIGO Garbage In Garbage Out – if a mistake is made in the input to a computer system, the output will also have mistakes in it

grammar check Checking the grammar in a document

graphic A picture or a chart on a computer screen

Graphical User Interface (GUI) An interface which enables the user to work with icons and a mouse, e.g. a WIMP interface

graphics card A graphics card is a device which controls the quality of output on a monitor.

graphics package A piece of software used for the production of, or editing, graphics

graphics tablet An input device which allows free drawing using a hand held pointer on a board

hacking Illegally interfering with information stored on a computer system

handwriting recognition A system for computer input which involves writing on a touch sensitive screen using a pen or stylus

hard copy A printed copy of your work, usually on paper

hard disk A backing storage device made up of metal disks coated with a magnetic material. It is sealed against dust and dirt

hardware The physical parts or devices which make up a computer system

header An area at the top of every page of a document. A book header may show the chapter number

headset An output device used in virtual reality

hierarchical filing system A filing system which has multiple directories

high level instructions Instructions written in a high level language

high level language A computer language with instructions written in normal or everyday language

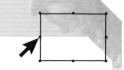

hotspot A hotspot is a special area on a web page, which is normally invisible when viewed in a browser - the mouse pointer changes shape when it is moved over a hotspot

HTML HyperText Markup Language -the language used to write web pages

human computer interface (HCI) The way in which the computer and the user communicate

hyperlink Hyperlinks are links between World Wide Web pages, documents or files. They are activated by clicking on text, which acts as a button, or on a particular area of the screen like a graphic.

icons Symbols or pictures on a screen - part of a graphical user interface.

identify and rectify errors Finding and fixing mistakes in a computer program

implementation Implementation is changing the program design into instructions that the computer can understand and the production of internal documentation.

import To bring in data from one file into another, sometimes between two different types of packages

initial costs The costs of buying and setting up a computerised system. Also called capital costs.

inkjet printer A printer which forms images using dots produced by tiny jets of ink

input To enter data that needs to be processed

input device A device which allows data to be entered, like a keyboard or a mouse

insert To put new information in

integer A whole number, with no fractional part or decimal point

integrated package A piece of software made up of separate parts which can share data. Each part has a similar HCI

intelligent robots Robots which are programmed to behave as though they had a form of intelligence

interactive processing a way of using a computer in which the operator's instructions are processed continuously, like a conversation

interactive system A system which carries out interactive processing

interface Part of a computer system that allows different devices to communicate with the processor by compensating for any differences in their operation

Internet The Internet is a wide area network spanning the globe. It can be thought of as many different, smaller networks connected together.

Internet ready computer A computer system with an internal modem and suitable communications software such as a browser and an email client program.

Internet Service Provider (ISP) An Internet Service Provider is a company that provides a host computer, which the user can connect to by dialling in. The host computer manages the communications, and also stores data such as electronic mail, web pages and files for its subscribers. This host computer is connected to the Internet and subscribers can communicate with other computers on the Internet.

interpreter A translator program which is part of the systems software of a computer. An interpreter changes a high level language into machine code one instruction at a time

IPO An abbreviation for input, process, output

ISP An abbreviation for Internet Service Provider

joystick An input device consisting of a handle and one or more buttons usually used for controlling a game

justification A way of arranging text on screen or on hard copy. Justification may be left, right, centred or full. Same as alignment

key field A field used to uniquely identify a record in a database

keyboard An input device consisting of a set of buttons or keys marked with characters

keyboard shortcuts A combination of keys that can be used instead of having to select an item from a menu.

keyword A word which is used to search for an item in a database

Kilobyte (Kb) One thousand and twenty four bytes (1024 bytes)

knowledge system A system which contains rules and facts about a particular topic

laptop computer A portable computer which folds and has an LCD screen and keyboard in a single unit. It is powered from batteries and may be operated while travelling.

laser printer A type of printer which produces a high quality image of both text and graphics

light guide A line painted on a factory floor that an autonomous guided vehicle can be programmed to follow

light pen An input device which is used to scan bar codes or to input data to a screen

Liquid Crystal Display (LCD) A type of flat screen display which is used in calculators, palmtop and laptop computers because of its low power consumption and light weight

Local Area Network (LAN) A network confined to a single room or building

log on The way of identifying the user to a computer system (or to a network)

logic error A mistake which causes your program to produce an unexpected result, for example, using an incorrect formula

loudspeakers Output devices which allow sound to be produced

machine code The processor's own language made up of binary numbers (0 and 1 only)

magnetic guides A cable buried in a factory floor which an autonomous guided vehicle can be programmed to follow

Magnetic Ink Character Recognition (MICR) An input process which can read characters written in magnetic ink

magnetic stripe A narrow band of magnetic material on which data is held. You can see a magnetic stripe on the back of a credit card,

magnetic tape Plastic tape coated with a magnetic material used as a backing storage medium

mail merge The process of automatically loading personal details from a separate mailing list and placing them into the correct places in a standard letter

mail shots Letters prepared by mail merge and sent out to individuals on a mailing list - also called direct mail or junk mail

mailbox A place where electronic mail is stored while waiting to be read or downloaded

main memory The memory in a computer system, linked to the processor

main memory size The number of storage locations available in a computer system

mainframe computer A computer system that can process a very large amount of data at high speed.

maintenance Maintenance involves changing a program, for example, to improve it by making it work better, or adding extra features.

mark sense card A card with lines drawn on it to indicate one or more choices.

MAXIMUM(..) A function used to find the maximum value in a range

medium An object upon which software and data may be held, such as a CD-ROM

Megabyte (Mb) One thousand and twenty four Kilobytes (1024 Kb)

memory management Part of the operating systems which controls where programs and data are placed in the main memory of the computer.

menu A list on screen from which choices may be made by the user

menu driven software Software which needs the user to make choices from a menu to make it work

microphone An input device which allows sound to be put into a computer system

microprocessor The processor of a microcomputer

MINIMUM(..) A function used to find the minimum value in a range

mobile robot A robot that can move around the floor

modem A device used to connect a computer system to a telephone line. Modem is short for MODulator-DEModulator

monitor A monitor is an output device, which accepts a video signal directly from a computer and displays the output on a screen. A visual display unit (or VDU) is made up of a monitor and a keyboard. The screen is the part of a monitor or VDU, which displays the output.

motor Part of a robot or automated system which can help it to move

mouse An input device with a ball underneath and one or more buttons - used to control a pointer on screen

multi-access More than one person using a mainframe computer system at the same time

multimedia The presentation of information by a computer system using graphics, animation, sound and text

multi-programming More than one program running on a computer system at once

multi-user database A database that may be accessed by many users at the same time

netiquette A way of behaving when connected to the Internet or sending email messages

network Two or more computers joined together so that data can be transferred between them

network interface card A device which allows a computer system to be connected to a local area network

network manager The person in charge of the network. He or she will be responsible for all of the computer systems attached to the company network

notebook computer A portable computer which folds and has an LCD screen and keyboard in a single unit. It is powered from batteries and may be operated while travelling.

number Data consisting of numbers which may have fractions or a decimal point

off-line Not connected to a remote computer system or a network

on-line Connected to a remote computer system or a network

on-line help Help which is available in the form of information screens when using a computer program

on-line tutorial A series of guided lessons on how to use a computer program

open loop A control system which does not involve feedback

operating system Programs which control the operation of a computer system. Part of the systems software

optical character recognition (OCR) Characters can be read in automatically from a page of text

optical storage A form of non-magnetic storage e.g. CD-ROM, which uses tiny holes called pits

output Data passed out of a computer system

output device A device which displays data from a computer system such as a monitor or a printer

package A computer program and its associated documentation

palmtop A hand held computer. A palmtop computer has an LCD screen but may not have a keyboard. A pen is used for input on the screen

paper, screen Forms of data output

password A secret code that you use to gain access to private information on a computer system or to log on to a network

peripheral Any device that may be attached to a computer system for input, output or backing storage

photographic A type of data produced by a digital still camera. A bit-mapped graphic image

pixel Stands for picture element. A tiny dot used to make up a picture on a screen

plotter An output device which draws on paper using pens. Used mainly for CAD

point of sale (POS) A computer terminal or 'till' in a shop where the goods change hands

pointer A shape displayed on screen which is used to select from a menu usually controlled by a mouse or trackpad

portability of software. When programs written on one computer system may be used on a different computer system with minimal alteration

print file To obtain a hard copy

printer An output device which produces hard copy usually on paper. Examples are ink jet, and laser

printer driver A program which takes the codes in a document and translates them into the appropriate code for the printer in use. A type of device driver

problem description The problem you are given to solve described in your own words

problem statement The problem you are given to solve

Procedure A sub-program which is identified by name, like take_in_words or display_results

processor The part of a computer which carries out the process

program A list of instructions which tell the processor what to do

program listing A hard copy or a screen display of the instructions which make up a computer program

programmer A person who writes computer programs

prompt A phrase which appears on screen to ask the user for input

pseudocode A way of representing the design of a program using ordinary language

pull-down menu A menu on a WIMP system which may be operated by using a mouse pointer and button

RAM Random access memory - a set of microchips that stores data temporarily. The data is lost when the computer is switched off

Random Access Memory (RAM) A set of microchips that stores data temporarily. The data is lost when the computer is switched off

random/direct access Being able to locate a data item straight away, wherever it is stored on disk or in main memory

Read Only Memory (ROM) One or more microchips that stores data permanently. The data is not lost when the computer is switched off

real time A system which responds immediately to input

record A data structure with one or more fields of information

registers Memory locations inside a processor

relative reference When a formula in a spreadsheet is changed relative to its position, during copying or replication

reliability of data link A data link is reliable if it is not likely to be affected by interference which may change the signal

remote data entry When data is input from a terminal at some distance from the host computer

replicate Copy

Resolution (dpi) The amount of detail which can be shown on a screen (or a hard copy) - measured in dots per inch (dpi)

resource allocation When the operating system allows a program to have access to a particular piece of hardware

rewriteable optical disk A type of non-magnetic storage such as a CD-RW

robot A device which can carry out repetitive tasks under the control of a computer program

ROM Read Only Memory – one or more microchips that stores data permanently. The data is not lost when the computer is switched off

ROM and RAM Two types of main memory in a computer system

ROM software Software which is distributed or stored on read only memory

rotate graphic To turn a graphic around

routine A programming instruction which carries out a particular task

rows Horizontal parts of a spreadsheet

RTF Rich text format – a standard file format for the transfer of data between application packages

running costs The cost of using a computer system - includes electricity, paper, ink, toner, maintenance

sample run A hard copy or a screen display of the (input and) output from a computer program

scale graphic Change the size of a graphic by enlarging or reducing

scanner An input device which allows printed text or graphics to be displayed on the screen. May be used with OCR software

screen The screen is the part of a monitor or VDU, which displays the output.

screen layout The way a program looks on a monitor screen

scrolling Moving the display on the screen by using the cursor keys, mouse or trackpad

search and replace A feature of a general purpose package which allows a word to be replaced automatically throughout a document. May be global or selective

search engine A search engine is a special site on the World Wide Web, which is designed to help you to find information.

searching Looking for an item using a database program and perhaps one or more keywords

security (passwords, encryption, physical) Methods of making sure that data is private or that only authorised people can see the data

sensors A device which detects something and provides input to a computer system. A temperature sensor is an example

sequence The order in which a set of instructions is carried out or the order in which a set of data is stored on backing storage

sequential access Reading a set of records in the same order as they were originally stored

shareware Shareware is not free, apart from a short trial period, during which you are allowed to evaluate the software.

simulation A computer program used to model a real life situation

single entry multiple use Entering data only once on a central computer and making the data available to different users

smart card A smart card has its own processor, and is able to store much more information than fits on a magnetic stripe.

software The programs that the hardware of the computer runs

software development process Analysis, design, implementation, testing, documentation, evaluation and maintenance

software upgrade Obtaining a more recent version of software, by downloading or installing from disk

sort on more than one field A complex sort

sort on one field A simple sort

sorting Putting a list of items into order, for example numeric or alphabetic

sound card - Input In order to input sound into a computer the sound must be changed from analogue into digital. The sound card carries out the analogue to digital conversion in a process called sampling.

sound card – Output In order to output sound from a computer the sound must be changed from digital to analogue. The sound card carries out the digital to analogue conversion

specialised input device An input device which is adapted for a particular purpose, such as use by a disabled person or for virtual reality

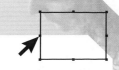

specialised output device An output device which is adapted for a particular purpose, such as use by a disabled person or for virtual reality

speed (ppm) The rate at which a printer can print, measured in pages per minute (ppm)

spelling check A feature of a general purpose package which compares the words in a document with the words in its dictionary and offers alternatives

spreadsheet A program which divides the screen into rows and columns. Cells in a spreadsheet can contain text, numbers or formulas

staff costs The cost of employing staff

standard file formats A way of storing data so that it can be understood by, and transferred between, a number of different application packages

standard letter A general letter with spaces for personal details (such as a person's name). Used in mail shots

standard paragraph A piece of text (held on backing storage) that you can combine with others like it to make up a complete document

static linkage A change to the data in one file will not affect the same data in other files

stationary robot A robot that cannot move around the floor

storage location A place in a computer's memory where an item of data may be held

stored program A set of instructions which is held in a computer's memory

structure chart A way of representing the design of a program using boxes linked by lines

structure diagram A diagram made up of different-shaped boxes containing text and linked by lines. It is usually used to explain the structure of a computer program

SUM(..) A function used to find the total of a range of values

syntax error A mistake in a programming instruction - for example PTRIN instead of PRINT

system A computer system

system error A mistake in the computer's operating system program which may stop the computer working

systems analysis Examining a method of working

systems analyst A person who examines a method of working and decides the best way of doing it using a computer system

systems software A set of programs which controls the operation of a computer system

table A table is made up of data arranged in columns and rows, like a spreadsheet, and data is placed in cells

tablet PC A flat computer with a large touch sensitive LCD screen as the main input device. It is powered from batteries and may be operated while travelling.

tabulation A method of producing tables in a word processed document by using the TAB character

teletext Pages of information transmitted with a television signal which may be received by a suitable television set or a computer and adapter. A one-way system only

teleworking Working from home and communicating with your employer or workplace by using electronic mail

template A template is a readymade blank document, with placeholders for items like text and graphics. Using a template can speed up the creation of a document, because much of the page layout has already been done for you.

Terabyte (Tb) One thousand and twenty four Gigabytes

terminal A piece of hardware consisting of a keyboard and a screen. A 'dumb' terminal does not have a processor

test data Data used to test a computer program to find out if it gives the correct results

testing Checking whether or not a computer program works as intended

text Characters or symbols displayed on a screen or printed as hard copy on a printer

text messaging Text messaging is a method of electronic communication using a mobile phone.

Thin Film Transistor (TFT) A type of liquid crystal display screen used for high quality output

tools Devices which may be attached to the end of a robot arm (also known as end effectors)

touch sensitive screen A screen with sensitive areas on it. The user presses particular areas to input into the computer, such as a palmtop

trackball An input device with a ball which is turned by hand, moving a cursor on a screen around. Works like an upside-down mouse

trackpad A flat touch sensitive area used instead of a mouse to control a pointer

translation Changing a program from one computer language into another, usually from a high level language into machine code

transmission media The media used to transmit data, for example, copper wire or optical fibre

update For example, adding new data to a file

USB Flash Drive a solid-state storage device made up of flash ROM. It connects to the computer via the USB interface

user friendliness Programs that are easy to learn to use and help you understand as you are using them are called user-friendly programs.

user friendly An interactive computer system which helps the user by giving clear prompts, menus and help screens when needed

user identity Your name or a code which identifies you to a network. Usually used with a password

utility A program which helps you to perform a task such as delete a file, format a disk

validation Checking that data is sensible. A range check is a way of validating data

values Numeric data in a spreadsheet cell

verification Checking that data has been entered correctly. Entering the same data twice is a way of verifying data

video A type of data – movies

video conferencing Video conferencing is the use of communications links to conduct meetings between people who are geographically separated.

virtual reality Reproducing the outside world digitally within a computer system and displaying it to the user in such a way that allows them to interact with it. Users use data gloves and a headset

virus A 'rogue' program which can spread through computer systems and may damage files

visual display unit (VDU) An output device consisting of a monitor and a keyboard. May be used as a terminal

voice output Speech produced by a computer system usually by special software and a loudspeaker

voice recognition Software which can recognise speech input by the user via a microphone

web page A single page of information on a web site

webcam A webcam is a small digital camera, which is attached to a computer and positioned on or beside the computer's monitor in order to capture images which may be transmitted across a network. Webcams make applications like video conferencing possible.

wide area network(WAN) A network which covers a large geographical area like a country.

WIMP environment Windows, Icon, Menu, Pointer

windows Areas of the screen set aside for a particular purposes such as displaying files or documents

wireless A method or a way of transmitting data without using a physical connection, e.g. radio waves or infrared

wizard A wizard is a feature of a package that helps you to step through the process of document creation.

word The number of bits a computer can process in a single operation

word processor A program used for writing and editing text

word-wrap Text formatting used in a word processor which stops words at the end of one line being split over two lines (it moves partially completed words to the start of a new line)

World Wide Web The World Wide Web (WWW) is a collection of information held in multimedia form on the Internet.

WYSIWYG Stands for 'What You See Is What You Get'. When what you see on a screen is exactly the same as the way it will be printed

Index

A

absolute reference 48-49

access 140, 146, 176

accuracy of information 192

accurate, complete and up-to-date
   information 13, 192

adaptability 200

add

   audio to
   a presentation 86

   to a web page 101

   clip art to a presentation 85

   graphic to
   a presentation 85-86

   web page creation 100-101

   hotspots to a web page 103

   record to a database 56

   table to a presentation 102-103

   video to
   a presentation 86

   video to a web page 101

addressability 287

advantages and disadvantages of
   electronic mail 127-128

advantages of Expert Systems 112-113

alignment 26-27, 42

alter

   cell format and attributes 41-42

   column width 42

   output format 61

   page size and layout 28

   record format 56-57

   screen input format 61

   text alignment 26-28

   style 27

   tool attributes (eg line width) 67

amend 3

analogue I/O 205

analogue to digital converter 205

analysis 290-291

anatomy 203

animation 12, 88, 103

applications of Expert Systems 109,
   111

applications package 1, 142, 260-261

Arithmetic/Logic Unit (ALU) 281

ASCII 12-13, 79, 284

assemble elements of presentation
   including text and graphics 85
   89

audio 86, 88, 101, 251-252

availability of information 14

AVERAGE (..) 46, 47

B

background job 273

backing storage 251-263

backing storage medium 251-258

backing storage requirements for
   different applications 260-261

backup 13, 175

bar code 171

basic hardware for Commercial Data
   Processing 177-178

basic hardware for General Purpose
   Packages 223-224

binary 205, 281-283

biometrics 142, 173

Bit 281

broadband connection 156-157

Byte 14, 283

C

cable 137

CAD/CAM 210-214

calculation – automatic and manual in
   a spreadsheet 44

calculation of storage requirement of
   b/w bit-map 285

capacity 227

capacity of backing storage 90, 227,
   259

capital costs 242

CD-Recordable (CD-R) 255-256

CD-Rewriteable (CD-RW) 256-257,
   259

CD-ROM 144, 254-255, 259, 260

   cell

attributes 42

   format 41

   protection 43

Central Processing Unit (CPUs) 177

change layout 78

change text appearance 3

changes in nature of job 201

character set 284

charting 44-45

check digit 174

chip 221, 222-223

circuit board 222-223

client and server network 144-145

clip art 77, 78, 85, 86

columns 38, 42, 43, 79

commercial software 160-161

common

   features of high level languages
   265-266

   features of most general purpose
   packages 2-3

   HCI 7

   tools 66

comparison

   of backing storage 258-259

   with manual system 13, 168-169

   of operators 207-208

   of printers 242-243

compiler 266, 267

complex formulas 41

complex search 159-160

   for information on CD
   ROM/WWW (Internet) 59

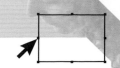

single entry multiple use 169

smart card 142, 172-173, 191

social implications 17-19, 178-181, 201

social legal and ethical issues 113-115, 146-148

software 177, 222
  development process 290-302
  integration 7-10
  upgrade 19

sort 59-60
  on more than one field 60
  on one field 60

sound card
  input 236
  output 246-247

specialised
  input device 231, 236-237
  output device 247-248

speed
  of access 156, 163, 176
  and accuracy of processing 14
  automated systems 200
  data transfer 258-259
  ppm 242
  of processing 168

spelling check 30-31, 32

spreadsheet 10, 38-53

staff costs 20

standard
  file formats 12-13, 79, 131, 284
  letter 33-34
  paragraph 32-33

static linkage 8-9

stationary robot 204

storage location 222, 287

storage, retrieval and communication
  of large quantities of information 13

stored program 206, 222, 280

structure chart 292

structure diagram 292

SUM (..) 295-296

syntax error 295-296

system error 295-296

systems
  analysis 202
  analysts 179
  software 264-269

T

table 29, 102-103

tablet PC 225-226

tabulation 29

technical implications 182-191, 201

teletext 71

teleworking 146-147

template 7, 34-35, 76-77, 91, 99-100

Terabyte (Tb) 283

terminal 177, 178

test data 297

testing 297-300

text 11, 12
  messaging 125-127, 148
  wrap around graphic 80

thin film transistor (TFT) 245-246

tools 6, 66-67

touch-sensitive screen 231

trackball 232

trackpad 233

translation 264-265, 266-267

transmission media 138-139

types
  of check (eg length, range) 174-175
  of file 274-275
  of translator 266-267

U

unauthorised access to data (hacking) 180

update 175

USB Flash Drive 258, 259

USB Flash ROM 258

use
  of keywords 61-62
  of a variety of input devices for multimedia 237
  of a variety of output devices for multimedia 248

use wizard or template
  desktop publishing 77
  presentation 92
  web page creation 99-100

user friendliness 3

user friendly 3

user identity 136, 179

utility 160

V

validation 175, 293

values 38

verification 175

video 12, 86, 89-90, 101
  conferencing 163, 236
  disk 101

virtual reality 215-216, 237

virus 131-132, 180-181

visual display unit (VDU) 177, 244

voice
  output 247
  recognition 26, 234

volume of documents 168

W

WAN- telecommunications link 136, 138-140

web page 97, 152

webcam 235

wide area network (WAN) 136, 138 140

WIMP environment 4-7

windows 5

wireless 137-138, 145, 163

wizard 7, 45, 77, 92, 99-100

word 287

word processor 17, 25-37, 81

word-wrap 26

World Wide Web 86-87, 97, 153

WYSIWYG 98-99

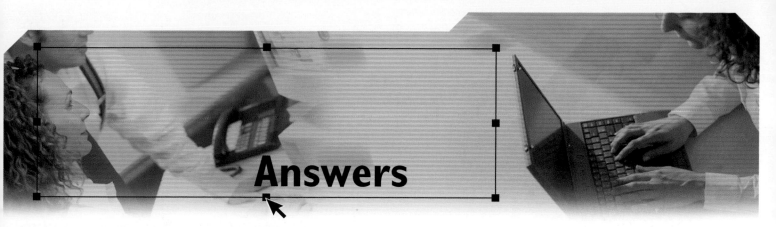

Answers

1 General purpose packages

Foundation level questions

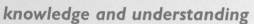

knowledge and understanding

1 Text, number and graphics.
2 Word processing, spreadsheets, database, graphics.
3 Insert, amend, delete, copy.
4 Human computer interface.
5 Windows, Icon, Menu, Pointer.
6 A file or document, an application, a utility like the trash.
7 I think that Microsoft Works is user-friendly because it has lots of menus and the help is easy to use. I think that COMAL is not as user-friendly because it only gives you some help and not as much as Microsoft Works does.
8 He can use the on-line help to ask it how to print.
9 A mail shot is a letter sent out automatically to people on a mailing list.
10 Keep regular backup copies so that your data does not get lost.
11 So that they can check that it is correct.
12 It is a package containing two or more general purpose packages in a single program
   a. AppleWorks.
   b. Word processing, database, spreadsheet, drawing and painting.

c. An integrated package can share data between each part. It can also have two different parts of the package open at once. It may have fewer features than a separate general purpose package.

problem solving

1 A word processing package contains a spelling and a grammar checker. It is easy to correct mistakes before a document is printed.
2 a. A general purpose package.
   b. An integrated package.
3 a. Chapter title.
   b. Page number.
   c. It is easy to keep track of each chapter and page number.
4 a. Word processing.
   b. Spreadsheet.
   c. Database.
   d. Graphics.
   e. Desk top publishing.
   f. Presentation.
   g. Web page editor.
   h. Expert system.

General level questions

knowledge and understanding

1   An application package may be single purpose or general purpose.

2   You must add your own information before it is of any use to you.

3   Information can be processed more speedily and accurately and it is easy to make amendments to the information.

4   You can change the layout to suit any purpose.

5   A computer program, associated files and documentation.

6   The program itself, a manual, a tutorial guide or demonstration program.

7   a. Help in the form of information screens which can be accessed when using a computer program.

    b. A series of guided lessons which teaches you how to use the package.

8   A graphical user interface.

9   The toolbar is a line of screen buttons which represent the actions that are available to be carried out within an application package.

10 Hacking.

11 a. School, doctor, dentist, bank.

    b.

> Bank of Ardmillan
> Marineville
> KA49 1SM
> Dear Sir
>
> My name is Aidan Robb and I understand that your organisation holds personal information about me in relation to my bank account.
>
> I would be grateful if you could send me a printout of the information. This will allow me to check it for accuracy and update it if necessary.
>
> Yours sincerely
>
> Aidan

12 a. Your seat could be double-booked.

    b. You could be wrongly arrested.

    c. The employee could pay too much tax.

problem solving

1   It removes an application and all files associated with it from a computer system.

2   Photographic data is a graphic produced by a digital still camera, webcam or scanner. Graphic data is a general term for any type of graphic.

3   By using an input device such as a microphone.

4   Print from page 3 to page 3.

5   The use of general purpose packages causes an increase in the amount of paper used, because most people like to have a hard copy of a document.

Credit level questions

knowledge and understanding

1 Animation is data made up of moving graphics. One method of producing animation is rapidly changing between two or more still images, like a flick book.

2 Animation is the creation of apparent movement through the presentation of a sequence of slightly different still pictures. Video data is made up of a sequence of moving or 'live' action images.

3 It means changing the human computer interface to suit a person's preferences.

4 A sequence of key presses used instead of selecting an option from the menu.

5 a. Someone whose personal data is stored.
    b. Someone who stores another's personal data.

6 • See data held on themselves, within 40 days, for payment of a fee.
   • Have any errors in the data corrected.
   • Compensation for distress caused if the act has been broken.
   • Prevent processing for direct marketing by writing to the data controller.
   • Prevent processing by automated decision making

7 a. Hacking and the distribution of viruses.
   b. Illegal copying of software and other materials.

8 a. When two copies of the same data are held in different parts of an integrated package, and the data in one part is updated, no change will take place to the data in the other part.
   b. When two copies of the same data are held in different parts of an integrated package, and the data in one part is updated, the data in the other part will be automatically updated to reflect the change.

problem solving

1 Computer animation is used in the film and television industry to mix computer-generated images with live action.

2 This is true because all information in a computer is stored as numbers.

3 It is easier for many people to access the same information when computers are networked.

4 Changing the highlight colour when an item is selected.

5 No because some help is provided on disk.

6 In a spreadsheet, when a graph is created from some data. If the data is updated in the spreadsheet, then the graph will automatically change. This is dynamic linkage. If the graph does not automatically change, for example, if it is pasted into a word processing document, then this is static linkage.

7 More up-to-date information may be obtained, and a wider range of help topics may be available. It is also possible to download software updates.

8 It is faster than using a mouse or other device to select an item from a menu.

9 a. A word processor and a printer. No need to go to great expense, for example, for a desktop publishing package if it is only required six times a year.
   b. A database, because the data can be stored and amended in future.
   c. A word processor, since it is not worth making up a database and a standard letter for such a small task.
   d. A spreadsheet, since it can automatically calculate dates as well as numbers.
   e. Create a database file with fields which match those on the response sheet, and then enter the ticks from the printed sheet. Create a report from the database showing the field totals. Alternatively, a similar form could be created in a spreadsheet and totals obtained.

2 Word processing

Foundation level questions

knowledge and understanding

1 Enter and edit text, word-wrap, formatting, search and replace, spelling check, grammar check, standard paragraph plus a suitable description.
2 Word-wrap is when a word processor takes a new line automatically and moves partly completed words at the end of one line to the start of the next line.
3 Left align, centre, align right, justify.
4 A4 and A5.
5 Bold, italic and underline.

problem solving

1 A dedicated word processor can only do word processing and no other task. A computer running a word processing package can run any other program to perform a different task.
2 The printer in use.
3 Some of the text would be lost or get chopped off the edges of the printout.
4 Because it may make the document difficult to read.

General level questions

knowledge and understanding

1 A paragraph, together with others like it, which may be loaded from disk in order to make a complete document.
2 Solicitors and estate agents.
3 The end of one page and the start of the next page in a document.
4 A grid of columns and rows which can hold text.
5 A spelling check has a dictionary of correctly spelled words, and a grammar check uses a set of rules.

problem solving

1 a. Use global search and replace or 'replace all'.
  b. Words containing the words 'he' and 'she' may be altered by mistake.
  c. Selective search and replace.
  d. Search for whole words only.
2 The highlighted word may be correct.
  a. A grammatical error, for example 'to much'.
  b. A grammar checker.
3 If you want to tabulate a single word, it is not worth going to the trouble of creating a table.

Credit level questions

knowledge and understanding

1 A letter containing blanks for use in a mail merge with a database.
2 The process of combining the data from a database with a standard letter.
3 The process of sending out standard letters in the post.

problem solving

1 Create a standard letter using a word processor; create a database with the required fields; select the required records, namely all pupils in S1; mail merge (insert fields into standard letter); print the letters; post the letters (mail shot).
2 I would choose a spelling check because I do not agree with most of the errors shown up in a grammar check.
3 So that it may be used again at later date and time will be saved because the page layout and other preferences will already have been set up in the document.
4 Text scanned using OCR software may contain mistakes.

3 Spreadsheet

Foundation level questions

knowledge and understanding

1 Formulas, formatting, cell attributes, cell protection, insert rows and columns, replication, calculation, functions, charting, plus a suitable description.
2 Numbers (values), text or formulas.
3 They can be used to show 'what if' situations.
4 Automatic calculation means that when a value changes, the rest of the formulas in the spreadsheet will be automatically recalculated. Manual calculation means that the spreadsheet will not recalculate until the user tells it to.

problem solving

3 The sum function.

General level questions

knowledge and understanding

1 a. Calculate the average of the values in cells D5 to G5.
   b. Display the maximum value in cells F4 to K4.
2 It is copied into another cell.
3 Change alignment, change column width.
4 Currency and date.

problem solving

1 Use cell protection.
2 The equals sign was missed out from the start.
3 It is easier to see any trends in a chart than in a table of numbers.
4 a. Any formula using this value will not work, because the number is treated as text.
   b. Alter cell attributes to currency.

Credit level questions

knowledge and understanding

1 a. Absolute referencing.
   b. Condition.
2 A chart wizard.

problem solving

1 Relative referencing should be used when you want the formulas to change relative to their position in the spreadsheet. Absolute referencing should be used when you want the cell reference to always refer to the same cell regardless of its position.
2 =IF (T7>4,"Well done","Average").

4 Databases

Foundation level questions

knowledge and understanding

1 a. A record of crimes and convictions.
   b. Tax details, salaries.
   c. Car registration details.
   d. Names and addresses of people to whom cards are sent each year.
   e. Names and addresses of subscribers to the magazine, renewal dates.
2 a. A data file is a collection of structured data on a particular topic.
   b. Each record may consist of one or more fields.
   c. A field contains a single item of data.
   d. To look for information in a database.
   e. To put records into a particular order.
3 A suitable set of field names for each topic.

problem solving

1 Field, record, file.
2 One each for first name, second name, street, town, postcode, at least five fields. To give more sorting options.
3 The same number or records as the number of pupils in the class.
4 If the information was to be updated.
5 Save the updated file and re-sort the file into the correct order.

General level questions

knowledge and understanding

1 A simple search is a search on one field. A complex search is a search on more than one field.
2 Number, text, graphic, date and time.
3 A search on a database uses a general purpose package and a search on a CD-ROM uses the CD-ROMs own program.

problem solving

1 Text and date.

Credit level questions

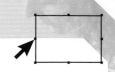

knowledge and understanding

1 The text that you use to search a file for a particular entry.

problem solving

1 a. To make it easier for a user to enter data, to speed the process of data entry.
  b. To suit a particular purpose, for example to print only selected fields.

2 a. If my name and address took up 50 characters, then 300 x 50 = 15,000 bytes.
  b. Taking a telephone number as 11 characters, 300 x 11 = 3,300 bytes. Add 15,000, giving a total of 18,300 bytes.

5 Graphics

Foundation level questions

knowledge and understanding

1 To draw pictures.
2 Draw graphic, enter text, common tools, alter tool attributes, scale graphic, rotate graphic, scan and edit graphic, crop graphic. Plus appropriate descriptions.
3 Rectangle, polygon, line, circle, fill.

problem solving

1 To make it easier for the user to produce shapes instead of having to draw them freehand.

General level questions

knowledge and understanding

1 a. To change the size of a graphic.
  b. To turn a graphic around.
  c. To change the properties of a tool.
2 Line width and fill pattern.

problem solving

1 Line thickness.

Credit level questions

knowledge and understanding

1   The level of detail in a graphic, high resolution gives more detail than low resolution.

2   Set image type on scanner software, preview, select scanning area, scan, save image to disk. Load image into graphics package, edit image, save final image to disk.

problem solving

1   a. Paint because you need to change the individual pixels in the graphic.

   b. Draw because the plan will be a line drawing.

   c. Draw because the logo will be made of distinct shapes which may need to be scaled.

   d. Paint because you need to change the individual pixels in the photograph.

2   You can edit the individual pixels in a paint package but not in a draw package.

6   Desktop publishing

Foundation level questions

knowledge and understanding

1   A computer system, desktop publishing application package, laser printer, scanner and a digital camera.

2   MS Publisher or any other DTP package.

3   The correct order is:
- The text is typed.
- The graphics are created.
- Templates are designed.
- The text is imported.
- Data from other programs is imported.
- The graphics are inserted.
- The completed pages are then saved to disk.
- The final document is printed.

problem solving

1   A wizard or assistant could be used to help a new user speed up document production.

2   A template may be used over again to create a new document.

3   Clip art is ready made, and saves a lot of time compared to drawing each picture yourself.

General level questions

knowledge and understanding

1. a. Scale graphic means to resize a graphic, e.g. 50%.
   b. Import graphic means to take in a graphic which was created in a different package or on another computer.
2. Scaling a graphic means reducing or enlarging the whole image, but cropping a graphic means removing part of it to make it smaller — it's only a reduction process.
3. Graphics resolution is a measure of picture quality — high resolution means finer detail is displayed.

problem solving

1. a. The file format is wrong.
   b. Convert the file format to one that you can import.
   c. Scale or crop the graphic to fit.
2. She could do this by using email.

Credit level questions

knowledge and understanding

1. Banner headlines, columns and drop capitals.
2. The purpose of a drop capital is to draw the reader's attention to the beginning of an article.
3. A header appears on every page of a document, but a particular headline is only at the top of one page.
4. The style, size and weight are three features of a typeface.
5. A style sheet allows the same style to be applied to different parts of a document to keep the style of text consistent. This makes a document easier to read.

problem solving

1. Text wrap around graphics can be used to save space and also to create pleasing effects on a page.
2. The file format may not be recognised by the application and the text formatting may be lost.

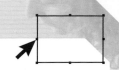

7 Presentation and multimedia

Foundation level questions

knowledge and understanding

1 Multimedia is the presentation of information by a computer system using graphics, animation, sound and text.
2 A presentation package is an application package which is used to create a presentation.
3 The presentation is made up of information displayed on a number of separate slides.
4 PowerPoint.
5 When slides in a presentation are displayed one after the other in order.
6 Clicking on the mouse button.
7 A resource (or a type of data) which is to be used in a presentation.
8 Assembling the elements of a presentation.
9 A template is a ready made up document containing guides or placeholders, which can accept objects such as text or graphics.
10 A wizard is a program which leads the user step by step through the creation of a document.
11 A multimedia projector.
12 A presentation set to run automatically without a presenter.

problem solving

1 A beginner or first time user.
2 Because of the Copyright, Designs and Patents Act, you could be breaking copyright laws.
3 a. It is possible to give a presentation without a presenter if the slide show is set to run automatically.
   b In a kiosk.

General level questions

knowledge and understanding

1 Text, graphics, audio and video.
2 A hyperlink is a link to a web page, another document or a particular slide within a presentation.
3 Sound library, audio CD, microphone, downloads.

problem solving

1 The advantage of a multimedia projector is that no hard copy need be produced, unlike for an OHP, and mistakes may be corrected easily. The advantage of an OHP is that no expensive projector is needed and it is much less likely to break down.
2 By using a drawing or other graphics packages.
3 If a presentation has too many sounds then users may become distracted and can miss the point that the presenter is trying to make.

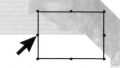

Credit level questions

knowledge and understanding

1 Audio may be captured using a microphone or by importing from an audio CD.
2 Images may be captured by using a scanner or a digital camera.
3 A hyperlink may be described as non-linear because it does not lead to the next slide in a particular sequence.
4 A transition is the name given to the effect shown on screen when moving between slides.
5 Animation is the way in which elements of a presentation may be programmed to move around the screen.
6 A slide master is a slide which controls the layout of other slides in the presentation.
7 Multimedia authoring packages may be programmed to a greater extent than presentation packages. Multimedia authoring packages may also be used to create stand-alone applications, unlike presentation packages.

8 Non-linear editing is when video clips are rearranged into any order, not just the sequence in which they were originally filmed.

problem solving

1 Jemima could do this by using the clip art library contained within the presentation package or by downloading suitable images from the World Wide Web.
2 Mrs Grofaz should put the text on the slide master.
3 A digital video camera.
4 Large backing storage requirements.
5 A large, fast hard disk drive.
6 You set up each slide in the presentation to have a consistent style.
7 Begin by working out the adventure story on paper, and deciding on the possible choices at each stage. Set up each choice within a separate slide in a presentation package and link the slides with hyperlinks.

8 Web page creation

Foundation level questions

knowledge and understanding

1 A text editor or a web page editor.
2 A wizard is a program which guides the user through the creation of a document.
3 A template is a ready made document.
4 Text may be entered by typing directly from the keyboard or by importing from a word processor or using copy and paste.
5 A graphic may be obtained from a web page editor's clip art library, imported from a graphics package or downloaded from the World Wide Web.
6 HTML or hypertext mark-up language.
7 WYSIWYG means what you see is what you get.

8 A WYSIWYG page editor allows the user to enter HTML code and have the web page created at the same time. Alternatively, you can create the page in the editor and look at the code which is created.
9 Netscape Communicator.

problem solving

1 a. To help create a web page.
   b. If she wanted a pre-defined layout without having to set it up herself.
2 From the World Wide Web.
3 All web pages are written in HTML. The text editor allows you to enter this.

4 You can see the page taking shape in WYSIWYG. With a text editor you can only see the HTML code.

5 Use the 'Save as web page' option.
6 It reduces the file size so that the picture will be quicker to load on the web page.

General level questions

knowledge and understanding

1 Hyperlinks are links to another web page or to another file stored on the World Wide Web or on a local disk.
2 An embedded video is a video file, which has been copied into the same file as the web page, increasing the file size.

problem solving

1 One method is to create a hyperlink, which will load the audio file. A second method is to embed the file, or make it part of, the web page.
2 The disadvantage of embedding a file is that the file size of the web page is greatly increased and may be slower to load.

Credit level questions

knowledge and understanding

1 Tables are made up of data arranged in columns and rows, and data is placed in cells, like a spreadsheet.
2 A hotspot is a special area on a web page, which is normally invisible when viewed in a browser. A hotspot has a hyperlink, or a piece of programming code associated with it, which can react to a user's action, such as moving the pointer over the hotspot or clicking the mouse button.
3 Hotspots are mainly used to display hidden images, and graphics which have hotspots are called image maps.

4 A web site's home page is its main menu page or index. A browser's home page is the web address, which it is set to load when the browser application is opened.

problem solving

1 Tables help to organise lists of data on a web page. They may also help improve the design or appearance of the page.
2 The mouse pointer changes shape when it is over a hotspot.
3 The home page is the main menu or index to the site. The purpose of the home page is to allow the user to find easily any of the other pages.

9 Expert systems

General level questions

knowledge and understanding

1 An expert system is made up of the facts and rules, known as the knowledge base; this is like a giant database, but is more flexible in that it contains rules as well as facts; the coding or program, this is known as the inference engine or expert system shell; the screen, or explanatory interface, which is used to ask the question of the user.

2 Artificial intelligence is a computer program which makes a computer behave as if it had a form of intelligence.

3 Eliza works by recognising patterns in the sentences typed in by the user and responds mechanically with preset adapted responses.

4 The purpose of an expert system is to contain the knowledge of a human expert, and to be able to represent and describe this knowledge in a useful way.

5 Two applications of expert systems are in medical diagnosis and in car repair.

problem solving

1 An expert system shell can be used for a different task by loading a different knowledge base.

2 If my pals are all taking a packed lunch then I will take a packed lunch. If I am playing football or need more time then a packed lunch is quicker than standing in the dinner queue.

Credit level questions

knowledge and understanding

1 a. The present role is that of an assistant in practice management.

b. The main reservation within the profession is about allowing the assistant to make decisions in place of professionals.

c. The expert system can draw on a potentially limitless databank of case histories and can give an immediate calculation of the probability that its diagnosis is accurate.

d. Such developments could limit the general practitioner's role much more to surgical procedures or to matters of strategy.

e. i. This represents a threat to jobs.
   ii. This is a change in role due to technological innovation.

f. A trained mind is necessary to trigger new lines of enquiry.

g. The immediate future role of expert systems in medicine is as a passive assistant to the doctor.

problem solving

1 Two advantages of expert systems are that they contain the accumulated knowledge from more than one person about a particular subject, and that they are more consistent than humans. Two disadvantages are that they are inflexible and can only act within the rules that they have and that they have no common sense.

2 a. Do you like me?

b. i. You sound like a nice person.
   ii. Do many people like you?

c. It is not a true test of intelligence because the computer can only follow pre-programmed responses, even if the interrogator is deceived by the answers.

10 Electronic communication

Foundation level questions

knowledge and understanding

1 Electronic communication is the process of sending and receiving electronic mail, text messaging and file transfer.
2 Electronic mail is a way of sending messages from one computer to another, over a transmission medium such as a network cable.
3 Access to the Internet, an electronic mail address or mailbox, a computer system, an email client program or an Internet browser is required for electronic mail.
4 A sensible subject line will increase the chances of your message being read.
5 An email client program can send and receive email messages.
6 Outlook Express.
7 Text messaging is a method of electronic communication using a mobile phone.
8 SMS stands for Short Message Service.
9 161 characters maximum length, including the header.
10 A mobile phone, an account with a service provider and to be in an area of sufficient signal strength to communicate.

problem solving

1 An email message will bounce if the email address of the recipient is incorrect.
2 A message will be sent to inform the sender that the email was not delivered.
3 A 'pending' message will be delivered when the recipient's mobile phone is switched on or within range.

General level questions

knowledge and understanding

1 You can cram more words into a message with a fixed limit, it is faster to type the message than if you had to type the whole word(s).
2 The point of Netiquette is politeness and respect for others.
3 a. It is called unsolicited email because it comes from people you have not asked to send you anything.
   b. It is called spam after the Monty Python sketch of the same name.

problem solving

1 You do not need to be on-line to compose an email message.
2 Electronic mail can send longer messages. Text messages are limited to 161 characters. Electronic mail can send attached files of any type. Text messages can send ring tones and logos.
3 Email can send much longer messages than text messages. Email can only go to an email address. Text messages can only go to a mobile phone number. Email clients have more features than mobile phones. Text messages may only be received if the mobile phone is on and within range. Email messages may only be received if the user logs on to their mailbox, but there is no limit to distance; either a person has access to an email account or they don't. A person is more likely to have a mobile phone with them than a portable computer for receiving email when they are on the move. The cost of sending a text message varies depending on the user's contract, but the cost of an email is the cost of the time it takes on-line to send it.

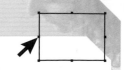

4 Because a mobile phone handset's main use is as a telephone

5 a. 'D qk brn fx jmpd ovr d lzy dg'.
   b. The storage space required will be:
      i. 44 bytes
      ii. 29 bytes.
   c. The storage space saved will be 15 bytes.

6 Use a filter, change your email address, make your address difficult for spammers to guess.

7 If you reply to spam, you are confirming that your email address is a valid one.

8 Messages should be short to save the recipient's time when reading them. It is good Netiquette.

Credit level questions

knowledge and understanding

1 File transfer is the sending of files along with an email message.

2 An attachment is a file which is sent with an email message.

3 An email filter is a program that can organise your email into separate folders, such as junk mail.

problem solving

1 File formats should be considered to ensure that the recipient can load the file correctly.

2 The email attachment may have a virus.

3 It spread so quickly because it infected the computer's email address book.

4 a. 50 computers to start with, then 50 x 10 new addresses = 500 addresses, total 550.
   b. Second generation original 550, then 500 x 10 = 5000 addresses, total 5550.

5 Phonetics is how words sound when they are pronounced, and not how they are spelt. When some words are abbreviated in a text message, they still sound like the word they are meant to represent, for instance L8 = late.

11 Local area networks and wide area networks

Foundation level questions

knowledge and understanding

1 A network is a linked set of computer systems that are capable of sharing programs, data and sending messages between them.

2 A stand-alone computer is one which is not connected to a network.

3 A local area network (LAN) covers a small area such as a room or a building and is usually owned by an individual, a single company or an organisation such as a school.

4 A wide area network (WAN) covers a larger geographical area, such as a country or a continent.

5 Each computer on a local area network is called a station.

6 a. Logging on is the process of identifying yourself to the fileserver.
   b. Logging on involves entering your user identity and your password.

7 'Sneaker-net' is the name given to file transfer by carrying disks between computers rather than using a network.

problem solving

1 Logging on is called going on-line because once you have logged on you are connected, or on-line, to the computer system.

2 Two advantages of a local area network are resource sharing and file sharing.

3 Wide area networks are not normally used for sharing peripherals because the output from a peripheral like a printer needs to be available to the user to collect locally.

General level questions

knowledge and understanding

1 A transmission medium is used to carry data between computers on a network.

2 Two types of wireless networking are infrared communication and microwave transmission.

3 a. Network privileges are a particular user's level of access on a network.

   b. The network administrator controls a user's network privileges.

4 a. A telecommunications link is a way of sending data over a distance.

   b. A wide area network uses telecommunications links.

5 The purpose of network security is to make sure that users can only see the data they are meant to see.

6 Three methods of network security are passwords, encryption and physical.

7 You should change your password regularly to make it difficult for others to guess.

8 Encryption means putting data into a code to prevent it being seen by unauthorised users.

problem solving

1 Copper wire is cheaper to buy than optical fibre.

2 It would be a waste of time if the computer is connected to a network, as it could still be hacked into remotely.

3 Optical fibre cable cannot be tapped into like copper wire.

4 Absolute security is not possible because all the security measures do ultimately is to slow down someone's access to data rather than prevent it entirely.

5 Because these passwords are easy to guess.

Credit level questions

knowledge and understanding

1 Different levels of access are required by different users, in order to administer the network or to oversee the files of a workgroup.

2 You should choose a password which is difficult for others to guess, not a name or a date of birth, but random numbers and letters.

3 A client and server network is a method of network organisation in which network stations or clients make use of resources available on one or more servers.

4 The most common client machine is a desktop computer.

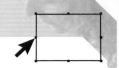

5 a. The function of a file server is to provide central disk storage for users' programs and data on a network.
   b. The computer has to be switched on and running all the time.
   c. CD-ROM server, Internet server.
   d. Printer server and print jobs.
6 A network interface card is a circuit board which allows a computer to connect to a network.
7 WiFi.
8 Multi-access is when many users are on-line to a computer at the same time.
9 Teleworking is working from home and not in a centrally located workplace.
10 'Information-rich' individuals are connected to the Internet and 'Information-poor' people are not connected.
11 One ethical issue is invasion of personal privacy. One legal issue is hacking.
12 a. A greater number of social ties, more diverse social ties and more support.
   b. One study suggests that spending even one hour a week online could increase depression
   c. Professor Hampton sees the Internet as a key part of peoples' lives.

   d. A wired neighbourhood in the suburbs of Toronto.
   e. The residents pulled together to replace what they had lost.
   f. Your own opinion.

problem solving

1 Bluetooth has a longer range than infrared and is not a line of sight transmission.
2 WiFi has a longer range than Bluetooth.
3 They save the print data temporarily to hard disk to allow background printing which means that the user can continue with another task.
4 A wireless network interface card is most likely to be found in a laptop or notebook computer.
5 For teleworking: travel is eliminated, so there is more time for work and less pollution. Against teleworking: less face to face contact with colleagues.
6 One reason is to prevent others from seeing your password on the screen, the other reason is to give the user feedback that a character has actually been entered.
7 Verification — both passwords should match before the new one is accepted by the system.
8 10 metres.

12 Internet

Foundation level questions

knowledge and understanding

1 The Internet is a wide area network, which spans the globe.
2 A vast quantity of information on any topic you can think of.
3 World Wide Web, electronic mail and file transfer.
4 A browser is a program that allows the user to browse or surf the World Wide Web.
5 An Internet ready computer consists of a computer system, a modem and suitable communications software such as a browser and an email client program.
6 A modem changes the digital signals from a computer into sounds or analogue signals, which can be sent along a telephone line.

problem solving

1 A bookmark allows a stored web address to be accessed.

General level questions

knowledge and understanding

1 The World Wide Web is a collection of information held in multimedia form on the Internet.

2 a. Hyperlinks are links between World Wide Web pages, documents or files.
   b. A web page is a single document on the World Wide Web.
   c. HTML is hypertext markup language which is used to make up web pages.

3 A dial-up connection is a connection to the Internet made by a computer dialling a telephone number using a modem.

4 A broadband connection is a high speed connection to the Internet which is always on.

5 Dial-up is slow and the line cannot be shared to make an ordinary telephone call. Broadband is a fast connection to the Internet and calls can be made at the same time as connecting to the Internet.

6 a. On-line means connected to the Internet.
   b. Off-line means not connected to the Internet.

7 A search engine is a special site on the World Wide Web which helps you to find information.

8 A search engine works by creating an index or database of web pages which can be searched.

9 A hit is the name for one match in a successful search of the Internet using a search engine.

problem solving

1 A wizard helps to connect the computer to the Internet.

2 By entering the web address directly into the browser.

3 Phrases can help to narrow a search and increase the chance of a successful match or hit.

4 Each search engine indexes their pages in a different way.

5 A broadband connection is constantly connected to the Internet.

Credit level questions

knowledge and understanding

1 A uniform resource locator or web address.

2 www.bbc.co.uk/scotland/revision/Computing.htm

3 A question written down as you would ask it.

4 What is the traffic like on the M8?

5 a. Receiving programs from another computer on the Internet.
   b. Sending programs to another computer on the Internet.

6 Freeware, shareware and commercial.

7 Freeware.

8 Shareware and commercial.

9 Accessing the Internet with a wireless connection using a portable computer.

10 Laptop and palmtop.

11 Video conferencing is the use of communications links to conduct meetings between people who are geographically separated.

12 A typical video conferencing set-up requires a computer system and a webcam in each location, together with a network connection between everyone involved.

13 a. Streaming video is the process of receiving video images over a network and displaying them on a computer screen.
   b. A weblog is a web page made up of short, frequently updated entries that are arranged in chronological order, like a diary.

problem solving

1 'sea fishing OR fresh water fishing'.

2 Buy a license or purchase 20 individual copies.

3 A palmtop computer or a mobile phone.

13 Commercial data processing

Foundation level questions

knowledge and understanding

1. Because of the volume of documents, speed of processing, speed of access, repetitive tasks.
2. Data collection, data preparation, input, processing and storage, output.
3. A set of lines on goods which holds a series of numbers with details about the goods.
4. A card which can be marked by writing on it. The marks can be detected by a mark sense reader.
5. A narrow band of magnetic material on which data is held.
6. A file is a set of records.
7. A record may contain one or more fields.
8. A field is a single item of data on a record.
9. The screen and on paper.
10. A mainframe computer system and terminals.
11. E-commerce is doing business electronically, for example, over the Internet.
12. On-line banking is banking using the Internet.
13. On-line shopping is shopping using the Internet.

problem solving

1. Because the price may be different in different shops or at different times of the year.
2. In case the original copy is lost or damaged.
3. It is more convenient because you do not have to travel to the shop.
4. It is cheaper for banks because they can employ fewer staff in local branches.

General level questions

knowledge and understanding

1. Information is data with structure. Data becomes information when you know what it means.
2. Magnetic ink character recognition.
3. An extra digit which is calculated from the original number and put on the end of that number.
4. A range check makes sure that numbers are within a certain range, for example, from 1 to 10.
5. Interactive processing is when data is processed or updated as the transaction is entered, and any enquiries are replied to at once.
6. a. A programmer writes programs or checks for commercially available applications.
   b. A systems analyst looks at all the jobs a company does manually and decides which jobs can be done best by computer.
   c. An engineer installs new computers and maintains existing ones.
   d. A network manager is the person in charge of the network. He or she is responsible for all of the computer systems attached to the company network.
7. EFT is a way you can pay for goods without using cash.
8. The place in the shop where the goods change hands.
9. The cost of operating a computer system such as paper, electricity, ink/toner, maintenance.
10. Physical — locking disks in a safe; software — encryption.
11. a. Use of computerised stock control linked to laser reading checkouts.
    b. Bar codes.
    c. Electronic funds transfer at point of sale is when money is authorised to be debited from a customer's bank account at the checkout terminal.

d. Your card is swiped or put in a slot beside the till, an authorisation check may be carried out depending upon the total amount of the bill, funds are transferred electronically from your bank account (or directly from the card if it is an electronic purse) and transferred to the shop's bank account.

problem solving

1
  a. Alex Jones   11 December 1979
  b. Mary Campbell   25 November 1954
  c. Miriam Horowitz   30 August 1949
  d. Joseph Timmons   19 April 1972.

2
  a. 710156
  b. 527069
  c. 307036
  d. 002118
  e. 012253.

3   201203 on its own is meaningless to people, therefore it is data. If the number is reorganised as 20/12/03, then it could be read as information in the form of a date, namely 20 December 2003.

4   To make money for the seller and to obtain more potential customers for the buyer.

5   They will receive more junk mail.

6   It is difficult to forge.

7   A range check for their birthday.

8   To check that it has been read correctly.

9   A suitable bank card.

10
  a. The customer is given an itemised receipt which makes it easier to check that the bill is correct. The shop's computer keeps a record of how much of each item is sold.
  b. Payment into the shop's bank account is guaranteed. The chance of theft is reduced because there is less cash in the till.

11
  a. I would be pleased that I could monitor the work rate of my employees.
  b. I would be concerned that I was being watched all the time.

Credit level questions

knowledge and understanding

1   A report of total sales for each month, breakdown of sales by type or by area.

2   A method of reading in characters to a machine by using a scanner and appropriate software.

3   A method of checking that data is sensible or allowable, for example, a range check.

4   A method of checking that data has been entered correctly, usually by typing data in twice.

5   Sequential access — data may only be read back in the order in which it was written.
Random/direct access — data may be read back in any order.

6   A database which may be accessed by many users at the same time.

7   Hacking or the distribution of viruses.

8   Entering data only once and using it many times.

problem solving

1   The data could be hacked into, stolen, or changed.

2   In a network of automated telling machines, or when booking tickets, because fast, direct access is required.

3   The number from the bar code is used to get the price from memory in the shop's computer.

4   Each time an item of goods is sold, then one is removed from the stock number in the shop's computer system.

5
  a. He could use this information to target shoppers with mail about related products and special offers.
  b. The Data Protection Act prevents shops from using information in this way.

6   You could say that the 'cashless society' has arrived because the vast majority of people use bank cards rather than carry large quantities of cash around. However, it could also be argued that cash is still necessary for use in small purchases or by people like young children who are not allowed to use bank cards.

14 Industrial applications/automated systems

Foundation level questions

knowledge and understanding

1. An automated system is a system where you provide the input, and the machine or computer carries out the process and provides you with the output.
2. a. A washing machine, a video recorder.
   b. Welding cars, transporting goods in a factory.
3. Bomb disposal.
4. a. Car manufacture, baking.
   b. Yes.
   c. They will have to be trained to operate computers and how to program automated systems and robots.
5. a. A device which detects a physical quantity like light or heat.
   b. A signal from a sensor to a control computer.
   c. Computer aided design.
   d. Computer aided manufacture.
6. Waist, shoulder, arm, wrist.
7. A tool.
8. A motor.
9.

Stationary	Mobile
Car welder	AGV
Mushroom harvester	Bomb disposal robot
Polisher	Turtle
	ASIMO

problem solving

1. Retraining.
2. So that they can carry out different tasks.
3. Mobile can move, stationary stays in the same place.
4. a. The traffic sensor senses when cars are waiting.
   b. The float rises when the tank is full and the valve shuts off the water supply.
5. a. The company can produce good quality products in less time.
   b. The employee can learn new skills and does not get bored.

General level questions

knowledge and understanding

1. Robots can work all day without a break.
2. To make sure that the correct signals are sent between the computer and the robot.
3. An autonomous guided vehicle.
4. By light guidance, where the AGV follows a line painted on the factory floor.
5. a. Simulation is using computers to model something that happens in real life.
   b. Virtual reality is reproducing the outside world digitally within a computer system.
   c. Real-time processing is processing which happens immediately without any delay as soon as the input is received.
6. Robots are programmed to move slowly so that people can get out of their way. Robot vehicles are fitted with bump sensors and will stop instantly if they bump into anything.
7. Fewer workers will do manual labour. Heavy or repetitive jobs will be done by machine. The skills which the workers have will change from manual work to control, programming and maintenance.
8. More leisure time may happen if work is done more efficiently. Less leisure time may happen if the employers demand increased productivity.

problem solving

1. Dirt has no effect on the magnetic field generated by the wire.

2 Laser guidance is not affected by dirt on the factory floor.

3 Automated systems are more accurate and efficient than humans. They will make long term savings by reducing the number of employees.

4 Robots can be programmed precisely. They do not get bored or make mistakes.

5 The robot could be shown what movements to carry out by using lead through programming. The human actions would be recorded and could be replayed by the robot.

6 a. The computer does not know anything about sizes of mushrooms.

 b. The camera sends information about the size and position of all the mushrooms in the tray to the computer.

 c. No mushrooms would be picked. They would be left to grow.

 d. The saw must be turned on and off at the correct time.

7 Money is saved in fuel and maintenance of a real aircraft.

Credit level questions

knowledge and understanding

1 Adaptability means that automated systems may be programmed to carry out different tasks.

2 A control language is computer language designed specially for robot control.

3 Control languages have the advantage that they have specialised commands for control such as TURNON and TURNOFF.

4 The computer only understands digital signals and the robot understands analogue signals, so an interface contains an A to D converter to allow signals from a sensor on the robot to be fed back to the computer.

5 ROM software is preserved when the power is switched off. It is quick to load.

6 An avatar is a digital representation of a person in virtual reality.

7 An embedded system is a tiny computer inside another, larger piece of equipment, like a washing machine.

8 A car and a mobile phone.

9 a. Hazard avoidance camera.

 b. ROM software.

 c. Rock grinder.

problem solving

1 a. To convert analogue signals from a sensor into digital for the computer to understand — a traffic sensor.

 b. To convert digital signals from the computer into analogue for the robot to understand — a welding robot.

2 A systems analysis is needed to design the computer system requirements for the workplace and, once installed, monitor the process.

3 ROM software cannot be changed unless the chip is removed and replaced.

4

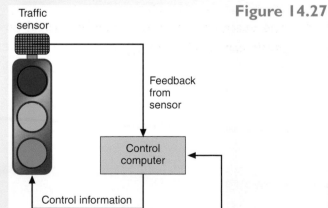

Figure 14.27

15 Hardware

Foundation level questions

knowledge and understanding

1.
   a. The physical parts of a computer system.
   b. The programs or data which a computer system uses.
2.
   a. A computer which is normally operated sitting at a desk.
   b. A battery operated computer which may be used sitting on your lap.
   c. A small battery operated computer which can be held in one hand while it is being operated.
3.
   a. Mouse and keyboard.
   b. Monitor and printer.
   c. Floppy disk drive and hard disk drive.
4.
   a. Mouse.
   b. Trackpad.
5. A labelled diagram of a desktop computer system.

6. In the main memory.
7. A processor which can fit on a single chip.
8. Silicon.

problem solving

1. The programs and data need to be held in main memory so that the processor can have quick access to them.
2. Save the program to backing storage, for example a hard disk.
3.
   a. Read only memory.
   b. So that the game is not lost when the computer is switched off.
4. The screen.
5. By being connected using a cable or by using a wireless connection.

General level questions

knowledge and understanding

1. One byte.
2. A very large computer which can process vast quantities of data at high speed and which occupies a whole room.
3. The quantity of data that may be stored on a particular backing storage medium.

problem solving

1. It is an idiot because it cannot do anything without a program to tell it what to do. It is very fast because it can process billions of instructions every second.
2. In the computer's main memory.
3. One byte of data.

Credit level questions

knowledge and understanding

1 The way it is formatted.
2 Accessing data in the same order that it was saved in.
3 Accessing data by going straight to it in whatever backing storage medium is being used.
4 Tape.
5 Because the data can be accessed in any order, not just the order in which it was written.

problem solving

1 Because you can go straight to the item of data you want, without having to go through all the other data first.
2 Chips are becoming smaller and have more processing power.

16 Input devices

Foundation level questions

knowledge and understanding

1 An input device is a device which allows data to be entered into a computer system.
2 Keyboard, mouse, microphone, sound card.
3 a. An input device consisting of a set of buttons or keys marked with characters, for entering text and numeric data and commands to a computer.
   b. An input device which allows you to draw freehand using a stylus on a pressure sensitive flat plate.
   c. An input device on a screen or monitor which is able to detect the position of the user's finger or a stylus.
   d. An input device which has a ball underneath it, and one or more switches on top, used to control a pointer on screen.
   e. An input device which has a ball on top, and one or more switches beside it, used to control a pointer on screen.
   f. An input device which has a flat pressure sensitive plate, and one or more switches beside it, used to control a pointer on screen.
   g. An input device with a large lever and switches, used for controlling the movement of characters in a computer game.
4 a. Keyboard.
   b. Mouse.
   c. Joystick.
   d. Graphics tablet.
   e. Trackpad.
   f. Touch sensitive screen.
5 Because of the order of characters in the top row.

problem solving

1 There is no room to use a mouse.
2 Trackballs need regular cleaning to operate properly.

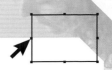

General level questions

knowledge and understanding

1.
   a. An input device which scans documents using light reflected through a glass plate.
   b. An input device which changes sound into electrical signals.
   c. A camera which uses a light sensor and saves the images to a memory card.
   d. A movie camera which uses a light sensor and saves the movies to video tape.
   e. A camera which can transmit pictures over a network such as the Internet.

2. Text and graphics.

3.
   a. Memory card.
   b. Video tape.

4. Microphone.

5. Megapixels.

problem solving

1.
   a. To monitor a premises remotely over the Internet.
   b. To video conference over the Internet.

2. Each key transmits a different number, which is related to the character code in ASCII.

Credit level questions

knowledge and understanding

1. Multimedia is the presentation of information by a computer system using graphics, animation, sound and text.

2. A card which allows sound to be input from a microphone or other source.

3. A way of reproducing the outside world digitally within a computer system.

4. An input device which may be used by people who have difficulty using ordinary input devices such as a mouse or keyboard.

5.
   a. A Braille keyboard, a 'magic wand' keyboard.
   b. Data glove.

6. A microphone, a digital video camera, a multimedia keyboard.

problem solving

1. The process of identifying and responding to voice commands.

2. It is useful for young children who are unable to use a traditional keyboard.

3.
   a. Scanner and graphics tablet.
   b. Graphics package to edit and save the output of the scanner; CAD package to produce the technical drawings.

4.
   a. Smell and taste.
   b. It would be too difficult to provide a virtual smell. It would be too difficult/may be unhygienic to provide a virtual taste.

17 Output devices

Foundation level questions

knowledge and understanding

1   A printout.
2   The plotter uses a pen and a printer doesn't. They both use paper.
3   A visual display unit has a screen and a keyboard. A monitor only has a screen.
4   a.   An inkjet printer works by squirting small droplets of ink onto paper through tiny holes in the print head.
    b.   A laser beam is used to project the image of the page to be printed onto a drum and transferring the image onto the paper by using toner.
5   A laser printer uses toner.

problem solving

1   An inkjet printer.

General level questions

knowledge and understanding

1   a.   The capital cost of a printer is how much it costs to buy the printer.
    b.   The running cost is how much it costs to use the printer.
2   a.   Pages per minute.
    b.   Dots per inch.
3   Cyan, magenta and yellow.
4   Cathode ray tube.
5   Liquid crystal display.
6   Thin film transistor.

problem solving

1   a.   The capital cost of a printer depends upon the resolution and the speed. A fast printer capable of printing at a high resolution will cost more.
    b.   The running cost depends upon the cost of the electricity, the paper and the ink or toner and any maintenance required.
2   It is more economical to use individual colour cartridges because a three colour cartridge may need to be replaced when only one of the three colours is empty.
3   The screen can be used to preview photographs when printing from a card or directly from a digital still camera.
4   To save having to load the photographs into the computer first.
5   • They are much smaller and lighter than a CRT and they use much less power.
    • TFTs do not flicker like CRT monitors, nor do they give out static electricity or any other form of radiation.
    • TFTs do not suffer from the reduction in viewable size that CRT monitors do.

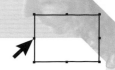

Credit level questions

knowledge and understanding

1 By multiplying the number of horizontal pixels by the vertical pixels and taking the dot pitch into account.
2 The dot pitch is the distance between adjacent dots of the same colour.
3 A card which plugs into a computer system and controls the sound output.
4 A card which plugs into a computer system and controls the graphics output.
5 Speech generated by a computer.
6 A headset.
7 Giving a multimedia presentation.

problem solving

1 Passive matrix displays suffer from 'ghosting' on the screen when the picture changes.

18 Backing storage

Foundation level questions

knowledge and understanding

1 Floppy disk and hard disk.
2 Floppy disk drive and hard disk drive.
3 Digital audio tape.
4 For backup of hard disks.
5 Because the actual disk is made of flexible plastic.
6 A DVD-ROM can hold much more data than a CD-ROM.

problem solving

1 Hard disks can hold much more data than floppy disks and can access data faster than floppy disks.
2 To hold the programs and data when the computer is switched off.
3 Backing storage holds programs and data, backup is an extra copy in case the original is lost or damaged.

General level questions

knowledge and understanding

1 Formatting is preparing a disk to hold data.
2 Invisible circles of magnetism called tracks are created on the surface of the disk.
3 The read/write head makes contact with the spinning metal disk and the disk may be damaged.
4 A drive which can read and write CD-Rs and CD-RWs and read DVD-ROMs.
5 Dye.
6 Different occasions on which a disk is written to.
7 Universal Serial Bus — an interface standard.
8 A flash ROM media which uses the USB interface.
9 a. A floppy disk.
   b. A hard disk.
   c. A USB flash drive.

problem solving

1 Floppy disks have a small capacity and some manufacturers no longer fit floppy disk drives to their computer systems.
2 One advantage is that one super disk can hold the contents of around 70 or more floppy disks.

One disadvantage is that you cannot use the super disks in an ordinary disk drive.

3 Because they use laser beams to read the data stored on them.

4 One power to record the data and another, lower power to read the data

5 CD-RW may be erased and re-written, CD-R may be written to until it is full.

6 The pits on a DVD-ROM are smaller than the pits on a CD-ROM, the tracks are closer together on a DVD-ROM, DVD-ROMs may be double layered and double sided, more efficient error correction means that there is more space to hold data.

7 You cannot save onto it and you cannot format it when it is write protected.

Credit level questions

knowledge and understanding

1 Data is stored on a CD-Rom using pits and lands and the pits and lands are read by a laser beam.

2 A CD-ROM drive has more efficient error correction and its read/write head moves faster than the head on an audio CD player. Both drives can play audio CDs.

3 Scratches on the label side may cause oxidation of the metal layer.

4 To find a program by using sequential access, you have to look through all of the tape from the beginning. Using direct access you can go straight to the program required.

problem solving

1 Its large storage capacity.

2 The user can decide whether or not they wish to have all of the application installed or just the basic features, either because they only need the basic features, or because their computer system is short of backing storage space.

3 To save space on backing storage.

4 In order to know whether or not it will be able to be read by a particular computer system.

5 To ensure that a CD-R is not written to at too high a speed, which may result in failure or an unreliable copy.

6 A loudspeaker has a magnet which can change the magnetic particles on a floppy disk but will have no effect on a CD-ROM which uses pits and lands to store data.

19 Systems software

General level questions

knowledge and understanding

1 A language which is like normal or everyday language.

2 They must be translated before they can be run; they are specialised for solving problems.

problem solving

1 The computer only understands its own language, machine code.

Credit level questions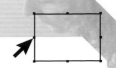

knowledge and understanding

1. a. An interpreter is a translator program which changes a high level language into machine code, one instruction at a time.
   b. A compiler is a translator program which changes a high level language program into machine code in a single operation.
   c. Source code is the original high level language program.
   d. Object code is the machine code program produced by the translator.

2. The portability of software is whether or not you can run a computer program that you write on one computer system on a different computer system without altering it.

problem solving

1. Compiler.
2. Software companies can have higher sales if their programs can be easily changed to run on more than one type of computer system.
3. In case the program needs to be changed or maintained in the future.

20 Operating systems

Foundation level questions

knowledge and understanding

1. An operating system is a program which controls the computer.
2. A directory or a folder.

problem solving

1. a. When the computer is switched on.
   b. When the computer is switched off.
2. Put them into two separate folders or directories.

General level questions

knowledge and understanding

1. a. A real-time system is one in which the speed of response is vital.
   b. In an interactive system the computer responds directly to commands.
2. A data file contains data but a program contains a list of instructions.
3. The filing system.

problem solving

1. a. Real-time.
   b. Interactive.
   c. Real-time.
   d. Interactive.

Credit level questions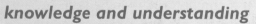

knowledge and understanding

1.
  a. The way in which the operating system organises the files on backing storage.
  b. The way in which the operating system makes best use of main memory.
  c. The way in which the operating system lets the user know if any mistakes have occurred.

2. A filing system with a root directory and one or more sub-directories.

3. A program which allows the operating system to communicate with a peripheral device.

4. A printer driver translates the codes in the word processed document into the correct code for the printer being used.

problem solving

1.
  a. By using the gaps in the processor time when the computer is waiting for the user to press a key.
  b. If you are using more of the available processing power then the processor is not as idle as it might be, it is being used more efficiently.

2. On disk you can go directly to the program required. On tape you have to search through from the beginning until you find the program.

3. RAM.

4. Memory management.

21 Low level machine

Foundation level questions

knowledge and understanding

1.
  a. A single binary digit.
  b. Eight bits.
  c. 1024 bytes.
  d. 1024 kilobytes.
  e. 1024 megabytes.
  f. 1024 gigabytes.

2. A list of instructions.

3. A list of instructions stored in the computer's memory. By changing the program, you can change what the computer does.

4. Bit, byte, kilobyte, megabyte, gigabyte, terabyte.

problem solving

1. In the main memory.

2. Megabytes or gigabytes.

3. To carry out the instructions in a computer program.

4. Input — disk to disk drive; process — formatting; output — formatted disk.

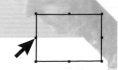

General level questions

knowledge and understanding

1 The computer's own language.
2 By using the binary system (1 and 0).
3 256.
4 Pictures displayed on a computer where each dot is represented as a pixel on screen.
5 a. A letter, number or symbol on a computer system.
   b. The set of characters which a computer can process and store.
   c. A dot on a computer screen.
6 American Standard Code for Information Interchange.
7 Each character has its own unique code.

problem solving

1 Because it can only carry out instructions it has been given, it cannot think for itself.
2 Many other computers use ASCII, so it is easy to exchange text between different computers,
3 I'm fine, how are you?
4 a.
```
XXXXXXX
X       X
X  X
 XX
X   X
X       X
XXXXXXX
```
b.
```
XXXX
X       X
X       X
X       X
XXXX
X  X
X    X
X      X
```

(X = shaded pixel)

Credit level questions

knowledge and understanding

1 Control unit, arithmetic/logic unit, registers.
2 See figure 21.2.
3 Do calculations and make decisions (logical operations).
4 Controls different parts of the computer. Makes sure that each program instruction is carried out in the correct order.
5 Hold the programs and data while they are being processed.
6 A word is the number of bits that the processor can process in a single operation.
7 A place in memory where an item of data is stored.
8 The way in which the processor can access each storage location. Each storage location has its own unique address in memory.

problem solving

1 Each storage location has its own unique address in memory.
2 Seven bits because $128 = 2^7$.
3 a. A computer which can process 32 bits of data in a single operation,
   b. Ravinder's computer will be able to hold more or larger programs in memory at the same time than Prabhu's computer.
   c. Prabhu, because his computer can process 64 bits in a single operation which is twice as many as Ravinder's computer's 32 bits.
4 a. 48 bytes.
   b. 29.29 kilobytes.
   c. 538.15 kilobytes.
5 One bit.
6 1073741824 storage locations (see table 21.2)
7 All the processing and storage devices of the computer have two states, on and off. The binary system has two states, 1 and 0.

22 Programming

Foundation level questions

knowledge and understanding

1 Use meaningful variable names and internal commentary.

2 To ensure that it is free from error.

3 To give the user instructions on how to best use the program.

General level questions

knowledge and understanding

1 By using a structure diagram.

2 It means when the program asks the user a question or tells them something.

2 Ensure that errors such as 'no paper in the printer' are trapped and do not crash the program.

problem solving

1

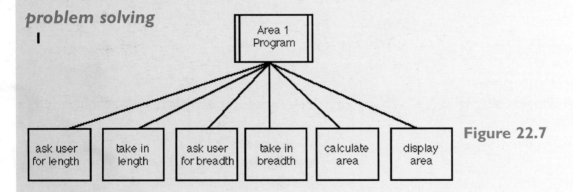

Figure 22.7

Credit level questions

knowledge and understanding

1 Analysis, design, implementation, testing, documentation, evaluation, maintenance.

2 • Normal test data is data which is within limits and which the program should accept.
  • Extreme test data is data which is on the boundaries and which the program should accept.
  • Exceptional test data is wrong and the program should reject this data.

3 A way of describing the design of a program using ordinary language.

4 To show how the program should be installed and maintained if necessary.

problem solving

1 Logical errors do not prevent the program from running, they just cause the program to work differently from what was intended.

2 Input should be validated so that it makes sense, for example, it is within a certain range.